Singing the City

Check out Stone Arch Books adventure novels!

Fire and Snow
A Tale of the Alaskan Gold Rush

Ethan and his family leave their comfortable home in Seattle to seek their fortune in the snowy North. Ethan must brave an avalanche, cross an icy river, and battle a deadly fire before he can decide if the hunt for gold is worth the risk.

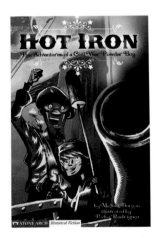

Hot Iron
The Adventures of a Civil War Powder Boy

Twelve-year-old Charlie O'Leary signs aboard the USS Varuna as it steams its way toward the mouth of the Mississippi River to fight the Confederate Navy. Will his ship survive the awesome Battle of New Orleans?

Radar Riders

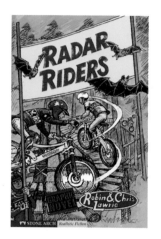

The Ridge Riders need a new place to race, so they build a wild new course. It takes all their skills, and some techno-wizardry, to keep them on track before they run into some unexpected twists and turns.

White Lightning

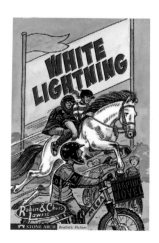

Someone smashed the Ridge Riders' practice jumps, and they suspect Fiona and her horse-riding friends. The boys are so mean to Fiona that she leaves. Then Slam gets a flat tire and has to race back home to get his spare, and he only has 50 minutes! Now a horse would come in handy!

Read other adventures of the Ridge Riders

Cheat Challenge

Slam Duncan and his friends, the Ridge Riders, don't know what to think when they come across a sword buried deep in their mountain-biking course. It's part of a new racing course contest called Excalibur. Then Slam accidentally gets a look at the map of the course, but he knows he can't tell his teammates the map's secrets.

Snow Bored

The Ridge Riders are bored. So much snow has fallen on their mountain biking practice hill that they can't ride. Luckily, Dozy has a great idea. He turns an old skateboard and a pair of sneakers into a snowboard. Before long, everyone is snowboarding.

Writing Prompts

1. Everyone has fears. What are some of yours? Write a story in which you overcome your greatest fear. If you can't think of one of your own fears, make one up!

2. Slam is forced to face his biggest fear so that he can help save Jack. What would have happened if he had been too scared to go up in the helicopter?

Discussion Questions

1. What does Jack mean on page 11 when he says "Discretion is the better part of valor"? Do you agree with him or not? What are some ways that you can use discretion to be brave?

2. Are you afraid of anything? How can someone get over their fears? What do you think of "Fear 3.1," the imaginary computer program Dozy invents for Slam?

3. Slam belongs to u scout troop, and it's with that group that he learns about rock climbing. Are you in any groups or teams? What do you learn from them?

Internet Sites

Do you want to know more about subjects related to this book? Or are you interested in learning about other topics? Then check out FactHound, a fun, easy way to find Internet sites.

Our investigative staff has already sniffed out great sites for you!

Here's how to use FactHound:

1. Visit *www.facthound.com*

2. Select your grade level.

3. To learn more about subjects related to this book, type in the book's ISBN number: **1598893483**.

4. Click the **Fetch It** button.

FactHound will fetch the best Internet sites for you!

Glossary

crevice (KREH-viss)—a crack or split in a rock

crossbar (KRAWSS-bahr)—on a bike, the metal bar that runs between the wheels

cursor (KUR-sur)—the arrow or line that shows your position on a computer screen

deaf (DEF)—not able to hear well or hear at all

discretion (diss-CRESH-uhn)—the ability to decide

harness (HAR-niss)—a set of straps that keeps someone safe

paramedic (pa-ruh-MEH-dik)—a person who is trained to do emergency medical work

psychology (sye-KOH-luh-jee)—the study of human behavior, the mind, and emotions

radioed (RAY-dee-ohd)—sent message by radio

valor (VAL-ur)—bravery

About the Author and Illustrator

Robin and Chris Lawrie wrote the *Ridge Riders* books together, and Robin illustrated them. Their inspiration for these books is their son. They wanted to write books that he would find interesting. Many of the *Ridge Riders* books are based on adventures he and his friends had while biking.

Robin and Chris live in England, and will soon be moving to a big, old house that is also home to sixty bats.

Librarian Reviewer
Chris Kreie
Media Specialist, Eden Prairie Schools, MN
MS in Information Media, St. Cloud State University, MN

Reading Consultant
Elizabeth Stedem
Educator/Consultant, Colorado Springs, CO
MA in Elementary Education, University of Denver, CO

First published in the United States in 2007
by Stone Arch Books,
151 Good Counsel Drive, P.O. Box 669,
Mankato, Minnesota 56002.
www.stonearchbooks.com

First published by Evans Brothers Ltd,
2A Portman Mansions, Chiltern Street,
London W1U 6NR, United Kingdom.

Library of Congress Cataloging-in-Publication Data
Lawrie, Robin.
    Fear 3.1 / by Robin and Chris Lawrie; illustrated by Robin Lawrie.
    p. cm. — (Ridge Riders)
    Summary: After a minor mountain climbing accident, Slam develops
a fear of heights that interferes with his bicycle racing and other activities,
until his friend Dozy suggests that he think of the fear as a computer
program that he can quit whenever he wishes.
    ISBN-13: 978-1-59889-348-9 (library binding)
    ISBN-10: 1-59889-348-3 (library binding)
    ISBN-13: 978-1-59889-443-1 (paperback)
    ISBN-10: 1-59889-443-9 (paperback)
    [1. Fear—Fiction. 2. Mountaineering—Fiction. 3. All terrain
cycling—Fiction. 4. Bicycle racing—Fiction.] I. Lawrie, Chris. II. Title.
III. Title: Fear three point one.
PZ7.L438218Fea 2007
[Fic]—dc22   2006026633

1 2 3 4 5 6 12 11 10 09 08 07

Printed in the United States of America

FEAR 3.1

by Robin and Chris Lawrie
illustrated by Robin Lawrie

STONE ARCH BOOKS
MINNEAPOLIS   SAN DIEGO

The Ridge Riders

 Hi, my name is "Slam" Duncan.

This is Aziz. We call him Dozy.

Then there's Larry.

This is Fiona.

And Andy.

* I'm Andy. (Andy is deaf. He uses sign language instead of talking.)

Our home is a town called Shabberley, which is overlooked by a huge forest on a hill called Westridge.

That's where we train and where downhill bike races are sometimes held.

But we do other stuff, too. For instance, Fiona is a horse rider. Larry knows lots of stuff about computers. And me? Well, I used to liked rock climbing. Until the other day . . .

I belonged to the local scout troop.
We did lots of camping and wilderness skills
and that kind of thing, but my favorite activity
was rock climbing on:

Westridge Cliff

We always had plenty of
supervisors and training, and
we always checked equipment
carefully.

But sometimes there were problems.
It was a part of the cliff I had
climbed many times before.
I was 100 yards up.
I had just placed
my foot in a
crevice and was
reaching for a
handhold.

Then my
foothold
gave way.

Luckily, my safety harness
and rope held, but I was
really scared.

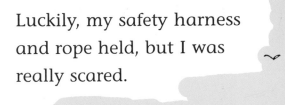

The next day was race 3
of the Westland Super Series.
11 o'clock. First run.
I was waiting at the starting line, with Dozy
and Andy behind me. I thought
I felt fine.

Beep BEEP Beep BEEEEP

Go!

WESTLAND START
SUPER SERIES

??!!

?
?

Suddenly, I
couldn't move. I
felt like my feet
were nailed to
the floor!

What's wrong?

I was shaking all over, so before the next run,
I went back to the food tent for a drink.
I felt a little better until I
overheard my friends
talking.

Lost his mind.

Can't cut it anymore.

Mutter, mutter.

In spite of all this, I managed to do
okay for my second run. I was
really starting to feel
much better, until I
got to the first
dropoff on
the course.

I froze again. I couldn't do it. I decided
to walk that one, and the next one, too.
I came in 14th. What a disaster!

There was only one thing to do —
serious training on the big drops
above Westridge Cliff.
It was a long, long
walk up, but
it was the best
place to get
over my
fear of heights.

AARRGGHH!

All I did was make myself even more scared.

After a really bad crash, old Jack, the forest ranger who lived in a trailer on top of the cliff, walked over and said . . .

Later that day . . .

Dozy came up to the cliff dropoffs the next day to try to help me with my problems.

But I couldn't relax at all. And then I bent my front wheel. I was thinking angrily about the long walk back with a useless bike when I heard a crash!

I felt sick. I don't remember going
to the door and opening it.

Jack was lying on the floor
with blood coming from his head.
Dozy took one look and was on his bike.

I had to get help up to Jake's trailer ①, but I was faced with a horrible choice. I could either climb down Westridge Cliff ② without ropes and then run into the town ③, which would take about 20 minutes.

Or I could get back home using the slow trail through the woods ④, which was easy to ride but hard to run. If only I hadn't broken my wheel! If only Dozy hadn't taken off!

I just couldn't decide what to do. In my mind's eye I saw two newspaper headlines:

Then I remembered Jack's advice.

I got halfway down and froze with
fear. I mean, I really went crazy.
My fingernails were bleeding, my
knees were shaking, and I was
starting to slide.

18

19

20

Suddenly I felt better. The program was closed. The monsters were gone. My right foot felt for a toehold. My left hand found a crack. One move at a time, I inched my way to the top.

We got on Dozy's bike.
Dozy stood over the crossbar and pedaled like crazy. We were back in town in 20 minutes.

Hello, we have an emergency. Can you come to the Hanson Garage in Shabberley? There's an old man who's hurt on Westridge. Better bring a four-wheel drive.

I climbed into the ambulance to show them the way, and a few minutes later we were struggling up Westridge.

The ambulance driver called for a helicopter. It landed in a nearby field.

The pilot ran over and asked me to show him Jack's trailer on the map of Westridge.

I'm a terrible map reader.

Well, you'll just have to come with us, then.

24

But when we got there, it didn't make sense.

And so, there I was, with nothing between
me and the trees, 100 yards below.

I thought
I was going to
lose my lunch.

I opened the computer program.

I looked at the monsters.

I moved the cursor to "File."

I clicked "Quit."

I took a deep breath and jumped out of the door of the helicopter.

RESCUE

I gripped tight onto the rope while the paramedic lowered me down. The paramedic came down after me.
With my feet on the ground, I knew where I was, and we soon found Jack.

29

Jack had turned a really funny color, and his breathing was very odd.

The paramedic radioed our exact position to the helicopter. The pilot hovered over the van, and lowered a special stretcher, called a Stokes litter, to lift Jack out.

First Jack was lifted up on the stretcher, then me on the rope, then the paramedic.

Ten minutes later, we landed on the helipad at Shredbury Hospital. Jack was rushed in on a stretcher.

The next day, we went to see Jack in the hospital. He looked a whole lot better.

Well, Slam. It seems to me you showed both discretion and valor. I'm very grateful to you and Dozy.

But on the way out:

Dozy, why don't you use "Fear 3.1" to fix your fear of blood?

I tried once, but when the program opened I'd already passed out!

James:
A Call to Grow Deeper

My earliest childhood memories take place in the hot summer months. My two brothers—both older than me—would gather the kids in our neighborhood for a giant game of Capture the Flag. My oldest brother, Kendall, would lead one team, and my brother Mark would lead the other team. Since we lived in an agricultural area, we'd climb the fence on the edge of town and stake our territories at the two ends of a dry canal.

My brothers became neighborhood legends. For camouflage they covered their faces, arms, and legs with mud, and they strategically assigned team members to various locations—some to stand guard, others to attack and capture. They also made weapons out of clothespins and large rubber bands. If you got shot with a rubber band, you were "captured." Since I was so much younger than all the other kids I was usually one of the guards. But I was always placed somewhere out of the way. I could never keep up with my brothers. I couldn't run as fast. Or shoot as well.

Eventually we all grew up. One brother joined the army. The other became a marine. If you met my brothers today, you'd meet two men who still possess a warrior's heart. But Kendall now lives his life in a wheelchair. At age 19 a car accident claimed his legs…and so much more. When it comes to suffering, you could say I've had a front-row seat. I've watched a cruel fate twist my brother's dreams into a life no one ever imagines when running through fields as a kid.

So before we begin this journey through the book of James together, I have to be honest. When I first met James, I didn't like him. I barely got two verses

into his book before rolling my eyes. Right away he says stuff like, "Consider it pure joy…whenever you face trials" (1:2 NIV). In my mind, I translated "trials" as "suffering," and I had a hard time swallowing it. Granted, I was only 17 the first time I read James's words. But still, they sounded too much like a platitude. And I don't care much for platitudes. I heard plenty in hospital hallways when well-meaning folk tried to minimize the pain my family was experiencing.

Consider it pure joy? Whenever you suffer?

When I read his words, I wanted to slam the Bible shut. But something caught my eye. A different font on the page said James was the younger brother of Jesus. Suddenly I saw this New Testament writer in a different light. James was the sibling of Suffering. Perhaps we had something in common after all. I knew what it was like to watch your big brother suffer, but I didn't know how to find any joy in that suffering. It didn't make sense.

So I kept reading.

Near the end of his book, James says, "What is your life? You are a mist that appears for a little while and then vanishes" (4:14 NIV). Now, some might see a negative connotation in this verse. At first glance it appears to say our lives are of little value because we're likened to a vapor that quickly disappears. But that's not what James is saying. He's comparing the length of our earthly lives to the unending expanse of eternity. In other words, our earthly lives are quite short when compared to all of eternity.

This shift in perspective changes the way a Christian can view suffering. Suffering is real, and I will never minimize another human being's pain. But all suffering is bound by time. Relief is coming. And a new life—with a new body!—awaits those who believe.

I grew up attending church, but my brother's accident sent each member of my family reeling in their own way. I became a teenager who sat on a spiritual fence, unsure of which way I should go. Could I trust God? Especially after the suffering I'd witnessed in my family? James told me I could. He also told me, the same as he told everyone else, that our beliefs should influence our behavior. Saying I believe in God isn't enough. Faith isn't an abstract, fanciful idea.

Real faith is lived in real time with real action. Sitting on a spiritual fence isn't an option. I must choose. Either God's way or my way.

After reading the book of James, I got off the fence. I chose God. And I've never been the same since.

> Real faith is lived in real time with real action.
>
> #WordWriters

More than 25 years have passed since I first met James. And every time I venture back to the familiar passages in his book, it's like going home. Because there's something comforting about listening to someone tell it straight. James isn't interested in impressing people with a lyrical style. He wants to help believers become more like Christ, and he does so in a straightforward manner. His book reads like a collection of proverbs; in fact, many of his admonitions echo Jesus's words from His Sermon on the Mount.

James is more practical than poetic, and I appreciate his candor because God used his words, his testimony, to help me grow deeper in my faith. Knowledge about God isn't enough. Our faith must coincide with our actions. That is my prayer for us as we journey through this book together. The book of James is a candid call to grow deeper in our faith.

Day 1

The Source of Our Identity

Open my eyes so that I may contemplate wonderful things from Your instruction.

Psalm 119:18

When I heard my name called, I stood with confidence and shook the hands of my interviewers. I had made a list of every question possible, and I'd rehearsed my scripted answers so they wouldn't sound rehearsed. This interview would be a cinch.

But the first question wasn't even a real question. Someone on the panel said, "So, Denise, tell us about yourself."

What? Can't they read the application that tells them my job history? This is a teacher interview. Don't they want to ask me about my philosophy of education? Or how I would respond to a misbehaving student or an upset parent?

My interview training told me to be natural and say what came to mind. So with all the eloquence in the world, I said, "Um, I like football."

They laughed. While I wanted to crawl under the table. But then they asked, "What team?"

It ended up being the best interview ever because I ditched the formal answers. I quit trying to impress my potential employers, and I just told them about myself. I like the Green Bay Packers. I like drinking tea and making quilts too. These things may not seem to go together, but they're all true of me.

Now, if someone had asked me the same thing a long time ago, I might have said I'm a pastor's kid. Because it's easy—almost automatic—to identify ourselves based on who we're related to or what we do. So when we read the first verse in the book of James, the way he describes himself is telling.

Read James 1:1.

James could easily refer to himself as the brother of Jesus—you know, the Messiah, the Savior of the world. He could easily remind his listeners that he grew up with Jesus and arguably knows more about Him than anyone, save their mother, Mary. But James doesn't identify himself by his familial relationship. He doesn't pull the family trump card. Instead, he calls himself "a slave of God and of the Lord Jesus Christ." A slave. Some translations say "a bondservant." Both terms mean a person who yields and surrenders to the lordship of a master. James is calling Jesus his Lord, his Master, his Savior.

This is a huge shift from his younger years.

Read John 7:1-5 and Mark 3:7-21.

James was late to the believing party; in fact, Jesus's whole family thought He was out of His mind. It wasn't until after Jesus's resurrection, when He appeared to the disciples and His family, that James and the rest of the family believed in Jesus as the Messiah.

Read Acts 1:1-14 and 1 Corinthians 15:3-8.

After the crucifixion, Jesus's family is specifically mentioned as being with the disciples when Jesus "presented Himself alive" and gave "many convincing proofs" (Acts 1:3). Then in Paul's letter to the Corinthian believers, we learn Jesus appeared to His brother James. We don't know what was said in this meeting. It was a private conversation between two brothers, between Creator and creation. But after this meeting, James was a changed man, and he became the uncontested leader of the early church in Jerusalem.

Because of Jesus, I am changed too. Yeah, I like

> Because of Jesus, I am changed. It's the most important thing you could ever know about me.
>
> #WordWriters

football, quilts, and tea. Yeah, I grew up wearing the moniker PK for pastor's kid. But the most important thing you could ever know about me is that I belong to Jesus. He is the true source of my identity. And while it may sound strange to our modern ears, this is who I am: a slave of God and of the Lord Jesus Christ.

Diving Deeper

Who are the recipients of this letter?

When you meet someone for the first time, how do you introduce yourself? What is the first thing you want people to know about you?

When have your friends, your coworkers, or your own family members struggled to believe in you? What happened?

As you turn to page 124 and write out James 1:1, thank Jesus for being the true source of your identity.

Prayer: Thank You, Lord, for believing in me, even when I failed to believe in You. Thank You for never giving up on me. Thank You for calling me Your own and for grafting me into Your family. In You alone, I discover who I really am. Amen.

A Call to Grow Deeper
~ through tests and trials ~

The blogging world has as many different kinds of blogs as it does bloggers. But most blog posts fall into one of two categories: "how to" or "me too." The "how to" post typically offers a bullet-point list of helpful tips—practical advice for everyday living. The "me too" post is more narrative—usually a story from real life the reader can relate to, meant to inspire and encourage.

If James were writing today, his letter to believers would fall into the "how to" category. His words are highly practical and applicable to our modern lives. In the first section, James tells us how to persevere when difficult trials come our way. He offers a road map for the journey of life. It begins with the acknowledgment that everyone will experience tests and trials, and that our destination is spiritual maturity (1:2-4). Then he advises us to ask God for wisdom for the journey (1:5-8). Next, he reminds us how temporary this life is and that our real reward awaits us in heaven (1:9-12). Last, he explains where temptation comes from and how to overcome it.

The Test of Faith

Open my eyes so that I may contemplate wonderful things from Your instruction.

PSALM 119:18

When I was growing up, my mom made a trip to the local library every week. I loved tagging along. The lady behind the counter even gave me my own library card. I could check out any books I wanted from the children's section. Every visit felt like Christmas.

I still love going to my local library, and whenever I visit a new city, I always want to check out its library. There's a certain solemnity to libraries; they're like sanctuaries. My favorite "library," of course, is the Bible, which holds the most important 66 books in the history of the world. But these books aren't arranged in chronological order.

Even though Genesis appears first, the book of Job was written years earlier. This means the first story told in the canon of Holy Scripture is a story of suffering. It's the first thing God wanted us to know, that life will be hard. Jesus Himself said, "You will have suffering in this world" (John 16:33). And just in case we missed it, God said it again on the first page of the first book written in the New Testament, in James. While the Gospel accounts appear first in the New Testament, James wrote his book several years before Matthew, Mark, Luke, or John wrote theirs. Not even Paul had penned a letter yet.

So the first story written in the Old Testament is about suffering.

And the first topic written about in the New Testament is suffering.

Well, we already know life is hard. So what is God saying here?

---------------- *Read James 1:2-4.* ----------------

Do you feel like rolling your eyes? I wouldn't blame you. I've already admitted I had a hard time with this passage when I first read it. Sure, I want to develop perseverance and endurance. But without the tests and trials, thank you.

I don't know many people who enjoy tests. Even as a teacher I never enjoy giving them. Some argue a teacher needs to give tests to know how well her students are learning. But the truth is, I already know how well my students are catching on to the material by the way they engage in discussion, by the kinds of questions they ask, and by the papers they write. The information a paper test gives me basically confirms what I've already observed in the classroom. But the results of a test *can* be instructive for my students. If we go over the answers together, and if they have a chance to take the test again, they'll likely do better the next time around.

God uses tests the same way. He already knows how we're doing in our faith-life. So if we fail in a certain situation, our failure informs *us* of where we are spiritually. Our failures can be instructive, especially when we invite God into the situation and ask Him to give us the grace and guidance we need to do better.

> Our failures can be instructive, especially when we ask God to give us the grace and guidance we need to do better.
>
> #WordWriters

I love the way Eugene Peterson translates this same passage in The Message Bible. He says, "You know that under pressure, your faith-life is forced into the open and shows its true colors." The tests and trials we experience, even the suffering we endure, are opportunities not only for us to grow in perseverance, but also for our faith to shine in an unbelieving world. I've known people—and perhaps you have too—who've endured deep pain and trauma with a genuine peace that surpasses all human understanding. That kind of peace is other-worldly; it can come only from God. This is one of the ways God is glorified.

Why tests and trials? James says they develop our perseverance and help us grow deeper in our faith. How can we overcome these tests and trials? James answers this question a few verses later by reiterating Jesus's words from the Sermon on the Mount.

Read Matthew 5:1-12 and James 1:12.

Jesus began His famous sermon with a collection of truths we now call the Beatitudes. He framed His words with the idea that a believer's suffering will end in blessing. Jesus said, "Those who mourn are blessed, for they will be comforted" (Matthew 5:4). Then He said, "You are blessed when they insult and persecute you and falsely say every kind of evil against you because of Me. Be glad and rejoice, because your reward is great in heaven" (Matthew 5:11-12). The Bible doesn't command us to be lovers of pain; rather, Jesus wants us to remember that, when we persevere, our suffering will lead to rejoicing one day—when He rewards us in heaven. So we can see where James gets the idea. He says, "Blessed is the one who perseveres under trial because, having stood the test, that person will receive the crown of life that the Lord has promised to those who love him" (1:12 NIV).

The believers in Jerusalem were experiencing tests and trials. They were being persecuted for their faith, and false things were being said about them. If Yelp had been around back then, some naysayers would have given the church in Jerusalem a bunch of one-star reviews. So when James talks about tests and trials, he's referring to the suffering the believers are enduring for their faith. His words are for us too. How can we consider it a joy when we experience tests and trials? We remember the end goal: to become more like Jesus. Because one day He will give us the crown of life.

Diving Deeper

According to James, what do perseverance and endurance produce?

When have you faced a test of your faith and failed? What did you learn about yourself? What did you learn about God's grace and forgiveness?

When have you faced a test of your faith and responded in such a way that you made God smile? How was God glorified from this experience?

While writing James 1:2-4 today, give God praise for the way He's been glorified in a difficult test or trial you've endured.

Prayer: Thank You, Lord, for forgiving me when I've failed. Help me to make wiser choices in the future so if I ever face the same situation again, I can respond in a way that brings glory to Your name. Help me to grow and become mature and complete so my true colors reflect You. Amen.

The Road Map for Life

Open my eyes so that I may contemplate wonderful things from Your instruction.

PSALM 119:18

When my oldest daughter, Simone, graduated from high school, she chose to attend college in Texas. That's about a thousand miles from where we live in California. She's always had a heart for adventure, so when the time came, we loaded the minivan and prepared to trek across four states. But before we pulled out of the driveway, I asked Simone, "You have your ID?" *Check.* "Your laptop?" *Check.* "Your suitcase?" *Check.* "Directions?" She gave me a blank stare, as if to say, "Don't you know how to get there?" Yes, I knew how to get there, but she needed to know how to navigate the route to college herself. We sat in the driveway while she Googled directions.

In his letter James gives something of a road map for the journey of life. He tells us up front that we'll experience hardships along the way, but our destination is spiritual maturity, which means becoming like Christ. So the first thing we should ask God for is wisdom.

> We find wisdom in the riches of God's Word.
>
> #WordWriters

Read James 1:5-8.

For this journey called life, we need a few things—like food, clothing, and shelter. We also need family and friends who stay by our side throughout the journey. More than anything, we need God's wisdom to help us make good choices, and James says we can ask God to give us wisdom.

God isn't stingy when it comes to wisdom. In fact, stinginess isn't in His character. God is a generous giver. Again, James echoes his big brother's words.

Read Matthew 7:7-12 and James 4:3.

Some have tried to interpret Jesus's words to mean we can ask God for anything we want and He'll give it to us. But James says we won't receive what we ask for when we ask with wrong motives. God isn't a slot machine, where we can put in a quarter, pull the lever, and expect a jackpot.

Jesus called His Father a giver of good things. If we need bread, He won't give us a stone. If we need fish, He won't give us a snake. These illustrations convey the necessities of sustaining life. Earthly wisdom tells us the "good things in life" are a bigger house, nicer clothes, and a fancier car. But these possessions don't give us life. Only Jesus can give us life. And He promises to deliver when we go to Him, diligently asking, seeking, and knocking. We mustn't doubt either. We must believe Jesus is who He says He is.

After driving my daughter a thousand miles to college, I helped her get settled in her dorm room. While I put her purple sheets on the bed, she set up her laptop on the desk. Then she pulled her Bible from her bag and set it on the stand next to the bed. I had forgotten to ask her if she remembered to bring the most important thing of all. But she remembered. She knows where to turn for wisdom—to God and His Word. In that moment I knew it would be okay for me to drive a thousand miles back home, without her.

Diving Deeper

If we lack wisdom, what does James say we should do?

What image does James use to illustrate a person full of doubt?

When you need wisdom, where do you turn first? A friend? A spouse? A counselor? The Bible?

When have you asked God for wisdom in a specific situation? What did He show you?

While writing out James 1:5-8, ask God to give you wisdom, trusting and believing He follows through on what He says in His Word.

Prayer: *Thank You, Lord, for being a giver of good gifts. You are the source of all that is good and true. In You alone I find life. Help me to turn to You whenever I need wisdom. Help me to grow as a believer and not be a doubter. Amen.*

The Sands of Time

Open my eyes so that I may contemplate wonderful things from Your instruction.

PSALM 119:18

Snapdragons are my favorite flower. They grow tall and vibrant in many colors. But the main reason I love them is because they remind me of my grandma. She kept a large water pitcher on her back porch, and every time I came to visit, she'd let me fill it up with the garden hose. When the pitcher was full of water, I'd need both hands to carry it, but I relished walking around her yard, watering her flowers.

Grandma's red geraniums grew in pots; her orange marigolds covered the beds. Along the sidewalk her yellow and pink snapdragons tried to out-reach the fence behind them. I'll never forget the morning she showed me their secret. The blossoms, she said, resemble a dragon's head, and if you squeeze them just right, they open and close like a dragon's mouth.

To my dismay, I didn't inherit my grandma's green thumb. I've given up trying to plant flowers in my own yard. The heat and drought in California don't help much either. So I've settled for hardy perennial plants. They're not as beautiful, but they live longer.

> Neither riches nor poverty matter in eternity. What matters is the human soul.
>
> #WordWriters

In today's passage, James compares the benefits of wealth to the beauty of a flower. With time, the benefits of wealth wither like a flower in the heat.

Read James 1:9-12.

In addition to persecution, many believers in the early church knew the hardship of poverty. The divide between the haves and the have-nots was just as real in the first century as it is today. But James says both are temporary. Neither poverty nor riches matter in eternity. What matters is the human soul.

When we believe in Christ, follow His Word, and endure the trials of life, we'll receive a priceless crown—a crown of life, promised to those who love Him. James isn't saying financial struggles aren't real. They're real. And they're hard. But they're temporary. As temporary as a blossom in summer's heat.

Read Matthew 6:19-34.

We see where James gets the idea. Jesus used the illustration of a flower too. The world as we know it is fleeting, like sand in an hourglass. We're sojourners in a foreign land, but one day we'll be home in God's presence and money won't matter. So as long as we're here, we're prudent to ask God for wisdom more than we ask Him for money. Wisdom from above gives us a long-term perspective. We needn't grind our teeth over the apparent inequity we observe every day. At the end of days, a person's wealth won't get them anywhere. The condition of a person's soul will be the only thing that matters.

Diving Deeper

What does God promise to give those who love Him and endure trials?

Why does James say a person in humble circumstances should "boast in his exaltation" but a rich person should "boast in his humiliation" (1:9-10)? What point is he trying to make?

James says the heat dries up the grass and the flower's beautiful appearance is destroyed. Why does he include the illustration of a flower in a field? What is he trying to communicate?

James reiterates the temporal nature of this earthly life. How does that influence the decisions you make? How does it influence the confidence you place in the earthly security money provides?

Write out James 1:9-12. Then draw a circle around verse 12. It's a great verse to memorize!

Prayer: Thank You, Lord, for looking past the material possessions people accumulate and the status people attain in the world. You see my heart. And what I want more than earthly riches is to know You more. That is my prayer. More of You, Jesus. More of You. Amen.

The Pit Stop of Sin

Open my eyes so that I may contemplate wonderful things from Your instruction.

PSALM 119:18

I round the corner to find sweet Brynn standing in the kitchen with cookie crumbs all over her face. She immediately points to her little brother and says, "He made me do it!"

"Are you saying your little brother *made* you drag the chair from the table over to the kitchen counter to climb up the cupboards to reach the bag of chocolate chip cookies?"

She nods profusely.

Finger pointing begins at an early age. We don't even have to teach it. It's ingrained in our human nature to want to blame someone else, or something else, for our choices. We can trace this behavior all the way back to Adam and Eve. Adam not only pointed his finger at Eve and told God *she* was the one who gave him the forbidden fruit to eat, but he also tried to blame God by saying, "The woman *You* gave to be with me—she gave me some fruit from the tree, and I ate" (Genesis 3:12, emphasis added).

See? It was all God's fault!

Not really. But it was a nice try, anyway. The truth is, we're not that different from Adam or Eve or a five-year-old with her hand in a bag of cookies. We want to blame someone else for our actions. James addresses this common behavior, and he tells us exactly who's to blame.

----------------- *Read James 1:13-18.* -----------------

James wants everyone to be clear about where sin originates. Sin never comes from God. Never. We're all tempted, he says, when we're "drawn away and enticed by [our] own evil desires" (1:14). This doesn't mean all desire is bad. Some desires are good and beautiful. The desire to be known and loved and accepted is part of God's imprint on our souls. It's a God-given desire. But God has given us parameters to meet those desires in ways that bring healthy fruit to our lives. When we choose to meet those desires outside of God's parameters, we sin, which means we've missed the mark of God's divine design for our lives. Sin originates with us.

There's also a difference between tests and temptations. Tests are meant to bring out the good. Temptations are meant to bring out the bad.* God's intentions for us are always good. Satan's intentions for us are always bad. Temptation may come from someone, or something, outside us. It may come from Satan himself. But we're the ones who allow temptation to take root in our minds and hearts. We're the ones who allow temptation to fertilize the seeds of desire. We're the ones who choose to fulfill our desires outside of God's plan for our lives, which is why we need God's grace in the first place.

> God's grace turns the pit of sin into a pit stop.
>
> #WordWriters

I love hearing stories of God's grace—how people met Jesus and how He changed them from the inside out. Few things are more beautiful than listening to a soul give God glory for the life He's redeemed. Every once in a while, though, I'll hear a hint of finger pointing in the story. Sometimes the testimony includes a long backstory to explain how the person was vulnerable to making a wrong choice in the first place. Perhaps there was a neglectful or abusive parent or spouse. Perhaps there was a job loss and a serious financial burden. It's understandable how these painful circumstances can lead us to a vulnerable place in our hearts and minds. It's also characteristic of Satan

---

* John Phillips, *Exploring the Epistle of James* (Grand Rapids, MI: Kregel Publications, 2004), 43.

to tempt us when we're at our lowest. He will work overtime to cause havoc in our lives—all for the express purpose of creating the "perfect storm" for sin. But when all is said and done, the choice is still ours to make. When we choose sin, we can't point our finger at anyone but ourselves.

I'll be the first to stand up and say I'm a sinner. I need God's grace. We all do. That's why His mercy is so amazing. He doesn't give us what we deserve; He gives us a second chance. James says, "He gave us a new birth" (1:18). There's nothing we can do that God can't forgive. Nothing! No hidden secret or past shame can bar us from God's forgiveness. His grace turns the pit of sin into a pit stop. His grace sets us free. It's His gift to all who believe. His good and perfect gift.

------------------------------ *Diving Deeper* ------------------------------

Does God ever tempt anyone? What's the difference between a test and a temptation?

What happens when someone gives in to temptation? How does James describe the progression of sin?

Why did God choose to give people a chance for a second birth? How would you describe this second birth to a friend who doesn't know Jesus?

Today write out James 1:13-18 and give thanks for the new birth you have in Christ Jesus.

Prayer: *Thank You, Lord, for the new birth You've given me. Because of You, I am changed. Your forgiveness has set me free. I'm a new creation. May all who see the change in me know You're the reason for the change they see. Amen.*

A Call to Grow Deeper ~through the implanted Word~

The moment we accept God's grace, we're forgiven. The slate is wiped clean. But how can we avoid making the same mistakes in the future? How can we overcome new temptations that come our way?

God gave us a powerful tool for overcoming temptation. He gave us His Word. When we read the Bible, the Holy Spirit renews our minds, replacing old thought patterns with new ones. The apostle Paul put it like this: "Therefore, if anyone is in Christ, he is a new creation; old things have passed away, and look, new things have come" (2 Corinthians 5:17). When we immerse our minds in the truth of God's Word, we begin to think differently, which leads to making different choices. Better choices.

The Strength to Overcome

Open my eyes so that I may contemplate wonderful things from Your instruction.

PSALM 119:18

When my kids were little, I made a poster to help them memorize the famous passage on love in 1 Corinthians 13:4-8. I made each phrase a different color. First, we focused on the red words: *Love is patient, love is kind. It does not envy, it does not boast.* Then we worked on the orange words: *It is not proud, it is not rude. It is not self-seeking.* We proceeded in this colorful fashion until my kids had memorized the entire passage. We called it the "First Corinthians Game."

One morning, while gathering laundry at the top of the stairs, I heard my son say to his big sister, "Let's play First Corinthians!"

His sister responded with a bored voice, "No thanks."

Undeterred he said, "Okay. I'll do it."

I stopped to listen and savor the moment. In his tender four-year-old voice he began, "Love is patient, love is kind. It does not envy, it does not boast. It is not proud. It is not self-seeking."

His sister interrupted, "It is not rude. You're supposed to say, it is not rude."

He had accidentally skipped that phrase, but he stammered back, "No! It is not self-seeking!"

Then she yelled, "That's wrong! You're supposed to say it is not rude!"

My moment of maternal bliss ended. I had to march downstairs and break it up. Their words to each other were neither loving nor kind. Obviously, they missed the point.

Later, I couldn't help but laugh at the irony. Sometimes we work so hard at getting it "right" that we miss the point too. Studying the Bible is about

transformation, not information. It's about implanting God's Word in our hearts so we can love others with the same compassion Christ has shown us.

> I don't want head-knowledge without heart-compassion. I want to love the way Jesus loves.
>
> #WordWriters

Read James 1:19-25.

The day my kids argued over a memory verse is a great example of being hearers of the Word and not doers. Sadly, it's not always little kids who make that mistake. It's a common malady, and I'm no more immune to it than the next person. We're all prone to letting something in one ear and out the other. Yet, being a doer of the Word means our beliefs influence our behavior. Jesus said as much in His Sermon on the Mount.

Read Matthew 7:24-29.

Jesus describes two homes being rocked by a storm. The home on a solid foundation withstands the pressure of the storm, but the home built on sand collapses. Our response to the storms in our lives will be the same. We can respond to a test or temptation with a quiet strength and humble dignity, but only when we've girded ourselves with God's truth. That's exactly how Jesus responded to Satan's temptations in the desert. He rebuffed Satan by quoting Scripture (see Matthew 4:1-11). The more we listen to the truth of God's Word and act on what it says, the more we can overcome any test or temptation that comes our way.

James says Scripture is like a mirror. A mirror reflects the outer person, while Scripture reflects the inner person. Nobody looks into the mirror and ignores a smear of ketchup on their chin. Neither should we ignore the truth God speaks to us when His Word reveals an area in our lives we need to change. Perhaps there's a splotch of jealousy in our hearts or a smudge of gossip in our talk.

My kids reminded me of an important truth that day. As much as I love to study God's Word and memorize life-giving passages, a mere recollection

of Bible verses isn't enough. The truth of Scripture must burrow deep into my soul, yielding a harvest of genuine service for Him. I don't want to acquire head-knowledge without heart-compassion. I want to love the way Jesus loves, and I want to teach my children to do the same. Memorizing Bible verses is a great benefit to us. It's a practical way we can embed God's truth deep into our hearts and minds, but it's also important that we understand the meaning of those verses and how we can apply them to our lives. James makes it clear: Knowing the truth means living the truth. There's no way around it.

Diving Deeper

What should we be quick to do? What does James want us listening to? Why is this so important?

What should we be slow to do? How can a quick response with our words be potentially harmful?

Why does James compare the Word of God to a mirror? What do both tell us about ourselves?

Writing the Word is a powerful way to implant God's truth deep into our hearts and minds. With God's Word in us, we can begin to overcome trials and temptations. Today let's write out James 1:19-25.

Prayer: *Thank You, Lord, for giving me Your Word. I pray my heart is softened every time I open the pages of my Bible. Help me to be quick to listen. Help me to respond to the promptings Your Spirit gives when I read the Word. Speak, Lord. Your servant is listening. Amen.*

The Heart of God

Open my eyes so that I may contemplate wonderful things from Your instruction.

PSALM 119:18

I used to think orphans were simply people without parents. Characters like Harry Potter and Oliver Twist came to mind. Little dancers from the musical *Annie* came to mind too. Didn't they all have happy endings?

When I married an orphan, my understanding changed. Life isn't about happy endings. Life is about the journey. And the journey without parents is hard. I never would have imagined how hard if I didn't witness it for myself—every day, every year, at every family celebration, every holiday.

I never met my in-laws. Two separate, unexpected accidents took their lives while my husband, Jeff, was still young. He became his youngest sister's legal guardian and raised her from the time she was 12.

Jeff and I had a traditional wedding ceremony, but we omitted the part where each mother lights a candle. It wasn't possible. As unbelievably special as that day was, there was still a taint of sadness to it. Jeff's parents weren't there to celebrate with their firstborn son.

I remember our first Thanksgiving together. It was such a little thing. I had washed and peeled and boiled the potatoes. But when it came time to mash them, I couldn't remember how much milk and butter to add. So I called my mom. From 400 miles away she told me how much milk and butter to use. I hung up the phone and poured the measured milk. Across the room, however, I caught a brief expression on Jeff's face. He didn't see me. But with children scampering and uncles chattering, I noticed, before it quickly masked over to the face everyone else recognizes. And I knew.

Some people don't have a mom they can call about mashed potatoes. Some people can't call home.

-------------------- *Read James 1:26-27.* --------------------

Widows and orphans are among us—in our schools and our churches, as well as in orphanages overseas. If we gather in His name, yet fail to care for the widows and orphans in our midst, James says our religion—despite our other good works—is not acceptable in God's sight.

God gets it. He really gets it. This is why He commands in Scripture, over and over again, to care for widows and orphans (see Exodus 22:22; Deuteronomy 24:17-21; 27:19). My faith in God's goodness is renewed by the compassion He shows and the compassion He commands because, nowadays, I get it too. The apostle Paul said, "Where, O death, is your victory? Where, O death, is your sting?" (1 Corinthians 15:55 NIV). The sting of death is real. But because of Christ, death is not an ending but a passageway.

> Because of Christ, death is not an ending but a passageway.
>
> #WordWriters

In my husband's extended family, Jeff is "the nephew." When he married me, Denise, we became "De-niece and De-nephew." I'm a firm believer in God's sense of humor.

-------------------- *Diving Deeper* --------------------

If someone doesn't control his or her speech, how does James describe that person's religion?

How does James define pure religion?

Does your local church have a ministry to reach out to the widows and orphans in your congregation and local community? Who are the widows and orphans in your community you could begin praying for today?

Write the names of the widows and orphans you know in your community in the margins of these pages. Commit to praying for them regularly. Then write out James 1:26-27.

Prayer: Thank You, Lord, for caring so deeply for widows and orphans, not only around the world, but here in my own community as well. Open my eyes to see the needs around me. Help me to be a bearer of Christ's light, and to love others as You love us all. Amen.

A Call to Grow Deeper
~ through love and mercy ~

When it comes to nutrition and physical health, most health experts agree on two essentials for healthy living: (1) eating balanced meals with lots of fruits and vegetables and (2) getting some form of physical exercise every day. In other words, take good food in, then exercise it out. I don't mean to oversimplify. Achieving physical health is harder than it sounds—especially if you're like me and you happen to love pizza and potato chips and anything with chocolate.

In the same way, there are two essentials for healthy spiritual living: (1) consuming a steady intake of God's Word every day and (2) doing what it says. Again, I don't mean to oversimplify. Indeed, some of the Bible's commands may be hard to do. But at the core of every instruction in the Bible is the need for a heart motivated by love and moved through mercy.

In the next portion of his letter, James gives some practical examples of what it means to put our faith into action through love and mercy.

The Exterior We See

Open my eyes so that I may contemplate wonderful things from Your instruction.

PSALM 119:18

I entered the large auditorium, excited to attend my first conference for church leaders. More than two thousand people congregated to be equipped and encouraged. Nearly everyone present was a leader in his or her church back home. I had just turned 21, and I looked forward to the sessions I would attend on youth ministry. Some of the "biggest names" in ministry were there.

I spent the next three days watching people all around me hustle from one session to the next, eager to get a seat up front, hoping to shake hands with the "famous" pastors in our midst. Even in the foyer outside the auditorium, crowds gathered around the VIPs—the very important persons. The VIPs all had something in common: They were pastors of mega churches. Their churches had large numbers, both in terms of weekly church attendance and the square footage of the buildings they met in. The largeness of their ministries attracted others; it seemed everyone wanted to be like them.

My wide eyes took it all in. The ladder of ministry success stood before me. I observed how it all worked. Rubbing elbows. Making connections. Accepting invitations. I joined the fray. I got excited about numbers. Even in youth ministry, the bigger the better. Or so I thought. Until it all fell apart and my world came crashing down around me. Disappointment. Disillusionment. Not only in others, but in myself.

For the next several years, I preferred the sidelines in ministry. Partly because it felt safer there, but partly because I didn't want to be that person ever again— that person who desires to increase her numbers, to increase her perceived importance. Instead, I prayed for God to conform my desires to His.

Fast-forward almost 20 years. I entered a large ballroom, excited to attend my first blogging conference. Several hundred Christian women writers gathered to be equipped and encouraged. Nearly every person present had a website, which meant she had a group of people back home who followed her and wanted to hear what she had to say. Some of the "biggest names" in the industry were there.

> What if we noticed people's eyes instead of their ties? What if we appreciated people's hands instead of their rings?
>
> #WordWriters

I spent the next three days feeling as though I had stepped into a time machine, watching people all around me hustle from one session to the next, eager to get a seat up front, hoping to shake hands with the "famous" authors and bloggers in our midst. The VIPs were the same, just with a different name. They had large numbers, in terms of "likes" and followers online. The largeness of their online presence attracted others; it seemed everyone wanted to be like them. But this time I didn't join the fray. I sat near the back and struck up conversations with whoever was near. I learned the names and stories of bloggers and writers most people have never heard of. And I loved it. I made friends with women from all over the country.

Read James 2:1-4.

I like James. He's no respecter of persons, and as the leader of the church in Jerusalem, he wants a congregation of believers who treat people with gentle care and genuine respect. No matter who they are. No matter how they're dressed. What if our churches today followed James's admonition? What if we noticed people's eyes instead of their ties? What if we appreciated people's hands instead of their rings?

I still love attending conferences. But these days I go to conferences with a different intention, with a different heart. The teacher in me loves the atmosphere of learning that takes place at conferences. But the main reason I love to go are the amazing people I meet who are serving in God's kingdom in

incredible ways. Some of these ministries may not be big and flashy; probably few people have ever heard of them. But Jesus often chooses the most unsuspecting people to share His love with a hurting world.

----------------------- *Diving Deeper* -----------------------

James uses the example of showing favoritism to someone who is impressively dressed. What are some other ways people show favoritism?

James describes people who show favoritism as discriminating judges with evil thoughts. Does this description seem unduly harsh? Why do you think James uses such strong language to make his point?

When have you observed someone being shown favor because of their outward appearance or impressive status? How did it make you feel? When have you shown favoritism?

How can you be a person who doesn't show favoritism in your community?

When you write out James 2:1-4 today, ask God to give you a heart for those who may get overlooked by others.

Prayer: Thank You, Lord, for not overlooking me. You saw me when I was at my very worst, and You still loved me. Your love for me isn't conditional on my appearance or achievement. You love me as I am. Help me to love others with the same grace and favor You have shown to me. Amen.

The Royal Law in Scripture

Open my eyes so that I may contemplate wonderful things from Your instruction.

PSALM 119:18

I sat next to the wall, unable to sing. While my eyes followed the lyrics on the screen, I made the words with my mouth, but nothing came out. I clapped my hands when everyone else clapped theirs, and I bowed my head when someone on stage prayed. But all I could think about was the empty chair next to me. I was relatively new at this church, and I'd hoped this women's retreat would be an opportunity to connect with some of the women. I agreed to be roommates with three total strangers. I showed up to all the meetings. I participated in the small group discussions. I even made small talk at all the meals. But the seat next to me was still empty. Like it had been all weekend.

Friday night. All day Saturday. And now Sunday morning. This was our last session before driving back home. The speaker shared the parable of the good Samaritan: *A man was beaten and left on the side of the road. A priest saw the man but walked on by. So did another citizen. Finally, a foreigner saw the man, treated his wounds, took him to an inn, and cared for him.* As I listened to the speaker tell this story from the Bible, a lump of cynicism collected in my throat. Part of me wanted to cry. Another part of me wanted to stand up and share a few pointed words with the women in the room. We're supposed to be good neighbors, like the good Samaritan. Except we prob-ably don't come across too many people lying half dead on the side of the road. If we did, we'd surely do something. Otherwise, this parable doesn't seem very

> Jesus takes this favoritism thing pretty seriously, so we should follow suit.
>
> #WordWriters

applicable. Walking right past the new gal at the retreat doesn't seem like the same thing. We can't see a half-dead heart sitting alone by the wall.

My hurt turned me into a judge. I judged all the women there. They were wrong. I was right. They were cruel. I was kind. It was very black and white. But then I felt a familiar nudge inside me; I needed to ask for God's forgiveness. It's not for me to judge. Besides, maybe my expectations were a tiny bit unreasonable. I didn't make an instant best friend, but I did meet a number of ladies I didn't know before the retreat. I did have some nice conversations over the weekend. And I'd certainly recognize some familiar faces the next time I attended a women's Bible study. Maybe the weekend wasn't a total loss after all. Maybe I just needed to invest a little time in sowing some seeds of friendship.

Read Leviticus 19:18; Luke 10:25-37; and James 2:5-9.

Once again we see James quoting Jesus, who's quoting a famous passage from the Old Testament: *Love your neighbor as yourself.* This is the royal law in Scripture. Jesus takes this favoritism thing pretty seriously, so we should follow suit. My neighbors aren't just the people who live on my street either. They're the people I see every day and throughout the week. They're the women I see at weekend retreats. That weekend I was so focused on finding someone to be *my* friend. Maybe there was someone that weekend who needed me to be *her* friend.

Diving Deeper

Who did God choose to be rich in faith?

If we show favoritism, what will we be convicted of?

When have you felt left outside a clique? How did you respond? What did you learn from this experience?

Have you ever felt convicted for showing favoritism yourself? What happened? What did you learn from this experience?

As you write out James 2:5-9, ask God to show you one "neighbor" you could express kindness to today.

Prayer: *Thank You, Lord, for loving everyone the way You do and for wanting us to do the same. Show me the areas in my life where I might be inclined to show favoritism. Help me to forgive those who show preferential treatment to someone over me. Help me to see my neighbors as You see them and to love them well. Amen.*

The Top 100

Open my eyes so that I may contemplate wonderful things from Your instruction.

Psalm 119:18

I read three things every day: the Bible, nfl.com, and packers.com. But during the offseason, the "news" for football is pretty slow. So what do sportswriters write about? They write articles that rank players.

First they rank quarterbacks. Then they rank running backs. Then they rank wide receivers. The sportswriters go through all the positions on a team. Once they're done ranking players by position, they rank teams—by division, by conference, by league. Then they rank the all-time greatest quarterbacks in football history. Then the all-time greatest teams. On and on the ranking goes.

Why am I talking about football news during the offseason? Because it represents a universal human experience. When we have nothing of real substance to focus on, we compare and we rank. It's what we do. We size everybody up, then determine where we fit in the lineup. I'm not just talking about pro football. Even in the Christian world, we rank other Christians according to the size of their ministries, businesses, bank accounts, homes, and even their blogs. These are real headlines: The Top 100 Christian Blogs, The Top 100 Christian Colleges, The Top 100 Christian Songs, The Top 100 Christian Books, and The Top 100 Christian Nonprofits. There are more, but you get the idea. The ranking and comparing is almost endless. And we've been doing it forever.

In James's day, the believers were converted Jews, steeped in the religious traditions they grew up in. These Jewish traditions were added to the laws God established through Moses. So the Jews used their traditions and laws to rank and compare themselves to others. It's how they established their moral reputations and social standings—by how well they observed their traditions and laws.

Read James 2:10-13.

Christianity is the great equalizer of people. We're all lawbreakers. Every single one of us. My sin will be different from your sin, but we're all sinners in need of mercy. Jesus doesn't rank our sin either. I'm not a "better Christian" because I've never murdered someone. As soon as we start thinking in terms of "better than" or "lesser than," we've strayed from the truth of Scripture because every human soul is in desperate need of mercy. James reaches the pinnacle of his letter when he says, "Mercy triumphs over judgment" (2:13). You can see where he gets it too.

> Christianity is the great equalizer of people. My sin will be different from your sin, but we're all sinners in need of mercy.
>
> #WordWriters

Read Matthew 5:21-30.

When Jesus stepped onto the scene, He rattled the religious teachers, who clung to their traditions. Jesus said we don't get a free pass just because we've never murdered someone. He said if we've ever held hatred in our heart for another person, then we're subject to judgment. Ouch. I need mercy already.

James writes his letter to encourage us to grow deeper in our faith. This growth begins when we have a right view of our sinful nature. The apostle Paul added to this sentiment when he said, "Do nothing out of rivalry or conceit, but in humility consider others as more important than yourselves" (Philippians 2:3). Hmm. Those words are worth pondering. How well do I consider others as more important than myself? Or am I busy ranking and comparing to see where I fit in the mix?

We don't need to join the ranks of the rankers to feel good about ourselves. God alone determines our worth. He made us, and He called us good. That's good enough for me.

Diving Deeper

If someone fails in one point of the law, why does James say that person is guilty of breaking all of it?

James quotes Jesus when he says, "Do not commit adultery" and "Do not murder" (2:11). How did Jesus raise the bar on these commands?

What does James mean when he says mercy triumphs over judgment?

When has someone shown you mercy? What was it like being on the receiving end of such mercy?

While writing out James 2:10-13, ask God to help you grow in being a giver of mercy.

Prayer: *Thank You, Lord, for wiping my slate clean, for giving me a fresh start. Thank You for calling me Your daughter. I'm so grateful for the mercy You've shown me. Thank You for seeing Your children equal in value and worth. You are truly the God of love and mercy. Amen.*

A Call to Grow Deeper
~ through faith in action ~

In ancient Greek theater, the actors on stage were called hypocrites. This wasn't an insult; it's how they described the profession of acting. Nowadays the word *hypocrite* has taken on a derogatory meaning; it implies a fraud. James says a Christian is a fraud if her faith doesn't grow into action. He's not saying salvation can be earned through good deeds. God's grace is a gift. We can do nothing to earn it. James simply means that genuine faith results in good deeds. The latter is a natural by-product of the former.

In this next section, James is explicit. He says faith without action is impossible. And he uses an unlikely pair of people, Abraham and Rahab, as his prime examples.

The Fruit of Faith

Open my eyes so that I may contemplate wonderful things from Your instruction.

PSALM 119:18

When I was eight, my family moved across the country. Everything we owned was in a moving truck. We awoke one morning to discover our moving truck had been stolen and everything we owned was gone. So instead of moving into our own home, we had to move in with Grandma until we could accumulate some basic necessities for living. Grandma lived in a small town, and everyone had heard about our plight, so folks would put bags of hand-me-down clothes and household items on Grandma's front porch, ring the doorbell, and leave. Even though I literally had nothing to wear other than one or two changes of clothing, I hated sorting through those bags. I'd find dirty clothes with stains and holes. Sometimes I'd even find a sock without a match.

One day a lady came to the front door with a box of dishes. She sounded so cheerful. She said she heard we didn't have any dishes, and she had just bought a new set herself, so she didn't need her old dishes anymore. She was so happy someone could use her old dishes. It must have been God's special timing, she said, that she happened to buy new dishes that week. She handed my mom the box of dishes and left. I followed my mom as she carried the box to Grandma's kitchen table. When she pulled out a plate and a bowl, I must have grimaced. They were the ugliest dishes I'd ever seen. My mom never said a word. She set them on the table, walked to her borrowed bedroom, and closed the door. I could hear her crying on the other side.

We were pretty squeezed in Grandma's two-bedroom house. Eventually we were able to move into a rental of our own, but for the next two years, we ate off those dishes. I hated every meal. They reminded me of our poverty, of our lack

of agency. We couldn't afford to buy new dishes. I wondered about the woman who gave us her old dishes. She must have had an entire home full of possessions she picked out herself, while our home was an odd mish-mash of donations. What if she had given us, a destitute family, her new set of dishes instead of her old ones? How might that have brightened an otherwise dreary day every time we sat down for dinner?

Read James 2:14-19.

Many believers in the early church knew the sting of poverty, but we're told in the book of Acts how they shared with one another generously (see Acts 4:32-35). As they experienced greater persecution from nonbelievers, they moved to other areas. So when James writes his letter to all the believers, he encourages them to put their faith into action.

James doesn't mince words. He says it like it is. It's not enough to tell someone in need, "I wish you well," but then do nothing for their physical needs. It's not enough to say we believe in God. True faith is evidenced by caring deeds. And when we do put our faith into action, let's do so with generous hearts. Let's not "give" our unwanted junk to other people. The most important thing we could ever give another human being is dignity.

> The most important thing we could ever give another human being is dignity.
>
> #WordWriters

Diving Deeper

How does James describe faith without works?

Why is James so adamant that people's faith lead to good deeds?

What are some ways you can minister to the physical needs of someone in your community?

Write out James 2:14-19 and ask God to show you one person or one family in your community you could reach out to today.

Prayer: Thank You, Lord, for caring so deeply for the poor. Thank You for all the ways Your sons and daughters have shown kindness and generosity to those in need. May the Holy Spirit convict me whenever my faith is stifled with inaction. Help me, Lord, to be a generous giver. Amen.

The Friend of God

Open my eyes so that I may contemplate wonderful things from Your instruction.

PSALM 119:18

I can't remember a time when I didn't know the name Jesus. I went to church every Sunday, so Jesus was a name I sang about, a name I prayed to, and a name I believed in. But it was still a name that represented an abstract idea like "the Son of God." I didn't know Jesus personally. I didn't have a relationship with Him. Not until I was 17, when I met Jesus through reading His Word. Looking back, I know this is part of His abundant grace in my life. Jesus knew I'd need Him to make it through the next few years.

In my early twenties, a dark despair consumed me. I wanted to give up. On life. On everything. That depression would have destroyed me, if not for Jesus. Without a doubt, I came to know Jesus as my Deliverer. By the time I turned 30, Jesus had exchanged the ashes of my life for something whole and new and beautiful. With each passing year, I grew to know Jesus as my Redeemer.

In each season, God has revealed Himself to me in new ways. If I could summarize the decades of my life, I'd say this: In my teens, I knew Jesus as my Savior. In my twenties, I knew Jesus as my Deliverer. In my thirties, I knew Jesus as my Redeemer.

So when my forties rolled around, I asked God one day, "What's next for us?"

I heard a familiar Voice speak to my spirit: *I want to be your Friend.*

Read James 2:20-26.

In this passage, James continues his homily on the connection between faith and action, and he uses two prime examples from Scripture: Abraham, the father of the Israelite nation, and Rahab, a Gentile prostitute. His choice of examples is intentional. Abraham is a greatly revered Hebrew male, whereas a non-Hebrew female prostitute represents the complete opposite of everything their culture esteems. And yet, both Abraham and Rahab are considered righteous for the good works they did, showing their trust in the one true God.

Read Genesis 22:1-19 and Joshua 2:1-21.

God called Abraham His friend and included Rahab in the lineage of the Messiah. God, the Creator of the universe, wants to be friends with us, and He's gone to great lengths to bridge the gap between us. God not only said He loved us, He also showed His love for us by the work of the cross. So when it comes to faith in action, we see God modeling the connection for us. If we say we love God, we must also show we love God. And the way we show our love for God is through our actions.

> To say we love God is to show we love God.
>
> #WordWriters

In the first four decades of my life, I experienced the full spectrum of friendships. Perhaps you've experienced it too. There's the instant friend—we seem to have everything in common and connect immediately. There's the long-distance friend—we share a history and pick up where we left off whenever we're together. There's the surprise friend—we don't have much in common but we like each other's company anyway. There's the work friend—we see each other regularly at work and our jobs are more enjoyable because of the other's presence. There's the hard-to-love friend—we sometimes wonder why we're still friends because there's always something prickly between us. There's the seasonal friend—we were friends for a season but when the season ended, our

friendship sort of faded. Then there's the forever friend—we know our hearts are knit together and we're for each other no matter what for the rest of our lives.

Jesus is my forever Friend. He wants to be yours too.

-------------------- *Diving Deeper* --------------------

Why was Abraham called God's friend?

How are Abraham and Rahab similar? How are they different?

Why does James use the examples of Abraham and Rahab to illustrate that faith without action is useless? What can we learn from each of them?

What does it mean to you that you can call God your Friend? What does your friendship with God look like?

Today write out James 2:20-26 and thank God for being the forever Friend He is.

Prayer: *Thank You, Lord, for being my Savior, my Deliverer, my Redeemer, and my Friend. Thank You for the sacrifice You made to make our friendship possible. Help me to show my love for You in all I say and do. Amen.*

A Call to Grow Deeper
~ through kindness and peace ~

My son, Parker, loves video games, so we have to monitor how much time he spends each day on electronics. Whenever the timer beeps, indicating his 30 minutes are up, he usually asks for a few more minutes because he's so close to making the next level. That's the allure of video gaming; there's always another level to achieve, another level to explore.

By the middle of James's letter, he moves to another level. He's already talked about treating everyone—rich and poor, stranger and friend—with love and mercy. And he's already talked about demonstrating our faith in action by caring for the practical needs of others. Now he's going to up the ante. To grow in spiritual maturity, James says, we must take our faith to a higher level by controlling our tongue and growing in wisdom.

The Power of Words

Open my eyes so that I may contemplate wonderful things from Your instruction.

PSALM 119:18

I can remember, as a kid, lining up my stuffed animals along the edge of my bed and teaching them the alphabet. With each letter I wrote on my small chalkboard, I explained the sound it makes. I suppose it's no surprise I became a teacher of books. But there's only one Book with *living* words, with the power to transform lives. I know, because it has transformed mine, and I want everyone to experience the same life-changing truths.

James gives a sound warning, though, to anyone who teaches the Bible. He says, "Not many of you should become teachers, my fellow believers, because you know that we who teach will be judged more strictly" (3:1 NIV). For a long time I read this short verse as an aside, as though James were a character in a Shakespearean play who stops for a brief moment to speak directly to the audience and then resumes the action in the play. James tells us how teachers of God's Word will be held accountable for what they teach. Then he seems to move on to the next topic: controlling the tongue. You know, because there's always a gossip somewhere.

> Only one Book has the power to transform lives. I know, because it has transformed mine.
>
> #WordWriters

But that's not what James is doing. The entire third chapter is a continuation of his discussion on the importance of teaching biblical truth.

---------------------------- **Read James 3:1-6.** ----------------

James gives two examples: a bit in a horse's mouth and a rudder on a ship. Both are small instruments used to steer and guide something much larger. The tongue is the same. It's a small body part that steers and guides much of our lives. For a teacher, the tongue can be used to steer and guide the lives of others—for good or for ill. This is serious business. Look at what Jesus had to say about this topic.

---------------- **Read Matthew 5:17-20.** ----------------

Jesus said it plain and simple. We need to practice what we preach, and what we preach needs to be aligned with the whole counsel of God's Word, including both Old and New Testaments.

So who are the Bible teachers today? We can start with preachers on Sunday mornings, but they're not the only ones. Anyone who claims to speak biblical truth will be judged by God more strictly. That includes midweek Bible study leaders at churches and in homes. Speakers at conferences and special events. Radio talk-show hosts and podcasters. Writers and bloggers. Even the layperson who goes on a diatribe on Facebook. All who use their voice and their influence to teach biblical truths will be judged more strictly. That includes me. I promise you I never take it lightly. The words that end up on these pages are scant compared to the words of Scripture that have been consumed and prayed over.

This is why it's so important for all believers to study God's Word daily. Listening to solid teaching is beneficial, but the Bible is the primary means God uses to renew our minds so we can discern what is good and true (see Romans 12:2). The most important book we could ever read is God's Holy Book.

Whether or not we're teachers in an official capacity, our words not only have the power to guide others in a certain direction, but they also have the power to destroy. James says the tongue is like a small spark, which can set a whole forest on fire. I live in Southern California, where fires wipe out hundreds of square miles of forest and brush every summer as a result of extreme temperatures.

Every fire begins as a small flame and grows beyond control. This is why James says "not many" should become teachers.

-------------------- Diving Deeper --------------------

How does James describe a person who is able to control the tongue?

James compares the tongue to a bit, a rudder, and a spark. How else does James describe the tongue?

When have you experienced someone's words becoming like a fire that destroyed everything in the vicinity? What happened? What did God teach you from this experience?

While writing James 3:1-6, invite God to renew your mind with every word from Scripture you record. This is such a huge benefit of writing the Word!

Prayer: Thank You, Lord, for caring so deeply about the purity of Your Word. Whenever I tell others about You, help me to honor You in everything I say. I pray the words of my mouth and the meditation of my heart are pleasing in Your sight. Amen.

The Spring of Sweet Waters

Open my eyes so that I may contemplate wonderful things from Your instruction.

PSALM 119:18

We'd only been back from our honeymoon a few weeks when we had our first real argument. When I feel hurt or upset, I usually withdraw. I'm quiet and sullen. I don't normally make a big stink, but that day I did. I was mad about something. I can't even remember what I was mad about. At the time I must have thought it was important. It probably wasn't. All I remember is what I learned that day.

I stomped around the house and slammed a few cupboards and yelled a few words. It was real mature of me, I know. My husband followed me from room to room, putting picture frames inside drawers, removing knickknacks from the mantel, tucking car keys into his pocket. Finally I stopped blathering and asked, "What are you doing? I'm really upset, and you're…you're redecorating!"

In his typical calm voice he said, "I know you're upset. That's why I don't want anything to get, you know, damaged."

Then I really exploded. "What are you saying? You think I'm going to break something? I might be mad, but I've never in my life broken anything when I was mad. Why on earth would you think something like that?" Then I remembered what he told me a long time ago about his stepdad having a violent temper. I stopped breathing and stared at him. My heart sank as I realized what my words were doing to him. We were coming from vastly different family backgrounds. My dad was a yeller, but he never hurt anybody. With my husband's stepdad, yelling was just the first stage. It would escalate from there. I told my husband how sorry I was for my words and my harsh tone.

How is it we can speak so unkindly to the very people we love most on the

planet? Or is it just me? James has much to say on this topic. His words are worth memorizing.

Read James 3:7-12.

James offers several images. First he mentions animals. We can tame the wildest animal, but we can't tame our own tongue. He calls the tongue a restless evil. We use it to bless God and curse men. But this should not be.

Next James mentions a spring of water. Bitter and sweet water can't come from the same spring. It's impossible. And yet, that's exactly what we do with our words. It's the same with trees and vines. A fig tree can't produce olives, nor a grapevine, figs. Our words reflect who we are at our core. My grandma used to say, "People are like tea bags; you find out what's inside when they're dropped in hot water." What's inside us *will* come out. Eventually. Lord, help us.

I don't want to be the kind of person who spews bitter words. If my heart is like a spring of water, I want my words to be sweet waters. Is change possible? Yes!

Read Luke 6:43-45.

Jesus said a tree is known by its fruit. In the same way, we are known by the fruit in our lives. Our words and deeds are our fruit. Is the fruit in my life sweet and nourishing? Or bitter and rotten? Do my words edify and uplift? Or berate and tear down? One of my favorite proverbs says, "Wise words are like deep waters; wisdom flows from the wise like a bubbling brook" (Proverbs 18:4 NLT). My heart's desire is that I become a spring of sweet waters, and deep waters. It's possible too. When we're immersed in truth, we overflow with grace.

> When we're immersed in truth, we overflow with grace.
>
> #WordWriters

--------------------- Diving Deeper ---------------------

Why does James include a list of animals? What point is he trying to make?

Why does James talk about fig trees and grapevines? How do these examples serve as illustrations?

When have you praised the Lord one moment and spoken a harsh word to someone in the next? This is a common experience for all people. What does James say about this?

What are some ways you can be intentional about filling your heart and mind with gentle, wise words?

As you write out James 3:7-12, ask God to fill you with more of Him.

Prayer: Thank You, Lord, for loving me as I am while also loving me too much to let me stay as I am. With Your help, change is possible. Grow in me a deep hunger and thirst for Your Word. I want my words to reflect a heart immersed in Your grace and truth. Amen.

The Wise Among Us

Open my eyes so that I may contemplate wonderful things from Your instruction.

PSALM 119:18

My computer blinks a new headline across the screen: "How to Gain 3000 Followers in One Day." Popularity has always been a numbers game. But with the advent of social media, the path to popularity has completely changed. We no longer consider people popular because they have a lot of good friends in their everyday lives. Nowadays we consider people popular if they have a lot of followers on Instagram and Twitter, and in certain social and professional spheres, the competition for increasing your following has become fierce.

The headline catches my attention because there's a story in the Bible about 3000 people becoming followers of Christ in one day, and I wonder if the article alludes to the biblical account.

Read Acts 2:1–42.

When I read the article, "How to Gain 3000 Followers in One Day," I discover it doesn't reference the story in the Bible at all. The article is a list of tips and tricks for getting people to follow you. The story in the Bible, however, describes the day of Pentecost—when 3000 people decide to follow Jesus. Peter and the other disciples don't have a clever marketing strategy. They don't have a catchy slogan. Peter simply stands up and tells the truth. He tells the crowd about Jesus. The Holy Spirit does the rest.

James is there too (see Acts 1:14). He witnesses the birth of the early church, and he becomes the leader of the church in Jerusalem. By the time

he writes his letter, the church is growing steadily, but God's church has always been made up of humans, so it's no surprise that James observes some folks vying for positions in leadership.

Read James 3:13-16.

Who is wise and understanding? James says it's not the person who wows us with intellect. Nor is it the person who impresses us with achievements. Those who are truly wise and understanding are known by their conduct, by their good choices. In other words, if people want to be in a position of authority and leadership, then their lives must exemplify a humble, gentle heart. Bitter envy and selfish ambition cannot reside in a heart of wisdom. Clamoring for a larger following and jockeying for position are not characteristics of wisdom either. Humble, gentle hearts don't focus on growing their own following. They simply tell others about Jesus and let the Holy Spirit do the rest.

Let's tell others about Jesus and let the Holy Spirit do the rest.

#WordWriters

Diving Deeper

What is the evidence of a truly wise and understanding person?

What are the effects of earthly, ungodly wisdom?

When have you struggled with bitter envy or selfish ambition? We've all struggled with this at some point. When bitter envy and selfish ambition infiltrates the human heart, how can God's Word clean our hearts and make us new?

Do you know someone who possesses a humble, gentle heart? What makes this person different? How could you begin to emulate this person?

With each word of James 3:13-16 you write, ask God to cleanse your heart and fill it with His truth.

Prayer: Thank You, Lord, for loving me, even when my heart's desire is to promote myself. Thank You for providing a way to make my heart new again. Give me a heart that wants to invite others to follow You and know You more. Amen.

The Cultivator of Peace

Open my eyes so that I may contemplate wonderful things from Your instruction.

PSALM 119:18

While rounding a corner in the grocery aisle, my young son nearly plows into a woman coming from the opposite direction. I kneel to his eyelevel and explain, "Son, I want you to yield to others. Yield means you let someone else go ahead of you. Okay?" He nods as we move on to the cereal aisle.

While rounding a corner on a neighborhood street, my teenage daughter nearly plows into a car coming from the opposite direction. I ask her to pull over and explain, "Honey, that green light back there wasn't an arrow. When it's a solid green light, you have to yield to oncoming traffic before turning left." She nods as we continue the driving lessons.

Yield. The word keeps peppering my conversations, especially with my kids. I want my kids to learn to yield to others, not only when they're out shopping or driving, but in all aspects of life. When we yield to others, we show a regard for others. As I've been talking to my kids about yielding, God has been talking to me about yielding too.

> When we yield to others, we show a regard for others.
>
> #WordWriters

Read James 3:17–18.

If ungodly wisdom is revealed in bitter envy and selfish ambition, then godly wisdom is revealed in yielding to others, encouraging others to get ahead of you. Whether we're talking about career advancement or personal

achievement, a wise person has a pure heart and genuinely wishes the best for others. Wise people don't succumb to scarcity thinking, believing they should get as much for themselves as they can while they can because there's only so much to go around. Wisdom is portrayed in gentle otherness.

James and Paul are two great examples in the Bible of towering leaders in the early church who yielded to one another with a gentle, peace-loving heart. When describing wisdom, James once again uses the example of fruit-bearing. A wise person, he says, is "full of mercy and good fruits" (3:17). The apostle Paul also shares a list of good spiritual fruit in his later letter to the Galatians.

Read Galatians 5:19-26.

When you read the two passages side by side, you can see how similar they are in spirit. It's obvious the two men spent time together. Scripture tells of at least three separate occasions when Paul joined James in Jerusalem (see Acts 9:26-28; 15:12-19; 21:15-18). Even though both men displayed a strong disposition for leadership, they didn't compete with one another. They didn't strive to be more popular than the other. They didn't envy the ministry success of the other. Both men were cultivators of peace while maintaining the purest devotion to God's unwavering truth. They knew each man had his own calling from the Lord. James was called to lead the church in Jerusalem. Paul was called to preach the good news of the gospel to non-Jews beyond the city walls of Jerusalem.

That's how we can rise above the common milieu of competition too. When we know the calling God has placed on our own lives, then we're free to cheer and support the calling God has placed on the lives of others.

Diving Deeper

How does James describe wisdom from above?

What is sown by those who cultivate peace?

How does competition destroy friendships? When has a friend competed with you? What happened to that friendship?

Do you know someone who is a beautiful example of being a cultivator of peace? How can you become a cultivator of peace in your relationships?

When you write out James 3:17-18, ask God to help you yield to others and become a cultivator of peace.

Prayer: Thank You, Lord, for leaders like James and Paul who show us how to be for one another and not in competition with one another. Grant me wisdom that is pure and gentle, full of mercy and good fruit. Help me to become a person who willingly yields to others and cultivates peace in my relationships. Amen.

A Call to Grow Deeper
~ through a teachable spirit ~

If I'm given a choice between two classes—a class of students who are struggling academically or a class of students who are high achievers—I prefer to teach the students who are struggling. In my experience, the highest achieving students, the ones who always get perfect scores on tests, are sometimes the least teachable students. For these students, the classroom isn't a place to learn; it's a place to perform. They see the teacher as a dispenser of tests on which they expect to get perfect grades. I've seen exceptions to this, of course, but for the most part I enjoy coming alongside students who know they need help and are willing to listen. Being in a classroom with students who have a teachable spirit makes all the difference in the world.

In the same way, if we're to grow deeper in our faith, we must have a teachable spirit, which always begins with humility. James devotes the next portion of his letter to helping us recognize our need for a humble and contrite spirit.

The Call to Pray

Open my eyes so that I may contemplate wonderful things from Your instruction.

PSALM 119:18

Whenever I read through Jesus's Sermon on the Mount, I usually get stuck on the part about praying for your enemies—not because I don't want to pray for my enemies, but because I don't think I have any. I guess it all depends on how you define *enemy*. Being the list maker I am, I decided one day to make a prayer list of my "enemies"—the people I don't enjoy being around, the ones I avoid, those who have hurt me in some way.

My list surprised me. Every name came from one place: church. I scanned the list again. Not a neighbor. Not a coworker. Not a parent from my kids' school. Not a parent from my son's soccer team. Nope. The people who hurt me the most were from the one place that's supposed to be a safe haven. Church.

To be honest, I wasn't sure what to do with this list. Discouragement seeped into my soul as the real enemy hissed, "Why bother going to church at all? The people there are hurtful." I stared at my list, feeling a bit befuddled, until I remembered why I made the list in the first place. To pray. So I did.

Read Matthew 5:43-48.

When I prayed, something changed. Bible verses came to mind, which gave me a new perspective. Paul reminds us in his letter to the Ephesians that "our battle is not against flesh and blood, but against the rulers, against the authorities, against the world powers of this darkness, against the spiritual forces of evil" (6:12). The enemy is not sitting in a pew four rows over.

Read James 4:1-3.

When I read the verses that begin chapter 4, I'm tempted to skim over them quickly and move on. I'm not in the midst of any wars or fights, and I'm not contemplating murder. At least not at the moment. But if you've spent much time in churches, you've likely witnessed a skirmish or two. Maybe not with fists, but with differences of opinion and clashes of desire. We shouldn't be surprised when this sort of thing happens. Neither should we be shocked when someone inside the church wounds us in some way. That's exactly what the real enemy of our souls wants. Satan wants hurt feelings and misunderstandings to cause friction between us and other members in the body of Christ. So when we feel hurt, we should pray. When we sense discord, we should pray. When we disagree with a brother or sister, we should pray. Jesus laid out the appropriate steps for handling conflict in Matthew 18:15-17, and every matter should be bathed in prayer. A healthy believer will follow His instructions in Matthew 18 with lots and lots of prayer.

> God uses broken people, and He redeems our brokenness for His glory.
>
> #WordWriters

The church—the global community of believers—is God's chosen vessel. We're a broken vessel for sure, but that's precisely the point. God uses broken people. He uses you. He uses me. And He redeems our brokenness for His glory. This is why I continue to attend weekly church services. Not because church is always an awesome, lovey-dovey community. We're real people with real hurts, and we're all at different places in our spiritual journey. We need to extend one another grace—the same grace God has extended to us.

Diving Deeper

What is the source of fights and disagreements among us?

How do our motives affect our prayer life?

When have you experienced strife or discord within your local church body? How was the situation handled? How much was prayer a part of the process for resolution? What did you learn about prayer and conflict from this situation?

While writing out James 4:1-3, seek God's wisdom in a situation you may be facing today.

Prayer: *Thank You, Lord, for helping us understand where wars and fights come from. Search me, God, and know my heart. Ferret out my true motives and give me a heart that desires to serve others with the love and grace You've so generously shown to me. Amen.*

The Need for Grace

Open my eyes so that I may contemplate wonderful things from Your instruction.

PSALM 119:18

The front door stood ajar, so I walked in—even though I'd never been to this house before. I heard voices coming from the backyard and figured that's where the party was happening. My husband's cousin's wife was expecting her first child, and I had happily accepted the invitation to the baby shower. (I never pass up the chance to shop for a baby!) After everyone introduced themselves, the topic quickly turned to birth stories—stories of a baby born in the car, of a dad who passed out in the delivery room, and of a mom who mowed the lawn just a few hours before giving birth.

As much as I love birth stories, my favorite stories are the ones that tell of our spiritual birth. How we met Jesus. How He's changed us. Those are the best stories of all.

Our stories will differ, yours and mine. Some of us have experienced a dramatic rescue from a life of darkness to a life of light. Others of us haven't experienced a harrowing before-and-after story. That's okay too. Whatever our stories may be, we all have one thing in common: our need for grace. At some point, every soul has turned away from God. Perhaps we depended on ourselves instead of God. Perhaps we looked to someone else or something else to fulfill us. Eventually we recognized our need for forgiveness and turned to God.

> We all have one thing in common: our need for grace.
>
> #WordWriters

Read James 4:4-6.

If James were writing books today, he probably wouldn't become a bestselling author. His bluntness would likely turn people away. He begins this next section by insulting everyone. He calls everyone an adulteress! I can't imagine this approach being recommended in one of today's popular books on church growth. Nevertheless, it's what James does. I'm sure it garnered the attention of his readers. In almost every culture throughout history, adultery has been considered a dishonorable act, but under old Jewish law it was punishable by death. So why does James call everyone an adulteress?

James isn't trying to insult anyone; he's trying to make a point. Throughout the Old Testament, God uses the analogy of adultery to illustrate how humanity has betrayed God. God wants our total devotion, but when we turn away from Him, we commit spiritual adultery. We've all done it. All of us. Paul says we've all sinned and fallen short of God's glory (see Romans 3:23). So when James calls everyone an adulteress, he's trying to wake up the sleeping soul, the person who's dabbling in sin and rationalizing their actions by thinking that what they're doing isn't *that* bad. But James says friendship with the world isn't an option for a follower of Christ. Thankfully, God has provided an escape hatch for everyone caught in a cycle of sin.

Read Proverbs 3:34 and Matthew 23:12.

To those who acknowledge their own wayward soul. To those who bend a knee and ask God for forgiveness. To those who turn back to Him as the source of all that is good. God gives grace to the humble.

------------------------------ Diving Deeper ------------------------------

Why does James say so emphatically that friendship with the world is hostility toward God? How then are we to live in the world?

What does James mean when he says the Spirit who lives in us yearns jealously? Why does God desire our undivided devotion?

Why is it repeated throughout Scripture that God opposes the proud? How do you describe a prideful person?

Let's write out James 4:4-6 and thank God for the grace He so freely gives.

Prayer: Thank You, Lord, for providing an escape hatch for me when I was trapped in a cycle of sin. I'm so grateful Your grace has set me free. Please guard my heart from the sin of pride. Help me to grow in humility, looking to the interests of others before my own. Amen.

The Way of Repentance

Open my eyes so that I may contemplate wonderful things from Your instruction.

PSALM 119:18

When my husband and I were expecting our first child, we attended a class to help us prepare for the birth. We learned a lot of helpful things, but the instructor's best advice came in three simple words: *Match her mood.* Labor is a process that involves patience and pain. Yes, the joy of holding a new child awaits, but when a labor companion fails to recognize the stage of labor the mom is in, it can sometimes create a dissonance in the room. When the mom is intently focused on breathing through a painful contraction, that's not the time to laugh and celebrate the joys of a newborn. The laughter and joy will come. In the meantime, match her mood. When the mom is relaxed, you relax. When the mom is focused, you focus. When the mom is laughing, you laugh. By matching her mood you're recognizing and respecting the stages in the process.

Like the pains of labor and childbirth, repentance is a process with several stages. It involves patience and pain, but it's worth it because it brings the joy of new life. Yes, God forgives us the instant we ask Him to, but the natural consequences of our sin still linger. Far too often our sin makes a negative impact on others as well as ourselves. Healing will come, though, if we're patient enough to move through each stage of the process.

The main reason people hide their sin is they're afraid of the pain that will inevitably follow when they confess their sin. The deeper the sin, the greater the pain. For everyone involved. But God doesn't

> Repentance is a process that involves patience and pain, but it's worth it because it brings the joy of new life.
>
> #WordWriters

want us hiding our sin or living in fear. That's what Satan wants. God wants us set free from the shackles of shame that bind us, so James gives us a ten-step process to guide someone who's trapped in sin back into true fellowship with God and the church.

-------------------- *Read James 4:7-12.* --------------------

Whenever we see the word *therefore* in Scripture, it's an indicator we need to look back at what has preceded. In light of everything James has already written, we're invited to move forward in repentance. When we're struggling with sin, James says to do the following:

1. Submit to God. (Confess your sin.)

2. Resist the devil. (Choose to turn from your former ways.)

3. Draw near to God. (Stay close to God through prayer and the intake of His Word.)

4. Cleanse your hands. (Withdraw from outward sinful actions.)

5. Purify your hearts. (Renew your inward thought-life.)

6. Be miserable. (Take your sin seriously, not flippantly.)

7. Mourn. (Grieve over the pain you've caused God, others, and yourself.)

8. Weep. (Show an outward evidence of an inward grief over your sin.)

9. Change your joy to sorrow. (Know when it's appropriate to experience one or the other.)

10. Humble yourself before the Lord. (Remember the lowliness of your spiritual state apart from God, and be filled with gratitude for the newness of your spiritual state with God.)

At first glance, James appears to contradict himself. In the first part of his letter, he tells us to consider it a great joy whenever we experience trials. Now he

says we should change our joy to sorrow. Which is it? Well, each admonition has to do with our outlook. On the one hand, when we're experiencing a trial, we know everything in this world is temporary. One day God will right all wrongs. In this we find deep joy. On the other hand, when we're stuck in the pit of sin, we mustn't take our situation lightly or have a flippant attitude. James instructs us to change our joy to sorrow because it's appropriate to grieve the pain our sin has caused God and others, as well as ourselves.

How can we come alongside a friend who's struggling to overcome sin in her life? We don't criticize or judge; we match her mood as she moves through the ten steps James outlines. In this way we recognize and respect the stage of the repentance process she's in, knowing the joy of freedom and new life awaits.

Diving Deeper

What is the first directive James gives in this passage? Why does James make this the first step?

In verse 8, when James says to "cleanse your hands," he's referring to your outer life. When he says to "purify your hearts," he's referring to your inner life. Why is it necessary to do both?

James says we should be miserable and mourn; he says our joy should turn to sorrow. Is he saying believers should never be joyful? What is the context for these commands?

According to James, if we criticize one another, what do we become?

As you write out James 4:7-12, ask God to show you any areas in your life where you need to repent.

Prayer: *Thank You, Lord, for providing a way back to You when I've been going in the wrong direction. Help me to be quick to repent when I hurt Your heart. Renew my heart and mind with the grace and truth of Your Word. I'm so grateful for the new life You give. Amen.*

A Call to Grow Deeper
~ through prayer and surrender ~

The deeper life is upside-down and inside-out from everything the world tells us to do. The world says we should work harder, do more, and strive better. The world emphasizes everything *we* must do; the Bible emphasizes everything God has already done. When we're steeped in Scripture every day, the gravitational pull of the world loses its effect on us. Our faith deepens and our love widens.

James knows this, too, which is why he finishes his letter with a call to grow deeper through prayer and surrender. We grow deeper in our faith when we relinquish our plans to God, trust Him to provide, and wait for Him to come through.

The Impact of If

Open my eyes so that I may contemplate wonderful things from Your instruction.

PSALM 119:18

Every time I step into a store for office supplies I'm smitten. I enjoy all things stationery—pretty paper, new pens, colorful Post-its, and lots of desktop organizers. I especially love the aisle for calendars and planners. Making plans and filling in calendar squares holds a certain allure for me. Perhaps my fondness for planning and scheduling stems from the illusion I'm in control of my future. But deep down I know the truth. If I've learned one thing from my oldest brother's life, it's that none of us can count on tomorrow. Nobody ever plans on waking up the next day to face life in a wheelchair. James has a few words to say about this subject as well.

Read James 4:13–17.

In this passage, James describes a self-reliant person, someone who thinks they're completely in charge of their future and fails to consider variables outside of their control. God is never factored into the equation of this person's life. Such self-reliance is actually a form of defiance toward God. James calls this boasting, and he calls it evil.

Not everyone, however, lives in the realm of self-reliance. Some of us settle on the other extreme: the path of absolute apathy. With self-reliance, we look to self. With apathy, we look to nobody. Both

> Apathy is the antithesis of God's purpose for us.
>
> #WordWriters

embody a disregard for God. This is why James ends this passage saying, "It is a sin for the person who knows to do what is good and doesn't do it" (4:17). In other words, the sin of omission is just as harmful to the soul. I confess this is more my tendency.

In the introduction of this study, I mentioned how James compares our lives to a mist; some translations say a vapor or smoke, but the idea is the same. Mist evaporates quickly. We're here one moment and gone the next. Our lives are short when compared to the vastness of eternity. But that doesn't mean we should sit around doing nothing in the meantime. Apathy is the antithesis of God's purpose for us. God gave us life! And He gave each of us a unique purpose, a distinct way to bring Him glory. Thankfully, the answer to apathy is prayer. Through prayer we actively invite God into our decision-making process, and James models this prayer for us by saying, "If the Lord's wills, we will live and do this or that" (4:15). This is the impact of *if*.

If it's the Lord's will, I will go to this city or that.

If it's the Lord's will, I will live in this home or that.

If it's the Lord's will, I will work at this place or that.

When we pray in this manner, we acknowledge our limitations and yield to the supremacy of God's rule in our lives.

Diving Deeper

Why does James say our lives are like a mist (or vapor or smoke)? What is he trying to communicate with this use of imagery?

How does James say we ought to plan our futures?

Do you tend to be more self-reliant or apathetic? How can you recognize either one of these tendencies in your life?

How often do you include the phrase "if it's Your will, Lord" in your prayers? When prayed with sincerity, how does this phrase demonstrate a heart-surrender to God's ultimate plan for your life?

With each word of James 4:13-17 you write, take a moment and invite God into your plans for today.

Prayer: Thank You, Lord, for wanting to be involved in my every-day life. When I'm faced with decisions, help me to look to You for wisdom and guidance. I want to surrender to Your perfect will for my life, and I want to honor You in the choices I make. Amen.

The Responsibility of Wealth

Open my eyes so that I may contemplate wonderful things from Your instruction.

PSALM 119:18

I've never been a dog person, so whenever our kids begged for a dog, I would smile and say, "Maybe someday, but not today." I don't have anything against dogs, but they do have a tendency to be loud, and I prefer a quiet environment. Dogs also have a way of shedding everywhere, so unless you buy one of those expensive hypoallergenic breeds, you're inviting dog hair into your life. Besides, I'd rather take out my trash without needing to sidestep brown clumps of stink.

Despite my best defenses, my stance about dogs changed a few Christmases ago. The items on our kids' Christmas lists resembled the typical gifts most kids ask for, but my husband and I knew what they wanted would eventually end up in a trash or storage bin. So instead of piling presents under the tree, we wondered what Christmas might look like with simplicity, and we started doing the gift-giving thing a little differently.

Besides a few stocking stuffers, we decided to get one family gift each year—something the whole family could enjoy. That first year we bought a Wii, and we enjoyed playing games together. But we discovered our son has a serious affinity for all things electronic, and we felt it prudent to limit his time with video games. We wanted our kids to play outside more. So the following Christmas, we planned a camping trip and had a blast making memories together. By the third year, we were stumped. We wanted something that would encourage the kids to play in the backyard, but we didn't want to sleep in a tent in December again.

Meanwhile, the kids continued to beg for a dog, but all I could think about

was dog hair and pooper-scoopers and loud barking. "Maybe someday," I would say, "but not today."

To this day, I'm not sure what happened. But every time neighbors walked a dog past our house, I watched our son gravitate toward those slobbery creatures. Parker rolled on the grass with them. He laughed while they licked him. And he no longer resembled a boy consumed with a video game. I was sold. My husband and I searched the area and found a pair of golden pups. We brought them home to the craziest squeals of delight we'd ever heard from our children. I admit I expected the novelty of the puppies to wear off. I assumed the kids, over time, would move on to something newer and more exciting. But four years later I'm surprised at how much those silly dogs, Hunter and Spark, have become a part of...dare I say...our family.

Not too long ago Parker walked into the living room with a dog lapping at his heels and announced, "Mom and Dad, you guys are wrong. You always say money can't buy happiness. But money bought Hunter and Spark." Our son spoke in jest, but with a hint of seriousness too.

> Owning great wealth isn't a sin, but it is a great responsibility.
>
> #WordWriters

If we're really honest, we can't help but think the same thing sometimes. Money may not be the source of real joy, but we can't deny that money helps some things in life go a little smoother. No matter how much or how little we think we have, most of us would like to have a little more. One of the greatest struggles in this life is our tendency to see money as the answer to most of our problems.

In his letter, James speaks to these same kinds of doubts.

Read James 5:1-6.

Yikes! First James calls everyone an adulteress (4:4), then he tears into rich people. But he makes a distinction. Owning great wealth isn't a sin, but it is a great responsibility. And far too many rich people neglect this responsibility. It's this neglect James speaks of. The wealthy in his day hoarded their

money, indulged in it with luxurious lifestyles, and relied on it exclusively. They showed no need for God. Money was their god. Not only that, but they gained their wealth through dishonest means by exploiting the poor. Does anything like that still happen today? It sure does. And God feels just as strongly about it as James does in his letter. James is really echoing Jesus's words on the matter.

Read Matthew 6:19-21.

The wealth of this world will soon fade. Our money cannot save us, no matter how much we have. It's far wiser for us to invest in eternal riches. We do this by showing kindness to others, and such kindness can come in the form of a gentle word or a generous gift.

I confess I have an easier time showing kindness to poor people. Perhaps it's because I relate to the poor. It's much harder for me to show kindness to rich people. I'd rather point fingers and sit in judgment. I'll never forget what it's like to sift through garbage bags of crummy old clothes to find something to wear. And yet the same God who has forgiven me of so much asks me to forgive others—even rich people who neglect the responsibility they've been entrusted with. That's what James is asking of believers too. He's reminding us God sees everything, including the hearts of rich and poor alike.

Diving Deeper

Why does James say rich people should weep and wail?

When James says the outcry of the harvesters has reached the ears of the Lord of Hosts, what does he mean?

When have you harbored ill feelings toward the rich? How do James's words help you place all judgment in the Lord's hands?

When are you tempted to see money as the solution to a problem? How has God proven Himself to be a Provider of your needs?

While writing out James 5:1-6, thank God for providing for the greatest need we have—our need for grace.

Prayer: *Thank You, Lord, for assuring us that You see the hearts of men and women everywhere. Forgive me when I'm tempted to judge others, especially when I'm tempted to judge the rich. Help me to show kindness through gentle words and generous gifts. I want my heart to reflect Yours in the way I treat others. Amen.*

The Coming of the Lord

Open my eyes so that I may contemplate wonderful things from Your instruction.

PSALM 119:18

As the temperature outside hovered around 108 degrees, my kids grew more irritable by the minute. The heat made everyone miserable, including me. I'd already administered several timeouts that day when I noticed my then-six-year-old, Brynn, wasn't with the rest of the family. So I checked on her and found her lying on her bed, writing a letter. It was the first sweet sight all day.

> One day God will right all wrongs. A great reversal awaits.
>
> #WordWriters

When their dad got home from work, the kids rushed to the front door as usual, but this time Brynn thrust her letter toward her father. I hadn't read it yet, so I was curious to know what she wrote. Jeff unfolded the note, read it, and tried to suppress a smile. Her letter said:

> *Dear Dad,*
> *Parker wrote on his door*
> *He hit me in the stumuk.*
> *He wakt me on my head.*
> *I love you.*
> *Brynn*

All of her little brother's offenses were addressed earlier in the day when they happened, but Brynn obviously wanted something more. She wanted Dad to know, and she wanted Dad to do something about it, something of a retributive nature.

After reflecting on my daughter's letter to her father, I couldn't help but wonder if some of my prayers sound like tattling too. God wants us to go to Him with our concerns, but sometimes I grow impatient. When I feel I've been wronged by someone, I want God to fix it. I even pray the words of the Psalms that express this sort of lament. Psalm 7:8 says, "Vindicate me, LORD." This roughly translates to "Go get 'em, Dad."

In the early church in Jerusalem, many believers experienced the hardship of poverty combined with the oppression of the rich. Undoubtedly they wanted their Father in heaven to intervene on their behalf. But James offers a different perspective.

Read James 5:7-11.

Just as James begins his letter on the topic of suffering, he concludes his letter on the same topic. The believers are experiencing hardship and oppression, but James takes the long view. He says to "be patient until the Lord's coming...because the Lord's coming is near" (5:7-8). While the rich may be exploiting the poor, the poor can take comfort knowing the Lord sees all. We serve a God of justice. A great reversal awaits. The Lord's coming is near.

This great reversal of condition is best described in Jesus's words in the Beatitudes. We read them earlier in the study, but let's look at them again in this later context of suffering and the Lord's coming.

Read Matthew 5:3-12.

Notice how Jesus finished the Beatitudes; He reminded His listeners of how the prophets of old were treated. They, too, were treated badly.

James follows the same pattern Jesus set forth. He finishes this portion of his letter by referencing the prophets. He says, "Take the prophets who spoke in the Lord's name as an example of suffering and patience" (5:10). Then James specifically mentions Job, the prophet known for immense suffering. While no

one would volunteer to go through everything Job went through, we can see how God restored him with His compassion and mercy.

James's response to the cries of the believers is to be patient, knowing the Lord will bring justice in His timing.

------------------------- *Diving Deeper* -------------------------

Why does James use the illustration of a farmer waiting for the fruit of his crops? How are we to be like the farmer?

When we complain about something, why does that open the door for judgment?

When have you asked God to vindicate you in a certain matter? How did the Lord respond to your request?

How do Jesus's words in the Beatitudes affect the way you view hardship?

Write out James 5:7-11 and thank God for being a God of justice who will one day right all wrongs.

Prayer: *Thank You, Lord, for seeing the hardships Your people endure. Help me to grow deeper in patience as I look to You to be the source of all justice. I'm so grateful You are full of compassion and mercy. Help me to grow deeper in compassion and mercy too. Amen.*

The Words of the Wise

Open my eyes so that I may contemplate wonderful things from Your instruction.

PSALM 119:18

One of my favorite games to play as a kid—besides Capture the Flag—was Red Light, Green Light. I'd line up with a group of kids and wait for the leader to yell, "Green light!" Then we'd walk with the longest, fastest strides our little legs could manage. We'd stop when the leader yelled, "Red light!" If we didn't stop, we'd have to go back to the starting line.

> God has given us everything we need to grow: His Spirit inside us and His Word to guide us.
>
> #WordWriters

Throughout his letter, James returns several times to the theme of controlling our tongues. He even goes so far as to offer explicit examples of the kinds of things we should and shouldn't say. When he shares an example of what not to say, it's like he's saying, "Red light!" When he shares an example of what to say, it's like he's saying, "Green light!" Then, as he brings his letter to a close, James seems to stop mid-sentence while talking about Job's suffering (5:11) and our suffering (5:13) and reiterates the importance of speaking wisely.

Read James 5:12.

When people feel their first words aren't enough, they add more words to bolster their earlier words until they're spinning words into a tangled mess of

confusion or deception or both. Proverbs 10:19 affirms this truth: "The more talk, the less truth; the wise measure their words" (MSG). To counter this tendency, James says to simply let your "yes" be "yes" and your "no" be "no." No additional words are required. Not coincidentally, Jesus said the same thing.

-------------------- *Read Matthew 5:33-37.* --------------------

We can see James is repeating what Jesus said, word for word. Jesus also said, "Anything more than this is from the evil one" (Matthew 5:37). Uh-oh. I don't want any of my words to be from the Evil One! I need to remember this the next time I'm tempted to keep talking.

Before we move on to the next passage in James, let's go back to the beginning of his letter and play Red Light, Green Light. If you have a red pen or pencil, circle the following verses in your Bible. These are the words we should stop saying: James 1:13; 2:3; 2:16; 3:14; 4:11; 4:13; 5:9; 5:12. Now take a green pen or pencil and circle the following: James 1:5; 4:15; 5:12; 5:14; 5:16. These are the kinds of words we should speak.

James's letter is a call to grow deeper in our faith, and we can see how much our words are a part of the growing process. A person of integrity does what she says she will do. No qualifiers are necessary. But when we speak the "red light words," we go back to the starting line and have to begin building the trust of others all over again.

-------------------- *Diving Deeper* --------------------

Why shouldn't we add oaths to bolster our words? How do oaths serve to weaken our words?

Is the idea of speaking fewer, simpler words appealing or disheartening to you? Why?

When do you find yourself wanting to add more words and keep talking? Is there a pattern to the kinds of conversations you're having when you do want to add more words?

As you write out James 5:12, ask God to reveal those moments when you tend to add more words than necessary.

Prayer: *Thank You, Lord, for giving me such straightforward instruction through Your Word. You desire for me to grow deeper in spiritual maturity, and You've given me everything I need: Your Spirit inside me and Your Word to guide me. Help me to be a faithful steward of all You've entrusted to me. Amen.*

The Prayer of Faith

Open my eyes so that I may contemplate wonderful things from Your instruction.

PSALM 119:18

In my brother's hospital room, my mom sits in the chair next to his bed. Her pale hands match her ashen face. A deep, unspeakable sorrow pervades all expression. Any attempt at trivial conversation seems stilted and contrived. The bitter reality penetrates the air we breathe. Dad is gone a lot, and the visitors come less and less often now. At first, dozens of people gathered in waiting rooms. Everyone prayed for a miraculous healing. But as the days and months wore on, people's endurance waned. In time, they went back to their regular lives with nothing more than a sad story to tell.

I suppose it was like that for Jesus too. For a while, lots of people crowded around Him, waiting to see what would happen next. Would there be another miracle? Another exciting story to take home? The masses congregated to hear Him speak and watch Him heal, but eventually they all went home. They had fields to tend and children to feed. One by one, they left. Even His closest friends deserted Him. In the end, Jesus was alone on a cross, with His mother weeping near His dead feet. That's what our hospital room looks like now. My brother's body lacerated and bruised and made immovable by a hideous unseen force. And my mother close by, near her own son's dead feet.

To be honest, I'm glad everyone left. I was grateful in the beginning to see so many people come to pray and hold vigil, but after a while their prayers burrowed seeds of fury deep within me. They quoted verses like bumper stickers, but to no avail. I heard them pray, "Though I walk through the valley of the shadow of death, I will fear no evil" (Psalm 23:4 NKJV), but I can't understand the solace this is supposed to bring. My brother would give anything to be

able to *walk* through a valley right now. I also heard them pray, "By His stripes we are healed" (Isaiah 53:5 NKJV). Except my brother isn't healed yet, so they shouted even louder, but louder didn't work either. Finally I heard them pray, "The prayer of a righteous person is powerful and effective" (James 5:16 NIV). Of the hundreds of people who have prayed for my brother, I guess none of them are righteous enough to gain God's favor because my brother still can't walk.

When no one has a real answer, the only answer left is to wait. "Those who wait on the LORD shall renew their strength; they shall mount up with wings like eagles, they shall run and not be weary, they shall walk and not faint" (Isaiah 40:31 NKJV). But I'm not praying for wings; I'm praying for legs. Legs that work. How long will my brother have to wait? Six months? A year? A decade? A lifetime? What about those plans to prosper him and not to harm him?

The do-gooders and well-intenders come and go. They lift their hands to Jehovah Rapha, which means "God Our Healer," but I secretly wonder if God is asleep on the job. When I mention this to a visitor, I'm told God never sleeps. Well, what's He doing up there then? He's not healing anyone I know, and I happen to see a lot of people on every floor of this hospital every day who could use a little healing. God must be stingy with His power. In my 12-year-old mind, this is the only viable conclusion. God doesn't seem to be following through on what He said He would do if we pray.

-------------------- *Read James 5:13–18.* --------------------

James wraps up his letter with a call to prayer, which is an integral part of every believer's journey. To grow deeper in our faith, we must pray. Moreover, our prayers are infused with power when we pray the words of Scripture. I believe this in the core of my being. But certain passages can cause confusion or heartache or maybe even bitterness when our reality doesn't seem to match what we read in the Bible. For years I struggled with some of the verses I heard churchgoers quoting, and this passage in James is a tough one, especially if you've ever prayed for a loved one to be healed and God didn't answer your prayer. Skepticism—or worse, cynicism—can creep into the crevices of our

minds, planting seeds of doubt. The Bible says we should pray; the Bible also says, "The prayer of faith will save the sick person, and the Lord will restore him to health" (James 5:15). But some sick people are still sick.

This is why James's image of mist has been so helpful to me in my own faith journey. Prior to the passage about prayer and faith and healing, James reminds us of the bigger picture by saying, "What is your life? You are a mist that appears for a little while and then vanishes" (4:14 NIV). Everything we see and

> Everything in this world is temporary, but an everlasting world awaits.
>
> #WordWriters

touch, right here and now, isn't everything. There is a world beyond this world, a life beyond this life. And what lies beyond is what matters most, because this world, this life, is temporary. But an everlasting world awaits. The disciple John explains it this way: "Dear friends, we are God's children now, and what we will be has not yet been revealed. We know that when He appears, we will be like Him because we will see Him as He is" (1 John 3:2). This call to grow deeper in our faith is a call to grow more like Jesus. Right now we're in process. But one day soon our transformation will be complete—because when He appears, we will be like Him. In the meantime, we continue to pray. Fervently. Expectantly.

The prayer of faith trusts and believes that one day, in His timing, God will do everything He promised.

Diving Deeper

When we're suffering, what should we do? When we're cheerful, what should we do? When we're sick, what should we do?

What did Elijah pray for? How does James describe Elijah? Why is this description of Elijah important?

When have you prayed for someone to be healed? Did God answer your prayer? How did God's answer to your prayer affect your faith?

While writing out James 5:13-18 today, let's give thanks that a future glory awaits those who believe.

Prayer: Thank You, Lord, for the promises You've given in Scripture. When I struggle to believe Your promises, help me to see beyond the here and now. Help me to focus on You more than the thing I want from You. Help me to grow in those areas where unbelief still plagues me. Help me to be more like James and hold to the long view. I fervently wait for the day when I can see You face-to-face. What a beautiful day that will be. Amen.

Day 25

The Way Back Home

Open my eyes so that I may contemplate wonderful things from Your instruction.

PSALM 119:18

I was eight years old the first time I saw the Pacific Ocean. For years my dad would take my brothers to San Francisco to see a 49er football game, and my brothers told me how they crossed the Bay Bridge to reach Candlestick Park. Dad said you could see the ocean water in the bay. So every year I begged him to let me go with them to a football game, but what I really wanted to see was the ocean.

When my dad finally agreed to let me tag along, he gave me a ticket. Then he pushed up my sleeve, and with a black permanent marker he wrote three numbers on the inside of my arm, from my elbow to my wrist. Each number on my arm corresponded with the section-row-seat where we would sit in the stadium.

Dad said, "If we ever get separated, you don't have to worry. There are ushers at every entrance. All you have to do is show one of them the numbers on your arm, and they'll bring you back to where your brothers and I are sitting."

The thought hadn't occurred to me that I could get lost at a football game. I just wanted to see the ocean, but those numbers on my arm reassured me. They were like a secret code that would help me find my way back to my father.

Read James 5:19–20.

After reading through the "proverbs of James," we can almost hear a drum roll when we come to his parting words. He's covered a number of topics in his letter, but the one thing he wants believers to remember most is the last

• 119 •

instruction he gives: if someone we know has turned away from God, we should reach out to them with the grace and truth of Jesus Christ.

Notice how James says "if any among you strays" (5:19). He's talking to believers about believers—people who profess to believe in Christ but then turn their backs on what they know to be true and choose a life of sin.

There are two kinds of wanderers. The first kind not only has a head-knowledge of Jesus, but has surrendered to Him and experienced the power of His saving grace. This kind of wanderer has stumbled into a pit of sin and needs a brother or sister to help him turn back to God. The second kind of wanderer has a head-knowledge of Jesus, but has never truly surrendered to Him. This kind of wanderer can say all the right, churchy things, but this person's heart has never known a genuine transformation.

How can we know the difference? Jesus said we'll know the true believers by their fruit.

Read Matthew 7:13-23.

Good trees produce good fruit. Bad trees produce bad fruit. James reiterated the same principle when he talked about the fruit of righteousness being sown by cultivators of peace (3:17-18). What does this mean for you and me? It means, first and foremost, that we want our lives to produce good fruit, and we know apart from Jesus this is impossible (see John 15:5). We grow deeper in our faith when we study God's Word and do what it says. And when we do what God's Word says, the fruit of the Spirit grows in our lives.

> God has given us His Word to guide us back to our Father.
>
> #WordWriters

When a fellow believer has wandered from the truth of God's Word, James encourages us to pursue that friend and help him or her turn back to God. We can't force anyone to turn to God, but we can show our love and concern for a friend who's treading a dangerous path. Just as those numbers on my arm could

help me find my way back to my father, God has given us His Word to guide us back to our Father.

-------------------- Diving Deeper --------------------

Why is it important to reach out to a friend who has wandered from the truth? What happens when we help someone turn back to God?

When have you reached out to a friend who was turning away from God? How did your friend respond? What did you learn from this situation?

What are some of your takeaways from your time in James?

How has writing the Word made an impact on your study of the Bible and your time with God?

As you write out James 5:19-20, gives God thanks for providing a way back home when you were lost.

Prayer: Thank You, Lord, for the sacrifice You made on the cross so I could come back home to You. Thank You for giving us the Word to help us grow to become more like You. Help me to reach out to friends who may be wandering from the truth. Help me to show them the kind of love and care You have shown me. I pray that my faith will always lead to action, with a gentleness of heart. Amen.

Word Writers

Your Turn!

As you begin this journey of writing the Word,
I pray the truth and beauty of Scripture will be inscribed
on the tablet of your heart, drawing you nearer to Him.

~ Denise

James _____

James --

James _____

James

James

James

James _____

James

James

James _____

James _____

James

James _____

James _____

James _____

James _____

James

James

James _____

_____

_____

_____

_____

_____

_____

_____

_____

_____

_____

_____

_____

_____

_____

_____

_____

_____

James _____

James

James _____

James

James _____

James _____

James

James _____

James _____

James

James _____

James _____

James --

James _____

James

James _____

James

James

James

James ----------------------------------

James _____

James _____

James _____

James _____

James _____

James _____

James _____

James

James _____

James _____

_____

_____

_____

_____

_____

_____

_____

_____

_____

_____

_____

_____

_____

_____

_____

_____

James

James

Castle for Rent

John DeChancie

AN [*e-reads*] BOOK

New York, NY

Copyright © 1989 by John DeChancie.
First e-reads publication 2002
www.e-reads.com
ISBN 0-7592-3204-0

"To Thomas F. Monteleone

The splendor falls on castle walls
And snowy summits old in story:
The long light shakes across the lakes,
And the wild cataract leaps in glory.
Blow, bugle, blow, set the wild echoes flying,
Blow, bugle; answer, echoes, dying,
dying, dying.
— Tennyson

Table of Contents

Contents

Prologue

Cellar, Near The Donjon

In a Niche in a crypt deep within a great castle, a section of wall vanished and revealed a high-raftered, pelt-hung room which evoked the interior of a Viking hall — but not quite. Two creatures stood in the room, facing each other. They were not human, but approximated human form. Their faces were huge and wrinkled, their eyes narrow slits over a blunt snout split by a mouth not unlike a hippopotamus', save that the teeth were numerous and sharp. They had thick, squat bodies, exorbitantly muscled, with leathery blue skin. They wore pieces of shiny green armor that could have been plastic or fiberglass or some composite material — or perhaps sections of the carapace of a giant insect. Both creatures wore swords and daggers in ornate scabbards. The behavior and mannerisms of both creatures could generally be described as an exaggeration, perhaps even a parody, of behavior patterns peculiar to a certain type of overaggressive male human.

The sudden materialization of the opening had interrupted a conversation — rather, a confrontation involving bared teeth, threatening postures, and much angry grunting and gesticulating. The creature who faced the opening stopped in mid-gesture, his six-fingered hand raised to strike the other creature. A puzzled expression formed on his inhuman countenance. The other creature had backed off, hand darting to the curving grip of a pistol in a hip holster.

Slowly the first creature lowered his arm, then grunted and motioned toward the opening, which lay at his adversary's back. The other grunted threateningly in reply, warily maintaining his orientation and taking another step back. He wasn't taking any chances. The first grunted again, pointing emphatically toward the suddenly created doorway.

1

The second creature couldn't resist casting a glance to the rear. He did an almost comic double take and whirled about to face the opening. Their argument temporarily forgotten, the two approached the anomaly. The second creature drew his weapon — a strange thing with a short barrel and a large underhanging clip. Cautiously they peered out. There was nothing immediately outside the opening but the bare stone walls of a corridor running to darkness at either hand. The gun-bearing creature stuck his head out and looked one way then the other. He snorted.

Then he said: "Secret passage. Escape tunnel."

The other grunted something in reply.

The first holstered his weapon and stepped out into the corridor. "Runs directly to Proconsul's quarters, leads to outside."

"Convenient," said the first creature as it came through the doorway. "But where did wall go?" He examined the dark stone of corridor, still looking puzzled. "Wonder where stone comes from. Strange stuff." He thumped a blue fist against it.

The gun-toting creature sniffed the air, snout wriggling. "Something not right here."

The other glanced about warily. "Strange. Very strange."

They wandered about, sniffing high and low, probing cracks and crannies with fat, blunt fingers.

"Sorcerer's work," the unarmed creature pronounced, peering at multicolored glittering motes that lay deep within the stone.

"You think?"

"What else? I saw wall disappear."

"You are drunk."

"If I want excrement from you, I will squeeze it out of your head!"

"And I will make you eat it — along with your words, dungbreath!"

The two squared off and snarled at each other for a spell. Gradually the tension lessened as they were again distracted by the strange apparition.

"Sorcerer's work, I tell you."

"Nonsense. Escape tunnel, nothing more."

"Look at seam here, between stone and wood. Blurry." The creature put his hand up against the juncture and observed that the hand became indistinct, then withdrew it as from something hot.

2

"Look!"

Far down the corridor, a mote of light danced in the darkness. Soon footsteps approached.

The two creatures went into defensive stances.

"Hi, there!" came a voice from down the hall.

A human approached, a short bearded man in jeans and a T-shirt. He stopped a short distance away. He held an odd lantern: it was a long wooden handle with a huge glowing jewel affixed to the end. The jewel glowed an eerie blue-white.

"Hi! Mort Kaufmann's the name. Have you two just wandered into the castle?"

The one with the gun slowly straightened.

"What sort of creature are you?" he barked. "And what are you doing in stronghold of Proconsul?"

"The what of who?" Kaufmann laughed. "You got it wrong. I should be asking what you're doing here — but of course I know perfectly well what you're doing. You were just minding your own business when all of a sudden a wall in your — " He took a step forward and peeked into the opening. " — living room? Yeah, a wall in your living room suddenly went *poof* and a doorway pops out of nowhere. And you go through, and you wind up here, and you're wondering what it's all about. Right?"

The creature thrust the pistol toward him. "I ask you question! Speak, or I will drill hole in your hairy head."

Kaufmann backed off. "Hey, now look. I don't want any trouble with you guys. Just being friendly, is all. I'm just trying to help out. You know, you really shouldn't — "

The unarmed creature rushed him. The jewel-torch clattered to the floor and Kaufmann went flying. The corridor wall interrupted his flight with a sickening thud. The creature then picked him up like a limp rag and began to pummel him mercilessly.

The other creature went for the torch, scooped the thing up, and examined it. At length he looked over his shoulder and growled, "Don't kill it! Proconsul will want to interrogate!"

Kaufmann lay still on the floor, one arm at an anatomically improbable angle.

"Two-legged, hairy creature that talks. Fantastic! Where did it come from?"

3

"From this place, wherever."

"Look. It has red blood."

"I can see that, fool!"

"Can you also now see — *idiot* — that there is something more to this?"

The other regarded the torch again. "Perhaps so." It ran a sausage-like finger over the handle.

The unarmed creature pointed at Kaufmann.

"Come, we must report this. Bring creature." When the other gave no response: "That is my order!"

The other glared back. "I urinate on your orders. You have no authority over me."

"I have Proconsul's authority! I am his chief of staff. As captain of stronghold guard, you are technically under my command. Obey!"

"Slime-eating schemer! You backstabbed your way to power!"

The other smiled toothily. "I could have you shot." His hand was a blur as it slipped behind his breastplate, bringing forth a small pistol. He trained it on the captain. "I could shoot you right now."

"You are coward as well."

The chief of staff's smile faded. Slowly he put the pistol back into its hiding place. He brought back his hand to his side.

"Now make your move."

It was quiet. Both creatures remained motionless for several minutes.

The captain of the guard carefully unbent and relaxed. "This is foolish. I will fetch prisoner."

The chief of staff picked up the torch. Looking it over, he walked toward the opening. Just as he reached it he caught sight of what the captain was about to do.

The captain's pistol smoked and sputtered. A brief flame coughed from the end of the barrel. That was all. Dumbfounded, the captain stood looking at the useless weapon in his hand — briefly, until a dagger suddenly grew in his throat. He dropped the pistol, gurgled, and fell dead. Bright purple blood issued from the wound.

The chief of staff retrieved the knife and picked up the gun. He looked at one, then the other.

"Strange."

Throwing down the gun, he grabbed the human by the hair and dragged him back through the portal.

4

Six
(Approximately)
Months
(For Lack Of
Better Word)
Later

Over The Plains Of Baranthe

He Pushed THE stick forward. The nose of the jet fighter dipped, allowing him to view the entirety of Castle Perilous atop its high promontory. It was as it always had been, a vast dark edifice of eye-defying complexity, a jumble of towers, turrets, bulwarks, and other fortifications, all ringed by concentric curtainwalls. The central keep soared into the clouds. The castle sat like a magistrate high on his bench, delivering judgments to the plains below and the snow-capped mountains beyond.

The castle belonged to him, as it had to his father, his father's father, his father's father's, etc., and all his forebears unto many generations. It was his home (one of them, at least), his freehold, and his fortress.

It was the biggest white elephant in the world. In several worlds, in fact.

But he loved the place.

He sent the plane into a wide banking circle around the castle and spent a good quarter hour inspecting it. As old as it was, the castle looked as though it had been built yesterday. No weathering discolored its stone, no mortar crumbled from its joints and cornices. It looked spanking new; in fact, it had been magically reconstructed a little less than a year before.

Without warning, the jet's single engine died with a whistling whine, and the lights on the instrument panel blinked, then went out.

"Infernal machine," he said irritably, shaking his head. He worked his fingers in complex patterns and muttered an incantation. The engine coughed once, roared to life, but faded seconds later. He worked his fingers again, chanting monotonously.

No use, the engine was dead. The jet dropped like a stone. He could have effected a levitation spell to keep it up, but that was hardly fun. Sighing, he waved his hand.

The jet disappeared, and was instantly replaced by a helicopter. He took the control bars, checked his counter-rotation, and put the ship into a steep dive.

He leveled off near the ground and hovered. The earth was blackened as if by a great fire. The copter bore down. Charred skeletons lay among the dust of the plain — the remains of the last army that had laid siege to Castle Perilous. The siege had been long and bitter, and the castle had almost fallen. But the besiegers had met a horrible end.

The helicopter's motor sputtered and choked.

"Damn!" He was dangerously close to the ground. He worked his fingers fast.

The aircraft that appeared around him was an eclectic meld of curving silver metal and clear, tear-shaped bubbles. It hummed and crackled. He looked over the controls — he had flown one of these only twice in his life — then gingerly put the tips of his fingers on the control panel. The craft shot toward the virginal blue sky with astonishing speed.

He leveled off at ten thousand feet, the castle still bulking hugely below him.

"Now to do what I came up here for," he said.

There was a computer terminal, of sorts, to his right. He studied it briefly, then punched in some data. A small screen next to the terminal lit up.

He was busy for several minutes. Then he looked up and searched the skies.

By the end of an hour, his neck hurt horribly and his eyes burned from reading instruments. It was hard work. The craft's engines had failed regularly every ten minutes or so, and had to be bolstered by complex levitation spells. The last of these was now fading rapidly.

"*There* you are!"

A fuzzy gray splotch floated against the bright sky. It looked like a defect in a camera lens, nebulous, out of focus. He headed the craft for it.

Worried that the engine might fail just at the wrong moment, he transformed the craft back to a jet fighter just before entry.

The sky didn't change color by much — it turned perhaps a shade lighter. Below sprawled an immense city cut by two rivers and outlined by a harbor. A long, thin finger of land, bristling with skyscrapers, ran between the rivers.

"I should have known. All roads lead to New York."

Smiling, he banked and turned toward Manhattan. It had been a long time.

Presently the radio sputtered and blurped.

" — Kennedy Air traffic control to unidentified military aircraft! Calling unidentified military aircraft! You are intruding in controlled air space! Come in!"

"Yes?"

"Unidentified aircraft — descend to fifteen hundred feet immediately! You are in a controlled air corridor! Acknowledge, please!"

"In a moment."

"Negative! Negative! You must — "

He snapped the radio off. This would never do. He suddenly realized how unprepared he was. Awkward, really.

The plane around him began to fade.

Of course. He had forgotten how inhospitable this world was to magic. Things were damned difficult here as far as the Arts were concerned. It was ironic. The jet didn't work very well back home because the universe of the castle was not amenable to mechanical contrivances, even conjured ones. Here, the jet worked fine, but its very existence was tenuous at best precisely because it was entirely a magical construct. He was getting the worst of both worlds.

That left him in somewhat of a pickle, one he should have smelted far off.

A simple shield spell protected him from most of the air blast when the jet finally faded out of existence, but even that began to wear off quickly. He stretched out his arms and legs and went into free-fall posture.

Plummeting toward the cold gray expanse of the East River, he decided that he would have to think of something very fast.

Elsewhere

"I've Gotten To like the castle," Linda Barclay said as she munched a kosher dill. "But I still have really serious bouts of homesickness."

Sitting with his back against the tree under which he and Linda were enjoying a picnic lunch, Gene Ferraro bit into a cheese-laden cracker. "That's normal. I don't get so much homesick as bored with life here — I mean, in the castle. I'd like to get out into some of the more exciting worlds. Explore a little, you know."

"You're big for adventure. I'm not. I'm basically a homebody."

"And one of the most powerful sorceresses around."

"Only in the castle and in some of the magic-is-the-rule worlds. That's what I like about my life here, as opposed to back in the normal world. Magic is fun."

"Sure is. Normal world? No such thing. Our world is just one of many — and a pretty dreary one at that."

"It's so nice here." Linda looked out across the meadow. Bright sunlight brought out the delirious green of the grass, and a soft breeze stirred the budding tree above. It was fine, first-warm-day-of-spring weather.

"Yeah, but I'd still like to do some exploring." Gene looked over his shoulder. "Take that big house over there."

Linda looked at the top of the huge dome that barely showed above the crest of the hill to the right.

"Did you ever go over and take a good look at it?"

"No," she said.

"It's a monster. It obviously belongs to someone, as does this whole estate. But the place is deserted."

"I guess that's why everyone in the castle comes here to picnic. It's nice, and there's no one to bother you."

A bird chirped in a nearby tree. Wooly clouds plodded sheeplike across a blue-violet sky. Gene sighed and stretched out, hands laced together at the back of his head. A sword in its leather scabbard lay in the grass at his left side.

Linda said, "The way I hear, some of the castle's worlds are pretty depopulated, due to wars, plagues, and other nasty things."

Gene looked off into the sky. "'The castle's worlds.' Say it that way, and it sounds like none of these places would exist if the castle didn't. I wonder."

"I never heard that. Kind of weird to think that our whole Earth existed just because Castle Perilous created a time warp, or whatever you call it."

"Spacetime warp. That's a scientific way of putting it. But Castle Perilous and everything about it has to do with magic, not science."

"Maybe the magic is just like science, only with different laws."

Gene shrugged. "Hard to say." He yawned. An insect buzzed about his head. He ignored it.

Linda stretched out one leg and adjusted her tights, then recrossed her legs. She echoed Gene's yawn. "Stop that, it's catching."

Gene feigned a loud, ripping snore.

Linda chuckled. "Maybe I should Z out, too. It was cold in the castle last night. I shivered all night long."

"Yeah, it does get cold sometimes," Gene murmured, eyes closed.

Linda looked off down the slope of the meadow.

"Gene?"

"Yeah."

"Have you ever seen a world with blue-skinned, muscle-bound creatures that wear green armor?"

Gene's right eye popped open. "Eh?"

"Look."

There were three of them, trooping in step up the hill. They were armed with swords and pistols, and all three wore backpacks.

Linda, said, "Something tells me these guys don't live here."

"Right, they're definitely prospecting, checking the place out."

"Their armor's pretty."

"Yeah. Linda, does your magic work here?"

"I've never tried. I whipped the food up back in the castle." She looked off, her brow furrowed. "I think so." She made a motion with her hand. "Yeah, it works a little."

"Good. Then maybe those guns they're toting won't work." Gene's right hand went to the hilt of his sword. "Here they come, straight for us. Get ready to move fast."

At the last minute, the three strange creatures changed course to the left and marched by, their big webbed feet crushing the overgrown grass in purposeful steps. One of them regarded Gene and Linda coldly. The others looked straight ahead.

When they disappeared over the rise, Gene let go of his sword. "I wonder what that was all about."

Linda shrugged.

Gene snapped his fingers. "Wait a minute. I thought something was familiar about them! Don Kelly was telling me about how people have been seeing strange-looking new aliens around the castle. Blue-skinned, short, chunky guys, lots of them, usually going around in threes. They don't mix, keep to themselves. In fact, they're supposed to be kind of belligerent, if pressed. Those must be the ones."

"I wonder what their world is like."

Gene shook his head. "Each one of those guys must go two seventy-five, maybe three hundred pounds. At least. They look like good fighters. Too good."

"Do you think they're trouble?"

Gene shrugged. "No real reason to think they would be. They seem to mind their own business." He mulled it over. "Trouble is, they look like they have business."

Linda nodded. "Serious business."

They were silent for a while.

"Have we been here a year, yet?" Linda asked.

"Who's keeping trade of time? Yeah, I guess."

Linda let out a long breath. "It seems shorter. Sometimes I still think this is all a dream."

"I know what you mean."

"A year ago I'm in Los Angeles, leading a normal life. I have a dull job, but I live near the beach in Santa Monica. It's okay, I guess. But I get depressed sometimes. A lot of the time. And I take a lot of pills. Then one day, when I'm feeling especially down, I open my closet and find that someone's torn out the back wall. I walk through and find this place that looks like the inside of a castle."

Gene broke in, "And the opening closes behind you, and you can't find a way back to your closet. And then you find there are all kinds of people in this castle, some good, some bad, some strange, some not. And the place is absolutely crazy, with doorways that lead to a million different worlds and universes — "

"Crazy isn't the word. Insane. Bonkers. Stark raving Looney-Toons."

"Never a dull moment. And there's even a king in this castle, by the name of Incarnadine." Gene sighed. "Yeah. Sounds familiar, except I came in by way of an odd doorway in a parking garage in downtown Pittsburgh, Pennsylvania. Of all places."

"Want to go back?"

"Huh? To our world? The good old USA, where I was born, like the song says?"

"Well, I meant the castle. But answer the question any way you want to."

"I dunno. The only thing that worries me is my parents. They must have given up hope by now."

"And mine."

"Sure wish there was a way to get a message back."

"Just a message?"

Gene nodded. "I like Castle Perilous. It's the ultimate trip, to use an expression out of the sixties."

"Let's trip back to the castle. I want to take a nap."

"At once, milady." Gene got to his feet and strapped on his sword.

Linda packed the wicker basket while Gene folded up the square of white linen they had used for a ground cloth. Then they both headed up the hill. The portal leading back to the castle stood among some trees just over the rise.

"I'm glad Snowclaw finally found a way back to his world," Gene said.

"Poor baby. He was practically dying from the heat."

"Yeah. He was in pretty bad shape. His fur was coming off in hunks."

"I miss him."

"So do I."

35th and Madison

When Alice Sussman heard the name of the author who was out at the front desk, she had to run to the files. Sure enough, the Spade Books backlist did show five titles published under the name of C. Wainwright Smithton. The titles hadn't been reprinted in years — decades.

She went to her "who's who" shelf and consulted several reference books. C. Wainwright Smithton was mentioned once or twice but information was sketchy. He was British, but emigrated here, wrote for the pulps in the thirties and forties, and published a few science fiction novels over the next two decades. His work had attracted much critical attention. One book referred to him as an "elusive genius."

As senior editor of science fiction and fantasy, it was Alice's duty to show hospitality to important writers who dropped in to visit — even if no one had ever heard of them.

"Very nice to meet you, Mr. Smithton," Alice said as she took the hand of the handsome white-haired gentleman in the checked overcoat. "You haven't been in to see us in quite some time."

"Oh, thirty years, I should say," Smithton said with a laugh. "I had a little trouble tracking down Spade Books, until I learned it had been bought out by the Bishop Publishing Galaxy."

"Spade Books still exists, Mr. Smithton, and it's doing fine. In fact, it's one of our strongest fiction lines. Won't you please come back to my office?"

Alice got him settled down with a cup of coffee on the couch in her office. She took the chair.

"What can we do for you, Mr. Smithton?"

"Oh, you can give me a book contract with an advance in six figures and one hundred percent of subsidiary rights." He grinned.

She grinned back. "We'd love to see a proposal from you, Mr. Smithton. I'm sure you still have many fans out there who'd buy a book with your name on it. After all, you're one of the veteran writers in the field."

"I'd be surprised if any of my old fans were still alive. I haven't had anything in print for years and years."

"Yes, I know. We put out reissues of backlist titles every month. Your name has come up several times during our weekly editorial meetings. Uh . . . I'm sorry to say we haven't actually done anything about it yet, but — "

"Quite all right, Ms. Sussman. You couldn't have, anyway. The rights have long since reverted to me, and I was out of contact for so long. I'm not complaining. I've been out of the country for years. I just recently came back to New York to look into some financial affairs of mine. Unfortunately, things haven't worked out the way I'd expected, and, frankly . . . to use the modern idiom, I'm having cash-flow problems."

Alice sat back and crossed her legs. "I see. Well, we'd certainly like to do all we can to help. But of course — "

"I certainly don't expect a contract and a check today. A few days would be fine."

Alice chuckled. "That's asking a lot of the machinery around here. Generally it takes a few weeks to produce a contract, and another few weeks to grind out a check. Minimum."

"I understand. Of course, I wouldn't expect special treatment just walking in here after thirty years — "

"Well, we'd like to do anything we can. We'll certainly look into reprinting some of your books, Mr. Smithton. I'm afraid I can't promise you anything at the moment, but — "

"You're very kind. What titles do you think would go these days?"

She teethed her lower lip. "Well . . ."

"Fortress Planet, perhaps?"

"A classic, and one of my favorites," she lied whitely.

"You flatter me. Blood Beast of the Demon Moon?"

"Is that a horror number?"

"On the cusp. How about my fantasy, *Castle Ramthonodox*? Then, of course, there's my story collection, *Bright Comets and Other Obfuscations*."

"Your work has been somewhat . . . neglected."

"I'm a has-been, you mean. Forgotten."

"Hardly," she said.

"Oh, it's true. And I never was prolific — "

"Unfortunately, quantity does count, as well as quality."

" — but it seems to me that I never did receive the last few royalty statements that were due."

Alice sat up. "Oh."

"I realize that thirty years is a long time, and your records . . ."

"Well, as a matter of fact, we do have a number of open files. Authors whose estates or heirs we can't locate. It may very well be — " She got up. "Won't you please wait here while I check with our accounting and legal departments?"

He cashed the check at a local bank and walked down Madison Avenue, heading for a little curio shop he used to know in the Lower East Side.

It had been tough persuading Alice Sussman — and the people in accounting — to cut him a royalty check this very day. The domination spell he had cast over the entire office had barely worked. Back home, everyone in the Bishop Publishing Galaxy would have been his willing slave. They all would have leaped out a ten-story window for him, single file. Here — forget it. The spell had only oiled the machinery a little bit. But it had worked. Done the job.

Well, there'd been a little give-and-take. Allie (at lunch she told him to call her that) had just about insisted that he submit an outline and sample chapters of a new book. Instead, over chicken lo mein, he spun out the plot of a sequel to *Fortress Planet*, quite off the top of his head, and she loved it. Well, the spell helped there a little, he had to admit. He hadn't written a word of fiction in years, and it must have been dreadful bilge he spilled out. Anyway, she'd offered a $14,000 advance, and he couldn't bring himself to refuse . . . Besides, he was stranded here and needed the money.

All in all, New York hadn't changed as much as he'd expected. Numerous landmarks had disappeared, replaced by austere modern structures (he rather disliked the ubiquitous Bauhaus influence), but plenty of familiar sights were still left. He remembered this part of town well.

He began to notice that there were more distressed people milling about than he recalled seeing during the Great Depression. He passed a slovenly middle-aged woman who carried two great bags stuffed with debris. She was followed by an emaciated man in a filthy overcoat who seemed to have difficulty controlling his tongue. These and other unfortunates made up a good percentage of the sidewalk population.

Wetting a mental finger and putting it up into the psychic wind, he got a subtle but overriding sense of decay, of desuetude, of things coming apart. Pity. It was a good town, but it had once been a great town.

The curio shop was just where he remembered it to be. The shops around it had been long since boarded up. A derelict lay unconscious on the sidewalk a few doors away. In the other direction, a nervous-looking youth regarded him from the doorway of an abandoned storefront.

He entered to the soft tinkling of a bell. The place was stuffed to the ceiling with an amazing collection of miscellaneous junk, and he was astonished to recognize some pieces from years before. Obviously business had not been brisk. The place smelled of must, dust, and stale cigar smoke.

There was a sallow young man behind the counter. He did not smile when he asked, "Can I help you?"

"Is Mr. Trent in?"

"Why . . . yes, he is. Who shall I say is calling?"

"Carney. John Carney."

"One moment."

The young man slipped through a tattered curtain into a back room. There was a murmuring of voices. Then the young man returned.

"Mr. Trent will see you. This way."

He followed the young man into the back room. There, seated at an ancient rolltop desk, was a man in his early sixties wearing a gray suit of fashionable cut, along with a burgundy tie, a tailored shirt with a crisply starched collar, and oxblood loafers burnished to a mirror shine. Even in the dim light he cut an imposing figure. His hair was blond-white, his face thin. His eyes were ethereal blue disks over a thin blade of a nose. The mouth was small and precise. He regarded his visitor, eyes narrowing, straining for recognition. At length and with some astonishment, he said, "It *is* you."

"Hello, Trent."

Trent rose and offered his hand, nodding to the young man, who retreated through the curtain.

"Incarnadine," Trent said.

"Greetings, my long-lost brother," Incarnadine said in Haplan, the ancient tongue of the even more ancient tribe of the Haplodites. "How dost thee fare?"

"Thou art a sight for longing eyes," Trent answered. "Let's stick to English," he added, "or Alvin will start to wonder."

"Alvin looks okay. I'll bet he's heard many a strange thing back here."

"You're right. Have a seat." Trent dragged up a battered hardback chair.

Incarnadine sat. "It's been a long time."

"How did you ever manage to get here?" Trent said.

"Well, I've been meaning to crack the problem of the lost gateway for the longest time. Just recently it occurred to me that it could be one of the orbiting variety, the kind that don't necessarily stay inside the castle. So, I whipped up a flyer, searched the sky over the castle — and sure enough, there it was. Had a devil of a time chasing it down, though."

Trent lit a small brown cigar and puffed on it. "After thirty years, you decide to do this. Why?"

Incarnadine shrugged. "Any number of reasons. I miss New York . . . I miss this world. Lots of memories here." He smiled. "I thought you might have been stranded here when the spell stabilizing the gateway went on the fritz."

Trent looked hard at him. "You thought. And it takes you thirty years to decide to find out for sure?"

"What is time to a spawn of Castle Perilous? Sorry. Were you stranded? Are you?"

"You said yourself that you found the thing floating in the sky. Where did it leave out?"

"About three thousand feet over the East River."

Trent whistled. "And you were flying a magical contrivance?" He shook his head. "Tough spot to be in."

"Yeah. I'd really forgotten how hard it was to practice the Recondite Arts around here."

"What did you do?"

"Well, when the plane dissolved, I tried just about everything on the way down. At about three seconds to impact I tried a simple protection spell, and that saved the day. And my hide. I hit pretty hard, though. Fortunately, it was only a few strokes swimming to shore. I didn't get a drop on me."

"You were lucky. Still, I wonder why you risked it."

"We've been getting a lot of Guests from here in the past few years. Some of them would like a way back. I'm here to see if I can establish a permanent gateway again."

Trent's pale brow rose. "You did it for the Guests? Those losers?"

"It's the least I could do. I would have seen to it long ago, but — one, I've been busy. Two, most of the Guests like the castle and want to stay. But some don't, and I thought we owed them."

"How about all the rest?"

"Some have stabilized gateways. The others . . . well, someday I mean to do something for them, too."

"Most of those damn holes should have been plugged long ago," Trent said, scowling. "The place is nothing but a big, drafty fun house."

"Do you realize how much power it would take to keep all the aspects sealed up? Keeping the particularly nasty ones shut up uses enough already."

Trent chewed his cigar. "Well, I'm no expert on castle magic." He took the cigar out and tapped the ash into a ceramic tray. "So, you say it never occurred to you to find out what happened to me."

"I'm embarrassed to say that although I certainly wondered, I always thought you could take care of yourself in any situation."

"I see." Trent's smile formed a small crescent. "Actually it was years before I discovered the gateway had skedaddled. I like it here, as you knew."

"One of the reasons I never really worried about you."

"Well, you were never very solicitous of my welfare."

"Nor you of mine, Trent."

Trent grunted. "Let's be frank. We were rivals for the throne. Dad favored you, and that's all there was to it." Trent tapped out the cigar. "Look. We have lots to talk about. Let's drive out to my place. We'll have dinner, hash over old times. What do you say?"

"Sounds friendly."

"It is, Inky. Wait a minute." Trent got up, parted the curtain, and called out: "I'm leaving early. I'll drive. Get a cab home."

"Yes, Mr. Trent."

Trent unhooked a camel's-hair overcoat from an antique coat tree and pulled it on. "Let's go."

The car was a blue Mercedes sedan, meticulously polished and parked next to a sign that read ABSOLUTELY NO PARKING.

"Hell of a nice car to leave on the street," Incarnadine remarked.

"I have a few friends on the police force who look after it for me."

"Nice to have friends."

They got in and Trent started it up and headed east.

"I'm surprised you still have the old shop. Still need a front?"

"Nah, not really. You were very lucky to find me there. My employees open the place up maybe two, three days a week. Most of my business is strictly legitimate these days. Real estate, stocks, the usual. The shop's still a good write-off, though." He chuckled. "I've been depreciating the same inventory for decades."

"Still deal in art?"

"My old hobby. I own a gallery on the West Side. Keeps the creative juices flowing." Trent honked at a taxi that cut in front of him. "Tell me this, why the hell didn't you try to stabilize the aspect from the other side? Why did you risk coming through and getting stranded?"

"I tried everything I could think of back home, but nothing worked. Something's changed. The stresses between the two universes have shifted over the years. It's not the same. Probably why the old spell failed."

Trent nodded. "I see." He made a series of lefts and rights, then turned north on First Avenue.

They were in the midtown tunnel when Trent asked, "Do you think you can tunnel back?"

"I'm going to give it the old college try. If I flunk out . . . can you take on a new employee?"

Ice Island

Snowclaw had been kneeling all day on an ice floe, waiting for a huge sea animal called the *jhalrakk* to come within range of his harpoon. But the jhalrakk had other ideas. It was content to stay where it was, just out of reach, half submerged in the shallow icy waters of the inlet. It had been feeding all day, ingesting vast quantities of water and filtering out what was edible. Only when it had its fill would it move out to sea again, and maybe — just maybe — its course would take it near Snowy's position.

Snowclaw knew it was a big jhalrakk (the word was sort of a growl, done with a snap of the jaws). He'd wanted to bag a big one all his life. This might be his chance.

It was cold. It was always cold here; the perennial question was *how* cold. Today, it was *very* cold. Bone-freezing cold. You had to watch when you took a leak outside, so as not to wind up stuck to one end of a pisscicle. It was *cold.*

Snowclaw hadn't moved for a very long time. Slowly he brought his four-digited hand to his belly, where the fur was a little thinner and finer than that which covered the rest of him, but just as milk-white. Bone-white claws extruded from the ends of his fingers. He scratched carefully, exhaling.

His feet, which were huge and padded with thick spongelike tissue at sole and heel, were cold. His left knee was cold. His butt was cold.

Damn, he thought. I'm *cold.*

He didn't know whether he'd be better off bagging the jhalrakk or not. If he did, he'd be all night gutting it, cutting it, and dragging the carcass back to his shack. And tomorrow would go to rendering blubber, seasoning hide, and doing a hundred different other things with

21

all the products and by-products that jhalrakks produced. He didn't look forward to any of that; it was all hard work. He just might freeze if he had to stay outdoors any longer. On the other hand, if he didn't bag something soon, he would starve. But at least he wouldn't have to break his back doing all that damn work.

It had been a very lean hunting season. He needed a little luck, or he didn't know what he was going to do.

The jhalrakk suddenly began moving. Snowclaw tensed, his left hand coming up to grip the front of the harpoon's shaft, his right moving back along its length.

The jhalrakk was heading straight for the floe. Snowclaw rose to a crouch and brought the point of the harpoon in line with the sharp, spiny back of the jhalrakk as it cut through the water, steaming toward him like a great ship, the kind Snowclaw would spy far out to sea sometimes. The spine rose, revealing the broad rubbery expanse of the beast's flanks. Then the head came out of the water. Its six eyes seemed to focus right on Snowclaw. The beast's great maw opened, revealing row on row of needlelike teeth.

Snowclaw swallowed hard and ran his tongue across his frost-white fangs. He stood up.

Come on right at me, big fellow.

Snowclaw made his shot. The harpoon skidded off the blubbery flank of the jhalrakk and plopped into the water. Snowclaw grabbed the line but his numbed hands couldn't stop it until it had paid all the way out, pulling taut against the iron anchor spike which had been pounded into the ice. Snowy growled and pulled on the line, but the jhalrakk had run over it, and now the big animal was diving. The beast slid out of sight, disappearing into the frigid, blue-black depths of the inlet.

Big it was, the largest that Snowy had ever seen. The jhalrakk was now underneath the floe. Snowy prayed that it would stay submerged and pass on out to sea. But the way it had looked at him . . .

The floe lifted out of the water, tilting sharply to the right. Snowclaw threw himself flat and hung on to the iron spike.

The floe soon became almost vertical and seemed about to tip over. Snowy knew he was in for a dunking, anyway, so he let go and slid into the water, hoping that he could swim away before the huge slab of ice flipped over on him.

It didn't. Snowclaw surfaced and watched the massive ice island slide off to one side and slip back into the water edgewise. The jhalrakk appeared satisfied that it had done enough damage. With a mocking wave of its flukes, it moved off serenely toward the open sea.

Snowy couldn't recall ever hearing of a jhalrakk big enough to lift an ice floe; a good-size one could overturn a large boat, for sure. But a huge, weighty mass of ice? It was ridiculous.

He swam back to the floe and climbed painfully back up on the ice. The wind hit him, making his waterlogged hide feel like a suit of fire. He pulled in the line, only to discover that he'd lost his best harpoon. With a savage growl, he yanked out the spike and threw it and the line as far as he could out to sea.

Some time later, grumbling, cursing, and generally bad-mouthing the world and everything that crawled or swam or walked in it, Snowclaw waded through deep drifts on his way to the only really warm spot he knew. He hadn't thought he would ever go back, but he was at the end of his tether. Maybe the time he'd spent away had made him go soft. He was losing his touch. You couldn't have asked for a more perfect setup shot on that jhalrakk. And he'd missed. Blown it completely.

He was just about frozen through, and could barely move, his fur a stiff mat of ice. The wind was howling out of the north throwing light snow, and night was falling. He could barely see through the icy rime forming over the fur around his eyes.

He found the crevasse and the steps he'd cut out of the ice going down into it. Minding where he put his feet, he descended the treacherous staircase.

The mouth of the cave was only a few steps from the bottom of the stairway. He went in, and the temperature immediately rose a few degrees. A few more steps inside the cave brought a warm draft from within. It felt like heaven.

There was a Gothic arch at the end of the tunnel, passing him through to a stone-walled corridor.

He was back in Castle Perilous.

The first time he'd stumbled in here, he and his hairless buddy Gene had met up and trooped around together. They'd wandered through the damn place for weeks, hopelessly lost. But after a while they'd become seasoned Guests of the castle, acquiring a sixth sense

that allowed them to navigate the vast edifice with a reasonable chance of at least finding a way to the lavatory.

He made a series of lefts and rights, moving through bare hallways lit by jewel-tipped light fixtures in their wrought-iron mounts.

At length he smelled food: human food, which ordinarily he found rather tasteless. But if he talked nice to the cooks, they would whip up something more to his liking. If Linda was around, she'd do it for him no questions asked.

He found the Queen's dining room and walked in. There were a number of hairless types — humans — at the table, his old friends among them.

"Snowclaw!"

Linda jumped up, ran over, and hugged him. He hugged back, careful not to crush the little human female, of whom he was greatly fond.

"Snowy, you're soaking wet!"

"Yeah, I been swimming."

Gene Ferraro thumped him on the back. "I *knew* you'd come back."

"You knew something I didn't," Snowclaw said. "Not that I didn't miss you, Gene, old buddy. How's it going?"

"Oh, been pretty quiet around here."

"Find a way back to your world yet?"

"Nope," Gene said. "Still working on it."

"That's too bad. We'll have to mount a search party. After all, you helped me find my aspect."

"It was nothing. Yours is one of the stable ones."

"So far. You know what they say, though. Any aspect can close up on you, anytime."

"Yeah, but I wouldn't worry about it."

Linda asked, "Why did you come back, Snowy?"

"Couldn't make it in the real world. I'm hungry."

Snowclaw scanned the table for anything he could eat. He grabbed a candle out of its sconce, dipped it into gooey white salad dressing, and took a bite. The thin man sitting in front of the empty sconce looked up and smiled bleakly at him.

"Sorry, pal," Snowclaw said. "Was that yours?"

"No, quite all right. You ought to try the silverware."

Gene said, "I'm glad you showed up, Snowy. I've been giving some thought to going exploring. Just picking an interesting aspect and heading off into it. Feel like going with me?"

"Sure, let's go. Just so it's someplace warm."

"I thought you didn't take to heat."

"I'm slowly becoming a convert to your way of thinking."

"Well, let me finish breakfast, and we'll scout around and see if we can find something interesting. Have a seat, Snowy."

Snowy said, "Linda, can I talk you into whipping up some grub for me?"

"Sure thing. What would you like?"

"Oh, the usual."

"You mean that fishmeal mush you like? The icky green stuff?"

"If it won't make you puke."

"Don't be silly. You have to eat the food your body needs. Hold on a minute."

Linda closed her eyes briefly, extending her right hand palm-down over the table. A large wooden bowl materialized under her hand. It was filled with icky green stuff.

"Thanks, Linda," Snowclaw said, taking the bowl and scooping out a gob of mush with his fingers. His fierce yellow eyes lit up as he sat down and began to eat in earnest.

"I don't know about you two running off like that," Linda said. "I'm going to worry about you."

"We'll be fine," Gene said, helping himself to more chicken a la king.

Snowclaw had sat down next to a chubby young man with a straggly beard who was staring at him with a mixture of awe and repugnance. Snowclaw caught his stare.

"Something bothering you, friend?"

"Huh?" The young man's face turned a shade paler. "No! Not a thing. Really. Uh . . ."

Linda intervened with, "Snowy, this is Barnaby Walsh. He's a new Guest. Barnaby, I'd like you to meet our friend, Snowclaw."

"A pleasure to meet you, Mr. Snowclaw."

"Same here. Pass that salt, would you?"

"Certainly. Here you are."

"Thanks."

Linda said, "Barnaby is an American, just like us."

"That's real nice."

"Uh . . ." Barnaby smiled sheepishly. "I don't understand. I mean, obviously Mr. Snowclaw is . . . well, he's not a human being. But I can

understand him perfectly. He even sounds American! But how could that be?"

"The translation spell," Gene said.

"The what?"

"It's operative throughout the entire castle. It's a magic spell that gives you an instantaneous running translation of any language. Snowy's speaking in his own tongue, just like everybody else here. Take Mr. Hoffmann over there, for example. He's German, and he speaks no English. Right, Mr. Hoffmann?"

"That's right."

"I don't get it," Walsh said. "He just spoke English."

"No, he didn't. He said it in German. Didn't you, Mr. Hoffmann?"

"Ja."

"Well, I heard it that time," Walsh said.

"You can turn the translation off if you want to. For instance, just listen to the sound of Snowy's voice for a while. He grunts and barks and growls, but you understand him perfectly."

"But how?"

"It's magic!" everyone at the table chorused. Then they all laughed, except Walsh.

"I think I'm going insane," Walsh said, covering his face with his chubby hands.

Linda reached out a hand. "Now, Barnaby, don't lose it. Come on. If I could adjust, so can you. I was in worse shape than you when I wandered in here."

"It's just all so fantastic. So unbelievable."

"It's real. Just go with it. Don't fight it. It's fun, mostly. Things can get a little dangerous sometimes, but magic is the rule here. Anything goes."

"Do you really think . . ." Barnaby steadied himself with a gulp of coffee. "Will I really develop magic powers?"

"Everyone who becomes a Guest does. Castle Perilous is like a big dynamo, spinning off this fantastic energy. We act sort of like conductors. But each person's powers are unique. Everyone can do something different."

"You mean I might not be able to materialize things, like you, but I'll get some other power?"

"Right. For instance, Snowy here can teleport like a champ."

"Really? No kidding."

Snowclaw nodded. "Yeah, I can zip all over the damn place just by thinking about it."

"And Gene is the greatest swordsman in this and a few other worlds."

"Zat is becawse ah am French."

"You're French?"

"Of course. Why else would ah have zis ridiculous accent, eh?"

"French accents are not necessarily ridiculous," said a gentleman named DuQuesne. "I wish you could hear what most Americans sound like when they try to speak French."

"Whoops, looks like I put my foot in it again," Gene said. "Sorry, Monsieur DuQuesne."

M. DuQuesne laughed. "I was teasing you, Gene."

"Well, I don't mean to go treading on nationalist feelings. I mean, we've all got — " Gene caught sight of something and trailed off.

He was staring over Linda's head. Linda turned to see three blue-skinned creatures enter the dining room and stop to survey it imperiously. They could have been the same three who had shown up on the picnic grounds.

They sauntered over to the table. One of them looked over the wide selection of comestibles spread from one end of the table to the other.

"Scavenger leavings," it said with disgust. "Garbage."

No one argued with the creature.

The middle one had picked up a turkey leg to sniff. The creature tossed the thing over its shoulder contemptuously.

"If you speak to the cook," Gene suggested to the first creature, "I'm sure you'll be taken care of."

The creature didn't answer. It stalked the length of the long table, sizing everyone up. It stopped at a place opposite Gene and stood arms akimbo, glaring, flashing its gleaming teeth. "What if I think your cook is garbage as well?"

"Then you'll starve, pal." Gene shrugged. "Those are the breaks."

"Breaks?" The creature's head turned slightly to one side, as if giving ear to an unseen interpreter. Then it nodded. "Understand. Yes. Luck. You are lucky I am under orders. I will not kill you now. But I might take some pleasure kicking your miserable carcass about this room."

"You'll take pleasure in this first, friend," Gene said, laying a hand on the hilt of his sword. His heart was jumping into his mouth as he said it.

"*That* would give me immense pleasure."

"Suits me," Gene said. "And now suits me as well as later."

The creature smiled the wickedest, toothiest smile Gene had ever seen or could ever have imagined. "You are brave. Surprising, inasmuch as your race is so cravenly peaceful."

Gene laughed. "He don't know humans very well, do he?"

Nobody else laughed.

"Gene . . ." Linda's warning was also a plea.

"Reconsidering," the creature said, "it might be worth being court-martialed to see this hovel tastefully decorated with your entrails — if you have any left after I am finished with you."

"Well, there's only one way to find out, big fella."

Snowclaw stood up. He towered at least two feet over the creature. "You're in my light, Blueface." Snowclaw placed a hand flat against the creature's shiny green breastplate and shoved. The creature went staggering backward but managed to stay on his feet.

Gene gulped uncomfortably. Any other living thing would have gone crashing into the wall.

The three intruders drew their swords almost in unison. Gene jumped up and followed suit, as did a number of armed males at the table. Snowclaw snarled and leaped toward the first creature, coming to a karate fighting stance, milky claws at their maximum extension.

"Halt!"

The voice had come from the arched entrance to the dining hall. There stood another blue-skinned creature, scowling in the direction of the one Snowclaw had shoved.

The first creature came to attention with its sword at present-arms. The others followed suit.

"There will be none of this," the creature at the door said.

"Yes, Squad Leader," the first creature acknowledged.

"You will report back to headquarters immediately. Consider yourself under arrest."

"Yes, Squad Leader."

"Go."

The three soldiers left. The squad leader lingered at the doorway for a moment, its cold eyes taking the measure of the room and the beings contained therein. Then, abruptly, it turned and marched off.

Everybody breathed again.

"Gene, I don't believe you did that." Linda rolled her eyes and put her hands to her head.

Gene looked unhappy. "It wasn't me, it was the magic. This castle turns me into a cross between John Wayne and Cyrano de Bergerac, and something compels me to act out the role. Besides, that guy was getting on my nerves."

"Yeah, they're kinda pushy, aren't they?" Snowclaw said.

"What *were* those . . . things?" Barnaby Walsh asked, his face the color of Chinese bean curd.

"I don't know what you'd call them," Gene said. "'Blueface' is as good as anything."

"Where do they come from?"

Gene shrugged. "One aspect or another."

"I've never seen them before," Hoffmann said. "But I've heard other Guests mention seeing them."

"Still want to go exploring, Gene?" Snowclaw asked.

Gene frowned and shook his head. "Not until we find out what these blue guys are up to."

"Goody, goody. I hope there's a rip-roaring fight in it."

Barnaby Walsh gave Snowclaw a look of dismay.

"I could use a good fight," Snowclaw told him. "I really like it when the fur flies and the guts go spilling all over the place." Snowy licked a gob of mush from his thin pink lips. "Kinda pretty."

Walsh belched. "Excuse me," he said, getting up from the table. "I don't feel quite — " He riffed again, tottering away.

"Was it something I said?" Snowclaw asked.

Long Island

Trent's house was of dark red brick with black wood trim, and stood on wooded grounds somewhere in the wilds of Nassau County, sea gulls pinwheeling in the sky above it. The interior was tastefully and expensively appointed. An accelerated course in the history of modern painting covered the walls, and various avant-garde sculptures graced tabletops and display pedestals. The furnishings were mostly modern, with dashes of tradition for flavor.

Trent's study was book-lined and warm, a cheery fire going in the hearth.

"So, you say you've had some trouble up at the old place recently?"

Incarnadine took the glass of sherry from Trent and nodded. "It was a full-scale siege. Nearly successful, too."

"Really? Who was it?"

"Vorn."

"Prince Vorn of the Hunran Empire?" Trent seated himself in the leather easy chair opposite Incarnadine's. "I wouldn't have thought Castle Perilous was worth the bother."

"He didn't think so, either. Melydia worked her business on him, and he followed her like a lost, hungry puppy."

"Amazing. Melydia, huh? She still has it in for you. Hell's fury has nothing on that woman."

"Had."

Trent's eyebrow's rose. "Dead?"

"In a sense. She got to the Spell Stone, and — "

"Gods!"

Incarnadine smiled. "Yes, she finally figured it out. She got to it, somehow, and unraveled the transmogrification spell."

"But . . ." Trent was appalled. "That could have meant the end of everything."

"Almost did."

Trent waited. "Well, for crying out loud, tell me what happened!"

"It's a long story. She messed up just enough to give me an edge. I did a little research, and found a good handle by which I could recast the spell almost immediately."

"That must have taken some doing. But then, you must have seen . . . it. However momentarily."

"Oh, yes. I saw it."

Trent sat back. "Ramthonodox," he murmured.

"The Ancient Beast, the Primal Demon. Ramthonodox, Hell-spawned enemy of man. Old Brimstone Breath himself."

"It must have been an awful sight, in the true sense. Inspiring awe."

"It was. It did."

"Yet," Trent went on, "perhaps thrilling, in some strange, sub-liminal way?"

Incarnadine considered it. "I wasn't very thrilled at the time."

"Not the tiniest bit? The primal force, the unlimited power of it — "

"Maybe a little. Evil has its attractions. But pure evil is a little heady even for the likes of us. Besides, evil really isn't a force, is it? It's more like entropy; the undoing of things."

"Depends on your philosophical point of view, I suppose. Still, it must have been . . . stimulating, in any event." Trent took a sip of whiskey. "But you managed to fix up the spell and reconstitute the castle. So Castle Perilous is still a place to hang your hat in, not a demon running around loose."

"Right. I'm here, aren't I?"

"So you are. What about Vorn and his minions — I presume he brought his army with him, and not just an overnight bag?"

"There was a slight but unavoidable delay in recasting the trans-mogrification spell."

"Oh, I'll bet," Trent said, grinning malevolently.

"Ramthonodox had a good time out there on the plains. Nothing left of Vorn or . . . well, there wasn't much left of anything after old Rammy was through."

Trent shook his head slowly. "And Melydia?"

"Strangest thing. After it was all over, I heard her voice in the castle. Can't exactly figure out what happened to her. Got caught up in the spell somehow."

"Justice. The poetic kind, too."

"Perhaps."

"Well." Trent smiled at his brother. "It's nice to see you again, Inky."

"You haven't called me that in . . . hell, I hate to think how long."

"About a century and a half? Longer."

"Not since you and I were at university," Incarnadine said.

"Which one? The one in Hunra, where we learned magic, or at Cambridge, where we read natural philosophy?"

"I never liked Hunra much, I must say."

"Neither did I. It was a good thing Dad was so keen on us learning the ways of nonmagic universes."

"Of which this one is the most nonmagical," Incarnadine said.

"Well, Dad had a fondness for Earth generally, and for western European culture specifically."

"Not surprising, since this culture bears some resemblance to our own. He once told me he spent some time in England. That's why he gave us all English names, he said." Incarnadine sampled the sherry, then continued, "I've always thought he must have been Merlin."

"You think?" Trent thought it over. "Fantastic. I'd never considered it. But when you consider the time frame — " He shrugged it off. "Dad never did tell us how old he was, and I'm not particularly interested in researching his exploits."

There was a pause as Incarnadine stared into the fire. Then he asked, "Do you still hate me, Trent?"

"Whatever led you to believe I hated you?"

"Just a feeling."

Trent looked away. "I don't hate you, Inky. You did come between me and my ambitions . . . once." He sighed. "But that was centuries ago. I'm happy here. You can see that. The gateway disappeared, and I didn't know it for five years. I never planned on going back, you see."

Incarnadine nodded. "But when I die?"

"Do you plan on dying soon?"

"No."

"Well? Yes, I suppose I'm next in line for the succession, but I'm not interested. If I were — " Trent grinned cordially. " — I'd simply kill you now."

"You could, I suppose. Easily. No one knows I'm here. Officially I don't exist in this world."

Trent got up and went to the bar. "Forget it. I've no interest in taking possession of a huge, drafty old castle that's a cross between a carnival sideshow and a sci fi movie." He made himself another whiskey and soda. "Besides, I own my share of useless real estate up in the Bronx. At least I can hire a guy to torch an abandoned apartment building."

Trent's oriental servant opened the door and poked his head in. "Dinner, sir," he said.

"Thank you, Phan," Trent answered as the door closed, then downed his drink in three swallows. "Well, shall we go in and eat?"

Dinner was superb, and mostly silent. There did not seem to be much more to talk about until coffee was served.

"Good food," Incarnadine said.

"Phan does a good job. He was raised in a French Catholic mission in Phnom Penh — learned to cook Parisian."

"Best *coq au vin* I've ever had."

"I'll tell him." Trent lit a cigar and puffed thoughtfully. "When was the last time you heard from anyone else in the family?"

"Oh, not so long ago. Dorcas dropped in a while back."

"How is our dear elder sister? She still married to that fat potentate who copulates with animals?"

"Nobody ever approves of in-laws. Besides, it's a religious ritual, common in his land."

"Disgusting. How about Ferne?"

"She hasn't shown up in years. I fear for her. She was a wild one."

"Oh, I've a notion Ferne's okay . . . somewhere. And Deems?"

"Deems is still King of Albion, and loves it. He'll never leave the place. I don't blame him, it's pretty nice." Incarnadine drank the last of his coffee and sat back. "Then there's Uncle Jarlath — "

"To hell with Uncle Jarlath and the rest of the fossils. I couldn't care less."

"In that case, that's all the news from back home. What's new with you? Is there a woman in your life? Or women?"

"Forgive me, Inky, but I don't feel like exchanging warm personal data with you just now. If you don't mind."

"Of course."

"I'm sorry. I didn't even ask about your current family. Uh, you do have one, don't you?"

"They're fine."

"What's the new one's name? I mean the wife."

"Zafra."

"Hmm. Sounds very nice."

"She is."

Another lull occurred before Trent said, "Where are you staying, Inky?"

"Hotel. I'm looking for an apartment in the city."

"In Manhattan? You'll be lucky to get on a five-year waiting list for anything reasonable. Unless you're talking about spending big money."

"I'm somewhat financially embarrassed at the moment."

Trent smirked. "Tricky getting used to a hard-physics world again, isn't it?"

"Very. The credit card I materialized to pay for the hotel disappeared a microsecond after I put it back in my wallet — which vanished not very much later."

Trent's look was detached, analytical. "If you're that far along already, maybe I would be taking a big risk trying to knock you off right here and now." Then the smile resumed. "Just kidding, brother."

Incarnadine's hand came up from beneath the table gripping a large revolver. "Just in case you're not," he said. "This won't last a minute, but a second is all it would take."

Trent laughed. "One thing I would never, never want to do, Inky, is underestimate you." Then he suddenly frowned in mock indignation. "Really, Inky, that was uncalled for."

"Sorry." The gun disappeared. "You've been making what I took to be veiled threats all afternoon. Sorry if I've misinterpreted."

"You have. I should apologize, though. Inky, I don't want to hurt you, or get in your way . . . or do anything, really, but continue leading my life. All I ask is that you leave me alone."

"That is not an unreasonable request," Incarnadine said. "I might ask the same of you."

"Then let's bury the hatchet. Let's agree to disagree, live and let live, and all the rest of that stuff."

"Let's." Incarnadine rose from the table. Trent did not.

"Inky, I've been meaning to comment — your disguise is pretty good. It's not magic, but it's a fair makeup job. How did you do it?"

"I went into a costume shop, bought some stage makeup, this wig, and the moustache. A few age lines here and there, a touch of pancake . . ." He shrugged. "Yours *is* magic, I suppose."

Trent snapped his fingers and the years melted away in an instant. Incarnadine beheld Trent as he had looked the last time they had seen each other, sometime in the late 1950s.

"Pretty neat," Incarnadine remarked. "You seem to have no trouble with the Arts here."

Trent shook his head. "Rudimentary stuff."

"Effective, though. I should ask you to give me lessons. But now, Trent, I have to go."

"Phan will drive you back to New York."

"I wouldn't think of it. Can you call me a cab?"

"We're out pretty far. Inky. Phan can run you into Great Neck, though, and you can get a train for the city."

"That suits me."

"It's been nice."

"Goodbye, Trent."

"And keep in touch," Trent added, smiling pleasantly.

Wilmerding, Pennsylvania

Ohmygawd. saturday night and no date. Jesus, Mary, and Joseph. Invoking all deities, great and small.

Sheila turned the water in the tub on and yanked up the thingee on the spigot that made the water come out of the shower head.

Oh Jesus H. Christ on the proverbial crutch. Sorry, sorry, don't mean to offend any supernatural personages. Can't afford that, not with the way things have been going. Oh hell.

She looked in the mirror. Same face. It doesn't go away, doesn't change. Still Sheila. Who did you expect?

Another Sa-tur-day night and I AIN'T got no-BOD-y . . . da da da da da dee dee dum dum DUM —

She let the ratty old robe drop and looked at herself. Her breasts seemed to sag just a little lower than they did the last time she'd looked at them. Mygawd, could this process be taking place *overnight?* Did they go — plop — just like that? Or was it her imagination?

She couldn't quite see her butt, though she knew she was okay in that department, at least. Thank heaven for small favors. She wasn't going completely to pot. Her weight was fine.

Oh, for Christ's sake, stop this damn fixation about the body, okay? So you're getting older. It's inevitable. Completely natural process. Everything's fine. Just . . . fine. So you've had two horrible marriages. Great. So you hate your job. Okay, so you hate the goddamn world. So what? That's life, kid.

The bathroom filled with steam and her image grew misty and faded. Faded away.

She wiped the mirror with two fingers and saw one green eye peeking back at her. Still there, Sheila?

36

Still there.

She got in and the water was a little hot, so she adjusted it. She let the spray sting her until it cooled down, perversely enjoying the discomfort.

No date. No men in her life. No men anywhere. No guys at work she wanted to *work* with, let alone go out with. The bar scene was deadly. 99.99999 percent of the men she *did* meet were: (1) pinheads; (2) multiple-attempt losers (like herself!); or (3) married. Most of them, it seemed, were (3). Why was she always·meeting married men she liked? Some weird psychological thing, no doubt.

She poured a cold gob of Herbal Essence into her hand, slapped the stuff on her head, and smooshed it around until it lathered.

Two disastrous marriages. Actually the latest had been the worst. Frank was . . . still *is*, from all reports . . . nuts. He had problems; *serious* problems. Her lawyer files, he gets the papers at work, and what does he do? He leaves work, goes straight to the house, breaks in (the locks had all been changed), and proceeds to trash the place from top to bottom. All the furniture, slashed, ripped, broken apart. Carpeting slit down the middle with a linoleum cutter. Dishes smashed, the stereo stomped on and wrecked, the bed . . . the *bed*, for Christ's sake, a complete shambles. The crazy bastard didn't miss a piece of communal property. Property settlement! Hah! What property?

What if she had been home at the time? Ohmygawd. He would have killed her.

Sure, she got a judgment against him for the damages, but who knew when he'd pay up, if ever? The schmuck was broke. Meanwhile, she had a house full of broken junk, this monster mortgage, a shit job at Mellon Bank, and she was stuck in Wilmerding.

Wilmerding.

Wilmer . . . *ding*.

She rinsed, then poured out another gob of goop and lathered again. Gonna wash that jerk right outta my . . . yeah, right.

No date. So we bathe, *madame*, and we brush on a little Clinique, and spritz on a touch of . . . oh, what would be good for tonight? — some cheap smelly crap, real whory stuff, and then, *mesdames et messieurs*, we go down to Chauncey's and watch the pretty lights and listen to the music and nurse a glass of Chablis until some insurance underwriter sidles up and asks us to dance to a disco (migraine-inducing rhythm track overlaid) redub of an old Beatles number. . . .

A sudden cold blast of air hit her, and she began to shiver. Her heart thumped against her breastbone. *Somebody had come in! Somebody had opened the bathroom door!*

But the draft was coming from the wrong direction, from the wall. Suds-blind, she reached out.

And there was no wall. She felt the shower curtain to make sure that she hadn't gotten turned around somehow. No! But . . . there was nothing but empty space to her right, where the side of the one-piece molded-fiberglass tub and the section of water-stained wall above it should have been. She stretched her arm and swung it in a wide arc. Nothing! She was freezing. She bent and reached out as far as she could.

She slipped, stumbled, and fell onto a hard cold floor.

There came a sudden quiet.

Soap burning her eyes, she struggled to her feet. She wiped and wiped at her face but stuff wouldn't get out of her eyes and she yelled in pain.

After an agonizing few moments she could see a tiny bit.

What the hell — ?

She was standing in a room with walls of stone and a ceiling like a church or something. There was a table and two chairs, and cold fireplace, and a sort of couch. Nothing else. She was standing on a gray stone floor, naked, dripping wet, and covered with suds. And freezing to death.

She whirled. She stood about two feet from a blank stone wall. The shower, the water . . . her house, were gone. Gone.

Slowly she turned around, her soap-reddened eyes in a zombie stare.

Gone. One second she was . . . and then she . . .

She screamed. But it didn't do any good. Nothing changed. She was still naked, cold, wet, scared, and in a situation she didn't understand.

She screamed again, then decided not to do it a third time.

She searched the wall for any sign of an opening, a hole, a seam, a crack, something, anything — any trace of a connection or bridge or transition between her existence of not half a minute ago and her existence now. There was nothing. The wall was as solid and as unyielding as stone walls rightly should be. She searched again. No change; no bathtub, no bathroom, no house, no Wilmerding. This was someplace else. Someplace else entirely.

There was a doorway to her right and she approached it cautiously, her sudsy feet precarious on wet, slippery stone. She poked her head out into a hallway, looked one way, then the other. Nothing but a corridor lit only by a few windows up and down it.

Grimacing from the chill and hugging her rib cage, she went out into the hall and trotted to the nearest window.

She was in a church, a cathedral, or some huge Gothic stone edifice. She could see a forest outside, and mountains. It was a bright day. Last time she had looked outside, it was a dark winter Saturday night. Now it was broad daylight. Different place, different time.

A castle — yes, the building looked more like a castle. A huge one, from what she could see. The window must have been forty stories off the ground.

She was cold. She toddled off down the hallway, at length discovering a huge wooden door to the left. She tried the wrought-iron handle; the door wouldn't budge. She passed another window and came to a dead halt, as if hitting an invisible barrier. No, she couldn't have seen what she thought she'd seen. She backtracked and looked out.

Yes, she'd seen it. There was a desert out there, vast and dry and empty. A molten sun beat down on endless salt flats, scorched and featureless, upon which there grew not a weed, nor a blade of grass.

She went back to the first window. The forest — as lush and green as before — was still out there, as were the glorious snow-capped mountains that rose in the distance.

She returned to the second window and stared out, forgetting her nudity, forgetting herself.

Presently the drying soap began to itch, and she turned away and continued down the hall. She again grew aware that she was cold.

"Help," she called, as calmly as possible. "Somebody help me, please."

No one answered. She came to a casement window with panes of leaded glass, but declined to look out. She called out again, and again no answer came.

She tried another door, then another. The third was unlocked, and she peeked in.

It was a bedroom. The bed was huge and looked quite comfortable, covered with blankets and quilts and decorated pillows. There were night tables on either side which held lamps, and a big wooden chest

lay at the foot of the bed. A tall pine wardrobe stood off to the right, and a dressing table lay near the huge open window. She went to the window and looked out.

The castle spread out endlessly beneath her, a tumult of walls and towers and courtyards and buildings. Beyond the farthest wall there was a sheer drop and then a wide plain. On the horizon, black mountains bulked against the sky like storm clouds.

The window had thick velvet curtains which she untied and let fall. The room darkened. She checked the door and found that it had an old-fashioned lock turned by a huge old-fashioned key. She twisted the key until she heard a click, then ran for the bed. She tore the covers down and slipped in. The sheets had been warmed by the sun, and she luxuriated in the comfort of it, sighing with relief.

She looked around the room. Ohmygawd, what a place to spend a Saturday night. Naked — and no goddamn date!

She pulled the covers over her head.

Castle Keep — West Wing

Gene, Linda, and Snowclaw approached the door to Gene's room.

"I think we should make some systematic effort to search for their portal," Gene was saying. "Find out where they're coming from."

"Track 'em," Snowclaw said.

"Yeah, that's it. We follow a couple of them. Eventually they'll go back to their world and we'll at least know — oh, damn it. The maid must have locked my door. I don't have my key, either."

Linda asked, "Want me to materialize it?"

"Yeah, sure."

A key appeared in Linda's hand. "Is this it?"

"We'll find out."

Gene fit the oversize key into the keyhole and turned it. The lock clicked open. "Anyway, we have to keep a close watch on them, that's for sure," he continued, shouldering the door open and going in. He stopped in his tracks when he saw the naked woman dash away from the door and dive into the bed.

Linda bumped into him, then saw the strange female in Gene's bed.

"Oh, excuse me," Linda said, then turned and left.

The woman was peeking over the covers, eyes as round as half-dollars. Gene stood there gawking for a moment. Then he called over his shoulder, "Linda? Hey, wait — "

Snowclaw came in, and the woman shrieked and disappeared under the sheets.

Gene said, "Uh, don't be afraid. He won't hurt you."

"Who's your new friend, Gene?" Snowclaw asked.

"Never saw her before. Uh, Miss — ?"

There came a frightened mewling from beneath the covers.

41

Gene laughed. "You know, that's a line right out of an old Bela Lugosi movie. 'Do not be afraid. He will not hurt you.' Snowclaw, do you mind leaving the room? I think I can handle this."

"I gotta find a room for myself, anyway. Darned if I know how I'll ever get used to sleeping on those soft bouncy things you humans like. See you later."

Snowclaw left.

"Uh, Miss? Or Ms., or whatever. You can come out now."

"I don't have any clothes!"

"Yeah. I'm aware of that. Uh, I mean, you can *look* out, if you want."

"Oh my God. Oh my God."

"Now, calm down. Take it easy."

She was a redhead with green eyes. Pretty, too.

"He's gone," Gene said.

"What . . . *was* that?" Sheila asked in wide-eyed wonder.

"I don't know the name Snowclaw's species goes by, but obviously they're humanoid, intelligent, and probably descended from ursine stock rather than anthropoids, like we are."

"Huh?"

"Bears. Polar bears."

"Oh. He didn't look much like a bear."

"No, not much. Looks ten times more ferocious."

"Oh my God."

"I'm Gene Ferraro."

"Huh? Oh. Sheila Jankowski."

"Hi, Sheila. You want some clothes?"

"Yes. Yes, please! Thank you."

Gene went to the wardrobe, opened it, and rooted. "Here's a tunic that's a little too small for me. It's just a one-piece thing. Linda can whip up a nice outfit for you anytime. I'll be in the john, there, so you can dress." He threw the garment on the bed.

When he came out of the bathroom, she was dressed and standing by the window looking at him sheepishly, apprehensively.

"I'm sorry I messed your bed up," she said. "Sorry I used your room. But, you see, I didn't know — "

"I don't mind in the slightest," Gene said.

"I heard you at the door," she said, "and I ran to see if I could bolt it. I . . . I didn't know — "

"Forget it. You're probably confused, right? You're probably wondering what the hell this place is, and what you're doing here, and why the hell I'm wearing something out of a bad old Tony Curtis movie — you know, the ones where he strikes a heroic pose and says, 'Yonder is da castle of my fodder.' Right?"

"Well, what you're wearing looks . . . interesting."

Gene rapped a knuckle against the leather cuirass that covered his chest. "Not much protection in a swordfight," he said, "but chain mail's too heavy and armor is ridiculous. I like to be able to move."

"Do you get a lot of use out of that?" she asked, pointing at his broadsword.

"It's saved my life any number of times."

"I see." She didn't see at all. Not at all.

Gene grinned. "Welcome to Castle Perilous."

164 East 64th Street

He had bought a color TV set to substitute as a computer CRT screen because of the sound capability. The set was nominally of American manufacture, though most of the parts bore oriental symbols. Lots of things had changed in this country.

He reattached the back of the set, tightening the screws a few turns. The adjustments he had made were minor, but necessary. He turned the set around on the table and sat back.

He began the incantation in a low monotone, then modulated to a wavering chant. As he did this he performed accompanying hand gestures. The screen began to form vague images. He continued the recitation until the screen went blank again.

"Damn."

His fingers went to the keyboard of the computer terminal and punched a few keys. A table of numbers appeared on the screen and he consulted it.

"More nearer A-flat than A-natural," he muttered.

He picked up a small plastic disk, about the circumference of which a number of small holes had been punched. He put the device to his lips and blew. A musical note sounded.

"That's more like it." He hummed a note in tune with the one that the pitch pipe had emitted. "Yes."

He began the incantation again, this time in a slightly altered tonality. The CRT screen came to life with a flurry of random images, fleetingly visible, along with accompanying sounds. In time, the images congealed into a scene.

The angle of sight was high, looking down on a large bed. A man and a woman lay in it, the man half sitting, half reclining, bending

over the woman, who lay with both legs dangling over the high edge of the bed. The man was dressed in kingly robes, she in a maidservant's gown and cap. The man nuzzled her neck as he fumbled with the ties of her bodice.

"Deems? Sorry to bother you — "

"What!" The man sat up suddenly. The woman squealed, jumped up, and ran off-screen.

"Who calls?"

"Up here, Deems. To your left."

The man looked first to the right, confusedly, then to the left. Then he tilted his head up and peered straight out from the screen.

"Incarnadine! What the devil — ?" He exhaled and rubbed his forehead, looking down. "Gods! You gave me a terrible start, Inky old boy."

"Sorry, Deems. I realize it's an awkward moment to reach you."

"Devil of a time. A man's hardly more vulnerable when he's dallying with a chambermaid." He chuckled. "I'm only relieved it was you instead of — " He looked about conspiratorially; then, in a whisper "— instead of She-Who-Must-Be-Propitiated." Winking slyly he added, "If you know who I mean."

"How is . . . Flaminia?"

Deems looked pained. "Healthy as an ox, I'm sad to report. She scrutinizes my every move, hides the liquor, keeps a tight fist on my finances, and complains that I don't pay enough attention to her."

"I'm sorry for you, Deems."

"Don't be, old boy. Otherwise, things are fine."

"How are things in fair Albion?"

"Middling indifferent. The northern barbarians threaten; the nobles carp about high taxes; the peasants squawk about ruinous quitrents; the royal treasury is just about depleted; trade imbalances are draining gold away from the country like shit through a sewer pipe — " He grinned broadly. "Same old story. How goes it with you? Where are you calling from, by the way?"

"New York."

Deems was impressed. "How did you ever find the portal?"

"It took some doing. About six months of trying different things."

"Well, congratulations. How is the place? Did they ever get that global war settled?"

"Which one? There have been two of them in this century."

"Oh. Well, I forget just who the major combatants were. Actually I never cared much for that world."

"It's lost a lot of its charm in recent years," Incarnadine said.

"A shame. You're rather fond of the place, aren't you?" Without waiting for an answer, he went on to ask, "I say, is Trent still living there?"

"Yes, I found him, at the same location, in fact."

"Well, that's . . . good, I suppose. Hm. All this time and not a word from him."

"He seems totally uninterested in maintaining any family ties."

"I thought as much," Deems said, shaking his head disapprovingly. "A contrary bastard, that one. Always was."

Deems' image began to waver. Incarnadine made a few quick hand passes to correct the interference.

"What's wrong? Are you breaking off?"

"No," Incarnadine said. "If you remember, the Arts are somewhat of an iffy proposition in this world. I'm still working the bugs out of some new methods. Complicating things is the fact that the energy potential between the various universes has shifted over time. I'm still dealing with the implications of that."

"Ah, yes, I do seem to remember there was a very good reason why I didn't like New York and its provinces. No magic at all. Which made it an unacceptable alternative to Perilous, which fairly oozes with the damnable stuff."

"You never took to the Arts in a big way. Did you, Deems?"

"Never cared for hocus-pocus," Deems said with a shake of his head. "Never wanted any part of it. Makes me nervous."

"Although you need it occasionally."

"Occasionally," Deems conceded. "As do we all." He rubbed his belly and sighed.

"You've put on weight, elder brother."

Deems laughed. "Tell me something I don't know, little brother. I eat too much and drink even more. The Arts I'll have none of; the Vices, every one." He laughed heartily again, revealing large white teeth. When he was done he said, "What are you up to, Inky?"

"Something's going on at Perilous, I don't quite know what. I suspect meddling. If that's the case, I haven't a clue as to who's the guilty party."

"What sort of meddling?"

"A few of the spells sealing off some of the more troublesome aspects are completely gone. It could be that they deteriorated and simply fizzled out. It could also be that someone canceled them."

"And you suspected . . . whom?"

"Trent, first off. One of the reasons I came here. I've been trying to detect evidence of major magical activity in this universe. So far the data are inconclusive. If Trent is responsible, however, he may have taken great pains to cover his tracks."

Deems nodded. "And you suspect me?"

"Brother, you're at the bottom of the suspect list. Everyone knows you could have had the throne, but turned it down. Why then would you conspire now to take the throne from me?"

"I know of no reason," Deems said flatly.

"Nor do I."

There was a pause before Deems asked, "Then why this communication?"

"I wondered if you had any ideas. If you'd heard anything."

"From who?"

"Ferne, for one. Have you seen her recently?"

"I haven't seen Ferne in a god's age."

Incarnadine nodded. "And Trent has never communicated with you in all this time?"

"I would have told you, just out of courtesy," Deems said.

"Just making sure, Deems. Trent says he wants to be left alone, and I have no reason yet not to take him at his word. But all the same, I have to be sure."

"I can assure you that I am not in league with our little brother Trent."

"I didn't say you were, Deems. In fact, I said I wanted your help."

"I'll do anything I can."

"Thank you. Ferne always liked Albion. Would you cast about and see if you can locate her there?"

"I'd be happy to, though I doubt she's here."

"Nevertheless, if you find her, please tell her I wish to see her."

"I will," Deems said. "Anything else?"

"Do you have enough Art to attempt calling Trent from your world?"

"No, I doubt it."

"Then, are you up for a short trip home?"

"Not exactly, but I will come if you insist."

"Then do, and be my guest. When you are here, use the Universal Projector to call him and sound him out. Tell me what you think. I need a second opinion, a second reading, if you will."

"Very well. I hope I can remember the spell that works that old contraption of Dad's. I haven't used it in years."

"Go to the library and look it up. Osmirik, the new librarian, will help you."

"It will be good to be back at Perilous again. I could use a change of scene." Deems scratched his black beard. "But won't Trent instantly suspect you put me up to it? I mean, calling him out of the blue, after so many years?"

"He may. I think he most probably will think I put you up to it. In fact, you can tell him I did. I want everything to be aboveboard, for now."

"As you wish. Do you suspect everyone? Dorcas as well?"

"Hardly Dorcas."

"Well, that more or less leaves Ferne, Trent, and me — and you say I'm out of the running."

"Ferne and Trent. Yes. They might be in it together. I find that not improbable. They always got along well together. In fact, Trent was the only one of us who was at all close to Ferne."

"It would seem a simple case, then, with only three possible solutions. It's either Ferne alone, or Trent alone, or both together."

"Or someone else entirely."

Deems scowled. "Who?"

"An outside force or agent of some sort."

Deems pursed his lips and looked pensive. "Hm. I suppose it's possible. Castle Perilous has never lacked for enemies."

"True."

"But see here. What's the game? What does this unknown conspirator mean to accomplish by opening up dangerous aspects and letting the boogeymen out?"

"The unknown may have struck some bargain with these boogeymen. They invade me castle in return for spoils he has promised."

"Which he can't deliver, unless he knows something I don't," Deems said sourly. "Out of 144,000 worlds, there isn't a single damn

one that has any easy money in it. And I include the one you're in at the moment."

Incarnadine gave a chuckle. "Don't you remember all the time we spent panning for gold in Hyperborea, back when we were kids?"

"With not a penny to show for it."

"Now, I remember making enough to buy a very small sailboat," Incarnadine said. "A ten-foot sloop, as I recall. I think me thing may still be lying in a dusty corner of the castle somewhere. I used to take it out on Lake Asmodeus, in the Helvian aspect. I also have a memory of you buying yourself a silver-handled Almedian scimitar with the paydirt you gleaned."

Deems grunted. "I don't remember. It was a long time ago."

"Yes, it was."

"Tell me this, Inky. What could Trent have been doing, isolated in a blind universe all those years?" Deems' brow furrowed. "The thought occurs to me that *you* are now isolated in a blind universe. How the devil are you going to get back from there?"

"I'm going to do my damnedest to summon the gateway from this side and set up a more or less permanent link to Perilous. From a Manhattan apartment."

"Wasn't that where it was originally?"

"Yes. The site was not this specific apartment, but you remember the general location correctly. As to your first question about Trent — he says he hasn't, but I suspect he has been developing new magic on this side. He may have a way of summoning the gateway, using it, then letting it wander free again until he needs it. He may have had access to Castle Perilous all these years."

"Why has he waited all this time to make his move?"

"He may have been aiding Melydia. I rather doubt that, as Melydia was a major-league sorcerer herself, but she may have needed help at the interuniverse level."

"That is an interesting surmise."

"A wild guess. Perhaps Trent is patient. Or perhaps he's just recently perfected his techniques."

Deems folded his arms and looked dubious. "You really don't have much to go on, do you?"

"Frankly, no. That's why I was hoping you would help. When you return from Perilous, I want you to give me a rundown on what's

happening there in my absence. Ask Tyrone, the captain of the Guard, to give you a report. Tell him I sent you."

"If he believes me." Deems squinted one eye.

"He will. Before I left I told him to expect you."

"I was going to ask why you can't call Tyrone yourself, but now I see you simply want to verify my trip to Perilous." Deems' eyes twinkled. "You've been planning moves in advance."

"As necessary in life as in chess."

"Inky, I'll always defer to your chessmanship. How you outmaneuvered Melydia — that horror of a woman! — I'll never know."

"Luck played its part — along with clean living, proper outlook, eating three squares a day, and so forth."

Chuckling, Deems said, "And regular exercise — no doubt."

"When can you leave for Perilous?"

Deems shrugged. "Today, if you wish. I have nothing pressing."

"Good. Call me again in, say, two days."

"Very well. Anything else?"

"Not at the moment. Good seeing you again, brother."

"Same here, old boy. But if you don't mind — " Deems stood and reached out both arms toward the screen. The image jerked and the angle of view shifted until Deems' face was in close-up. "I'm going to forgo the refined pleasures of having a mirror by the bed. I don't really care to be surprised in quite that way again. There are plenty of other looking-glasses about the palace."

"My apologies."

"So, if it's all the same to you — "

Deems carried the mirror through high mullioned doors and into open air. "Goodbye, Incarnadine." Deems held the mirror out at arm's length, then let it drop.

The mirror turned slowly as it fell. The twisting perspective showed Deems standing on a balustrade high on the outside wall of the palace. He was looking down, smiling and waving. His image quickly shrank, sliding off to one side as the mirror turned to face the uprising ground. Briefly a tilted vista of the green and beautiful Albion countryside revealed itself until the screen of the CRT went black.

Keep — Queen's Dining Hall

Sheila took another sip of coffee. She felt a little better now. There were people here who seemed to be in the same boat she was in — lost and stranded in a crazy place without knowing how or why. It felt good to talk to them and find out more about what the heck was going on here. None of what she was hearing made any sense, but at least everyone seemed to acknowledge that it *didn't* make any sense. She could deal with that. Not with everything not making sense, but with the fact that no one seemed concerned that it didn't.

Yes, she felt a little better, now that she had some proper clothes to wear. She had declined the usual quasi-medieval costume that everyone here pranced around in, opting instead for jeans, a blouse, and a good pair of running shoes. She'd been told that it was wise to be quick on your feet in Castle Perilous. She was determined to be as quick as possible.

The dining hall was almost full. Apparently it was a holiday in this world, and the castle servants (it was sometimes hard to tell the servants from the Guests, except that the servants had a sort of English accent) had set a festive table laden with dish after colorful and elaborate dish.

Everybody was digging in, so Sheila did, too.

"Anybody know what the occasion is?" Gene asked.

"Something akin to our winter solstice, I think," M. DuQuesne said.

"I guess most worlds have solstices and equinoxes and all that stuff," Gene said.

"My world doesn't," the creature called Snowclaw growled. (It seemed to growl all the time.) "Course, I wouldn't know what an eekinocks was if it came up and kicked me in the butt."

Sheila couldn't get over how she could understand everything the white-furred, white-clawed creature said. In fact, it sounded a little like Uncle Walt, Mom's brother. Uncle Walt growled a lot, too.

Despite her fear, she found the creature to be very friendly. She just couldn't bring herself to look into its fierce yellow eyes.

She helped herself to a slice of roast suckling pig, then spooned out samples of a few of the side dishes. Everything had been delicious so far.

"Snowclaw, your world has to have an equinox," Gene insisted.

"How do you know?" Snowclaw scoffed. "You've never been there."

"Does it have a sun?"

"Well, of course."

"Then it has equinoxes and solstices. What I'm talking about is . . . well, really it's the relationship of a sun to a planet that revolves about it. You see, when a planet's axis of rotation is tilted somewhat to the plane of its orbit, what happens is that — "

"What's a planet?"

"Uh, a planet. It's a world. You know, a big spherical lump of dirt that spins around."

"Spins around what?"

"Turns. Rotates."

"Where?"

Gene blinked. "What do you mean, 'Where'? Out in space, of course. Look, when a planet spins on its axis, it — "

"What's space?"

Gene took a long drink from his beer stein. "Forget it."

"Anything you say, pal," Snowclaw said amiably.

M. DuQuesne said, "Snowclaw, does your world have a warm season and a cold season?"

"Sure does."

"Is the sun a little lower in the sky in the cold season?"

"It's a lot lower."

"Then, when the sun is at its lowest point during the cold season, and the days are very short, that's the winter solstice. When it's at its highest point in the sky during the warm season, and the days are long, that's the summer solstice. The equinoxes are in between, in spring and autumn, when night and day are about equally long."

"Oh. Well, sure, everybody knows that! Thanks."

Everyone looked at Gene. He shrugged. "Okay, so I'm not Isaac Asimov."

A man called Thaxton said, "Who's for tennis today?"

Another, older man who called himself Cleve Dalton said, "Thax old boy, you ask that every damn day, and I can't recall that anyone's ever taken you up on it. Where the devil are the courts, anyway?"

"Well, they're through an aspect just a little down the hall to the right. I suspect they're not really tennis courts per se. I mean, there are nets and such, but they actually seem to be — "

There came shouts from out in the hallway, and the sound of running feet. A man, one of the servants, came running through the main entrance looking frightened to death. He ran past the table and shouted, "They're coming! Run for your lives!" He sprinted to the kitchen entrance, threw the door open, and dashed through.

Everyone froze for a moment. Then Gene said, "It's gotta be the Bluefaces."

As if to corroborate his remark, three Bluefaces stormed through the main entrance with drawn swords.

"Stay where you are!" the middle one commanded. "You are now under authority of His Imperial Domination, High Proconsul of Greater Borjakshann, and you are subject to his every whim, wish, and caprice!"

"Hey, Blueface!"

Somewhat nonplussed, the creature raked an eye up and down the table until it found the speaker.

"Who dares defy authority of Proconsul?"

Snowclaw rose to his full height. "Me, that's who," he said.

The creature looked a trifle uncertain. "Any resistance will be dealt with harshly!"

"Yeah? What are you gonna do, bleed on me?"

The Blueface grinned with a satisfied malevolence. "For that bit of insolence, you will be put to death immediately!"

With a blood-congealing howl, Snowclaw sprang into a blur of motion. In one clean jump from a standstill, he was up on the table and running, huge clawed feet picking their way through the soup tureens and serving plates of prime rib, executing a neat end run around the carved ice centerpiece. At some point he became airborne,

taloned toes leading, the claws of his hands swiping at the air, mouth wide and bristling with wickedly sharp teeth, gleaming incisors almost big enough to be tusks. A fire of diabolical ferocity burned in his alien yellow eyes.

The Blueface barely had time to point its sword in the proper direction. To no avail. The splayed foot of Snowclaw's long right leg, which had extended slightly, hit the invader squarely in the breastplate. The sword went flying, and the creature went down, Snowclaw crashing on top of it.

Gene had delayed only an instant. He was up and charging by the time Snowclaw had made his leap.

"Everybody out through the kitchen!" he yelled.

Four more blue-skinned soldiers stormed through the door, and a few of the other males and one woman jumped up and ran to meet them, swords drawn.

Sheila just sat there, a morsel of beef Stroganoff still poised on the end of her fork, her mouth hanging open.

Ohmygawd. What the *hell* is happening now?

Someone grabbed her arm. It was Linda Barclay.

"Sheila! Run!"

Sheila got up and joined the clot of people that had jammed up at the kitchen door. She looked back over her shoulder to see Gene Ferraro crossing swords with one of the creatures, while the big white beast karate-fought with another. The Blueface who had done all the talking was sprawled on the floor with purple gunk running out of its mouth. Sheila suddenly got very sick, and very afraid.

Gene swung his weapon and lopped off the sword-arm of his opponent. Sheila saw the severed blue member splat to the floor. She thought she would throw up then and there, but when Gene's next stroke clove the creature's skull in two, spraying purple liquid all over the place, she was too shocked to react. Meanwhile, Snowclaw had lifted his adversary over his head; he threw the creature against the stone wall. The Blueface hit with a bone-pulping thud, hung against the wall for an impossible instant, then clattered to the floor.

Gene ran for the door. "Come on, Snowy, there's too many of them!"

Snowclaw batted at one of the new intruders and sent the creature flying, but when he saw more reinforcements streaming through the main entrance, he broke for the back door.

Sheila had been watching all this, half hypnotized by the savagery of it, half paralyzed with fear. Linda yanked her back through the door as Gene came charging through.

Linda, Sheila, Gene, and Snowclaw raced through the cluttered, now deserted kitchen and banged out through the opposite door. They were followed by three survivors of the group who had joined the fight. The woman was not with them.

Once outside the kitchen, they pushed a huge sideboard against the door to block it. Immediately grunts and crashing sounds issued from the other side.

"They killed Morgana," one of the men told Gene. "She chopped up one of them before getting it from behind."

"I saw," Gene said. "We'd better split up."

The other nodded. "My favorite aspect is down this way."

"Maybe not such a good idea," Gene said. "Better to get off into the remote parts of the castle. Of course, that's just a guess. You make your own decision."

"Good luck."

"Same to you." Gene turned to Linda. "You and Sheila coming with us?"

"Of course. Gene, you were marvelous. I can't believe how good a swordfighter you are. Maybe you really are Cyrano de Bergerac."

"No, I just have a nose for trouble."

Sheila hoped he was Cyrano, Duke Wayne, and Sylvester Stallone all rolled into one.

164 East 64th Street

He sat hunched over, his forehead in one palm, elbow on the desk, peering down at a sheet of paper that crawled with arcane mathematical symbols. A high pile of crumpled sheets lay to his right. Stacks of books lay about the desk, interspersed with pencils and other writing implements, three or four different types of electronic calculator, several empty aluminum soda cans, and a cup and saucer holding the dregs of two-day-old coffee.

He threw down his pencil, a weary scowl on his face. "Dung of a thousand kine!"

There was not much enthusiasm in the curse. "Shit," he added, with not much more.

He exhaled and peered into the coffee cup. He *yecched* silently, got up, and carried it into the kitchen, where he set about inducing Mr. Coffee to do its job. He spooned grounds into a fresh paper filter and slid me little drawer holding the filter into the machine, then poured cold water into the top of the device.

In the living room, the computer beeped a warning. He rushed directly to it and sat at the terminal.

He typed, NATURE OF EMERGENCY?

The disk drive rumbled. Then the screen displayed: *DANGER.*

RANGE AND DIRECTION? he queried.

NEARBY AND CLOSING FROM WEST.

GROUND OR AIRBORNE?

GROUND.

NATURE OR EMBODIMENT OF DANGER?

UNABLE TO DETERMINE.

"That's a fine how-do-you-do," he muttered. CAN PINPOINT PROXIMITY?

NEAR was all it answered.

"Damn program is full of bugs! Full of them!"

He halted waving his arms and considered his outburst. "I'm losing it. I'll have to pull myself together."

His eyes closed and his shoulders relaxed. He remained motionless for several minutes.

Presently the intercom buzzed. He opened his eyes, took a deep breath, and got up.

"Yes?"

"Mr. Carney?" It was the doorman.

"Yes."

"Express package for you. Should I send the guy up?"

"Just take delivery. I'll be down for it later."

"He says you gotta sign for it."

He considered the matter. The package would doubtless be the books he had ordered from a small specialty bookstore in San Francisco, whose owner had promised to get them out on the next plane yesterday afternoon. He was not yet acquainted enough with the minutiae of this world to judge the degree of risk.

But he really had to know, didn't he?

"Have him come up."

He sat down and closed his eyes again, preparing himself, until the door chimed.

The express man was young and looked innocuous enough.

"Hi! Mr. John Carney?"

"You got 'im."

The express man shoved the package toward him. It was heavy and he had to use both hands to accept it. Heavy enough to be books.

"Just sign here, sir," the man said, proffering a clipboard and pen.

"Just a minute."

He turned, walked into the apartment, and laid the package on the dinette table. As he did, he heard the door close behind him. The computer began to beep frantically.

He whirled in time to see the delivery man drawing a large-caliber, silencer-tipped revolver. He dropped behind the dinette table just as

the hit man fired, the bullet thunking into the package. He crawled behind an easy chair, then leaped out, diving toward the door of the darkened bedroom. The next two shots chipped wood from the doorframe above his head as he sailed through.

He crawled to the far end of the bed and remained on the floor.

Then, reaching into a place that was not exactly a place, which lay in a direction that was not quite up or down or to or fro, he summoned the thing that he found there, and it came forth. From what time or space or continuum the thing had come, he neither knew nor cared.

It stood above him, a mass of gleaming metal trimmed with strips of black synthetic material. Its arms ended in huge steel claws, and its head was a clear bubble housing whirling sensors and flashing probes. Thin, many-colored lines of light danced in crosshatch patterns on the walls of the dim bedroom, shifting and changing as the device took readings and measurements. In less than a second it was ready to move.

It clanked around the bed and rolled through the doorway into the hall.

There came a yelp, then another muffled gunshot and the spang of a bullet ricocheting off metal.

"DESTROY," the mechanical thing stated, raising its arms. The claws swung to one side and dangerous-looking rods protruded from the cavities within the arms.

"No!" he shouted from the bedroom.

"I'm leaving!" the express man shouted.

There came the sounds of hasty retreat. Then the front door slammed.

"NOT DESTROY?" was the query with a slight note of disappointment.

"No. Scan premises for enemy."

"SECTOR CLEAR."

He came out from the bedroom. The machine was already fading.

"WILL NOT BE REDEPLOYED?" the thing asked.

"Return to post," he ordered, which it was doing, anyway.

It was gone in the next instant.

He locked the door, slid the dead bolt, and affixed the chain. He retrieved the package. The books he had ordered were in it, one with a deformed slug inside that had bored clear through to page 457, which began a chapter titled "Incantations Useful in Interdimensional Quantum Transformations."

He went into the kitchen and poured himself a cup of fresh-brewed coffee.

Library

Osmirik carried THE heavy folio up the stairs to his favorite carrel, which was tucked into a vault on the first gallery. He liked the spot, snugly surrounded as it was by his favorite things, namely books; but now it would afford him safe haven in more than a spiritual sense. That is, it would if all his hastily made plans worked out. He meant to take advantage of one of the castle's architectural peculiarities. If all else failed, an exit lay close by, should the need for such arise.

Arise it doubtless would, and soon. The invaders would hardly overlook the castle's library, surely the largest depository of learning in this world. If they coveted the castle's secrets, only its library could provide the key.

What Osmirik sought was the key to fight the invaders, and that could only be found in certain ancient texts contained in this library and this library alone. This huge folio was one such text, a work written by Ervoldt, the ancient Haplodite King who had "built" Castle Perilous — or, to be more accurate, had caused it to be created, some three millennia ago.

He sidled into the narrow carrel. Sighing, he sat down and opened the leather-bound volume, which in gilt lettering bore the simple title *Ervoldt, His Book*. The language and script in which the work had been written was called Haplan, which he had diligently studied since beginning his tenure as chief librarian at Castle Perilous, almost a year ago to the day. (The post had been vacant for fifty years before he took it up.)

He turned to the first page, and his former wonder was renewed. This was no codex, no painstakingly handwritten work of a copyist. This was a printed text, which would not be surprising were it not for

the fact that it was over three thousand years old. The beautiful vellum paper was not even yellowed. Printing had not existed three thousand years ago, nor three hundred — except, obviously, in Castle Perilous, by whose magic all manner of things was possible.

The author's prefatory material was short. In fact, it was rather blunt:

> Ye who scan this Book be well advised; that its Scribe be no Man of Poesy, nor Aesthete given to Niceties of Phrase. For Such and their Ilk I care not Pig Leavings. I set down the Words as they come, as they are needed for their appointed Tasks, and as I see fit; no more or less do I set down. For I, Ervoldt, King by the Grace of the Gods, have a Story, and I will let nothing bar the way of its Telling. I will leave out nothing of Substance. Neither will I embellish. What is ugly, I will render ugly; what is beautiful needs little by my Hand. I will tell what I must, and no more, and when the Telling is done, I will be done. If any find Fault with this, or me, I say read another Book, and be damned.

Somewhat brusque, but to the point, and possessing a certain admirable muscularity of phrase. But Osmirik had no time for literary criticism. His task was to glean practical knowledge from this work, not to judge its author's prose style. Moreover —

There came a loud crashing from below. Osmirik jumped up, left the vault, and went to the rail of the gallery. Below, the huge main room was as deserted as before — nothing but row upon row of open stacks with a few tables interspersed — but now he could identify the source of the noise. Someone was trying to break through the massive oak of the front doors, which were bolted and barred from the inside. Very likely the invaders were on the other side.

Another crash, and Osmirik saw the doors shake. He dashed back to his nook and drew out the parcel that he had laid inside. It was crammed with victuals, enough to last him days. A chamber pot lay underneath the table, along with a supply of candles and some blankets.

He stood and ran his hand along the back of the stone ribbing that formed the inside arch of the doorway. Finding a small block of wood there, he pressed it. There came the rumble of sliding stone. He

stepped back as a massive stone barrier slid across to seal the vault off like a tomb. Osmirik exhaled and listened to the silence. This small chamber was one of hundreds used to store rare volumes of inestimable worth. It also made an excellent redoubt for a librarian.

The vault was completely dark. Cursing himself for not doing it before, he sought candle and flint wheel. At length he managed to get a flame from the wheel, lit a candle, and stood it in its sconce on the table. The tiny chamber filled with yellow light. The flame of the candle guttered. The place was well ventilated. He would be fine here, for a while. He had light, air, food, and books — and he could catch a few winks under the table. No one could find him, no one would bother him, not even the Hell-begotten blue demons.

Now, all he had to do was discover what particular hell had begotten them.

Keep

Gene stepped over the body of another castle Guardsman. He had lost track of how many they had encountered.

"The Bluefaces are everywhere," he said to Linda. "It's a well-organized and coordinated attack. Meticulously planned, too, I'll bet."

"What should we do?" Linda asked.

"Leave the castle. Have any preferences as to what aspect we dive through?"

"Oh, any nice place with trees and grass, I guess."

"Trees and grass? How about a source of food? Remember, when you leave the castle, your magic stays here. No more whipping up quick meals with a wave of the hand."

"That's going to be somewhat of a problem."

They continued down the hallway cautiously, Gene in the lead and Snowclaw bringing up the rear. Sheila tagged close to Linda, whose hand she occasionally sought when danger neared. Linda didn't look as scared as Sheila was. But then, Linda was used to this place. Sheila didn't understand how anyone could get used to a nightmare, but she was more than willing to stick close to anyone who could.

They walked on a little farther until they came to a crossing corridor, at which they stopped. Gene poked his head around the corner.

"It's clear." As he took a step forward, grunting sounds came from far down the hall to the left. Gene backstepped hastily, bumping into Linda. "Company coming!" he whispered.

They backtracked to an empty alcove and crowded into it. Sheila squeezed in next to Snowclaw, noticing how smooth and silky his fur was.

The rumble of heavy running feet sounded. Gene knelt, peered around the corner, and saw Bluefaces streaming through the intersection of the corridors.

"There must be thirty of 'em. No, fifty."

The thunder of footsteps receded, diminishing to distant echoes.

Gene took a breath. "They must have invaded with a force in the thousands. They've probably already taken over key points in the castle."

"We don't have much of a chance," Linda said.

"Not unless we find an acceptable gateway soon. If this keeps up, we might have to take the next one we run across."

"I'd invite you all to my world," Snowclaw said, "except that it's pretty darn cold there, and you hairless types might not take to it. Besides, the portal's on the other side of the castle."

"I'd put up with the cold," Gene said. "The more unattractive the world, the less chance the Bluefaces might be interested in it."

"Maybe so," Snowclaw said. "Well, you're all welcome to stay in my shack for as long as you like. I wouldn't mind the company." He scratched his belly absently. "We'd be a little crowded, though."

Gene said, "Snowy, I've always wanted to see your world, but I'm going to keep it as a last resort." Gene leaned against the wall and scratched under his cuirass. "Damn it, all the best portals are in the Guest areas, which is where most of the invaders are going to be hanging out, of course."

"The one with the golf course is nice," Linda said. "And the little dinosaur-humanoids are friendly."

"Primitive," Gene said, shaking his head. "Hot, and dangerous. Outside the little resort area, it's pretty rough out there in the jungle. And the Bluefaces will be all through there, I bet."

"And we saw them on the picnic world," Linda said. "So much for that."

"We must have looked into hundreds of portals since we've been here. There are 144,000 of them in the castle. Try to think of one that we can hide out in for a while."

"Well, there's the one with the forest and the waterfall."

"Same problem, it's near the Guest area."

"Right," Linda said. "I've always liked the one that sort of looks like a Japanese garden."

"Ditto."

"Oh, you're right. Well, how about — ?" Linda was stumped.

"Now, there was one with a little village nearby with nice sorts of native people. Little pale people with big golden eyes. They'd gladly put us up for a spell, I think. Damned if I can remember where the hell the portal was, though."

"I remember!" Linda said.

"Shhhh! Keep your voice down."

"Sorry. I was just thinking of one. It's not too far from here, if I recall. It's near the castle armory, and — " Her face fell. "Oh, dear."

"The armory's probably the first objective the Bluefaces took, along with the Guard garrison. You have to remember — "

Sounds of approaching footsteps came from the direction in which the Blueface troop had marched.

"They're coming back," Gene said. "Come on!"

They ran. At the next intersecting hallway, they took the right branch, running a spell until they came to a stairwell. This they descended one level, where they found quiet.

"Hell," Gene complained. "Look, we need to think, and plan. Let's get to someplace where we can do it, like Snowy's world. There, at least, we won't be bothered, and we can come up with some answers."

"Will we be able to get back into the castle?" Linda said.

Gene thoughtfully rubbed me stubble on his chin. "Good point. The castle's a big place, but maybe they have enough troops to block every portal. No telling."

"So, what do we do?"

Gene shrugged. "Keep moving until we find a good aspect, jump in, and hope the Bluefaces won't follow us."

"Back to square one," Linda said. She thought awhile, then said, "How about we hide out in the wilder parts of the castle?"

Gene looked dubious.

Sheila asked, "What do you mean, Linda?"

Linda squatted and leaned against a pillar. "Well, some parts of the castle are stable, like the Guest areas. You know, like where the dining hall is? Around there. But other parts of the castle aren't so stable."

"In fact," Gene said, "they're absolutely crazy."

Sheila nodded. Crazy. If what she'd already seen of the place was *sane* . . . Ohmygawd.

"And dangerous," Gene added. "But on second thought, not quite as dangerous, maybe, as what we're facing here."

"Maybe not," Linda agreed. "I think it might be worth the risk."

"Isn't there some way of . . . you know, *leaving* the castle?" Sheila asked. "Just going outside, the regular way?"

"There's not much out there," Gene said. "We've been told that most of the people who live in these parts stay in the castle. I don't blame them. It's pretty bleak."

"Oh." Sheila slumped against the cold stone of the wall.

Grunting voices came from the right.

"Let's move," Gene said calmly.

They ran from the voices, but made it only a short way down the corridor before hearing echoing footsteps ahead. They took the left branch of the nearest intersection, sprinted to the next crossing, stopped, and looked both ways before going on.

Voices behind them, now voices in front again. They backtracked and went left, ran and then dashed right, only to hear the flapping steps of flat, webbed feet everywhere they turned.

"It's no use," Gene said, stopping for breath. "Linda, you gotta use your magic. We have to go either up or down in a hurry."

"Stairs?"

"No, something faster!"

"What? I can't think of anything that wouldn't be mechanical, like an elevator or something."

Grunting sounds came from the left, then, after a moment, from behind.

"Think!" Gene whispered hoarsely.

Linda closed her eyes. A soft popping sound came from behind Gene, and he turned to look. A neatly cut hole had appeared in the stone floor. A shiny brass pipe, about three inches in diameter, ran from the ceiling down through the hole.

"A firehouse pole?" Gene shrugged. "Hey, why not? Let's go."

Gene was first. He slid out of sight quickly, and Linda followed.

"Let's go, little girl," Snowclaw urged gently.

Sheila leaned out, grabbed the pole, and jumped, locking her legs around the slippery brass shaft. The drop was heart-stoppingly fast, and only frantic contractions of her leg muscles finally slowed her. Despite her best efforts, she landed hard on her buttocks.

Gene dragged her up. "Again," he ordered Linda.

"Again?"

"Down another floor. Can't you hear them up there?"

Linda whipped up another pole as Snowclaw dropped down and corroborated, "They're coming!"

They all slipped down the new fire pole. This time Sheila was determined to land on her feet, and she did.

"Again," Gene said.

They dropped four levels in all before Gene realized it was useless.

"They're simply following us down," he said. "We're just not thinking, gang."

Linda said, "Then we're sunk. I can't make things disappear." She blinked, then smiled. "But I can make a ladder!"

The hole appeared, as before, but this time a wooden ladder angled up from it. They clambered down one by one. On the lower level. Gene and Snowclaw slid the bottom of the ladder across the flagstone until the upper end slipped out of the hole above. The ladder clattered to the floor.

They repeated this procedure three more times before coming to a quiet level.

Gene looked up. "Linda, I want you to conjure a sort of thing that looks like a drain stopper, but made out of heavy stone, one just big enough to plug that hole up there."

"A drain stopper?"

"Imagine a big heavy thing like a stone mushroom, with the stem plugging the hole."

"Got you."

The bottom of the plug fit neatly flush with the ceiling.

"Good job. I don't think they'll be able to lift that thing very easily."

"Great idea, Gene," Linda said.

"Should have come up with it sooner. But when you're on the run, it's hard to be creative."

"Man, you gotta think fast in this place!" Sheila said breathlessly.

"Even more so, down here," Gene told her. "Stay close, and watch your step."

"What's down here?"

"Expect the unexpected."

"Like . . . what, exactly?"

Bright daylight flooded the corridor. Sheila whirled and beheld what looked at first like a movie screen, except that the images were three-dimensional. Then her mind made the connection that this was some sort of opening that had suddenly appeared. Through the rectangular portal lay a short expanse of white beach, leading to foaming breakers. The surf was close, very close. In fact . . .

"You better get back, Sheila," Gene said.

She watched, transfixed, as a swell rose up, rode in, and broke very near the opening. Sheila squealed and backstepped as the surf foamed through the portal and across the floor, slopping over her shoes.

She squished down the corridor to where the others had sought dry floor. They were smiling at her.

"I see what you mean," Sheila said.

"Is that your first wild aspect?" Gene asked. "Strange, isn't it? The aspects you see through the windows aren't so startling. You look out and see weird things, but somehow, the window comfortably frames it. But when you see an aspect pop out of nowhere like that — "

"It kind of blows your mind," Sheila said, nodding gravely. "Why are they called aspects?"

"Just a term that's used around here. They're called aspects, portals, gateways . . . other things."

Suddenly the sunlight faded, and the sound of breakers stopped abruptly. They all turned to find that the portal had vanished.

"There it goes," Gene said, "just as mysteriously as it appeared."

Sheila shook her head slowly. "Where *was* that place? That ocean?"

"It could have been the beach at Malibu," Gene told her. "Or somewhere on the Gold Coast of Africa. But I looked, and I didn't see anything out there that would lead me to believe it was a way back to Earth. It could have been any one of tens of thousands of worlds. Probably a deserted planet, somewhere, in an uninhabited star system a billion light-years from — " He shrugged. "Wherever."

"Was the one I fell through like that?" Sheila asked.

"Probably. Just like the ones we blundered through."

Sheila stared off into the darkness. "Maybe it actually was a way back. Back home."

"We'll never know, Sheila. Best not to think about it. We're stranded here, in this world, this castle. You'd better start getting used to the notion of being here for a while."

Sheila grunted ironically. "A while? You mean for the rest of my life." Brow knitted, she massaged her bottom lip between her teeth. Then, murmuring to herself: "But I really didn't have much of a life, did I?"

Gene said, "I'm sorry. What did you say?"

Sheila took a deep breath and turned around. "Nothing. Nothing at all."

Gene smiled at her. "Don't worry. In time, you'll actually get to like it here. I look at it as sort of an extended vacation. Two weeks in August that never seem to end. But at some point it will, it must. A gateway will pop up in front of us, leading right into Times Square, and the vacation will be over. It'll be September, time to go back to school. Or to a new job."

Sheila studied him clinically. He wasn't a bad-looking fellow, rather tall, with curly dark brown hair and gray-green eyes. Not bad over all, except that she would never have given him a second look on the street, or in a bar. He had a boyish, immature way about him, even though he talked very well and sounded educated. She liked him. "You really believe we'll get back someday, don't you?"

Something deep in his eyes flashed when he smiled. "You bet. This is a dream — a shared dream. And someday we'll all wake up."

She managed to smile back at him, and it made her feel good.

"Anyone for lunch?"

Gene and Sheila looked. Linda had conjured an impressive buffet table laden with an endless assortment of cold cuts and salads.

"Come and get it before it goes up in a puff of smoke," Linda said.

Snowclaw swiped at a plate and came away with about three pounds of sliced roast beef. He shoved the mass into his mouth, chewed four times — no more — and swallowed. He shook his head wearily. "You know, I keep trying this stuff you guys like. It's good, don't get me wrong. But a little while later and I'm hungry again."

"Try a little mustard with it," Linda suggested, tossing him a jar of Dijon. Unbelieving, she watched Snowclaw pop it into his mouth. "Snowy, don't!"

The glass crunched horribly. "Hey, now you're talking!" Snowclaw said with a satisfied grin.

Keep — Lower Levels

Barnaby Walsh was exhausted. He was by nature a sedentary person, tending to avoid movement unless dire necessity demanded it, and this frantic chasing about, keeping one step ahead of the Bluefaces, was more than his ill-proportioned, overweight body could stand. In fact, he simply couldn't take another step. . . .

"We can't stop!" Deena Williams yelled at him.

"I gotta," Barnaby told her, slumping against the wall.

Deena ran back and yanked at a handful of his shirt. "Come on, man! They're right behind us!"

"I can't . . . run . . . anymore," Barnaby wheezed at her. "I'm completely . . . I can't — "

"You gotta! The Bluefaces are comin'!"

"But . . ." Barnaby tried to swallow the acrid dryness at the back of his throat. He choked and coughed, bending over double.

"Shhhh!" Deena looked worriedly back down the passageway. "Keep it quiet, or they gonna get us."

Barnaby recovered enough to say, "I can't go on. I'm done."

"No, you're not. Just keep puttin' one foot in front of the other. Come on, man, you can do it."

"No, honest."

He looked at her. She wasn't even breathing hard! But she'd been a trade athlete in high school, she'd said, before getting pregnant and dropping out. She had always dreamed of going to the Olympics. She was even dressed for the part, in a purple sweatshirt, red shorts, and white running shoes.

"Go ahead," he told her. "Take off. I'll just hold you up."

Scowling, she shook him hard. "Don't start that hero stuff with me, you hear? I'll slap you silly. Now, let's go, unless you wanna mess with them blue dudes."

"Okay, okay," Barnaby groaned. Grunting noises from behind gave him the added impetus to start moving again. He staggered forward, steadied himself with one hand on the wall, then boosted his pace to a painful, galumphing jog, his oversize wing-tip oxfords slapping against the flagstone.

They ran. The place was nothing but endless corridors shunting every which way, leading to nothing but more passageways and corridors and the occasional crypt or alcove, all of it giving the impression of having been laid out without design, purpose, or plan.

I'm no hero, Barnaby thought to himself. In fact, he was just the opposite. He was more afraid now than he had ever been at any time in his life. He had told her to go on without him as a sort of test. He didn't know what he would have done had she left. Alone, he might have simply gone insane.

They made their way down the stone-walled corridor, Deena at a sprint, Barnaby loping along. She reached a cross-tunnel and stopped until he caught up.

"Stairs," she said, pointing to the left.

Barnaby could barely see in the gloom. "Let's go," he said.

The stairwell was spiral. Deena started down the well, taking two steps at a time, her crisp white athletic shoes glowing in the darkness.

Barnaby said, "I can barely — " then stumbled and almost fell.

Deena halted a few turns down. "Watch yourself," she warned. "It's dark down here."

"Yeah," he said dully.

They continued down, and found to their dismay that the stairwell was endless. After five minutes of steady descent they stopped, not knowing what to do.

"Go back up?" Deena suggested.

Barnaby gave her an incredulous look.

"Guess not." She shrugged. "They gotta end sometime."

They kept on following the downward spiral for another ten minutes. The stairwell continued with no sign of a bottom.

"Shit?"

"It's ridiculous," Barnaby said.

"Silliest damn thing," Deena complained, hands on her hips and a look of offended dignity on her dark brown face. She sneered up, then down. "Damn. Well, if we didn't go back up before, we sure ain't gonna do it now. Let's go."

They stumped down the stairs for another five or ten minutes. The stairwell was bare and featureless, except for an occasional glowing jewel-torch and the odd niche here and there.

"I'm really starting to get pissed off," Deena said.

Barnaby couldn't help laughing. Deena caught it and began to giggle. She continued doing so, intermittently, for the next few minutes, but as time wore on, she fell silent save for occasional grumbling and cursing.

They marched down the spiral for a quarter hour before the stairs eventually ended in a low-ceilinged tunnel.

"Finally," Barnaby murmured, barely able to keep his legs moving. He was beyond fatigue now; he wondered how long his heart would last, how long it would keep feebly pushing blood through his bloated carcass, which now felt like something dead that had to be dragged along.

The tunnel went straight for a stretch, then made a forty-five-degree turn, followed by a right-angled corner. The passage continued for about sixty feet, ultimately feeding into another stairwell whose spiraling steps led nowhere but up.

"Oh, no!" Barnaby staggered backward.

"Damn," she said. "They *screwin'* with us!"

"Oh my God." Barnaby collapsed against the cold stone wall of the tunnel. He sank to his haunches and closed his eyes.

Deena sat on the steps and began tenderly massaging her firm, almost muscular brown legs. "They jerkin' us around."

Barnaby didn't speak; he couldn't. They sat in silence for a long spell.

"Damn," she said again, quietly. And then, after a long pause: "Well . . ."

"Don't even think of it," Barnaby said.

"Okay," she said. "Take your time. We ain't exactly got anywhere to go."

"Thanks."

"But up."

"Exactly."

She craned her neck, peering up the spiral. "Maybe it don't go up as far as the other one went down."

"Why can't I believe that?" Barnaby said.

"'Cause they *screwin'* with us, that's why," Deena said. Then she began giggling again.

Barnaby answered with a hideous laugh, which made Deena giggle all the more. Barnaby closed his eyes again and laughed till it hurt.

He choked it off when Deena suddenly yelped and jumped up from the steps as if from a hot stove.

"What the hell — ?" She stared in disbelief at the steps, which, inexplicably, had begun moving upward of their own accord, like some impossible stone escalator.

Getting to his feet, Barnaby acted as though he wasn't at all surprised. He caught the bottom step, mounted, and rose up the stairwell.

"Going up — lingerie, notions, merchandise return on the mezzanine."

"I'm comin'," Deena told him, stepping aboard. "I just wish this *was* Bloomingdale's," she added in a mutter.

They rose in silence, the paradoxical escalator making a barely audible humming noise. Gradually its speed increased, and the stairwell showed no sign of ending. Eyes wide with wonder, Barnaby and Deena continued their magical ascent. Air whistled past them down the spiraling shaft. The rate of climb kept steadily increasing. In a few minutes it began to take on alarming proportions.

"What was that you said about the mezzanine?" she asked nervously. "I want to get off."

"Yeah," he said, licking dry lips. "This seemed a peachy idea down at the bottom."

The noise increased to a thunderous roar, and the escalator's speed soon necessitated their getting down on all fours to fight a centrifugal force that threatened to push them into the stationary outside wall, which was rushing by at a rate guaranteed to impart a severe brush burn at the very least. But there was nothing to hold on to but bare stone.

It was like being inside a tumble-dryer. Soon, the walls became a blur and vertigo overtook both of them. Barnaby felt consciousness slipping away as his hands inexorably slid across the smooth stone of the steps. . . .

He reached the brink of oblivion, then came back, and he realized that the escalator was slowing down. He held on tightly until it came to an abrupt stop.

They lay motionless for a moment. Barnaby raised his head. There was a landing a few steps up. He slowly got to his feet, then looked back at Deena, who was rising. He held out his hand, and she took it.

"Come on," he said.

They mounted the last few steps and came out into an expansive room with numerous windowed alcoves. Daylight streamed through some of the windows. There were a few tables and chairs lying about, and one leather-covered settee, which Barnaby collapsed across, stretching out facedown. Deena sat down on the backs of his legs, and, fashioned like this, they rested for a full ten minutes.

Eventually he said. "My legs are falling asleep."

"Sorry, I couldn't get up."

"It's okay."

Deena rose and moved to a chair. Barnaby levered himself upright. "Jesus," he sighed.

"Yeah, ain't it the truth."

Presently Deena got up and wandered over to one of the alcoves.

"What the *hell is* this shit?" she wanted to know.

"What?" he asked, still too tired to move.

"You gotta see this."

"In a minute . . . or two, or three."

"Barnaby, you gotta see this crazy shit! This is insane!"

"Oh. Well, for the merely crazy, I wouldn't stir myself. But for the truly irrational . . ." He cranked himself off the settee, went over to the alcove, and stood next to her, looking out the open window.

Outside the window, there was no castle. The window itself was simply a rectangular hole in the middle of the air, suspended about five feet above an arid plain. In the distance lay a gigantic egg-shaped crystal bubble covering the polyhedral buildings and tall towers of a wildly futuristic city. Something about it made it look deserted. A slow wind moved across the plain; all was silent.

"Jesus," Barnaby said.

"Where the hell is that place?"

Barnaby shook his head slowly. "Who knows? Somewhere in time and space."

Deena snorted contemptuously. "Time and space, huh? I think it's *crazy.*"

"They told me about these floating aspects. They're a little less stable than the kind you can just walk through. But they generally stay put."

"I never seen one like this. Most of 'em have different scenery and stuff, but I ain't never seen one with a space city in it."

"You think it's somewhere out in space?" he asked in wonderment. "On another planet?"

"Damn if I know. Sure looks like it."

"I wonder . . ." He swallowed and massaged his throat with a thumb and forefinger. "I wonder who — or what — lives in that city."

"I don't know, and I don't wanna know. Let's look through the other windows. It's gonna be more crazy shit, I bet."

It was. The window to the right looked out onto a vast desert of wind-furrowed sand, and the next one down was a breathtaking view of an alpine meadow, snow-capped peaks in the distance. The next was dark — there was nothing out there but the distant cries in the night. The fifth window looked out on brackish marshes, and the next presented the green and pleasant aspect of a park.

"This is pretty nice," she said. "Let's take a walk."

He gulped. "Out . . . there?"

"Yeah, why not? Better than this crummy place." Deena stuck her head out, looking down. "It's only two foot off the ground. We can jump it easy. Come on." She swung one meaty leg up over the stone windowsill.

Barnaby was hesitant. "Do you really think we should?"

Deena brought her other leg up, sat momentarily, then jumped off. She landed lightly, bouncing up and down a few times to test the footing. "It's okay," she said. "Come on."

Barnaby climbed through the window and jumped down, falling to his knees in soft shoe-high grass. He got up. They were in a wide clearing; the surrounding woods were thick, but almost no underbrush grew between the tall, slender trees. The sky was soft blue, shading to yellowish white toward a bright sun directly overhead. The air was warm, and there was the smell of green and growing things in the air.

"Nice," Deena said.

"Yeah," he agreed.

They wandered together for a few paces, then went off separately, she to examine a bed of wildflowers, he to find a place to take a leak. He didn't want to go off very far, but the only cover nearby lay among a grove of tall bushes at the edge of the clearing. He wished something better were available, but duty called, so he struck off for the woods.

Glancing about nervously, he relieved himself. It was one of those extended sessions, long delayed, that never seem to stop. Finally it did, and he was zipping himself up when he heard Deena yell for him. He dashed out from the bushes.

The clearing was full of animals that looked somewhat like lions, were it not for me elaborate coral-colored, antlerlike organs that blossomed from their shaggy heads. Their coloring was tawny, lionlike, but their legs and bodies were longer and thinner, and they had no tails. There were about eight of them, and one was advancing toward him, growling with saber-teeth bared.

Deena was standing near the spot where the floating window had been, but there was no chance of her escaping. The aperture now hung a good ten feet off the ground. Apparently it had drifted.

Four of the creatures had her encircled, and several more were stalking into position to do the same to him. There was nowhere to run, even if he could have run, which was hardly his strong suit.

"Deena?" he called in a tremulous voice.

"Yeah," she answered. "We in deep shit now, baby."

164 East 64st Street

He was doodling with some field incantations that were proving especially thorny when he noticed a blob of light dancing in mid-air a little to the right of the dinette table. He recognized it for what it was, and answered the "Are you receiving visitors?" query by tracing a simple pattern with his finger.

The blob of light wafted closer, drifting over the carpet. It stopped and grew brighter, suddenly unfolding and spreading out to take the shape of a human figure, that of a beautiful woman.

"Hi, Ferne."

"Incarnadine." His sister's greeting came with a cheery smile.

He sat back and took her in. She was as pretty as ever, dark of eye and delicate of face, her hair a dark waterfall spilling to her shoulders. She wore a crimson velvet gown, ornamented in gold filigree. The garment left her shoulders bare. Her skin was very white, very pure, totally unblemished. There were wild highlights in her eyes, and over them an ironic, skeptical downturn to her brow.

"Where are you?" he asked.

"The castle. Deems told me where you are, and I can scarcely believe it."

"It's about time somebody did something about re-establishing the gateway to Earth."

"Yes, it was long overdue," she said.

"I haven't done it yet, though."

"No?" One dark eyebrow rose. "But you're close?"

"Another few days. The problems have been tricky, but I think I have most of them solved."

"Good. Then we'll be seeing you soon."

"I hope. You said Deems told you. Were you in Albion?"

"Yes, I just happened to drop into my estate there. I'm having the house remodeled, and I had to consult with the master carpenter."

"Odd. Deems appeared to be unaware of your having any permanent residence in Albion."

"Is he? He should be aware. I've never made any secret of it. But, then, I rarely tell Deems my business. May I sit down?"

"I'm terribly sorry. I'd offer you a chair — " He smiled. " — But of course, you're not really here."

"Don't trouble yourself." She reached out and made as if to grasp something, pulling it near. She lowered herself to a sitting position. What she sat on was completely invisible. She arranged the folds of her gown and leaned back. "There. Now we can have a nice chat. As I was saying, my estate isn't exactly in Deems' kingdom, it's in the Protectorate of Westphalen — next door. These days it's only nominally a protectorate, and Deems has little power there, aside from receiving an annual tribute. I've had the place for years, and I don't visit as often as I'd like."

"How did Deems find you?"

She shrugged. "I don't know. I got a message from him by special courier this morning. The note said you had requested that I call you immediately on the Universal Projector. It sounded important, so I threw a few things in a bag and got to the portal as fast as I could. And here I am, back at the castle and on the line to you, just as you requested. What's all the fuss?"

"I'm afraid Deems made it sound more urgent than it really was. I merely wanted to talk with you, Ferne."

"Well, I'm delighted, of course, and it's been much too long since we last had a nice, cozy chat. . . ." She batted her long eyelashes at him. "But there must be a little more to it than that."

"A bit more, I have to admit. Before I get to it, do you mind if I slide a chair under your image? I find it strangely unsettling to have unsupported bodies levitating about."

"Feel free."

He got up and fetched a dinette chair, positioning it so that it looked convincing in the part. "That's a little better," he said, resuming his seat. "Now, what I wanted to ask you is this. Somebody's been fooling around at the castle. Is it you?"

Her face remained expressionless for a moment. Then she threw back her head and laughed. "Oh, Inky, the word 'blunt' was invented for you. That's always been your favorite tactic, hasn't it? You always lay your cards right on the table. No bluffing, no subtlety, nothing."

"Yes, at first. When the tactic fails, as it usually does, then I get sneaky."

"Yes, I've noticed over the years that this is your usual opening gambit. But why, if it usually avails you nothing?"

"I didn't say it availed me nothing. I can get a lot out of reactions. I like to read them, weigh them. The emotional overtones to any reaction, however insincere or pretended, are always very interesting. And very informative."

"Really? Fascinating. And *my* reaction — just now?"

"Oh, very interesting indeed."

She smiled. "And informative, I hope."

"That laugh spoke volumes."

The smile faded. She seemed concerned. "And what did it tell you?"

He crossed his legs, chuckling.

She frowned. "I think you're making it all up." She studied his face. "Yes, you're bluffing. Making me think you have one up on me already, and we haven't even really begun to bargain."

"Bargain? Are we at odds, in some way?"

She lifted her delicate shoulders. "Haven't we always been?"

He considered it, nodding. "Well, yes, it does seem to me that we've butted heads one or two times over the years. Just why, I can't imagine, because I've never had anything but the fondest regards for you, dear sister."

"And I for you, dear brother." Her expression hardened. "Now let's cut the crap and get down to business."

He laughed. "I really didn't know we had any business." He laughed again. "I suppose I can totally discount the first two minutes of this conversation. All that stuff about getting a message, coming to the castle. What exactly have you been up to, Ferne?"

She sat up and looked straight at him. "Never mind that. Listen to me. Your castle has been invaded. Successfully, I might add. What remains of your Guardsmen are prisoners or deserters. Most of them are of the latter category, having fled through sundry aspects."

"As per their standing orders in case of a successful incursion into the castle," he said calmly.

"Of course. Very wise, actually, as they had no chance."

"Who are the invaders?"

"They originate from an aspect that Dad sealed off long ago, on a hunch that the inhabitants might be potential troublemakers. He was right."

"Well, now," he said, scratching his chin. "That could be any one of about a hundred aspects that Dad had doubts about."

"Does it really matter which one? They are a race of bipeds, very warlike, very aggrandizing. Overwhelmingly so. They discovered the gateway quite readily, and instantly realized the unparalleled strategic value of the castle."

He nodded. "Gateway to thousands of worlds ripe for conquest."

"Yes. And they have technology, good technology. And a little magic, too; more, since they've been in the castle. So no worlds are safe from them."

"They sound like a real going concern." He shifted in his seat and recrossed his legs. "Looks like you're putting your cards on the table, for once. I thought we'd be here for hours, playing cat and mouse."

"It would have been fun, but . . ." She gave him a sulky look. "Damn it, Inky, you have a way of putting me off my stride. That 'reading reactions' business was just a ploy to get me to think that you have something on me, when, in fact, the situation is entirely the reverse."

"You have something on me?"

"You're locked out, dear brother. On the outside looking in. You're in New York, and you'll never be able to summon the gateway to the castle, let alone stabilize it in a New York apartment. I have established the gateway. Elsewhere."

"So, you *have* been fooling about here. With Trent?"

She chuckled gloatingly. "I knew you'd fall for that. You detected meddling and instantly suspected Trent, so you hied yourself to Earth to check him out. And he was as oily and as sneaky as always, and looking worried about your showing up there after all these years, nosing about. So you thought, 'Trent is up to something.' And he may very well be, if I know Trent. But it doesn't have anything to do with what I'm doing."

"Brilliant so far, sis. By the way, did I tell you that you're absolutely stunning in that dress?"

"Thank you." She reddened slightly. "Damn you! You always know exactly what to say to bring me up short. That's why I'm not inclined to toy with you, Inky. YOU are much too dangerous for that, and I'm not ashamed to admit it."

"I see." He looked down, tapping one shoe against the other. "So, you've taken over Castle Perilous."

"Oh, not yet. We're only in the first stage of things."

"You're not in cahoots with these invaders?"

She wrinkled her nose in disgust. "They're perfectly dreadful beasts, and I wouldn't think of having anything personally to do with them."

"So you just busted the containing spell and let them spill out into the castle? Unwise, Ferne honey. Unwise."

"On the contrary, they've been very useful. They are a bargaining chip."

"Indeed? Tell me this. Just where are you in the castle, if the castle has been invaded?"

"Well, you don't think I wouldn't take precautions, do you? We've sealed off the old family residence. We're quite safe here, for the moment."

"I see. So the Albion aspect is protected."

"Naturally. And the Earth aspect is here, too, stabilized nicely. And the door is locked, Inky. Only I have the key."

"What did you mean by calling the invaders a bargaining chip? What are you bargaining for?"

"For a share of control of the castle. And its power."

"Of course. And you want to bargain with me."

"Who else, my liege lord?"

"Why do I figure in at all?" he asked. "According to you, I'm locked out."

"We need you."

"Who is 'we'?"

"Deems and I," Ferne said.

He looked off, nodding, understanding. "I see. Old Deems is finally having second thoughts about abdicating in favor of me. Why, I wonder?"

She laughed mirthlessly. "He doesn't want the throne. Through his profligacy and general ineptitude, he's screwed up things in Albion to the point where he finally had to ask me for help. Magical help. The kingdom's in a mess. Fiscally speaking, he's just about at the end of his rope."

Incarnadine folded his arms and nodded. "So, he wasn't kidding."

"Deems has trouble lying. There's no guile in the man at all. And not a great deal of brains. Imagine him trying to pretend that he didn't know how to reach me. Dead giveaway."

"You're right. I knew immediately that you and he were up to something. But by then it was too late. I was here, and, as you put it, on the outside looking in."

"You couldn't have timed things any better. I had no idea when the creatures would make their move to take over Perilous, but I had hoped you would follow the Trent lead and go to New York before the attack. And you went, beating them by about two days. It was a little close, but it worked out. Had you been present during the invasion, I don't think it would have made much difference. But your not being there was good insurance."

Incarnadine got up and went to the dry bar. He poured himself two fingers of whiskey, then tore the cap off a small bottle of club soda and mixed it in. "I'd offer you a drink, but . . ."

"I'm having one served to me here," she said, holding an invisible glass. The faint suggestion of a long-stemmed wineglass — a milky, wavering outline — took form in her hand as she brought it to her lips.

"I've often wondered," he said, "why the spell that projects the image won't project any other material thing but the subject's clothes. Why just clothes?"

"Dad's sense of propriety, I guess. How would it look, me sitting here in front of my brother naked?"

"Well, it wouldn't look all that bad," he said. "All in the family, you know."

"Inky, I'm surprised," she said coyly. "I never knew you harbored incestuous thoughts."

He feigned shock. "Hold your scandalous tongue, woman! That would be unspeakable. Not to say bad form. No, dear, chaste sister, I simply have always thought that you were a knockout. Purely a matter of aesthetics." He took a drink and walked back to the chair and sat down.

She shook her head. "You're just sandbagging me again. Forget it, Inky. It won't work."

"Ferne, your biggest fault is that you can't take a compliment."

"That may be. I'm much too suspicious to accept them at face value."

"Pity," he said. "But back to business. You say you need me. For what?"

"We need your Guardsmen to take back the castle. Deems' forces aren't adequate. Only you know where your boys are hiding. With them and Deems' army combined — and with a little help from the Recondite Arts — we'll be able to stuff the disgusting little devils back into their hole."

"You hope!"

Ferne shrugged. "I don't see why it can't be done. The invaders are troublesomely adept at fighting, true, but they're certainly not invincible. See here. You thwarted Prince Vorn and destroyed the combined military might of the Hunran Empire and its allies. Surely you and Deems can turn back an army that has but one access way into the castle! Close off the portal, and reinforcements and supplies are denied them! Then it becomes merely a question of mopping up."

He rolled his eyes. "Thank you, Karl von Clausewitz!"

"Oh, really, Inky, you're always carping over details. You'll think of something, I'm sure."

He took a good stiff drink. "Okay, say Deems and I beat back this horde of — what the hell do they look like, anyway? Want to give me a hint?"

"Disgusting, squat blue creatures with nasty teeth and big, flat webbed feet." She turned up her nose as she brought the ghost wineglass to her lips. "Horrible things, really."

Frowning, he massaged his forehead. "Gods. That rings a bell somewhere."

"Again, what does it matter? Their magic is primitive, and their technology won't work in the castle — "

"But they will undoubtedly establish bases through some of the portals. Once they fan out, they'll be unbeatable. Like termites in an old barn. Ferne, you don't know what you've done."

"I don't believe you."

"Of course you don't. Anyway, as I was saying, let's assume Deems and I do prevail and win back the castle. What's to prevent me from kicking Deems and his rabble out, and you along with them?"

"I'll simply 'bust' another containment spell and let more termites into the barn."

"Not if I see that you never set foot in Perilous again."

She smiled serenely. "You can't keep me out, Inky."

He sat back and emitted a grudging snort. "You're probably right." He drained his glass and set it aside. "So — after this great victory, you, Deems, and I will make a cozy triumvirate. Eh?"

"I think it sounds very friendly. Various contingents of Deems' forces will stay on to complement select units of your Guardsmen. The two forces will share duties equally."

Incarnadine rose and approached the figure of his sister.

"No, Ferne. It won't work. No deal."

"Think again, Inky. You can't get back. You can't summon the gateway now. The end on your side is nailed down in a remote spot. Even if it weren't, I very much doubt you could re-establish the portal. You said you had run into some difficulties."

"I admit it," he said. "It's a tough problem. I've been studying as much high-energy physics as magic."

"Exactly. It was only after years of study that I finally found a solution."

"You've been spending quite a good deal of time here, haven't you?"

"Oh, yes. Once I found I could summon the gateway from this side, I began dividing my time between there and Albion. I prefer the latter, by the way, but Earth is a dandy place to build up your magical muscles. Earth magic is the most powerful of all, precisely because it's the most difficult to work with, and to master."

"You can say that again. Still, it's no deal, sis. The only thing that doesn't make sense was that attempt on my life."

She fixed him in a questioning stare. "I can't imagine what you're talking about."

"Really? Well, somebody tried to take me out. I'll admit, you make a dubious suspect. From what you say, you'd stand to lose by my death — at least for now. Once the castle's back in our hands, it'll be another matter. Then I'll simply be a liability."

"I repeat, I don't know what you're talking about. You have a limited amount of time, my brother. You said it yourself — once the invaders establish a beachhead, they'll be hard to dislodge. Perilous will be a lost cause."

"And it will be on your head."

She shrugged. "The decision is yours. Share Perilous, and it will stand. Insist on being stubborn, and the Haplodites will have to find a new home."

He shook his head sadly. "Sister, I'm disappointed in you. I never thought you would stoop so low."

"Oh, stuff it. Look, Inky. Just say the word and I'll let you through, and we can get on with business."

"What does Deems get out of this?"

"Gold for his royal treasury. What else?"

"Oh, no," he groaned. "Ferne, I'm surprised at you. You know very well that Albion is the wrong kind of universe for alchemical changes. The stuff you'll whip up for him will turn phony in a matter of months."

"Who will care but Deems' creditors? And who will believe them?"

"Ferne, you shouldn't go around screwing up the economy of a world like that! You're talking about a lot of gold, aren't you? If I know Deems, you are."

She waved the matter aside. "It is of no moment whatsoever."

He sighed and sat down. "No deal, Ferne."

Her eyes flashed. "Then you'll rot there, little brother!"

He flipped a palm over. "New York is not exactly Siberia."

"Have fun, Inky. Take in a Broadway show or two. There are still some fine restaurants in New York. You might try Windows on the Park. It's at the top of the Gulf & Western building. The food is good and the view is breathtaking."

"I'll be sure to check it out."

"You'll be sorry, Incarnadine. I'll give you twenty-four hours to deal. After that, Perilous is a lost cause."

"I think I know what you're up to, Ferne."

"You couldn't possibly," she said. "Good-bye, Inky."

"Good-bye, Ferne."

Her figure collapsed to a ball of light, then was gone. The useless chair stood in the middle of the floor, as empty now of form as content.

He sat for a long while, silently contemplating areas of the walls and ceiling.

Keep — Near the South Tower

"This looks promising," Gene said as he peered across the threshold of an attractive aspect. There was sunshine out there, and green grass, some trees, and a small pond. It looked like the grazing meadow of a small farm, *sans* cattle. He sniffed the air and could have sworn he smelted fresh-cut hay. But there were no buildings visible, and something told him this was not an inhabited aspect.

"Trouble is," he added, "it'll look just as inviting to the Bluefaces."

Linda said, "Maybe we'll be safe if we get far enough away from the portal."

"But we don't want to get too far away from the castle. We might not be able to make it back."

"True. But we haven't found a better aspect so far. Aren't those apple trees over there?"

"Maybe," Gene said. "Looks like the wrong season for apples, though. I vote no. Anyone disagree?"

No one did. Gene and Linda walked away from the portal, Snowclaw and Sheila following.

"At least we haven't seen Bluefaces for a good while," Sheila commented.

"Damn, I wish I knew what I was looking for," Gene said, preoccupied with his thoughts.

"What would you be looking for," Linda asked, "if you knew what you were looking for?"

"An aspect that could turn up some kind of fancy, high-tech weapon that would be effective against the Bluefaces."

"The way I understand it," Sheila said, "technology doesn't work in the castle."

"Depends on what you mean by technology," Gene said. "I've heard tell of aspects where it's pretty hard to tell magic from technology. Maybe something from one of those worlds would do the trick."

"Everybody keeps saying that there are some pretty weird aspects," Linda said. "Maybe we'll get lucky."

"Fat chance," Gene said glumly. "I think we're sunk. We've lost the castle."

"It wasn't ours to begin with," Linda said.

"No, but it was the only home we had."

Sheila said, "My usual luck. I just start getting used to the place, and we get chased out. Thing is, I can't decide whether it's any great loss."

"The castle's a mixed blessing, Sheila," Gene said. "But it's given me one thing I lacked back in the real world. Adventure. Real, heart-pounding, thrill-a-minute, no-holds-barred adventure. They don't make that in the mundane world. They just make boredom, periodically relieved by stark terror."

Another aperture appeared suddenly in the wall ahead, this one revealing a scene of dense jungle. Gene halted in his tracks and put out an arm to hold his companions back.

"Wait a minute. This looks like trouble."

They stood and watched. Birdcalls echoed in the treetops, the undergrowth rustled here and fidgeted there, and tropical sun streamed green and gold through the high jungle canopy. But not much else happened.

"What were you saying about heart-pounding adventure?" Linda asked.

"Yeah . . . well." Gene pushed his broadsword back into its scabbard. "We're really getting the proverbial horns of the dilemma right in the butt. If we hide out in one of these wild aspects, we'll be safe from the Bluefaces, all right. But you can bet the damn thing'll close up and leave us stranded."

"Great choice," Linda said. "Die in some weird place, or stay here and get taken prisoner." She gave a tiny shudder. "If they take prisoners. I wonder if they think humans are good to eat."

Snowclaw said, "I've often wondered myself."

The great white beast's hairless companions regarded him gravely.

Abstractedly Snowclaw stroked the blade of the huge longsword that Linda had conjured for him. Then he flashed his teeth, chuckling impishly. "Just kidding, friends."

"Maybe we'll just have to take the chance and hole up in one of these," Sheila said, pointing toward the jungle.

"It's a thought," Gene said. "But not this one. We need one with some signs of civilization."

"That, I think, is going to be hard," Linda said. "Did you ever notice that most aspects are either uninhabited, deserted, or, if they do have civilization, it's primitive?"

Gene thought about it. "Yeah, now that you mention it. I've seen some strange things, briefly glimpsed through aspects here and there. But for the most part, you're right. If the aspect is easily accessible, there's usually nothing there except picture-postcard stuff. Pretty, but of no use. There must be a reason for it."

"Just think if the portal to Earth were, say, in the middle of New York City."

"Right, this castle would be co-op apartments by now. Maybe that's the reason that portals to worlds with advanced civilizations are so rare. Maybe the castle was designed that way in order to protect it from invasion from within, so to speak."

"Makes sense," Linda said.

"Come on, let's get going."

They moved away from the jungle aspect. Farther down the corridor they passed two large empty halls, one at either hand.

Gene thought awhile, then said, "Yeah, it makes sense. But what happened with the Bluefaces? Did the castle's defenses — whatever they are — break down? Or does this kind of thing happen periodically?"

"If this place is as old as they say it is," Linda said, "it would have been invaded long ago."

Gene shrugged. "Maybe it was. Maybe Lord Incarnadine is an invader himself."

"Haven't you ever talked to any of the servants? They all say — "

"Yeah, I know. They all say Incarnadine's been lord of Perilous for hundreds of years. And before that his dad was lord for a thousand years. I know — I'm just throwing hypotheses against the wall and seeing if any of 'em leave a stain." He ruminated for a few more paces. "Thing is, I *have* seen cities and high-tech-looking stuff through a few

of the floating aspects, most of which look mighty hard to cross." He shook his head slowly. "I can't figure it out."

"Halt!"

They had just begun to cross through an intersecting tunnel. Swords already drawn, four Bluefaces were double-timing down the left branch, breaking into a charge when Gene and his companions came into view.

"Run!" Gene yelled, turning Sheila around and shoving her back down the corridor. Linda and Snowclaw needed no prompting. They ran, passing the two empty halls and the jungle aspect, but before they reached the crossing passageway ahead, three more Bluefaces turned the corner, snarling and waving swords.

Linda skidded to a stop. She had less than five seconds to arrive at a magical solution to the problem. She fought an urge to panic and closed her eyes, hoping the decision she made would be the right one.

Snowclaw turned to fight the first group of Bluefaces and Gene raced to meet the threesome. Snowy's first victory was swift. His left hand struck like the head of a snake, tearing out the throat of the leader. He neatly sidestepped the falling body to bring his longsword to bear on the second creature.

Sheila backed against the wall and squatted, hands covering her head, mind gone numb with fear. Peeking between fingers, she saw Gene clash swords with two Bluefaces as a third maneuvered for position in the narrow hallway. Gene held his own for a spell, but three-on-one proved too much even for Gene's expert swordcraft. He backstepped, fending off all three now, parrying and riposting, his blade a silver blur. Snowy was similarly boxed in, his three opponents giving him a hard time.

Then something strange happened. Sheila blinked her eyes and looked again. Either she was seeing triple, or there were three Genes. And Snowclaw seemed to have suddenly acquired two comrades-in-arms who looked exactly like him.

With a helpless groan, Sheila covered her eyes again as the *whang* and *clank* of swordplay filled the corridor. When she looked again, the situation was even more confused. Now there were more Bluefaces, and still more duplicates of Gene and Snowclaw.

"A duel between us, sorceress!" one Blueface called out. He was standing back from the melee, and appeared to be speaking to Linda, who stood calmly in the middle of things.

"You got it, Blueface!" Linda answered. She stuck her tongue out.

From that point on, things got very bizarre indeed. The number of combatants seemed to increase every few seconds. In a short time the passageway became the scene of an armed engagement of major proportions, spilling over into the great rooms on either side. New sorts of combatants appeared: knights in armor, Roman legionnaires, and Greek hoplites crossed swords with an outrageous assortment of monsters. Tentacles snaked, talons raked, and claws tore, all to the tune of singing steel. The noise was deafening. Sheila dove to the floor and flattened herself against the wall. When someone or something stepped on her ankle, she gave a yelp and crawled off.

Someone grabbed her arm and yanked her halfway up. It was Gene.

"Get to the aspect and jump through!" he yelled. "And keep down!" He let her go.

Sheila crawled, keeping her head down but watching out for stamping feet and other, stranger extremities. She was kicked once in the leg, then took the heel of a boot in her ribs. She doubled up with pain; and then got her foot mashed. Whimpering, she rose to a crouch and hobbled away. She stumbled, fell, and got up again.

Someone seized her wrist and spun her around. It was a Blueface, sword raised and ready to strike. Sheila stood transfixed, hypnotized by the gleaming blade above her. She had never really considered what it would be like to be struck by a sword. The blade was huge and looked wickedly sharp, sharper than the Japanese knife in those ubiquitous TV commercials where the guy cuts a beer can open and then dices an avocado. She was now up against the awful prospect, the impending reality, of having that blade slice through her flesh. The amazing thing was that she couldn't scream. She simply stood there in this frozen instant, acutely conscious of her fate, almost dispassionately wondering if there would be much pain.

She never got the opportunity to find out. Another blade flashed round from behind and took the creature's head clean off, leaving its neck a pulsing fountain of purple blood. Almost in slow motion, the body dropped at her feet. Snowclaw — which one? — grabbed her arm and shoved her in the direction of the portal.

"Move, Sheila!"

She ran, but more fighting blocked her way. She cut to the right, sidestepped left, then stooped and ducked between the legs of a

strange giant creature covered in yellow feathers. The incongruous thought of *Sesame Street's* Big Bird came to her, unbidden, as she caught sight of an opening and sprinted for the portal.

She tripped over something and fell. A man in tunic and crested bronze helmet helped her to her feet, then saluted with his sword, turned, and rejoined the fighting. Sheila looked down at the body she had tripped over.

It was Gene, and he was dead, his skull split open and a huge gash in his neck. Sheila screamed and kept screaming.

Someone took her arm and shook her violently.

It was Gene. "Let's go!"

Dumbfounded, she swung her gaze back and forth between Gene's twin bodies, living and dead.

"Forget it!" he said. "Come on!"

As she was being dragged down the corridor, she couldn't take her eyes off Gene's paradoxical dead body. But she soon lost sight of it as the battle closed in around her. The next few seconds were lost to complete disorientation. Then there was light and a sudden wave of heat — it was like running out of an air-conditioned building on a blistering-hot day. The castle was gone and she was outside, in the middle of a humid and fragrant rain forest. The portal was an upright rectangle, like an odd movie screen, standing in the undergrowth, and through it she could see inside the castle. The fighting raged on.

"Run! Hide!"

Gene was shaking her, yelling into her ear.

"Get lost! Run!"

She was about to ask about Linda when she was rendered speechless by the sight of Gene's form suddenly growing blurred and indistinct. Then he disappeared altogether, and she was left standing alone. Astonished, she whirled around, again and again, her bewildered eyes searching frantically for any sight of him.

But he was gone. He had simply vanished.

He reappeared just as quickly. He and Linda came through the gateway at a run.

But before Sheila could register shock, they disappeared as inexplicably as the first Gene had done.

They were followed by Snowclaw, who also vanished without fanfare and without a trace. Two more of Snowclaw's doppelgangers

repeated the trick, each blinking out of existence shortly after crossing the threshold.

Then another Gene-and-Linda set came through. This one did not disappear.

"Here she is!" Gene yelled as he ran by. "Let's go, Sheila!"

He grabbed Sheila's arm and dragged her along. Sheila tripped, staggered, then found her footing. Gene let go of her arm and she ran after them.

Eventually they pulled ahead and she lost them in the sea of vegetation. She dashed on through the thick undergrowth, leafy tentacles grabbing at her feet, overhanging vines whipping at her face and snagging her clothing. She stopped and looked wildly about. Someone grabbed her sleeve and yanked her down.

It was Gene, crouched with Linda behind some bushes.

"Shhh!"

Sheila peered back at the portal. As she watched, several Bluefaces crossed over and promptly dematerialized. Then Snowclaw came running through. Apparently he was the genuine article. He stayed hugely real.

Gene jumped up and waved at him, whistling.

Snowclaw caught sight of Gene and started forward. A Blueface came charging out of the portal, saw Snowclaw, and jumped him from behind. Snowclaw rolled to the ground to avoid a wicked slash, and in so doing, shot out a foot to trip the creature up. The Blueface went down. There was a brief scuffle on the ground, then both creatures sprang to their feet, swords flashing in the tropical sunlight.

By the time Gene got there to help, the Blueface lay on the ground, wanting the top half of its skull. Gene led Snowy back to the hiding spot.

The foursome watched the portal for five full minutes. No one else came out. All was quiet.

"Maybe that last one was the only survivor," Gene said. "The only real one, that is." He found a tree trunk and leaned against it. "How are you guys?"

Linda said, "I wasn't in much danger. That Blueface was a strong magician, though. If we hadn't ducked out, I don't know." She shook her head ruefully.

"Sheila?"

Horror-struck, she was staring at Gene. "Gene, I . . . I *saw* you. You were — "

"Yeah, I know. It was pretty interesting."

Sheila's mouth hung open. She worked her jaws, trying to form words in reply.

Gene shrugged. "Well, philosophically speaking — "

Sheila burst into tears, and presently she found that Gene was holding her. She hugged him, pressing her face against the braided leather of his breastplate.

"It's okay, it's okay," Gene was saying, but she knew that nothing would ever be the same again.

"Oh, no!"

Blinking back tears, Sheila looked at Linda.

Linda's face was ashen. "The portal's gone," she said.

East 64th and Lexington

Trent's Mercedes Swooped to the curb and halted beneath a sign that read NO STOPPING ANYTIME. Trent got out and opened the trunk. Incarnadine threw his luggage in; then they both got in the car.

It was about three-thirty on a Friday afternoon, and traffic was already congealing into a hopeless clot. Trent drove south on Lexington to 58th Street and turned west.

"Think we can get through the Lincoln Tunnel in under an hour?" Incarnadine asked.

"Sure, no problem," Trent answered with the casual self-confidence that only a New Yorker can muster in the face of impending gridlock.

"I'd be willing to bet we never make it to the tunnel. This town was always bad, traffic-wise, but the situation seems to have reached absurd proportions."

"Come now, you're exaggerating."

Incarnadine laughed. "You really have become a native."

Trent shrugged. "Maybe." He dodged and weaved expertly through the taxi-thick rush, applying the car's horn in liberal doses. "Tell me again why I should help you."

Incarnadine sighed and leaned back in the leather seat. "I don't think I want to go through it again. If you can't marshal enough reasons on your own, your heart's probably not in it. If that's the case, let me off here, and we'll say no more about it."

"Hold your horses, I'm not backing out. I just want to hear again why I should take your side against Ferne. And Deems, though I don't hold a brief for him."

"I'm not asking you to take my side. I'm enlisting your aid in a campaign to save Perilous from the irresponsible machinations of our crazy sister. She's really gone off the deep end this time, Trent."

"You say she has something else in mind besides sharing power with you and Deems?"

"She wants to be nothing less than mistress of Perilous. She's wanted it for years, and has stated so to me on a number of occasions. Always with a laugh, mind you, and a pretty smile, as if she didn't mean it."

"Always. That's our Ferne. But who am I to thwart her ambitions? Look, Inky. I've lived in this culture long enough to have been influenced by certain so-called progressive ideas. In our world, as in this one, women traditionally get the short end of the stick when it comes to things like royal succession. She's older than you, but you are a male, and she was passed over. You inherited the Seat Perilous, the crown, and the castle. She's pissed about that, as rightly she should be."

"In the moral universe you're delineating, our sister Dorcas, as oldest sibling, should have taken the throne upon Dad's death."

"Dorcas is traditional-minded as hell, and you know it. She'd be on your side, for Christ's sake. Let's forget hypotheticals. It's Ferne who thinks she has a civil rights case."

"Ferne may have a case, but the way she's going about redressing her grievance is guaranteed to put more than Castle Perilous in jeopardy."

"Not if you gave in a little and let her share power."

"Can't be done, Trent. I mean, we're not talking about political power in the traditional sense here, are we?"

"Well, not exactly," Trent said. "As far as Perilous' local situation is concerned, the Pale is a Wasteland, and has been for centuries. Is there anyone at all living out there on the plains these days?"

"There are about two hundred tenant farmers and their families left, scraping by as always. They won't live in the castle for religious reasons."

"Only two hundred? Gods! Then the Pale is virtually deserted outside the castle. No, we're not speaking of governing a few hundred square *zeln* of marginal farmland. It's a matter of controlling whole worlds — at least potentially."

"Trent, you know Perilous can't control worlds. Not very well, at any rate. For instance, take this one. Could we rule Earth from Perilous?"

"Maybe not a complex, heavily populated world where magic is problematical. But other, simpler aspects where the ground rules are a trifle more liberal? Yes indeedy. We could run worlds like those."

"Why? To what purpose?"

Trent swerved to avoid a cab that had cut in front to pick up a fare. He chuckled. "Why? Something to do. Something different. A new kick. A little excitement to leaven the boredom that's inevitable in the lives of long-lived sorts such as we."

"You might take up batiking. Or beer can collecting. How about aerobics? Maybe holistic medicine?"

"Okay, okay. I was simply dying to see it from Ferne's point of view."

"I think I know what her point of view is," Incarnadine said. "She's nuts. Gone round the bend. Crackers."

"What makes you think that?"

"I'm pretty sure she intends to make a deal with the Hosts of Hell."

Trent honked angrily at a brave pedestrian, a man in a trench coat and wool cap, who had stepped out in front of the car. The man jumped back to the curb in the nick of time as Trent roared by. Incarnadine heard shouted obscenities dwindling in the car's wake.

"How do you know?" Trent said.

"I don't, for sure," Incarnadine answered, "but I'm fairly sure she tried to have me killed, and that means she's not dealing squarely with Deems. I don't think Deems would go along with assassinating me."

"Unless he is as desperate as Ferne said he was."

"Possibly. But I don't think Ferne wants to share power with anyone, let alone Deems, let alone me. She needs allies to take and hold the castle, and I think she thinks that only supernatural allies will do. She's probably right. Alone, she'd have to face her subjects, to say nothing of the Guard. And there's always the Guests as a wild card. And all of them are magicians, to varying degrees. That's what makes Perilous a fun place and makes plotters toss and turn all night. I do myself, sometimes."

"This all sounds complicated," Trent said uneasily. "Why is she stringing Deems along? Why does she need him?"

"If she had simply summoned the Hosts of Hell to take over the castle, Deems would have thrown in with me to fight them off. So would Dorcas, and, I think, even you."

Trent seemed to be grinning in spite of himself. "But I was stranded here, remember? Still am, as a matter of fact."

"Bullshit, Trent. I never believed it for one minute."

Trent laughed. "Okay, I never was good at keeping secrets."

"You shouldn't have shown off at dinner, when you let me see how you do your aging act. Obviously you've learned to adapt to this universe. How long did it take you to learn how to summon the gateway?"

"Oh, about five years, as I said. But once I could do if, I had no interest in going back to Perilous, or in living in any other universe but this one. I simply had settled down here and wasn't about to move. I have friends here, you know. I've put down roots."

Incarnadine nodded, looking out the window. Traffic thickened up even more as they reached the West Side.

"I still don't quite understand it," Trent said. "Okay, she wouldn't have won any popularity contests by teaming up with a bunch of demons. But can any of us prevail against the Hosts of Hell, singly or combined?"

"I don't know. The Hosts of Hell are a troublesome bunch."

"That's putting it mildly. If Dad feared anything at all, it was those guys. He warned us about them more than once."

"Dad knew their power. It's not for nothing that the strongest containment spell in the castle is the one blocking their aspect." Incarnadine rubbed his dark beard. He was glad not to have to go about in makeup all the time. Only his C. Wainwright Smithton persona required his looking elderly. "As I said, I don't know exactly what Ferne's up to. But I'm sure I'll find out sooner or later. As I take my dying breath, maybe." He opened his coat and loosened the collar of his shin. "Tell me this. Why *are* you helping me? Or are you?"

Trent took a long breath. "I guess it's occurred to you that I could be behind all this."

"Yes, it has. Forget it. That's a possibility I'll have to live with. I'm betting you aren't. Granted that you're not conspiring with Ferne or running her, why help me find the portal and get back to Perilous?"

"Because I don't want Perilous taken over by militaristic blue monsters," Trent said, "let alone demonic entities from some fever-dream universe who would rule Creation if they could get their claws on it."

"Makes sense. Another question. How sure are you about Ferne's having an estate in western Pennsylvania?"

"I thought you'd found out. You were the one who asked me about it."

"It was just a wild hunch. We've been getting a lot of Guests from that area lately."

"Well, it was a pretty good hunch. I've known about it for some time."

"How did you find out?"

"About ten years ago I woke up in the middle of the night with the strongest feeling that someone was doing major magic in this universe. I didn't have the vaguest notion of how to locate the source, so I worked on that problem awhile. Eventually I came up with a direction-finding technique, and the next time I got that same feeling, I went out in the car and got a triangulation fix on it. Over the years, I've managed to get a wider baseline and pinpointed it pretty accurately."

"What's the name of the town it's near, again?"

"Ligonier, Pennsylvania."

"That's where the portal ought to be nailed down."

"You would think. But the booby traps and fortifications around it are going to be a living nightmare."

Incarnadine nodded, smiling thinly. "Let's deal with the horrors as they come. First we have to survive the Lincoln Tunnel and the New Jersey Turnpike."

They ate at a Burger King on the Pennsylvania Turnpike near Reading. It was about eight o'clock, and the night was cold and dark.

"What's with the gadget?" Trent asked as he munched his Whopper.

"Checking some parameters," Incarnadine said as he tapped with one finger on the keys of a pocket computer. "Stresses, field strengths, other variables. I can't keep track of them by feel here."

"That's the first thing you've got to learn. You can't use technology as a crutch here. Otherwise your magic becomes a sort of pseudoscience."

Incarnadine smiled ruefully. "I know what you mean. But getting an intuitive grip on things is going to take a little more time. For me, at least."

"Don't worry, you'll get it eventually."

"I hope I get it before I get it, if you take my meaning."

"You haven't touched your french fries."

"I can't get used to this kind of food. Ring Lardner once told me that American culture could only get more bland and homogenized as time went on, and he was right."

"I like American food," Trent said. "It's fast, nice and greasy, and appeals to the kid in us all."

"Nothing wrong with hamburgers and fried potatoes. It's just that — uh, never mind. Can we go?"

"Of course."

They walked out into the brisk winter night. The parking lot was well lighted near the restaurant, but Trent had parked on the dim outskirts under a burnt-out light.

"Ring Lardner?" Trent said. "You were always one to hobnob with the literati."

"Forever courting the Muse's favored. I liked the old Algonquin Round Table crowd, back in the twenties and thirties. Those were the days."

"Who was that writer woman you had a fling with back then?"

"Dorothy Parker? Very briefly. She was fun, but she had a melancholy streak in her. You know, she once said to me — "

A windshield shattered in front of them, its sound almost masking the dull thud of a silenced gunshot that came from behind. Incarnadine dove over a hood, slid off the fender, hit concrete, and rolled to a crouch. He listened, seeing nothing. He heard running footsteps recede. Then a car door slammed, and tires squealed. He peeked over the front end of an Audi and saw a dark nondescript sedan peeling out of the lot. It screeched onto the turnpike re-entry ramp and sped away.

Trent came over, holding a compact submachine gun. He handed it to Incarnadine.

"You keep this. They could be laying for us down the road."

Incarnadine examined the weapon, then clicked on the safety and folded up the wire stock. "I guess this puts you in the clear."

"Maybe. I could have had one of my guys stage it."

"Possible, but unlikely."

"You're right." Trent yawned. "Let's go. We have a five-hour drive ahead of us."

"You look tired. Want me to drive?"

"When was the last time you drove an automobile?"

"1958, I think." Incarnadine said. "Why?"

"I have a pretty good autopilot spell. We can both nap. We're going to need some sleep before we tackle Ferne's place."

"Do you trust the spell?"

"It drives better than I do," Trent said. "Besides, I belong to the Triple-A. They'll tow the wreckage away, no charge."

"In that case, start with the hocus-pocus, O great Trentino."

Elsewhere

Deena stroked the shaggy mane of the animal she called Buster. The hair was thick, soft, and smooth. Buster looked at her with huge golden cat-eyes and communicated warm feelings of friendliness, bordering on affection. Certain filaments of the strange and complex organ which blossomed antlerlike from Buster's head appeared to undulate slightly. The organ, a light pink in color, looked somewhat like a stand of coral, with fine, featherlike hair covering some of the thinner tendrils.

"Yeah, I like you, too, Buster," Deena said. "I started to like you when I found out you wasn't gonna eat me."

Barnaby lay in the grass with his head resting on the tawny flank of the one they had named Jane. Her purring had a strangely tranquilizing effect, and he felt at peace. He was watching the floating rectangle of the portal, which had steadily but slowly descended over the last few hours. It was now only about seven feet off the ground.

"If I could chin myself, I could get up there," he said. "But I know I can't chin myself."

"Don't worry, it'll come down," Deena said.

They waited while the sun inched down the sky and a cool breeze came up out of the forest. The other animals lazed in the grass, some sleeping, others giving themselves tongue baths or simply staring off, preoccupied with quiet thoughts. That these creatures were intelligent was very apparent. Once he and Deena had gotten over their initial fright, it had also been obvious that these strange animals could communicate emotions via some sort of telepathy.

Barnaby wondered about them. Were they truly intelligent, or simply emotionally sensitive and empathetic? Their life seemed a bit too idyllic to require much problem solving. He did a mental shrug. The

jury was still out on dolphins and whales; who knew about these strange and marvelous creatures?

He checked the aperture once more. Still descending with clocklike slowness. He shaded his eyes. No, it had stopped. Or had it? It was difficult to tell. As long as it wasn't rising. Then again, a stay here might not be too bad. He wondered what it would be like. Were these animals carnivorous? They looked the part. He couldn't imagine them grazing and chewing cud. But they didn't seem aggressive enough to be killers.

Life might be pretty nice here. It was warm and sunny and quiet. He rather liked the place even though he didn't know much about it. He was very tired, and he needed a rest. The castle was simply too much for him. He had to find a place where there was no noise and no fighting and no huge white beasts with claws, no strange blue monsters. Just a nice quiet place where he could relax and not have to worry about . . . whatever. About getting back home. About castles and kings and knights of the Round Table and everyone running around like characters in an old Errol Flynn movie. Worse. None of it was real, of course. Couldn't be. It had to be a dream, had to be. Just a dream, and soon he'd wake up and he'd be back in familiar surroundings and everything would be fine. The world would be right again, no more nightmare, no more . . . dream. . . .

"Barnaby, wake up!"

"Huh?"

Barnaby sat up. Jane got to her feet and stared into the forest.

Deena pointed. "Somethin's going on over there. I smell smoke."

So did Barnaby. "How long was I asleep?"

"I dunno. I was asleep myself. Look."

A pall of gray smoke drifted above the trees, and the smell of burning wood came out of the forest on a hot, acrid wind.

"Forest fire!" Barnaby gasped. He turned and searched for the aperture. To his dismay, he found that it had risen to about ten feet. "Oh, no. My God, what'll we do?"

"We either get up to that window or run."

"I'll never make it, Deena."

"Neither will I. It's too high to jump up."

"Climb up on my shoulders."

"Okay, say I make it. What then?"

"Look for something up there. A rope, whatever you can find. We'll never outrun that fire. Come on. Alley-oop, and all that."

After some initial tries, Deena managed to climb and perch on Barnaby's shoulders. Shakily she tried to rise to a stand, but couldn't get purchase on Barnaby's sloping shoulders. He helped as best he could, letting her use his hands as supports. She tried again, slid off, and went tumbling in the grass.

All the animals had left the clearing except Jane and Buster, who stood looking on curiously, occasionally glancing back toward the rapidly approaching fire front. Streamers of thick black smoke now trailed through the clearing.

"That fire is racing a mile a minute," Barnaby said worriedly as the roar and crackle of flames came to his ears.

Deena mounted again, circus style, stepping up on Barnaby's angled thigh and leaping to a stand in one clean motion — but she lost her balance and fell again. It was the right approach, however, and they tried again. This time it worked, and Deena managed to balance herself precariously on Barnaby's shoulders.

"I got it!" she yelled as she hooked her fingers over the lower rim of the portal. "Push me up!"

"I . . . I can't — " Barnaby felt her weight come off his shoulders. He jammed the heel of his hand under her right shoe and lifted, then did the same with the left. He looked up and was struck by what would have been, to someone just arriving on the scene, the bewildering sight of a young black woman hanging on to a hole in the middle of the air. Grunting and puffing, Barnaby boosted her up as far as he could. Deena tried chinning herself, but her strength was not up to it. Her legs flailed out uselessly, with nothing to push against but air.

"I can't do it!" she cried.

"Yes, you can!" Barnaby glanced toward the source of the eye-searing smoke that now began to engulf the clearing. He could see flames quite clearly now as they licked at the underbrush and raved in the treetops. He looked up at Deena again. "Swing your leg up!"

Deena swung from side to side to get momentum, then kicked out with her right leg. The heel of her shoe caught the outside lip of the aperture, but slipped off, and she very nearly lost her tenuous finger-grip. She tried again with the left, to no avail. Then she got an idea and

began to swing back and forth through the plane of the window, as if on a parallel bar. She increased the arc of her swing, then tucked her legs in and let the sudden increase in angular momentum boost her to chinning level. Her right leg shot up over the windowsill.

"You got it!" Barnaby shouted. "Get your arm over!"

Deena got more leg inside the window until she hung almost upside down. Using her legs more than her arms, she pulled herself up to where she could hook her right arm over the sill.

Barnaby watched her disappear inside the portal. Then Deena showed her head.

"I made it!" she cried. "Now what?"

"Is there anything up there we could use?"

"There ain't nothin'! No rope, no nothin'. Not even any furniture. Oh, Barnaby, I'm sorry."

"Yeah," Barnaby said, turning to watch tongues of flame ignite the dry grass at the edge of the clearing.

"I'm gonna go get help," Deena yelled. "Maybe I can find a rope."

"Forget it!" Barnaby told her. "There isn't time. I gotta make a run for it. I — "

He looked down. Jane was nuzzling the backs of his knees. Buster had something clenched between his teeth. It was one chewed end of a very long and very thick vine.

"Thank you," Barnaby said in astonishment. He took the vine. It seemed long enough and strong enough. But now the problem was one of Deena's ability to haul him up. He didn't see how she could do it.

"Throw it up!" Deena yelled.

Barnaby took the vine in both hands and tested its strength. It had a tough, spiral structure that made it almost as strong as top-grade hemp. Barnaby coiled the vine — there was about twenty feet of it — and tossed it up through the aperture. Soon one end came trailing down.

"Tie it good!" she called.

"You'll never be able to lift me!"

"I got help!"

Barnaby looped the vine around his middle and tied what he hoped was a nonslip knot. "Ready!" he shouted.

Slowly he rose. When he was high enough, he readied up and threw both arms over the sill and pulled with all his might. Two sets of arms

grabbed him and hauled him up and through the portal. He tumbled to the floor and lay still, gasping and wheezing.

Having caught his breath, he sat up. Deena and a stranger were smiling at him. The man was dark-haired and bearded, wearing a green doublet and jerkin, green hose, and thigh-high boots of soft buff leather. A saber in a gilded scabbard hung at his side.

"Thank you," Barnaby said to the man.

"'Twas nothing." The man peered out the portal, through which smoke drifted.

Barnaby got up and looked out. Buster and Jane had reached the far end of the clearing. They stopped and took one last look back at the portal.

Goodbye, new friends.

Barnaby heard them as if they had shouted it. He waved, watching the two beautiful animals disappear into the brush.

A moment later, the clearing went up in an incandescent flash and they had to step back from the window.

"I owe you my life," Barnaby said. "My name's Barnaby Walsh."

The man took his hand.

"Kwip's the name," the green-clad, dark-bearded stranger said.

Elsewhen

The ruins looked Mayan only because of the jungle setting, but the architecture was just as strange, the carved glyphs just as enigmatic, the hidden crypts as dark and foreboding. Froglike inhuman faces stared out in bas-relief from the walls of buildings whose functions were difficult to guess. They could have been temples, or just as easily dormitories or warehouses. Inside, bare rooms were laid out in bewildering mazes. In one of the larger buildings there was a spacious, rotundalike chamber which did evoke a religious atmosphere, and it was there that the foursome stopped to rest after touring the ruins. The heat was awful, the jungle air a sodden, mist-hung pall that shrouded everything, stifling and oppressing.

The interior walls of the "temple" were profusely decorated in enigmatic frescolike paintings.

"Real interesting," Gene remarked sarcastically, dabbing at his forehead with his undertunic, which he had doffed, along with his cuirass, in the heat.

"I think so," Linda said, examining a curious mural which depicted strange bipedal beings doing even stranger things. She couldn't quite make sense of it.

"Well, I wanted civilization," Gene said, stalking around the huge polygonal room. "I didn't count on a dead one, though."

"No," Linda said, "I guess there's no chance of finding a super-weapon here."

"A knife, maybe, good for cutting out the hearts of sacrificial victims."

"Yuck."

"Don't worry. If they indulged in that sort of thing, they're long dead."

Snowclaw said, "*Ghallarst miggan.*"

"I was wondering how it was affecting you," Gene said, walking over to his white-furred friend.

Snowclaw sat down wearily on a stone bench and let his sword clatter to the floor. "*Hallahust ullum nogakk, tuir ullum miggast kwahnahg.*"

"Don't die on us, Snowy," Gene said, laying a hand on Snowclaw's snout and turning his head a bit. "Your eyes do look glazed."

"How can you understand what he's saying?" Sheila asked.

"I don't, not really," Gene said. "But you can get the general drift. I've been listening to his jabber for almost a year now, while at the same time listening to a simultaneous translation. You get to the point where the jabber becomes semi-intelligible."

"That's amazing," Sheila said. "Back in the castle I could understand Snowy perfectly, even though I knew he was doing a lot of barking and growling. But now it sounds just like a lot of barking and growling."

"Yeah, I know what you mean. It took me a long time before I could understand him at all this way."

"But I still don't see how."

"Well, I heard somebody say once that if you watched enough foreign movies with subtitles, you'd eventually learn the languages. I never believed it, but it seems to be true. Either that or it's some kind of holdover effect of the castle's magic. I really don't know."

"What's Snowy saying?"

"He says he can't stand the heat, and that he has to cool off somehow, and soon, or he'll get really sick. He may even die."

"Oh, no."

"Yeah, it's going to be a problem."

"*Hallosk ullum banthahlk nak gethakk.*"

Gene answered, "Sorry, chum. I wish there was something I could do."

Snowclaw said something else, and Gene nodded.

"What did he say?" Sheila asked.

"He said he'd be okay, but not to count on him in a fight. He's not feeling up to snuff."

"Poor baby." Sheila went over to Snowclaw and stroked the top of his massive head. Snowy encircled her waist with a sinewy arm and squeezed gently.

"Well, wonderful," Gene declared. "Here we are, stuck somewhere in the goddamn eightieth dimension. Just our luck. We had our choice

of worlds — universes, for Christ's sake! What do we do? We pick some wild, jerkwater aspect that appears in the castle every two hundred years, or something. We buy ourselves a one-way ticket to Rod Serling's game room, that's what we do."

"It won't do any good to complain," Linda said.

"Do you mind if I complain just a little bit?"

"Be my guest," Linda answered with a shrug.

Gene stared at the floor awhile, then said, "I'm sorry, Linda. You're right."

"Forget it, Gene. There really isn't much we can do."

"What we have to do is some thinking." Gene plopped down on the edge of a circular stone platform that could have been an altar, or perhaps a stage or dais. "Thing is, I don't have a thought in my head. How do we go about chasing down a portal that could appear anywhere in this world, if it ever appears again?"

"It may crop up somewhere near," Linda said. "We just have to keep a sharp eye out for it."

"Our chances are pretty slim, Linda. We might just have to face that."

Linda looked away, her face set grimly. "I'm not sure I can. I don't have any magic here. I'm back to being what I was back home. Sort of a nothing."

"Linda, don't say that."

"It's true."

Gene frowned reproachfully. "You're not being fair to yourself."

"Please don't lecture me."

"I'm sorry." Gene wrung his hands for a while, clenching his jaw muscles. Then he stopped. "Did you actually try your magic?"

Linda was staring off. She came out of her reverie and said, "Huh?"

"I said, did you try your magic here?"

"First thing. I got all kinds of weird feelings, but nothing materialized. How about you?"

"I don't think I'll be able to tell for sure until I get into some sort of combat situation, but I suspect I am no longer ze greatest sword een France . . . or anywhere else, for that matter."

Linda looked off again, head cocked to one side, as if hearing something in the distance. Her eyes narrowed. "Something tells me mere is magic here, somewhere."

"I sort of get that feeling, too," Gene said.

"But it's a different sort of magic. Very different. Not like the castle's."

"Yeah. Lot of help to us."

Brow furrowed, Linda fell into deep thought.

Sheila said, "Something tells me you guys will work it all out." She smiled wanly and gave a helpless shrug. "You guys are magicians. You can do anything. I've *seen* you do absolutely mind-boggling things, things that nobody would ever believe. And you did them as easy as falling out of bed!"

"Yeah, but that was back in the castle . . ." Gene broke off, something catching his eye across the room. He jumped up, crossed to the far wall, and stood with hands on hips, casting a critical eye over the strange mural. Moving nearer, he scrutinized several details, then stepped back again to take in the entire scene.

"There's something here," Linda said, slowly looking around the great chamber. "In this room." She stared curiously at the circular platform.

Sheila got up and walked to Gene's side.

"What does that look like to you?" Gene asked her, pointing to the middle of the painting.

"Where, there?"

"Yeah, that rectangle near where the thing with all the teeth is. Behind it."

"Yuck, what is that?"

"That's what I'm asking you."

"No, I mean the thing with all the teeth. What a horrible-looking thing."

"Some kind of demon or monster. And I think it's guarding that rectangle."

"What rectangle?"

"Well, it's hard to see with all the gingerbread. I missed it at first. Sort of ignore all that rococo stuff around it and inside it. See that box?"

"Oh, okay. Yeah, now I see it. Could it be . . ."

"Yep, I think that's the portal. And I think this place was a temple for the cult that worshipped it. Or whatever they did. It stands to reason that strange, inexplicable holes in the air would wind up being thought of as miraculous things. Doorways to the realm of the gods, whatever."

"Yeah, it stands to reason, all right. But what does the painting mean?"

Gene lifted his damp shoulders. "Who knows?"

Linda called, "Gene?"

Sheila and Gene walked back to the stone altar. Linda was standing in the middle of it.

"I feel something here," she said. "There's some kind of force, some kind of . . . *thing* going on here."

Gene turned around and looked back at the painting. "Hey, that's it! It's gotta be!"

"What is it?" Linda said.

"The portal materializes here," Gene said, pointing to the middle of the altar. "Look at the painting, underneath the rectangle. A circle. It's gotta be this thing we're standing on."

"That must be it!" Sheila jumped once and clapped her hands.

"If they built a temple around this spot," Gene went on, "it must mean that the portal appears here every so often." He sighed. "Of course, the question is *how* often. Every hour? Every other Tuesday? Once a year? Or maybe once a millennium."

They surveyed the room, looking at the other wall paintings. All were just as enigmatic as the one with the portal, if not more so.

"It'd take a team of archeologists to make any sense of this stuff," Gene said cheerlessly. "All the answers are written all over the damn walls, if only we could read them."

Linda said, "I guess the only answer is that we have to wait. Wait for the portal to appear."

Pennsylvania Turnpike, Near Bedford

"You up?" Trent asked.

Incarnadine touched the control button, and the leather bucket seat tilted up. "I am now." He rubbed his eyes. "What's that infernal buzzing?"

"Just a danger signal."

"Oh." Incarnadine looked back through the rear window. "Nothing but a trailer truck, it looks like, back about half a mile."

"That must be it. We're coming to a three-mile downgrade. If he's going to make his move, it'll be when we're going down this mountain."

"You seem fairly sure. It could just be a trailer truck."

Trent shook his head. "My spells rarely fail me. Get that gun out and get ready."

"Will do."

Trent increased speed. The cold rural night howled by, whistling through the car's air vents and a hairline fresh-air crack that Incarnadine had left between the window glass and the weather stripping on the door on his side.

A pair of bright headlights grew in the rear window. Trent's eyes shifted between the road and the rearview mirror. Incarnadine watched out of the mirror on his side. The truck drew up to the Mercedes, headlights glaring, its huge engine revved to a frenzy. It hung there a moment, then suddenly swerved into the passing lane. It went thundering by, plunging down the steep hill, a leviathan of the night, its flanks glittering with dozens of tiny red and yellow lights.

"What was that about fail-safe spells?"

Trent seemed discomfited. "Something may be up ahead, waiting for us. The car we saw back at the Burger King, maybe."

They drove on for several uneventful minutes. The road was dark in both directions.

"Are you sure your Earth magic is all it's cracked up to be?" Incarnadine asked.

Trent gave his head a quick shake. "Can't figure it."

Like the sudden deadly blooming of a nuclear fireball, the crest of the hill behind them lit up in a blaze of light. Something big topped the rise and rolled down the hill, approaching with unbelievable speed.

"I take it back," Incarnadine said. "Your lookout spell isn't fooling."

"Interesting," Trent observed. "What do you make of it?"

"Not your average tractor-semitrailer."

The thing behind them was twice as big as any conventional vehicle, its array of headlights like a blinding galaxy of suns. The windshield and windows glowed strangely blue, and yellow flames shot out of twin exhaust stacks at either side of the cab. Swooping down the hill at breakneck speed, the spectral truck howled like a psychotic beast chained in the fires of Hell.

Trent floored the accelerator and wheeled the Mercedes around a bend to the right as the road continued down the side of the mountain. The speedometer crept past 80 mph, edging into the red.

"Got your seat belt on?" Trent asked casually.

"When did they start putting these things in automobiles?"

Trent didn't answer as he mashed the accelerator into the floorboard. The thing behind them was still gaining.

"We'll never outrun it," Incarnadine said.

"You're right. I wonder if he means to crowd us off the road, or simply run over us."

"It looks quite capable of either tactic."

"Inky?"

"Yes, Trent?"

"I think we've had it."

The monster vehicle closed steadily. Trent began swerving between lanes, and the demonic semi followed suit. There was very little room for maneuvering; the right shoulder was narrow, edging an almost vertical wall of blasted rock. An aluminum barrier ran between the roadways. There was no emergency lane and no place to pull off.

111

Ghastly blue light flooded the interior of the Mercedes as the truck drew close. An ear-splitting horn blast rent the night, and gouts of flame belched from the twin exhaust stacks. The truck's contoured windshield looked like a phantasmal roaming eye, radiating otherworldly light. The truck tried to pass, and Trent blocked its path, eliciting another angry blast of the demonic horn. Incarnadine thought his ears would burst. The truck swerved right, and Trent dodged back into the right lane.

"Watch it," Incarnadine said.

"I can't let it get abreast of us."

The truck stopped weaving and crept closer to the rear of the Mercedes.

"You can't let it — " Incarnadine began to say.

The truck bumped into the rear of the Mercedes and backed off; then, engine yowling, it sprang forward and slammed into the car, its huge burnished grille looking like a shark's mouth, huge and hungry and slavering for the kill.

Another impact came, and the Mercedes began to fishtail. Trent countersteered and straightened out. Again, the demon semi lunged forward, but this time Trent whipped extra power out of the car's already overtaxed engine and pulled away.

"Steer for me, Inky!" Trent shouted. "I have to have my arms free!"

Incarnadine leaned over and grabbed the wheel with both hands. The car swerved just as he took control, and he fought to bring it back into line. At his left ear he heard Trent chanting a complex and mostly unintelligible incantation. Trent's fingers worked off to either side, moving in precise patterns.

The road underwent a sudden and quite unexplainable transformation. It changed color, from murky, half-seen gray to bright yellow. It also widened considerably, somehow acquiring a multicolored canopy like the roof of a tunnel. Streamers of color flowed past, along with geometrical shapes and strange designs.

Trent laughed triumphantly, taking back the steering wheel. "Shades of Stanley Kubrick!"

"Who?"

Incarnadine craned his neck and looked out the rear window. The truck was still tailing but had dropped back. As he watched, it continued to fall behind. Wherever the Mercedes was going, the truck either could not or did not want to follow.

Incarnadine looked ahead and whistled his admiration. "Neat trick, little brother. What do you call this?"

Trent flipped a palm over. "A shortcut. The tricky part is getting back to normal reality."

"Are we ready to do that yet?"

"Not quite. Enjoy the show."

Incarnadine sat back and watched the play of light, color, and pattern. Brilliant shapes raced out at them from an incandescent night, flowing past with ever-increasing speed. There was no longer a road now, just a long tunnel of reticulated luminescence. At its distant vanishing point, somewhere out near infinity where all the glowing lines converged, a brilliant starburst of light coalesced. It grew and increased in intensity. Incarnadine got the impression that it was getting closer.

"See that light?"

"Yes," Incarnadine said. "What is it?"

"I've never driven long enough to find out. Want to?"

"I would, under other circumstances."

"Right. Where's the demonic eighteen-wheeler?"

Incarnadine looked. "Nowhere in sight."

"Okay, hang on."

The tunnel of light faded gradually until at last the mundane turnpike again rolled under the wheels of the Mercedes. The terrain had flattened out somewhat. Clearly they were on a different section of the road.

"Good job, Trent. I liked your shortcut."

"And here's the exit. State Route 711, right?"

"I'm not sure I like the numerological implications."

Trent turned off the highway, gradually slowing on the long, curving exit ramp. The toll booths lay up ahead, on the other side of the overpass.

"There it is," Trent said, looking to the left.

The monster semi rolled by on the highway beneath, screeching its frustration. Incarnadine watched it come out the other side of the underpass and go hurtling down the road, a shiny black juggernaut trimmed in glistening chrome.

It rolled about a thousand feet down the turnpike before vanishing in a burst of crimson flame.

Keep — Family Residence

The room was full of antique furniture representative of many periods. On the walls hung ancient tapestries depicting stag hunts, tournaments, battles, and other manly pastimes. Many a quaint and curious artifact lay about: there were weapons, articles of military apparel, inscribed drinking cups, medallions, and other mementos, all prominently displayed in glass-fronted cabinets.

Ferne stood in the middle of the room at a table, upon which sat a most extraordinary device. It was large, taking up most of the tabletop, and in the main consisted of porcelain cylinders, glass spheres, copper tubes, and other less readily identifiable components. A small plate of frosted glass rose from the works inside a copper frame. The device was in operation. Blue sparks crackled within the glass spheres, and faint multicolored aureoles enveloped a few of the other components. The glass plate glowed with a milky light.

Ferne was bent over the device, twisting dials and knobs on a control panel. She studied a quartz gauge, noting the fluctuations of the small needle within. She adjusted a control until the needle stabilized, then threw a toggle switch.

The screen came to life with the images of three individuals sitting behind a long narrow table. They appeared human, and wore gray suitcoats over black turtlenecks. Their faces were pale and thin, and their eyes were cold, hand, and black. Short dark hair grew above their high foreheads.

"Your Royal Highness!" the middle individual beamed, smiling. "So nice of you to visit us."

"I am pleased to see you all," Ferne said. "May I sit down?"

"By all means, Your Highness. In fact, we beg your forgiveness for sitting in your presence, but we didn't — "

"You needn't apologize," she said, sitting down. "You doubtless know that this device merely projects my image."

"Of course. But it has been quite some time since anyone communicated with us in this manner."

"Quite so. I can't speak for my family, but know I haven't used the Universal Projector since I was a youngster."

"We remember. A most curious device."

"Yes. My ancestors mainly used it to bring wayward vassals into line. A sudden apparition in the night was usually enough to reduce any strong-willed underling to a compliant mass of jelly."

"One can well imagine. But why rely on a mechanical contrivance to effect such a purpose?"

"The device is not quite mechanical. It works by tapping interuniversal forces, which, as you know, are the source of all magical energy. But it makes unnecessary all the usual appurtenances and folderol — talismans, chanting, gestures, and the like. Long-distance image projection requires subtle spellcasting. This instrument facilitates the process greatly. The device is quite ancient, though, and is somewhat crude. But it does work."

The middle one smiled warmly. "In any event, we are always glad to talk with you, regardless of the means used."

"Thank you. May we now proceed to the main order of business?"

"Certainly."

"I assume you received my last communication."

The one on the left spoke. "Yes, Your Royal Highness. We have given your proposal a great deal of study."

"And?"

The individual on the right answered. "We find much of merit. We regret to say, however, that the terms are not entirely satisfactory."

Ferne's dark eyebrows curled down. "If I may ask, what specifically is not to your liking?"

"Well, there are a number of specific issues," the middle one said. "But we think it safe to say that the question of sharing power is the main stumbling block."

"Ah." Ferne nodded. "I had a feeling it would be."

The one on the right said, "Generally speaking, we do not feel that the rewards specified are commensurate with services rendered."

"You want more worlds under your exclusive control."

"Actually," the middle one said apologetically, "to be very blunt about it, we think that your offer was totally inadequate. Of course, we would be willing to negotiate on the final number, but we were thinking orders of magnitude higher."

"No doubt," Ferne said. "But I am afraid I can't budge from the terms of my offer. There is only so much power I'm willing to relinquish."

"But there are so many worlds. Surely you can't be thinking of administrating them all on your own."

"Of course not," Ferne said. "Not even a tenth part of them, nor a hundredth. My imperial ambitions are quite limited. This sharply distinguishes me from my brother, who has never had any imperial ambitions at all. I think him absurd. Surely an instrument such as Castle Perilous deserves better use than to serve as a hostel for vagabonds and beggars. Hardly fitting for what may be the most powerful artifact in the whole of Creation."

"We quite agree," the individual on the left said. "That is why we feel that such a resource must be shared. This has long been a bone of contention between your family and us. As for ourselves, of course, we have no 'imperial ambitions,' as you put it. We seek only to impose a benevolent order. The state of the universes is chaotic in the extreme. We merely wish to establish a semblance of rationality."

"Oh, I quite agree with those sentiments," Ferne said. "The universes are in a dreadful mess, and so is the castle. And the unfathomable thing about it is that this has been the case ever since the castle came to be! Apparently the will to power runs weak in my family."

"We would not agree. Your family has jealously guarded its power, and its secrets, for generations."

"Guarded its power, yes," Ferne said. "Maintained it, yes. But used it? No. Absolutely not. What I seek to establish is merely a measure of . . . well, of *intestinal fortitude*. And it's high time someone tried."

"We seem to agree on a few general principles, at least," the middle individual said. "Surely this can provide a basis for working out our differences."

"Perhaps, but time is running short. The invaders will very soon consolidate their hold on the castle."

116

With a casual shrug the one on the left said, "From your description of them, we don't think they will be much trouble."

"Do not underestimate them."

"We believe we haven't, Your Royal Highness."

"Very well," Ferne said. "You are the best judge of your abilities. And I am quite sure they are considerable. Also, do not underestimate me. I am fully aware that there is a good deal that remains unspoken between us."

The three individuals exchanged glances. "Such as?" the middle one asked.

"Many things. True intentions, motivations. Desires and goals. Also circumstances. For instance, I am aware that what I am seeing now is not your true appearance. I have also gotten the impression in my dealings with you that your world or your society is not composed of individuals, but is in reality a single mass entity of some sort. I am not sure of this, but it remains a possibility in my mind. I remember asking you about this very point long ago. Whenever I pressed for an answer, I got only evasions."

"There is of course a perfectly logical explanation for many of your doubts and reservations," the one on the right said. "Our universes differ widely in many respects. In fact, the differences are profound enough to greatly hamper mutual understanding."

"Doubtless so. I'm sure a mere mortal could never understand beings such as you."

"Forgive our saying this, but your terminology is somewhat inappropriate."

"Is it? Only you would know. But let us return to concretes. In return for the privileges I have accorded you, you will aid my brother Deems and me in our fight to take back our family stronghold from the invaders who have usurped it. If we are successful, I am willing to provide you with exclusive access to a few hundred universes of your choice. You will be free to do what you want with them. That is the sum and substance of my proposal. Do you accept or not?"

"In principle, yes," the middle individual said. "However — "

"That is all I am willing to offer. I am afraid I am not disposed to negotiate any further."

The three were silent for a moment. Then die individual in the middle said, "We will have to confer and give you our answer at a later date."

"I want it in an hour."

"We need time to — "

"I want your answer in an hour," she said tightly.

There was a pause. Then: "As you wish."

"I will call you."

She flipped the toggle, and the images faded. With some effort, she rose from the chair.

The far door opened and Deems came in.

"Did you communicate with them?" he asked, walking over.

"Yes," she said.

"Are you ill? You look peaked. Let me get you some refreshment."

"Thank you. Negotiating with them is draining. Don't you remember how it was?"

Deems went to a small cabinet and took out a bottle of sherry and two glasses. He filled both glasses and gave one to Ferne, who had seated herself on a recliner. "We all toyed with the Hosts of Hell at one time or another. Fascinating lot. Hideously dangerous, of course, which made them all the more alluring to the young and disgruntled. Yes, I well remember their incessant attempts to seduce one of us into letting them out of their hellhole." Deems sighed disconsolately. "And I suppose they've finally succeeded."

"Had they accomplished it when we were children, they would have overrun the castle."

"And would have taken control of Creation."

"Perhaps, although I think it's possible to overestimate them. They are powerful, but surely not godlike."

"Be that as it may, I hope you and Inky can control them, as you claim you can. There'll be hell to pay — quite literally, I should imagine! — if you're mistaken."

"You worry too much, Deems. You always did."

"What if Inky doesn't give in? Do you really need him?"

"No, not really. I think I have a few things over on Inky these days. Though his cooperation would make things a little easier, I admit."

Deems looked at her askance. "Why do I have trouble believing you?"

She laughed. "Don't be silly. I've told you everything. You have no reason to doubt me. Besides, what do you care about all this? You'll get your gold, one way or another."

Chewing his lip and looking dissatisfied, Deems sat down on an ancient thronelike chair and threw one chain-mailed leg up over the armrest. "Don't think I don't care about Perilous."

She laughed scornfully. "Deems, you've never cared for anything but drinking, wenching, and the occasional brawl."

"I don't deny that, but it doesn't mean I'd suffer lightly the destruction of my family's ancestral home."

"There won't be any destruction, Deems. Not unless Inky chooses to detransmogrify the castle."

Deems sat up. "Gods. Do you think he would?"

"Undoing the spell that maintains the castle and then immediately recasting the spell would be the optimum solution for him. In the process, everything and everyone in the place would . . . well, *vanish* for want of a better word. No one really knows what happens. In any event, it would be a new shuffle of the deck. Recast the spell, transform the demon back into a castle, and everything reverts to what it was before any of this started." She took a sip of wine. "Of course, there is one problem. All of that is vastly more easy to say than to do. He was lucky once, a year or so ago. I don't think he'd risk it again. He'll see the wisdom of compromise. Eventually."

"You must open the gateway for him."

"No! Let him stew a while longer yet. We have to convince him we mean business."

"What if he breaks through on his own?"

"If he does, we take him into custody. It's that simple."

"Nothing is simple with old Inky, Ferne. You ought to know that."

"Oh, I know. I know."

Deems sat back and stared moodily into his glass. "If you would have suggested to me that we would have to deal with the Hosts, I would never have gone along with this. I would have taken Inky's side — gold or no gold — and would have fought you tooth and nail."

"I realize that," she said. "But that's not what happened. Is it?"

Deems fell silent for a long spell. Then he took a deep breath. "Damn me." He drained his glass in one gulp. "I've been a bloody fool."

"It's a little too late to back out, Deems dear."

"I've got to talk to Inky."

"No! You can't reach him."

"The Projector."

"I wouldn't advise it."

"Advise me no advice, woman." He rose, crossed to the table that held the Projector, and began fiddling with the device's control panel.

"Deems, Deems," she said in mock lament. "The Projector merely channels a spell and gives it form. The operator has to provide the mental energy."

"I know there's a simple spell that sets up the device. Then it's merely a matter of calibrating — "

"Yes, you can find a book of standard utility spells — in the library. Your problem is fighting your way through hordes of invaders to get there."

Deems stopped fiddling and thrust his fists against his hips, glaring at his sister. "Damned meddling bitch!"

"How *dare* you speak that way to me."

"I'll speak any way I bloody well — " He broke off. Brow lowered, Deems eyed her as if seeing both her and the situation anew. "You never meant to bargain with Inky, did you? You want to keep him out of the castle. Do away with him entirely, if you have to. Isn't that true?"

Ferne settled back in the recliner and lifted the glass to her lips. "And if it is?" she said quietly.

"But . . ." He threw out his arms helplessly. "But you can't hope to prevail against the Hosts by yourself! Surely you don't think yourself the equal of Inky as a magician. No one is. He's the master of Perilous! Only he can tap the castle's deepest source of power."

"Because he's a man?"

Deems was brought up short. "Eh? Because he's a — ? Well . . . yes!" He shrugged expansively. "I *suppose*."

"You suppose."

"This is ridiculous! Females may succeed to the throne only in the absence of a suitable male heir apparent. You know that as well as I do. What of it?"

"That is the tradition. But it has no bearing on who may tap the castle's power. You silly men have simply got to realize — "

Deems silenced her with an upraised hand. "Stop confusing the issue! I see now what you've done, and why you did it. This was all a scheme to divide the family, clearing the way for your bid to power.

You haven't the least intention of sharing power — with Inky, or me, or anyone else! You want all of it!"

"I deserve it," she said. "I'm the only one who's not afraid to use it."

"But surely you realize that the Hosts don't mean to share with you, either!"

"I don't know about that. They have certain ambitions, but they can be placated for the time being. Pacified."

"Appeased, you mean?"

Ferne's blue eyes turned to ice. "I needed allies, powerful allies! Who was I to turn to? You? Trent? Or maybe my fat cow of a sister."

Deems grunted. "Dorcas is the best one of a bad litter."

"Pig shit. I needed allies, and I found them."

"Not yet. Not while they're still ensconced in their hellhole."

She laughed, throwing her head back.

Appalled, Deems regarded her. "What in the name of all the gods . . ." Understanding bloomed on his face. Paling, he brought his hand to his throat. "The gods be merciful. Woman, tell me you haven't already unbuttoned them."

She continued laughing and he knew.

Ashen-faced, he sat down and stared at the floor. When he spoke, his voice was empty. "Inky's the only card you hold. He's the threat you're holding over them. The threat that Inky will return and detransmogrify the castle."

"And I have him bottled up," she said, still giggling. "Corked." She burst into another bout of laughter.

"It was the security spell on the Hosts' portal that you undid first," Deems droned on. "One of the oldest in the castle. One of Ervoldt's spells. No wonder Inky was concerned. No wonder he raced off to earth to find Trent. Trent specialized in ancient magic. Inky probably needed his advice. Doubtless Inky suspected Trent of having done it, but in any event he had to confront him."

Recovered from her mirth, Ferne regarded her brother with raised eyebrows. "Deems, this new pastime of yours may prove your undoing."

"Eh?"

"Thinking. You've done so little of it in your life. This much exertion all at once . . . Well, it can't be healthy." She took another sip. "Anyway, you're wrong in all the details. Details are important, Deems."

Deems slowly rose and crossed to the liquor cabinet. He poured himself another glass of sherry, retired to the leather throne again, and sank into it.

Suddenly he bolted upright and set his glass down on a side table. He fixed his sister in a penetrating stare. "Here's more thinking for you. If the Hosts have had access to the castle for — how long? — six months? If they've had time to send out scouts, or agents, or whatever, may they not now be on Earth trying to do Inky in?"

"I doubt it."

"You doubt it? Great gods, woman! You mean to say the possibility exists?"

"Well, yes. Before I stabilized the Earth portal, it was free for anyone to use, if it could be located. But why would the Hosts send agents to Earth?"

"To keep an eye on you, of course! Tell me, are any of your servants at your Earth residence?"

"Of course, some of my bodyguards. Their job is to keep Inky from — "

"Listen to me. Have you hired any new servants within the last six months?"

She thought. "Yes. Those bodyguards, in fact." Suddenly Ferne became motionless, a strange light in her eyes. She stared off for a moment. Then she shrugged, and drank the last of the sherry. "I suppose the possibility *does* exist." Smiling sweetly, she held out her glass. "Do be a dear and fetch me more wine."

Temple

"Try it again," Gene said.

Linda put out her hands and closed her eyes. A china plate with a hamburger on it materialized on the stone floor of the temple.

Gene picked the hamburger up and bit into it, tasting it clinically. "Better than the last one," he pronounced. "Edible, but still not what you'd call gourmet."

"It's getting a little easier," Linda said. "But I doubt if I'll ever be as good as I was in the castle."

"Well, that goes without saying. The castle is a huge power source."

Sheila said, "Let me see if I understand this. You're saying that this world is one in which magic works. Right?"

"Right," Gene said.

"But it's not the same kind of magic that's in the castle?"

"Right again. Different universe, different laws."

"But you say you're slowly getting used to this different kind of magic."

Linda answered, "Sort of. But, again, it's not going to be the same as back in the castle. Everything is *real* easy there. Maybe too easy. We got spoiled."

"At least we won't starve," Gene said, holding up the half-eaten hamburger. Then he looked over at Snowclaw, who was sleeping on the narrow stone bench near the wall. "But that doesn't solve all our problems."

"It doesn't solve any of them," Linda said. "We can't stay here."

"Right," Gene said. "So, I say we try it."

"I'm not up to it yet," Linda said. "If I can't conjure a hamburger right, how the heck could I do a portal?"

"Well, let's look at it this way. There are an infinite number of possible hamburgers. Now, an *haute cuisine*, gourmet, taste-treat kind of hamburger is going to be pretty hard to find out of all those others. But there's only one portal to the castle from this world. One. It shouldn't be hard for you to find it and fetch it here. You follow?"

Linda giggled. "Gene, you always have a strange way of looking at things. I don't think I find things and fetch them. I just whip 'em up and they appear."

"No, I think you *do* find things. How else can you explain your ability to conjure things you've never seen before? Like the first time you whipped up food for Snowy, food that you'd never imagined, let alone set eyes on. What I think you do is this. You send out feelers or sensors into interuniversal space and locate stuff. Then, somehow, you pull the stuff in."

Linda looked dubious. "How do I know where to find what I want?"

"I don't know. I'm not saying this is the actual way it happens. It's just one way to think about it. Skeptical-rationalist that I am, I can't bring myself to believe that you create something out of nothing. It must come from somewhere. There must be a law of conservation of . . . whatever. Mass, energy, you name it, even in magical universes. What you do is merely find stuff and transport it. It takes energy, and the castle supplies that. But the amount of energy you'd need to create something even as small as a quarter-pound hamburger would be stupendous! E equals mc squared — you know?"

"Yeah, I think I get you. But what's going to supply the power here?"

"This temple, maybe. You said you could feel it. It's a different kind of power. Think of it this way: the castle's AC, but this world is DC. Actually it's probably better to say that they're both AC, but not in phase — but forget that, forget that. Do you get the drift?"

"Gotcha," Linda said.

"I understand it," Sheila said. "I think you ought to go ahead and try, Linda."

"I'm game," Linda said.

Gene got up and searched the stone floor. "I saw some markings over here. Yeah, here's one of them. See this circle?"

"There's another over there," Linda said.

"Yeah, there are four of them, positioned around the altar. From what I can glean from the murals, four priests stood in those circles when they conjured the portal."

"If that's what they did."

Gene threw out his arms. "Hey, look. What do we have to lose?"

"Famous last words."

"It'll work, it's gotta. What I'm proposing is this. There are four of us. We each stand in one of these circles, and we all do our best to conjure together. It might work if we try to reproduce as many aspects of the conjuring ceremony as we can."

"Can't hurt."

"Wait a minute," Sheila said. "I hope you don't expect any magic from me. I know I don't have any."

"You never can tell," Gene said. "It usually sneaks up on you."

"Well, okay. It can't hurt."

"Yeah. You know, it is starting to sound like famous last words. But we gotta try it. Okay, everybody. Sheila, wake up Snowy, will you?"

Sheila did, and Snowy woke up with a start. Snarling, he lashed out with one arm. Sheila ducked, narrowly missing having her head taken off.

"Whew! Is he better after he's had his coffee?"

"Sorry, Sheila," Gene said. "He's suffering pretty bad in this heat."

"Oh, it's all right. He didn't mean it. Did you, Snowy?"

Snowclaw rubbed his eyes. He growled again, then groaned and got up.

"How are you feeling, big fella?" Gene asked.

Snowy made a gesture that said, "*So-so.*"

As best he could, Gene tried to explain what they were about to do. Snowclaw seemed to understand.

They all took their positions. Silence fell in the temple. Outside, distant hooting calls echoed in the jungle, punctuating a wider, greater silence. Dripping water plop-plopped somewhere off in a dark corner of the ruined building.

Sheila felt a warm rivulet of sweat trickle down her back, but she didn't dare scratch. Everyone looked deadly serious, and she didn't want to break the mood. She remained skeptical about the whole enterprise, but did her best to concentrate, calling up images of the portals she had seen. There hadn't been very many, and there wasn't

very much to visualize except for a hole in the air, which was a difficult concept to grasp, much less visualize. She tried thinking of the castle and how much she wished she were back there. Not because she liked the place, but because the castle seemed one step closer to the world she had lost.

But was that the way she really felt? Part of her wanted to go back home, but another part was curious about the castle itself. She had found new friends there, people who shared some of the same personal problems. Everyone had been friendly so far, for the most part. But that wasn't the entire explanation for her attraction to the place. Where else in the world — in the universe? (or universes?) — would one be likely to meet a wide variety of beings, intelligent beings, *who were not human*? She felt privileged, somehow, to have met Snowclaw. She hadn't seen many other nonhumans besides the Bluefaces, but she'd heard enough to have been struck by the wonder of it all.

Wonder. Yes, that was it. The place was *wonderful*, in the sense of being full of wondrous sights and things. It wasn't always wonderful in the colloquial sense — sometimes it was absolutely frightening and very unpleasant. But it was so totally different from her former existence. Life back home was boring, dreary, and full of small frustrations. And it wasn't entirely safe, either, what with wars, disasters, terrorism, crime, etc., etc., check any daily newspaper. So, what did her old life have to offer that her new life didn't? The food was better here, she had to admit that. Not here, in the temple, in whatever world this was, but in the castle, where she wanted to be now. She had to get back there, so that Gene and Snowy could beat the crap out of those blue guys and take the castle back — so Sheila could get something good to eat again! Yeah, she wanted to be back in the dining room with all that terrific food. Those blue guys sure were jerks! Spoiling everything —

"Forget it, Sheila," she heard Gene say.

"Huh?" She opened her eyes and looked around. Gene, Linda, and Snowy had left their stations and were walking toward her.

"Forget it," Gene said. "We'll try again. Maybe Linda needs to practice more."

Linda said, "Gene, look."

"What?"

They all beheld what had appeared at the center of the circular altar. Standing there was the upright oblong of the portal, dark castle stone visible on the other side.

"Let's go!" Gene yelled.

They ran through the portal in single file, Gene with sword drawn leading the way.

"Great White Stuff!" Snowy shouted as he came through. "I thought I was going to die in that heat!"

"You okay now?" Gene asked.

"Yeah, I'll be fine now. I'm never going to complain about this place again."

Linda was staring at Sheila. "You did it," she said.

"Me?" Sheila said. "How is that possible?"

"I don't know. I tried, and it didn't work. I couldn't summon the portal. You kept trying, and you did it."

"But — "

"Linda's right," Gene said. "It must have been your magic. How you got it in the temple is anybody's guess. But I'm guessing you had it here all the time and just didn't realize it."

Sheila lifted her shoulders. "Whatever you guys say. All I did is wish to be back here."

"Well, this is the only place I know of where wishes *are* horses and beggars go riding all over the goddamn place. You wished, and you got. Which brings up an interesting question."

Linda said, "Yeah! Maybe Sheila's talent is whipping up portals!"

Sheila said, "Huh?"

"Possibility," Gene said thoughtfully. He pointed to a blank wall. "Try to materialize a portal, say, right here."

"What portal?"

"Uh, well, let's go for the big money. The portal that leads back home."

Sheila's eyes widened. "Do you think that's possible?"

"Why not? Try it. Or any portal. Give it a go."

Sheila tried, but she just didn't know how to go about it.

"Something's wrong," she said. "Back in the temple it was different. Like you said, different universe, different laws. I can feel the magic *here*, though. Before, I don't think I did. Or at least I didn't know I was feeling it."

Gene looked annoyed. "This is getting complicated. You can do it back there but not here. Linda's the other way around. Now *you* have to get used to the castle's laws. Hell, why isn't anything ever simple?" He squared himself into a heroic stance. "Well, hell. Us John Wayne types ain't much for subtleties."

"What happened to Cyrano?" Linda wanted to know.

"That big-nosed pansy, fighting with those skinny swords? Hmph!"

"Gene, I think you're the one who's suffering from the heat."

"Hey, I'm hungry. How 'bout rustling up some grub, woman?"

"Right away, pardner."

"Yeah, *Samantha.* Wiggle your nose, cutesylike, and bewitch us something to eat."

"Okay, *Darin.*"

Snowclaw leaned toward Sheila and asked quietly, "Do all humans act silly like this a lot of the time?"

Sheila laughed. "Yeah."

It was Linda who saw the bodies first. The group had been walking down the corridor, and she was first to turn the corner. She stopped dead and put her hand over her mouth. Gene drew his sword, came round the corner, and halted. Frowning, he slowly put his sword back in its scabbard.

Sheila peeked around the corner. The hallway ahead was littered with dead Bluefaces, dozens of them, most in a profound state of dismemberment. The sight didn't sicken her as much as it would have only the day before.

Gene examined a few of the corpses, then turned to his companions. "Someone else is in the castle," he said.

Keep — Near the Well Tower

Kwip had been a thief most of his life, having apprenticed himself as a youngster by stealing fruit from hucksters' wagons in Market Square, in the town of Dunwiddin, his home. He recalled many a merry chase through the streets, keeping a half-step ahead of the constable and his men. Hardly fond memories. The life of a thief was bleak indeed; and it had never been bleaker the night he had paced his cell waiting for the hangman's noose at dawn.

Bleak, dark night of the soul. Night, as well, of his liberation. For a miracle had occurred. The far wall of the cell had disappeared, become a doorway into a great castle, one such as he had never seen or even dreamed of.

Better yet, here in this grand and mysterious place he was free to pursue his occupation amazingly unhindered, so it would seem, by the authorities.

Which detracted from the fun somewhat, he had to admit.

But there was a catch. Aye, a pip of a one. There was nothing *in* the damnable place. There was not a garnet, not a fleck of amethyst, nor a gram of silver to be found in the entire castle, much less diamonds, rubies, or gold; leastwise, there was none he could discover. The blasted sconces were brass!

But the food was fit for princes, and it cost nothing for a man to eat his fill and drink himself to stupefaction. The Guests, by and large, tended to be pleasant when they weren't minding their own business. Broadly speaking, the castle was a fine place in which to disport oneself.

If only he could find something worth stealing! Then the task would be to find a way back to his world. . . .

Ah, but then, he'd been over this same ground a thousand times since bumbling into the castle a year ago. There was no way back, or none easily found. And if he gave the matter enough thought, if he sat himself down and went about the task of sorting through his wishes, he usually found that he would as lief stay here. So be it.

Still, he hungered sore for some pastime to while away the hours, and questing for booty was as good as he could come up with. So it was his habit, at times, when the spirit moved him, to strike out into the far reaches of the castle in search of its fabled Treasure Room, which he had heard talk of. That such talk could be sheerest fancy, he well knew; but the quest was the thing. He needed it. It fortified him.

It was on such a trek that he had met the obese young man and his blackamoor mistress.

"You mean you ain't seen the Bluefaces yet?" the young woman asked him.

"Neither scale nor scutcheon of them. What manner of creature be they?"

She blinked her dark eyes. "They ain't got *no* manners to speak of."

"What I meant — "

"I know what you mean. They're scary, ugly blue guys with big feet and lots of teeth."

The young man who called himself Barnaby said, "That's about the size of it. No one knows what portal they came from. They began their attack about . . ." He scratched his head. "Jeez, Deena, how long has it been?"

She shook her head. "I dunno. It seems like days, but I know it hasn't been that long. Say ten hours."

"Has to be longer than that."

"Okay, say maybe twelve. Fifteen?"

"So, it's really just begun," Kwip ventured.

"Yeah, but how come you missed it?" Deena wanted to know.

"I was off in a far part of the castle. Outside the keep, along the outer walls. I had a fancy to explore some tall towers which stand thereabouts."

"Wow. You went wandering around alone? How'd you find your way there?"

"One gets used to the place. A servant showed me a tunnel betwixt the keep and the outer fortifications. I saw nothing of any disturbance."

Barnaby said, "Well, at least that means they haven't overrun the whole castle yet."

"'Twould be wondrous an they could. The castle's a vasty barn. Sometimes I think there's no end to it."

"I know what you mean. Still, the Bluefaces seem to be everywhere in the keep. At least that's the way it's appeared to us."

Kwip stroked his beard pensively. "Very likely you saw what you saw. They seem of a military bent, say you?"

"Very well organized, tactically pretty good, although they're not the best swordsmen in the world. It's just that they're very efficient soldiers."

"Such are dangerous, there's no doubt. Well, there seems to be nothing for it but to hie ourselves through a suitable aspect."

Barnaby nodded. "We tried to, but as you saw, our luck wasn't very good."

"No," Kwip agreed, "but I suspect inexperience were more the culprit than luck. There are any number of aspects. 'Tis but a matter of knowing which to choose."

"Well, we'd appreciate any help."

"Aye." Kwip was not keen on taking two fledglings under his wing. Such obligations tend to slow a man down. Still, he could not very well leave them to fend for themselves. He had no wish to trip across their corpses in a day or two. "I know a place," he said. "I sometimes take my mid-day meal there. It's well away from the Guests' quarters."

"Fine," Barnaby said. "We'd love to go along with you, if you'll have us."

"'Twould be my pleasure, sir."

See that you don't get underfoot, Kwip thought sourly. Damn me for a softhearted fool.

They exited the room and made their way down a narrow corridor which led to a short staircase. The stairs descended into a great hall furnished in chairs and tables and hung with colorful pennants. They moved through the room to a far door, which opened onto a hallway. Turning right, they walked a stretch, then swung left at an intersection.

"You seem to know where you're going," Barnaby observed.

"Be quiet!" Kwip whispered.

131

"Sorry," Barnaby mumbled.

Kwip held out an arm and Deena bumped into it, Barnaby bumping into her. Kwip tilted his head, listening a moment to far-off noises. Then he crooked two fingers and beckoned his companions forward again. They advanced down the hallway slowly.

A tremulous wail sounded in the distance. It was like nothing Kwip had ever heard. A chill went through him.

They stopped, Deena and Barnaby instinctively linking hands. Kwip turned to them.

"The invaders?" he asked quietly.

"I don't know," Barnaby said in an awed tone. "I can't imagine what *that* was. Sounded like some horrible . . . *thing.*"

Kwip lifted his eyebrows, nodding emphatically. "Aye, it gave me a start. But many a strange beast walks this place." He drew his saber and motioned with his head. "Come on, then. And keep a sharp eye out."

They moved off. A few paces down they encountered a spiral stairwell. Kwip led them into it.

"I know a shortcut," he said.

They hurried down the well, their footsteps making hollow, muddled echoes against the curving stone walls.

They came out into one end of a long hallway, the T of a crossing passage a few paces to the left. Barnaby edged to the right, peering into a dark alcove across the way. Kwip decided to check out the intersection and peeked around the left corner.

Kwip had never seen a demon, but he knew the creature for what it was the moment he saw it. He could barely comprehend what he saw. It was big, about seven feet tall, and its head and face were a horror that he would half remember for nightmares without end. The eyes were not human, but seemed to radiate an intelligent malevolence like heat from the glowing tip of a torturer's pincer. The face was generally triangular, and the mouth gaped, heavy with numerous black, ragged teeth — charred stumps in a burnt forest. Its coloring was generally red, mottled with blotches of bilious green and diseased black. The torso and legs were powerfully muscled, and the three-toed feet ended in great curving talons. The area between its legs gave no hint of its gender, if it had one.

What Kwip found eye-defying was that the creature glowed with a strange interior light. The thing did not seem to be composed of ordi-

nary matter. It was as if the figure were a three-dimensional painting, an artist's embodied rendering of a nightmare. A diffuse greenish glow surrounded the thing, and banners of shifting auroral color played about it here and there.

The sight hit Kwip as one telling blow. His pulse stopped, his blood froze, and his mind emptied of everything but a numbing fear.

The thing apparently had heard them coming out of the stairwell and had tried to creep up along the wall. It stopped when it saw Kwip, its mouth widening into a horrible travesty of a smile. Then it spoke one word.

"*Death,*" it intoned. Part of the vibrations of which the voice was composed rumbled at the bottom end of the range of human hearing. The remaining, more audible component sounded like clustered notes pounded out on the lower octaves of a spinet's keyboard, combined with shrieking overtones that rasped against the ear.

Shocked into immobility, Kwip watched the thing raise a huge bladed weapon that was a cross between an ax and a scimitar. Faint multicolored flames played about the curious, evil-looking blade. The creature's glowing eyes nailed him with a look that pierced his heart, their hot, withering gaze searing the very nub of his being.

Hands yanked him back, and the demon's blade struck the wall at a point directly across from where his head had been. With a cascade of violet sparks, the stone fractured, pieces of it sailing off. Smoke rose from the impact point.

The next thing Kwip knew he was running faster than he had ever run in his life, and the thing was chasing him. He was dimly aware of the young man and woman running beside him.

They ran for a short eternity, the corridor an endless treadmill. Finally they reached the branches of a cross-tunnel.

"Split up!" Kwip shouted over his shoulder.

"Barnaby, this way!" Deena yelled, grabbing her fat friend's shirt sleeve and swinging him round. The two raced off down the left branch of the crossing.

The demon let them go and chased after Kwip.

Library

Osmirik was tired. He had lost track of time. It seemed that he had been locked in the vault for days on end. He had not slept yet, and his eyelids felt like lead weights. He forced himself to read on. There was no choice. Indeed, the fate of the castle might hang on what information he gleaned from the stacks of curious volumes that lay about the table.

So far, he had had no luck. Ervoldt's journal had proved a difficult read. The difficulty lay not so much in what the ancient King wrote as in what he omitted as irrelevant or of limited interest to the reader. What was sound editorial judgment on Ervoldt's part was vexatious obscurantism to the scholar. True, judicious paring had made for a lean and powerful narrative. Osmirik had marveled at the King's account of how he trapped the demon Ramthonodox and transmogrified it into a great castle. But exactly what supernatural means had he used to accomplish this feat? Ervoldt had written simply: "The Enchantment hath such Convolutions as to make the Brain fairly reel. I shall not bemuse the Reader by setting it down herewith."

Such bemusement was devoutly to be wished! But this was not the spell that Osmirik sought. There was another mentioned in the sections in which Ervoldt described his magical construct, Castle Perilous. The first of these chapters began with a typical understatement: "I found the Castle possessed of numerous Peculiarities."

Indeed. Ervoldt went on to describe the inherent dangers of the castle's unusual fenestration; Perilous had, in effect, 144,000 open windows, through which any manner of invader might trespass. There followed a catalogue of the aspects which the King explored, listing what was found therein and assessing its potential as a threat. The catalogue was short; apparently Ervoldt meant only to include a sample

of what he had found. "It took me a Year and three-quarters, trudging through and through the Place. Much did I see." Obviously the King had covered a good deal of ground.

Ervoldt went on to describe some particularly troublesome aspects, outlining what measures he took to ensure that they would be no danger to the castle. There was one aspect which he had found especially alarming:

> I did then discover a Cosmos like no other I had seen. Vast and drear and fearful it was, a place of blackness and despair, yet Beings dwelled there, having such horrific Lineaments and foul Mien that I bethought them Demons, to be numbered among the very Hosts of Hell. I did but escape with my Life out of that Place, and laid a Spell of Entombment on the Way that led therein, and the Gods forfend its unbinding, at peril of the world — nay, of Creation itself! I say, beware this Place, in which is contained a surfeit of malign Cunning.

This was the only reference Ervoldt made to the Hosts of Hell, and to the nature of the spells used to seal off especially dangerous aspects. Osmirik had searched through volume after volume of arcane magic, chasing down spells similarly named. He had found restraining spells, binding spells, immobility spells, and confinement spells, but nothing that carried the connotation of the Haplan verb *tymbut*, which Osmirik had translated as meaning "to place within a tomb or burial place." Ervoldt's offhand mention suggested that the spell was common, one that could be found in the standard spell manuals of the day. Indeed, the King had mentioned other sorts of spells, and those Osmirik had located. But he could find no trace of a spell specifically designed for the purpose of sealing something or someone in a tomb or burial place.

It was a puzzle. Why would Ervoldt use a spell of this kind? What, indeed, could be the common use of such a curious enchantment? Why would anyone be interested in sealing the dead inside their tombs? It was a common practice to equip burial places with magical defenses to ward off ghouls and grave robbers, but these certainly were not meant to inhibit the dead from getting up and walking out. . . .

135

Osmirik rubbed his eyes and looked about the tiny, candlelit chamber. He had stacked almost two hundred books inside it, and he had just about riffled through them all. He sighed, leaned back, and stretched his arms, his cramped muscles throbbing. Then he gave a protracted yawn. It would be so good to lay his head down on the table, just for a moment, just to rest. . . .

No. Lord Incarnadine had charged him with this vital mission, and he could not fail his sovereign liege.

He groped in the satchel for something to eat, coming up with a loaf of bread and a wedge of cheese. He used his dagger to slice the cheese, hands to tear off a chunk of bread. There was a bottle of wine under the table, but he was wary of opening it. A few good swallows, and he'd be out like a candle.

He ate voraciously at first, then slowed down as his mind returned to the problem at hand. Had live entombment been a common capital punishment in ancient times? If so, it was not widely known, but would explain Ervoldt's not bothering to be specific about the method used. Of course, he may have wanted to keep the spell a secret to guard against someone's tampering with it.

Of course. That had to be the reason. Still, it could be a simple and fairly common enchantment. . . .

Something clicked inside his mind. The only motivation for laying such a spell on a tomb would be an inordinate fear of the dead. Necrophobia was widespread in ancient times, and was no rarity even today. The ancient Hunrans, who were in Ervoldt's day called Tryphosites, had a cult of the dead — rather the opposite of a cult, for the Tryphosites believed that those who died became evil spirits in the afterlife, occasionally returning to Earth to work their devilment on the living.

Yes!

He tossed the bread and cheese aside. If Ervoldt had used an existing spell, he might have borrowed it from the Tryphosites, whose magic he must have studied.

Osmirik slammed his bony fist against the table. There was a book on Tryphosite magic in the library. But he would have to leave the vault to fetch it! That would be the bravest of deeds. The blue-skinned Hosts of Hell were certainly out there. Yet he had to do it. He had to run the risk of losing his immortal spirit to demons from the fiery bowels of Perdition.

Something nagged at him — a triviality, really. The blue creatures had not struck him as proper-looking demons. They were brutish, monstrous, and ugly as sin — but not quite what one would expect of genuine evil spirits.

No matter. They were dreadful enough. So be it.

He rose and went to the outside wall, feeling along the stone ribbing for the switch that would send the stone slab rolling back into its slot in the wall. He found it and rested two tremulous fingers on it.

A cold sweat broke out along his forehead. Keeping his fingers lightly on the switch, he bent and blew out the candle.

It was worse in the dark. He did not know if he could bring himself to do it. Could he face Evil itself? Could any mortal? He stood awhile in agonized indecision. Then he lowered his hand.

He groped along the table for the flint wheel, found it, and struck a spark. The oil-soaked cotton flamed, and he lit the candle.

He would have his last meal, then venture out of the vault to meet his fate. Surely no one could expect him to face an eternity of torment on an empty stomach. Besides, he needed time to cogitate. There must be an alternative, one he was simply not thinking of. Now where the devil was that bottle of wine . . .?

Pennsylvania

The Temperature Rose a bit as they drove farther west and crossed a weather front, but it was still chilly. The sky was cloudless, spangled with cold winter stars. The road wound through dale and over hill, farmlets sleeping to either side. An occasional dimly lighted window alleviated the darkness, the loneliness.

"Do you know exactly where Ferne's estate is?"

"I'll be able to pinpoint the gateway," Trent said, "which amounts to the same thing."

Incarnadine looked out into the darkness. "Bleak," he said.

"What do you expect for the wilds of Pennsylvania on a winter night?"

"A roaring fire, a bottle of good wine, some good music. . . ."

"Sounds nice. Want to bag out of this and go and get some of that good stuff?"

"I could hardly do that."

Trent shrugged. "Let the gods-damned castle go to the devil. Choose a world and live in it, never leave."

"I've often considered it."

"Do it. Let Ferne have the old rat trap, let her be Queen of Creation."

Incarnadine took a long breath. "What you said about going to the devil — it's looking more and more as though that might be literally true."

"Well, that demon semi back there wasn't Ferne's style, if that's what you mean." Trent flicked on the high beams, and the trees along the road loomed like tall gray specters. "Do you really think it's the Hosts of Hell?"

"I have no doubt. Naturally they'll be laying for me — us — at the portal. We'll need all the magic you can muster. Otherwise, we're sunk."

"Well, I hope I'll be able to summon the portal when we get close to it. Going to be rough, though. They've got it nailed down pretty tight on this end."

"Do you think proximity will make any difference?"

"Hard to say. All I know is that doing it from New York was impossible."

They came into a small town, turning left at a junction with another highway. Now and then, pairs of headlights came at them, receded into the night.

"Getting close?" Incarnadine asked.

"Yeah. It's off on your side somewhere."

A turnoff to the right came up and Trent took it. The road took a slight dip directly off the highway, then bore gradually uphill, a split-rail fence running along its right side. They passed a very large and very imposing stone barn, then a few other outbuildings.

"Some big farms around here."

"Gentlemen farmers, it looks like," Trent said. "The country estates of the super-rich."

Other farms rolled by. Trent took a side road to the left that arched over a hill, then ran along a winding valley, crossing a stream via a stone bridge. Then it twined upward through stark, bare-limbed trees. They went by the entrance to a gravel-paved side road that was barred by a steel-pipe gate. A mailbox stood off to one side.

A quarter mile farther down the road, Trent said, "That was it."

"Are you sure?"

"Yes. Want to try a head-on assault?"

"No. That gate looked pretty sturdy. Let's see if we can't find a hole in their perimeter defenses."

The road branched and they bore to the right. The road wound through forest, a chain link fence paralleling it on the right.

"This looks like the back end of the property," Incarnadine said.

"That fence doesn't seem like much," Trent observed. "Not even barbed wire along the top. Electrified, maybe."

"I doubt it."

"Then they must be confident of their magical defenses."

"One would tend to think so, if that big ghostly rig was any indication."

Trent pulled off the road, parked on the narrow cinder-strewn shoulder, and turned off the motor. He doused the headlights. Quiet fell, save for the sound of a cold wind through the treetops.

"Want to try it right here?"

"Well, not in the car."

They left the Mercedes and walked to the chain link fence. Trent raised his arms and traced small circles with his index fingers, looking off, as if testing.

"This is going to be difficult." He looked around. "Hate to do it in the open like this. If somebody comes along . . ."

"They'll be mighty suspicious but will probably drive on. Let's give it a try."

Trent nodded, then began to trace elaborate patterns in the air. After a time, thin suspended filaments of light appeared, taking their shape from the path of his fingers, forming a luminous grid that hung between the two brothers.

"Nope." He lowered his arms and examined the pattern. He was not satisfied. "No. It won't work. They have it anchored too firmly. They own the door, Inky. And they have the key. We'll simply have to go in there and crash it down."

"So be it. Are you ready?"

With one finger, Trent drew a diagonal slash across the pattern: the Stroke of Cancellation. The luminous design faded quickly. "As ready as one can be to die, which is what the upshot of this enterprise is likely to be. But first, let me deal with this fence business."

Trent waved out a simple pattern, and the fence took it upon itself to give up a few of its chain links, to the accompaniment of much clinking and snapping of metal. A section of steel mesh split down the middle and fell away like a torn curtain.

"Neat," Incarnadine admired.

They walked through the gap and into the woods, following a winding deer trail. About fifty yards along they encountered a clearing. In the lead, Trent stopped.

"One other thing I can do is give us some power. We're going to need a shitload of it. I'm going to tune it so that you can channel it for any weapon or defense you see fit to use. So just wish, and it shall be done. Think you can handle that?"

Incarnadine smiled crookedly. "Two days ago I couldn't even spell 'magician.' Now I are one."

Trent stepped back and again began to make motions with his hands. At length the pattern became visible. It was wondrously complex, comprising red, blue, and green filaments. Arcane geometric figures decorated with elaborate filigree took shape within it, along with subtle curves describing arcs of mathematical precision and elegance.

A high-pitched, agonized yowl, as from a strange, half-human creature, came from somewhere ahead. Various grunting and snorting sounds arose from the woods.

"The natives are having nervous breakdowns," Incarnadine muttered.

After a time, the filaments all turned bright blue, growing brighter as the seconds passed. Trent worked furiously, eyes caged on his work, his pale brow furrowed, fingers flying. Incarnadine took a step back as the pattern began to emit great waves of heat. The filaments turned blue-white and kept increasing in luminosity. Finally they became stark, blinding white, humming and crackling with energy.

Finished at last, Trent staggered back, flinching from the intense heat. "Gods!" He wiped the film of sweat from his forehead.

"I'm impressed," Incarnadine said, studying the pattern. "That's the hairiest-looking Power Grid I've ever seen. Three-dimensional, too! How the hell did you execute all those icosahedrons so quickly?"

"I nearly burned my damn face off doing it." Trent exhaled slowly, straightening his clothes. "But she'll hold for hours." He glanced around. "It's rained recently, so there isn't much chance of a fire unless we overload it."

The roar of some great, hellish beast rent the night.

"That is a distinct possibility," Incarnadine said, looking off into the darkness.

"The only thing that will save us," Trent said, "*might* save us, is that they will be dealing with the same unfavorable conditions, with respect to magic in general, as we. On the down side, they seemed to have learned very quickly."

They left the anomaly blazing behind them like an overloaded Art Deco neon sign. The deer trail continued for another twenty yards, debouching into a hayfield that slanted up a low rise. They struck out

into the open, crushing dry, brittle grass underfoot. Light came from over the rise, outlining the top of the hill.

"We should stick to cover," Trent said.

"I suspect they know exactly where we are. Whoever or whatever we have to face, we might as well face them in the open."

Weighty footsteps sounded just over the hill, along with a deep-throated growl. Then a ferocious saurian head appeared above the line of the hilltop, its fiery eyes sweeping the field below. The rest of the monster came into view as it topped the rise. At least twenty feet tall, it vaguely resembled a Tyrannosaurus rex, but differed chiefly by virtue of its fully prehensile, thickly muscled upper limbs, at the ends of which sprouted huge curving talons. Its eyes glowed like yellow beacons, and faint red flames shot from its mouth as it took each whistling breath.

"On second thought," Incarnadine said.

They dashed off in opposite directions, both heading for woods on either side. The monster swung its gaze between them, pondering which quarry would make the tastiest morsel.

Then it made its decision and sprang forward to give chase.

Castle

They found more dead Bluefaces everywhere they went. Blue corpses littered the rooms and corridors, lay like butchered meat in the great halls and stairwells. They marveled at the slaughter, surprised to be feeling a tinge of pity. It seemed certain that none of the invaders were left alive. If any had survived, they were likely in hiding or had beat a hasty retreat back to their world.

"Serves 'em right, I guess," Gene said.

"They didn't have to kill all of them," Linda said.

"Yeah, but who are 'they'?"

"Good fighters," Snowclaw commented.

Gene whistled. "Sure are. That means we're in a worse situation than we were with these guys."

"Same difference," Linda said. "Both ways, we're out of the castle."

"I don't know," Gene said as he bent to inspect a charred and blackened corpse. "Incarnadine and his Guard might have been able to take the castle back from the Bluefaces. But against whoever or whatever did this, I'm a little pessimistic of their chances. Very pessimistic, actually."

They walked on a little farther, coming into a large empty dining hall. A few more dismembered cadavers lay about.

"We'd better find a good aspect fast," Gene said, keeping his voice low. "I think this is the King's Hall. Isn't it?"

"Looks like. That means we're near the Guest areas," Linda said. "But I don't see a darn thing."

"Let's get the hell away from here and back into the wild regions."

"But we need a stable aspect."

"I think it's boiling down to this — we're going to have to pick the least objectionable wild aspect we can find and make the best of it. I really think the castle is a lost cause."

Linda's face fell. "I suppose you're right."

"But before we do that, we have to make sure that this carnage *isn't* the work of the King and his Guardsmen."

"Do you think there's a chance?" Sheila asked.

"No. But we have to be absolutely positive before we exile ourselves again."

"We might be better off back in the jungle," Linda said. "If it weren't for Snowy not being able to take the heat."

"Linda's right," Snowclaw said. "Don't put yourselves in danger on my account. Go back to that place. With Sheila along, you'll be able to get back into the castle anytime you like. I'll stay here and scout around."

"I can't take the heat, either," Gene said. "Sorry, Snowclaw, that's real noble of you, but I'm not going to leave you here alone."

"Remember," Snowclaw said, "I have a stable aspect to slip into anytime I want."

Gene laughed. "I thought you said you couldn't make it back in the real world?"

"Well, maybe I did, and maybe I can't. But it's no big thing one way or the other. Actually I never really — "

Snowy was silenced by a horrible, blood-chilling yell that seemed to echo throughout the castle. They all stopped, stunned by the sound of it.

It took a few moments before any of them could speak. "My God," Linda whispered, her face gone a bit gray. "Gene, what was it?"

"Uh . . . I hope I never find out. This way."

Gene led them down a short hallway that made an L to the left. After peeking around the corner, he beckoned to his companions, and they followed him up another short corridor, passing a stairwell.

The horrible yowl came again, and this time it seemed to boom from around the corner ahead. They hastily backtracked and took the stairwell, which led up. But more strange cries assailed their ears up on the next floor, so they climbed six more flights until the sounds diminished.

Linda gasped, "Think . . . think we're safe?"

"I dunno," Gene said, a little out of breath.

More bellowing came to their ears, but from a distance.

"Maybe," Gene said. "Whatever that is, I do not want to meet up with it."

"You mean with them," Sheila said. "It sounds like there are hundreds of them, all over."

"I don't want to think about that today," Gene said airily. "After all, tomorrow is another day. I think." He slapped himself on the face. "Shut up, you're babbling."

"I'm going nuts, too," Linda said. "Gene, I'm scared. I want to get out of here."

"Righto! We'll take the first portal." He looked around and gave a sardonic grunt. "Wouldn't you know, when you *need* one of the goddamn things, suddenly everything's normal. Like Sunday in the park."

Sheila began, "I think . . ." Then she trailed off.

They waited. Then Gene said, "What is it, Sheila?"

Sheila closed her eyes, holding her breath. She held it for a good fifteen seconds. Then she breathed out and opened her eyes, looking disappointed. "Thought I had it. For a second there, anyway."

"Keep working on it. I'm for heading that way, folks, but if anyone has a better idea, I believe in democracy and the principle of one man, one vote. Or one being, one vote."

Everyone accepted Gene's autocracy and followed him down the dim corridor. They crept along, wary of every shadow, Sheila hanging on to a tuft of Snowy's fur.

Gene saw something ahead and stopped, holding out a hand. A strange, hulking shadow lay across the floor, the thing it shadowed obviously standing just around the corner. The thing, whatever it was, stood motionless.

They flattened against the wall and froze. Sheila could hear her heart banging against her sternum like some wild frightened thing. She felt only numbness and an overwhelming sense that they would never get out of the castle alive. This was it; this was the end of her life. And she could not bring herself to be frightened.

Silence hung like a boulder precariously balanced. Then a rumbling murmur came from around the corner. It rose in pitch to become something far removed from a human voice yet somehow akin to it, eventually turning into an evil chuckling, a mocking laugh.

Then the form stepped out from behind the corner. The eyes of it were evil, and held them all. It raised its fiery sword.

Linda screamed. Gene's hand went to his sword but he had trouble pulling it free, as if his arm had suddenly turned to rubber.

Snowy charged past and engaged the thing. Metal clashed and sparks flew. Snowy exchanged a few strokes with it before the blade of his longsword snapped in two, singing its distress as it glanced off the wall and clattered to the floor. The demon swung viciously and Snowy jumped, doing two quick backward somersaults before rolling to his feet. A long diagonal line of singed fur ran across his chest, wisps of smoke rising from it.

"Run, everybody!" Snowy yelled.

They needed no coaxing. Sheila ran as fast as she had ever run in her life, even passing up Snowclaw. A demonic howl came at their backs and sped them on.

It took some time to realize that the demon had stopped chasing them, possibly because the answering cry of one of his comrades came from up ahead. Two huge wooden doors lay at the end of an alcove to the left, and they all ducked through into a huge room full of books. One of the doors had a hole in it, looking to have been battered in. Gene and Snowy slammed the doors shut, then began piling heavy wooden tables in front of them, laying the first on its side to block the hole in the door.

Soon the pile of tables and chairs mounted beyond the top of the doors. Snowy was about to throw the last of the oak tables on top of the pile when there was a flash and the pile flew to splinters amid a shower of sparks. The smoke cleared, revealing two demons with fiery swords standing just outside the doorway. They bellowed triumphantly and jumped forward.

A huge steel door materialized in front of them, sealing off the entrance.

"That ought to hold the bastards!" Linda screamed, then burst into tears.

Gene held her, watching the door, listening to the loud banging sounds that had begun, coming from the other side.

"They'll cut through that steel eventually," he said.

"It's two feet thick," Linda said, drying her eyes. "Oh, Gene, they're the evilest things in the world. Horrible, horrible — "

"They won't get us, Linda. I promise. I won't let them."

They all backed away from the door. Sheila clung to Snowclaw, wanting to lose herself in the forest of his warm fur. She noticed the smell of burnt hair and ran her hand across the burn along his chest.

"Snowy, you're hurt."

"Nah, just got singed a little."

More horrendous banging sounded, but the door seemed to be holding for the moment.

It hit Sheila suddenly. She couldn't put it into words if she tried for a year, but something had happened. She understood the magic of the castle. It was like noticing a huge feature of the landscape for the first time, something so big and obvious that you wondered why you hadn't noticed it before.

She let go of Snowclaw. "Gene! I have it figured out! I can summon the portal!"

Gene nodded understandingly. "Do so. Like, immediately."

"Uh . . . oh. Yeah, sure!"

Sheila looked around. The library was huge. The main floor held rows and rows of open shelves stacked with books. There were more shelves spaced around the walls, interspersed with study nooks and carrels. Above were two stories of galleries, with more shelving and still more books. Other, smaller side rooms let off the main floor, and she crossed to one of these, stopping in front of the high pointed arch that formed its entrance. The arch would make a good frame for the edges of the portal.

Now all she had to do was summon the portal. Easy in principle, but now that she thought about it, her general knowledge of the castle's magic would have to be refined and adapted for this particular job. It would take some time.

A fearful crash sounded, and the steel doors shook.

Sheila turned back to her task. She would have to learn her new magic *real fast*.

Estate

As Incarnadine, Lord of the Western Pale, sprinted for the woods, he wondered which way of dying would be the quickest and least painful: being crushed to death under huge reptilian feet, being burned to char, or being eaten alive, torn apart in the maw of the gargantuan creature that was now chasing him. The question was academic, inasmuch as the creature would most likely combine all three methods. First tenderize the meat, parbroil it to taste, then gobble it down after a few brisk chews.

Flames from the creature licked at his back. Something crackled around his head, and he realized his hair was on fire. Slapping at his head, he willed a forfending shield to cover him and hoped it would be efficacious.

He dove into the woods and hid behind a stout oak, peering around its trunk. The monster was temporarily blocked by the trees. It roared out its disappointment over losing a quick meal, streams of thin red flame shooting from its nostrils. Then, extending its upper limbs, it took hold of two birch trees and pried them apart. The trees snapped like matchsticks and fell over. The monster began to bull its way into the woods, branches snapping as it moved.

Incarnadine examined the hand-held missile launcher that had materialized in his grasp. It was a long tube affair, set about with gadgets and gizmos. It was very heavy. He studied it for a moment. He was not familiar with its type, but the device did not look overcomplicated. Probably a Soviet design. He balanced the tube on his shoulder and put his eye to the aiming scope. He centered the beast's thorax in the cross hairs and waited for a clear shot. Finally getting one, he squeezed the trigger-grip.

The missile whooshed away, spewing yellow flame and leaving noxious fumes in its wake. Incarnadine did not see it hit, but heard the explosion.

When the smoke cleared, he saw that the beast was down, its massive head wedged between two tree trunks, the glow of its yellow eyes dimming quickly. Then, suddenly, the huge animal vanished with a bright flash. Nothing remained but trailing smoke.

The missile launcher also disappeared, but with less fanfare. Incarnadine walked out of the woods and rejoined his brother on the meadow.

"Nice solution," Trent said.

"Thanks. Better than conjuring a knight atop a foaming charger, or some such poetry."

"Whatever it takes."

They advanced up the sloping meadow, soon reaching the crest of the hill. Below them stood a large manor house done in the Tudor style, surrounded by trees, gardens, and numerous outbuildings. Dim light glowed behind curtained windows in the main house.

"So far, so good," Trent said. "What next, I wonder?"

As if in answer, a bright green shaft of energy lanced out from what looked like a large tool shed near the house. A blinding green aura enveloped the two brothers, outlining the bell-shaped forfending shields around each of them.

Trent made circles with his index fingers, moving first clockwise, then counter. "Okay, they don't have enough power here to get through our shields using the fancy high-tech stuff."

"Maybe we have a ghost of a chance after all."

"Maybe. The stuff they do have is nothing to sneeze at. Looks like it might boil down to swordplay, though. I can't figure it. They must not be connected to their continuum."

"Hope springs eternal. I thought they'd be running a channel right through the castle to here."

"That's what I figured. But maybe Ferne's still holding out."

"I don't see how she could be," Incarnadine said. "But more power to her. For the moment."

Another bolt, this one a bright magenta, shot out from the trees.

"Testing different frequencies," Trent said. "Maybe they'll find one that works. In the meantime, this will keep them honest."

Trent raised his arm and pointed at the source of the firing. A blue-white shaft of energy speared out from his fingertip and hit the shed, which disintegrated in a fiery explosion.

"Good shooting," Incarnadine said.

A sudden droning came from above — the motor of a plane. Looking up, they could see its outline against the stars. The plane banked, then went into a screaming dive.

"Sounds like a Stuka," Trent said. "The bombs we can live with, but it could strafe us with silver bullets."

Tiny sparks of flame budded along the black outline of the bomber, and the rattle of machine guns sounded. A few slugs chunked into the earth at Incarnadine's feet.

Behind them, something rose from the trees on a pillar of fire and streaked into the night, heading along a collision course with the plane. Within a few seconds, missile and plane met in the air about midway between the house and the top of the knoll. A brilliant star-burst of light blossomed at their joining. Almost simultaneously, a huge explosion tore up the meadow about twenty yards in front of where the brothers stood. A second bomb hit just behind them, splattering chunks of frozen brown earth.

"Think we should take cover?" Incarnadine asked when the smoke and dust had cleared.

"Not yet. I can't say I've been really impressed by anything so far."

"You didn't have that reptile chasing you."

"I concede the point. But I wonder why they're holding back? Toying with us?"

"Trent, it may just be that they're as chary of us as we are of them."

"Gee, think of that. Let's get closer."

"Hold on."

Many things began to happen. Great winged beasts appeared, defecating balls of fire as they flapped their huge pinions overhead. A motley troop of creatures — variously taloned and beaked, chitinous and scutellate, some with claws, others with pinchers — began charging up the hill. Amorphous shapes slithered out of shadow, leaping and gibbering. Vapors coalesced and churned with demonic energy, advancing like tornadoes. The grass was alive with fang-bearing homunculi that screamed and chittered their venomous hatred.

"A shooting gallery!" Trent said, both index fingers raised and spewing multicolored fire. "Have fun!"

"It may be our last chance," Incarnadine said as his first shot dehorned a seven-foot-tall ambulatory crustacean with delusions of horror-film stardom.

The spooks charged and the bolts flew. Smoke and fire rose from the hayfield as chitin smoldered and scales burned. Great flying creatures plummeted from the sky, trailing pink and yellow sparks and bright blue smoke. Vortexes exploded, and brilliant shafts of radiant energy intersected in the night. There came swarming congeries of fiery motes, and bright tongues of flame, the sky taking its color from their flashing luminescence.

Incarnadine flamed a four-pincered lobsterlike thing that had advanced to within a few yards of him, and when the creature vanished in a puff of vermilion smoke, the armored, insectoid little hellion that it had shielded leaped at him like a grasshopper. He fired, diving to the right and rolling to his feet again, only to confront another hobgoblin, this one a nine-foot-tall cross between a praying mantis and a sexually aroused ostrich. Incarnadine hosed it down, then played his beam of energy on the blasphemous horror that wriggled and twitched behind it.

The battle continued for some time, stratagems being employed on both sides. Creatures would feint at one invader and charge the other. The brothers cross-fired on oversize and airborne demons, and generally helped each other when they could.

Eventually the stream of apparitions petered out.

Incarnadine burned the last of the big ones, then mopped up what remained of the salamanders and other smaller incubi.

When done, he turned to see Trent shaking off a small legless thing with big yellow teeth that was worrying at the cuff of his trousers. He kicked it away and spritzed it with fire. The thing squealed hideously, blazing into nothingness like a scrap of flash paper.

Trent walked over to his brother, smiling, his breath trailing behind him in the cold night air. "So much for the fireworks. I wonder when the real battle's going to start?"

Something was forming in the air over the manor house, something big. It was an image, at first blurred and indistinct, gradually growing sharper.

It was a face, a human face, dark of eye and square of jaw. The thin lips curled into a pleasant smile.

"Hi!" the image said brightly. "Listen. Can we talk?"

Castle

"How's it look out there?" Barnaby whispered.

Deena poked her head out of the niche and looked up and down the corridor.

"Okay. I don't see any of 'em."

"Let's move."

Cautiously they exited the niche and inched along the wall, their eyes wide and fearful. A demon howled somewhere close, and they froze.

Deena pushed her face against Barnaby's chest. "They gonna get us," she whimpered.

"No!" Barnaby said. "We're going to get out of here. Let's move."

Deena dried her eyes and crept on.

Barnaby stayed behind for a moment, looking back down the passageway. Deena reached back for his hand, couldn't find it, and halted, turning her head.

"Barnaby!"

"Shh. Hold it."

"C'mon!"

Satisfied that they weren't being followed, he started forward. Deena took a step, bringing her head around in time to see a human hand growing out of the wall.

She screamed and jumped back.

The hand grew an arm, which in turn got connected to a shoulder. Then Kwip stepped out of the wall like a ghost in the flesh.

The two were dumbfounded.

Kwip put a finger to his lips. "It's me peculiar talent. I'm glad to find you."

"How did you get away from that . . . thing?" Barnaby asked.

"The demon? By the method you just saw. I've the Creator to thank that wall-walking's a talent they lack."

"Can we still get to that aspect of yours? Do you know where we are?"

"Approximately. Methinks we'd best hide out awhile. A blind chamber, preferably with something to eat and drink in it, a wine and cheese cellar, perhaps. But any room with a locked door will do."

"Sounds good to me," Deena said.

"Aye. Now, do exactly as I say. Come here, lad." He drew Barnaby to him by the hand. "Take hold of the back of me shirt and hang on for dear life. Join hands with your ladyfriend, and whatever you do, don't let go of her, either. Am I clear?"

They nodded.

"Good. Now, follow me, and hesitate at peril of your life."

They lined up, Kwip in front facing the wall.

A hellish screeching came from the left. They turned to see a demon rushing down the passageway at them.

"Follow me!" Kwip shouted, striding forward. He merged with the stone and was absorbed into it. Unbelieving but unwilling to be left behind, Barnaby and Deena followed.

The passage through the stone was like walking in water. Mercifully the experience was of short duration. They emerged into another hallway.

"That was *weird*," Deena said.

Kwip glanced around. "And again."

They ghosted through the opposite wall. This time they came out in a book-crammed chamber lit by a single candle that had almost burned itself out.

Kwip barked a shin against the tome-littered table that filled most of the floor space. "Gods of a pig's arse!" Rubbing his leg, he looked around. "Well, food for thought, at any rate. This will do, I suppose. No demon will get in here."

They heard a disgruntled moan. It had come from beneath the table.

Kwip drew his saber, knocking over a stack of books. Then a head appeared above the tabletop. The glazed eyes of a slight, balding man regarded the intruders.

"Greetings." The man belched. "If you don't mind my asking, how in the name of all the gods did you get in here?"

"It's the librarian," Kwip told his companions.

Osmirik squinted at him. "Kwip. Ah, Kwip, my good man." Osmirik struggled to his feet. Tongue a trifle thick, he licked his lips, scratching himself. Smiling, he said, "I'm glad for a little company. It was getting a bit lonely in here."

"Hiding out, then?" Kwip asked, sheathing his sword.

"Quite so. Ah, I see I have more than one guest." Osmirik smiled.

Barnaby introduced himself and Deena.

"Enchanted, my dear lady," Osmirik said, overdoing a bow. He was obviously a bit drunk.

Deena giggled, but enjoyed the scribe's elaborate gesture.

He continued, "An honor, goodly sir. Welcome to my humble lodgings, such as they are. There is food aplenty, if you wish refreshment, but I'm afraid I have nothing to offer you to drink." He held up the empty wine bottle and regarded it with much puzzlement, as if there were some question as to how the contents had disappeared.

"Thanks. We'd love some food," Barnaby said. "Is it safe here? Have you seen the demons?"

The librarian's face blanched. "I've seen them, sure enough."

"Here?"

"Not here. Those foul blue hellions won't get through that wall. It's as thick as a — "

"Blue hellions?" Kwip said.

"The demons. Blue creatures with intensively redundant dentition. Didn't you — ?"

"Those ain't the demons," Deena said. "You obviously ain't seen no demons yet. When you see one you'll know."

Osmirik sat down, looking grave. "I will?"

"Other beings have invaded the castle," Barnaby said. "These things are indescribably worse."

"Indescribably . . .?" Osmirik paled and reached for the wine bottle. Spying the dregs at the bottom, he upended the bottle into his mouth. He wiped his lips. "Demons or none, my duty is clear. I must venture out and get the volume."

Kwip looked at him incredulously. "Gods of a spavined nag. How the devil can you think of books at a time like this?"

"I must have the spell to give to my liege lord, Incarnadine."

"What spell?"

"The spell that will close up the demons' aspect. Seal it off, so they can't get through. I need the book that contains that spell."

Kwip nodded, rolling his eyes in appreciation. "Aye. Now, there's a book worth considerable thought. Whereabouts is it?"

"Out there," Osmirik said, pointing to the wall sealing off the arch.

"The library?"

"Aye, down in the open stacks. I must fetch it, be there demons or be there none."

"Well, there's but one way to decide aye or nay. I'll have a look-see."

"Be careful, they may see you!"

Kwip gave a wry smile. "I'm a man who doesn't fancy being seen. Never fear."

He drew up to the section of wall within the arch, stopping just short of touching it with his nose. He leaned forward, and his head and the top half of his torso disappeared into the wall.

He remained in this paradoxical state, half in and half out, for a longish moment. Then he pulled back.

"Something's up," he said, a strange expression on his face. "Abide. I shall return shortly."

He walked through the wall and was gone.

Library

SHEILA STOOD WITH her eyes closed and her arms straight down and rigid, fists clenched and knuckles white. She swayed from side to side like a sapling in a mild breeze. The others stood by and watched. Snowclaw reached out for her as she swayed, but stopped short of touching her.

They heard someone walking above, and turned to look. Gene drew his sword. The clanging and banging on the other side of the huge steel doors continued.

Smiling, Kwip came out of the stairwell to the first gallery. Linda and Gene met him halfway across the floor.

"Fancy you people being here," Kwip said. "How goes the world with you?"

"Not too darn good," Gene said. "Were you hiding out in here?"

"For the nonce, yes. I've been away. Apparently there's been trouble."

"A lot of it. Have you seen the demons?"

"Aye, and nearly soiled my breeches."

"Well, get out a fresh pair of undies, because they're right behind that door, making all the racket."

"Gods of a pig's arse! Then we'd best take our leave, hadn't we?"

"We're working on it. That girl there has a powerful talent. She can summon portals."

"The devil you say." Kwip looked over his shoulder.

"Well, she did it once. She's trying like hell to repeat it."

They watched Sheila teeter gently back and forth.

"I'd best go fetch them," Kwip said, then answered Gene's questioning look with, "The librarian and some others. I'll be back in a trice." He trotted back to the stairwell.

A loud bang sounded. Gene and Linda looked back at the steel barrier. A large protrusion had appeared on it, as if something had nearly punched through from the other side.

Another door materialized, covering the existing one.

"I can keep whipping up doors as long as we stay here," Linda said, "but once we cross the portal . . ."

"Yeah, and they'll follow us through." Gene bit his lip. "I hadn't considered that. Good God, can you imagine those things loose on Earth?"

"I don't want to think about it. Gene, we can't take the chance of summoning the portal!"

A wave of heat hit them. The clanging and banging had ceased, and now thin streamers of smoke rose from the door.

"Hell. They're burning their way through! Linda, we have to get out of here. Maybe Sheila can make the portal go away after we cross over."

"Let's hope so, or else we'll be responsible for the destruction of our world."

The door was glowing a deep cherry-red. Linda covered it with another layer of solid steel. The barrier now jutted out from the wall a good six feet. The heat dissipated momentarily, but then returned.

"That won't hold them very long," Linda said.

"Look!"

Linda whirled. The alcove that Sheila stood in front of seemed to have undergone a transformation. Then Linda realized that she was looking through a portal.

Kwip came out of the stairwell, followed by Barnaby Walsh, Deena Williams, and Osmirik the librarian. Without uttering a word of greeting or explanation, Osmirik broke for the open stacks.

"Hey!" Gene yelled, then turned to Kwip. "Where the hell is he going?"

"To fetch an important book."

"Book? Tell him we have to — "

"It's vital, trust me," Kwip said.

"Well, if you say so."

They all peered through the portal. On the other side was a pleasantly and expensively appointed living room. The walls were of dark wood paneling, the ceiling of dark oak beams. It looked like the interior of an English manor house.

"Looks like Earth," Gene said, smiling at Sheila. "Good work."

Sheila nodded. "It was pretty tough. Seemed like something was holding it back. Like someone had tied it down somewhere else in the castle."

"Maybe. I wonder where it's been hiding all this time?" He shook his head in wonder. "There it is. Home. God, I can't believe it."

Sheila glanced at the barrier, which had again turned red-hot. "I have to stay."

"Are you nuts?"

"No. I have to close up the portal from this side. I won't be able to do magic on the other side. It's outside the castle, remember?"

"But you found your magic outside the castle. Look, Sheila. I haven't given this a lot of thought yet, but obviously you're a major talent. Maybe your talent isn't limited to summoning portals. You also seem to have the knack for figuring out alternative magical systems, for want of a better way to put it."

Sheila thought about it. "Maybe I do."

"I think you could figure out Earth's system easy."

"If I have enough time, maybe," Sheila said. "But we can't take the chance. What if they get through?"

Gene grabbed her arm. "Look, there's no way I'm going to let you stay behind and face those things alone."

"No, Gene. It has to be. You take Linda back."

"Nothing doing. You're coming with us."

"Gene, I can't."

The ear-splitting groan of tortured metal filled the library. The door had turned white-hot.

"Sheila, go with him," Linda said. "I've rigged something up to buy us time."

They turned. The portal now looked like a bank deposit vault. An enormous steel door with a complex locking mechanism hung open on gimbals.

"It's three feet thick," Linda said. "It's set to close in fifteen seconds. Sheila, you'll have about five minutes to learn Earth magic. Run, everybody!"

Snowclaw, Linda, Barnaby, and Deena ran. Kwip, Gene, and Sheila stayed.

Gene said, "Look, if the demons take over the castle, Earth's done for."

"I suppose you're right."

An explosion rocked the place. Shards of molten metal spewed from a small hole that had appeared in the barrier blocking the library entrance.

Gene and Sheila ran for the portal. Kwip waited for Osmirik, who came charging out of the open stacks, book in hand.

When they reached the other side, everyone watched the huge steel door swing shut. It closed with a slam, and the complex locking mechanism hummed and whirred for a moment. Then it fell silent.

A few seconds later, the vault door disappeared. Through the portal lay a room somewhere in the castle. It was furnished with antiques and decorated with tapestries and other curios. A strikingly attractive woman in a dark red gown stepped into the frame of the aspect. Startled, she halted, regarding the group of strangers on the other side with some astonishment.

"Who in Creation might you people be?" she asked.

"We might ask the same of you," Gene said.

She stiffened. "Such impertinence. What are you doing in my house? Where are my servants?"

"Look, lady, we just missed being devil's food cake by a short hair. The demons were right behind us."

Her eyebrows shot up. "Demons? Where did you see them?"

"We just came from the castle."

"So it was you who moved this end of the portal. How did you manage it?" She cut short any answer with a wave of her hand. "Never mind. You must leave my house immediately. I cannot let you re-enter the castle this way. We are under attack here."

"We know. We don't want to go back. We're leaving right now."

"You there!"

The voice belonged to a thin young man in dark slacks and white open-collared shirt who had entered the living room by way of a door to the basement. He approached the group warily.

"How did you — ?" Then he saw the woman. He bowed. "Your Royal Highness."

"Anselm, show these people out. You know what to do."

"Of course, ma'am." Anselm showed a trace of a smile.

"I sort of figured that," Gene said, drawing his sword. Then his face fell, as if he suddenly realized something.

"Your sword will avail you nothing," Her Royal Highness said. "You are in the grip of forces beyond your understanding. Cooperate, or it will go badly for you."

"If you think I'm worried about this little pinhead," Gene said, jabbing toward Anselm, "think again."

Anselm's hand was a blur. It seemed to grow a wicked-looking automatic pistol. He pointed it at Gene. "You're the one who should go back to square one, friend." He grinned wickedly.

"You do have a point, Anselm old bean," Gene said, sheathing his sword.

"Very good, Anselm," the woman said. "How goes it?"

"All quiet, ma'am."

"Splendid. No sign of my brother?"

"None at all. May I ask how your battle fares?"

"Certainly. Deems and his men are holding their own in the outer quarters. Which is to say they are being slaughtered. But my spells sustain them. Even an armless corpse can be animated enough to block a demon's path. In the unlikely event my brother should discover the location of this portal, you will do your best to take him alive. Is that understood?"

"It will be done, ma'am."

"Good. I will put up the veil again."

The woman waved her hand and the portal became a dark oblong.

Anselm gestured with the gun. "Okay, down those stairs, all of you. But first get rid of all that steel. Throw them in a pile . . . there."

Snowy, Gene, and Kwip tossed their swords and daggers on the floor near a red leather easy chair.

"Right. Now, down the steps, single file. And I'll shoot the first one who thinks about . . ."

Outside, the night erupted in fireworks.

Gene yelled, "Rush 'em, Snowy!"

But Snowy had already begun his leap. Anselm squawked, stepped back, and fired. Snowy hit him first, then Gene jumped on top. The three of them rolled around the carpet until Kwip jumped on the pile. The tangle of arms and legs became a beast that shambled about the living room, upsetting end tables here and there.

"Jesus Christ!" Gene yelled finally, springing to his feet. Everyone unpiled, got up, and stepped back warily.

Anselm rose to his feet. Something strange was happening to him. Parts of his skin had cracked like an ill-fitting rubber suit. The cracks revealed an interior yellow-orange glow. The fissures veined out and widened, and the skin fell away in swatches, revealing the demon body within. The demon swelled to full volume as it shed its outer camouflage. The last of the skin and clothing dropped off as the eerily glowing creature topped seven and a half feet.

"YOU WILL DIE, HUMAN SCUM! ALL OF YOU!"

The house lights went out.

Estate

"What kind of deal did you have in mind?" Incarnadine asked the enormous apparition that had appeared above the house.

"I'm sure we can work something out, Inky old friend."

"I don't share your optimism. What do you have to offer, aside from what already belongs to me?"

"Well, we're not exactly offering anything, my dear Inky. In fact — "

"*I am not your 'dear Inky'!* I am Incarnadine, Liege Lord, Imperator and Gatekeeper of the Western Pale, and, by the grace of the gods, *King* and Sovereign Ruler of Ylium, Zephorea, Halmudia, Grekoran, and West Thurlangia! You have our leave to address us as 'Your Serene and Transcendent Majesty.'"

The face raised its eyebrows. "Touchy, aren't we? As I was saying . . . *Your Majesty.* . . you're not exactly in the best bargaining position imaginable. Now are you?"

"Why not?"

"We have the castle. In a very short time we will cut off the only access you have to it."

"Which means that you haven't overrun Ferne's position yet."

"A formality. What are mortals against us? Chopped liver, that's what."

"Well, what's taking you so long?"

"I have to admit your sister's not chopped liver. And neither are you, Ink — er, Your Majesty. Neither are you. Really, I mean it! Look, let's be frank. All cards face-up. I mean, *obviously* we have a stalemate here. I think it's high time we all sat down and had a serious talk about what we're going to do about the situation. Share ideas. Exchange information. Get to know each other."

Incarnadine nodded. "Sounds very cozy. I will also be frank. I'd sooner bed down with scorpions than sit at a bargaining table with the likes of you."

The face looked hurt. "Really, that's not very nice."

"You know that the moment I get back inside the castle, your game is through."

"I don't know that at all. You might not be aware of this, but the barrier your great-great-great-great — "

"You've actually kept track?"

" — great-great-great grandfather erected to keep us out of the castle is *gone*, Your Super-Terrific Majesty. Zip-bang, not there anymore. Okay? So, don't go making threats you can't follow through with."

Incarnadine was silent a moment, then said, "I really must compliment you on having mastered the local vernacular so quickly."

The face couldn't help being pleased. "That? It's nothing. This is one world we're going to insist on keeping. We work right into the mythology so well, it's as though it had been created with us in mind."

"If you look back far enough into your historical records, you might find that you did have a hand in working up the indigenous mythology, or at least inspiring it."

"Really? That's very interesting. But back to business. Isn't it clear that you will have to share power at some point? You people can't keep us back forever."

"I don't see why not," Incarnadine said. "In any event, I certainly won't be the one to give away the family business."

"Oh, you wouldn't be giving away all of it, now would you?"

"You would never be content with partial control, were I willing to grant it."

"Come now. I think it's about time you realized that your attitude toward us is really the result of years of propaganda. We get the worst press imaginable. Your family always had it in for us. It's not fair! We've done nothing, absolutely nothing to justify being treated so shabbily all these years. Discrimination! That's what it is, pure and simple."

"You have my sympathies. My advice to you is this — pull back your forces now. If you fail to do so, you will be destroyed."

The head shook sadly. "Really, Inky. I thought better of you."

Incarnadine raised both hands and began to trace a pattern in the air. "Foul spirit, destroyer of worlds, blasphemer and ancient enemy!

I bid you begone, in the name of all the gods of all the universes — get thee hence! Flee the wrath of the righteous, and trouble the innocent no more! Depart, I say!"

The face contorted with pain. The mouth opened, and a wailing cry pierced the night.

"Bastard human!" it screamed. "Filthy pile of excrement! You had your chance! Now you'll suffer everlasting torment! You'll all suffer horribly and die! You, your family, and all the get of the Haplodie! Die, you'll all die, die, die — "

Abruptly the apparition disappeared.

Trent said, "They really do fear you."

"Of course," Incarnadine said as he finished up the spell. "Their only hope was to take me out — here, in this world, where I was handicapped."

"Will it be necessary to push the castle through another magical transformation in order to get rid of them?"

"No, not with all the modifications I made when I recast the transmogrification spell. I can now draw all the power I want without the risk of blowing the spell by overloading it. Which was always a limitation, as you know. I installed a circuit breaker, so to speak."

"Nice touch," Trent said. "But we have to get you back inside the castle before you can tap any of that power."

"Not necessarily. Not if what I've been working on for the last few days proves fruitful."

"What's that? I thought you were trying to summon the portal."

"I gave up on that fairly quick. It was obvious someone had it nailed down. No, I came up with a gimmick that might allow me to tap castle power by means of an inductance effect through interuniversal space. I say might, because it hasn't worked so far. But now the portal is close at hand, and that might make a difference. I'm going to try it, anyway. I'll disconnect from your system first. Cover me."

"Go ahead," Trent said. "And good luck."

As Incarnadine made movements with his hands, things sprang into existence in the hayfield and in the general vicinity of the manor house. Swirling pillars of fire blazed up. Hordes of sword-wielding monsters charged. Various airborne improbabilities commenced their unlikely maneuvers. The sky opened up and began to rain fire and brimstone, and fingers of lightning jabbed at the earth.

"They're really slinging the crap now," Trent said edgily. "Everything they have, it looks like. This isn't going to be easy, Inky, castle power or no."

"Piece of cake, Trent old fellow," the King of West Thurlangia said as multicolored pyrotechnics spewed from his fingertips.

Hand in hand with Deena, Barnaby stumbled up the stairs. Darkness above. He reached a landing, turned, and kept climbing. He didn't like this option, but the demon had come from the basement, and he didn't relish going down there. He and Deena had to hide out somewhere, and the ground floor was out, having erupted into a melee soon after the lights had gone out.

They reached the top of the stairs and a long hallway, along which a few doors were set. Barnaby tried the first and found it locked, as was the second, but the third, which lay at the end of an L, opened onto a dark, sparsely furnished bedroom. They went in and closed the door.

"I'm hidin' in here," Deena said, sliding back the closet door. It was a walk-in closet, quite spacious enough to be considered a small room. Barnaby rolled the door shut, and they stood in darkness with their arms around each other.

"I don't know if I like this," Deena said.

Horrible noises came from the first floor: shouts, exclamations, the sounds of furniture smashing, and the odd demoniacal howl.

Barnaby eased the closet door open and looked out. The rectangle of the bedroom window flashed incessantly as the battle raged outside.

"Still shootin' out there?" Deena whispered.

"I don't think it's shooting, exactly," Barnaby said. "I don't really know what the hell it is. We couldn't be on Earth, because nothing like this goes on there."

"How do you know?"

Another voice in the closet said, "Can't you people see I'm busy in here? Damn inconsiderate!"

Deena tried to climb Barnaby like a ladder. Barnaby toppled backward into a tangle of clothes and coat hangers.

A match was lit and put to a candle. The form of a squatting demon became visible in the far end of the closet. Beneath its haunches the carpet had been rolled back, and a pentagram, executed in precise chalk lines, was inscribed on the oak flooring underneath.

It was a different sort of demon from the one they had seen before. Smaller, and having a somewhat rounder head, its coloring was a ghastly, cadaverous gray. Purple wormlike growths festooned the right side of its face, and festering sores afflicted its hide at various locations.

Its humanlike face registered extreme pique. "You think this is easy with all these distractions?" it demanded to know. "*You* try to cast an effective spell with all this commotion going on. And then if something screws up, it's *your* ass is on the grill. Try working under those conditions! And you just come waltzing in here without so much as knocking! Unbelievable!"

"Sorry!" Barnaby said after spitting out one end of a feather boa. He tried to get to his feet.

"Barnaby!" Deena screamed, pounding on his back. "Let's get outta here!"

"Capital idea!" the demon agreed.

It took some doing. The sliding door was stuck, caught on some debris. Finally Barnaby succeeded in rolling it back, and he and Deena crashed through into the bedroom along with a shower of hangers, peignoirs, shoe boxes, and other paraphernalia.

"I'm complaining to my union about this," came a muttering from the closet. "Just you wait and see!"

Downstairs, Sheila huddled behind a sofa, calmly shifting lines of force with the power of her will. There were lines that ran crosswise — north-south (magnetic fields?) — and lines that ran perpendicular, east-west, and she had no idea what those were. All she knew, in this early stage of her understanding of Earth's magical forces, was that allocating power was a matter of shifting those lines around. Of course, what she really didn't understand was the power source that seemed very near. She couldn't fathom why there would be such a strong one so close by. She knew now that certain points of the Earth's surface, certain features of the landscape, contained great power, and she sensed quite a few of those out there, somewhere, but this nearby power source was different. Anyway, she was tapping it, too. Probably badly, very inefficiently, but she was getting power from it.

She seemed to be able to see what was happening in the living room, even though she had her eyes closed. Snowy and Gene were

each battling a demon, the second demon having appeared shortly after the first one had revealed itself. Snowy and Gene were doing fairly well. They would be dead in an instant if Sheila were to stop helping them, feeding them the magical energy that transformed them into superhuman (in Gene's case; super-whatever in Snowy's) swordfighters.

Whoops! Another demon. Better do a Linda and split off . . . Snowy. Yeah, split off Snowy into twins. Wait. Was that demon another demon, or a doppelganger? If it was, it was a good one, so no matter.

By the way, where was Linda? Still hiding behind the settee; good. She was out of this, no magic at all. What about the others? The one with the beard was fighting. The small guy, the librarian, was — in the library! That guy really liked books! But there were others. A guy and a black girl? Sheila couldn't get a fix on them.

A fourth demon? Good Lord. Well, now she'd have to split Gene off, too.

They approached the house, firing continuously at unnamed and unnameable things which attacked from every quarter. A troublesome phenomenon was developing off to the left: thin, glowing tentacles like animated garden hoses snaking through the grass, trying for encirclement. Incarnadine tried bearing to the right, but two filaments met in front of him and completed the circle. Sheets of flame rose to form a dome of fire around the brothers. Incarnadine halted. He shouted a six-syllable word twice, the first time in a normal pitch, the second in falsetto. The dome broke apart, boiling away into pink smoke.

"Nice work!" Trent called. "Hey, I think it's going to be all ri — "

Trent leaped over the rapidly widening crack in the earth that had opened at his feet. Smoke and fire issued from deep within the chasm. The crack branched off and clove the earth near Incarnadine, who leaped to the right, then did a hop, skip, and jump over a series of smaller lateral fissures that gaped in front of him.

Then the earth settled down, and the brothers continued their advance.

Streamers of scintillation had begun forming in the air around the house. They did not look particularly dangerous to Incarnadine, and he decided they were probably by-products rather than defensive phenomena, but he kept glancing at them occasionally as he walked and fired, mindful that they could develop into something.

As he swung his sword again and again. Gene wondered why his castle-bred skills were still with him, here, on Earth. He was thankful that they were. He would have been reduced to cold cuts otherwise.

Gene parried a wicked crosswise cut, sparks shooting off his blade. He riposted with a lunge, then feinted to the demon's right side. He whirled, did a backflip, landed on his haunches, and slashed at the demon's legs, cutting them neatly in two at the knee joints. The body toppled over an upturned chair.

Gene lurched to his feet in time to beat off a lunge by another demon. He backtracked, steadied his footing, then parried three quick cuts, riposting to his opponent's head. He feinted to the thorax, then quickly jabbed at the eyes again. The demon backed off.

Snowy's sword was like the blade of a whirling fan. He was up against two opponents and holding his own.

He was thinking of how hungry he was.

"Somethin's happening out there!" Deena said, peeking out the dormer window.

They had found a relatively demon-free spare bedroom. Barnaby rose and looked out the window. It was hard to describe what was going on. There were two arenas of special interest: one, what was happening out in the field in back of the house; two, what was gathering around the house itself. The latter involved sparkling auroral displays that fluttered like sheets hung out to dry in a high wind. As he and Deena watched, the phenomenon grew more intense, partially blocking their view of the strange battle that raged in the backyard.

Barnaby sank to the bed. "I can't watch anymore. Is the door locked?"

"Yeah. No, let me check it."

Deena returned. "Yeah, it's locked. I — what the *hell* are you doin'?"

"I'm tired," Barnaby said as he turned down the bedding. "I'm going to try to get some shut-eye."

"You gonna what? You're crazy!"

Barnaby crawled between the covers. "What else is there to do? We can't get out of here. We might as well die in bed as anywhere else. Besides, if I'm dreaming all this, maybe I'll wake up."

"Well, move over."

Deena climbed in with him. They looked at each other, then pulled the covers over their heads.

"Singularity vortex!" Trent yelled over the noise of battle.

"Yeah!" Incarnadine agreed. That was what the sparkling streamers that had enveloped the house were beginning ominously to look like. The flux of magical energies in and around the house and its environs were starting to warp the fabric of normal spacetime. If the process continued, the house would drop right out of the continuum, possibly taking the portal along with it. Incarnadine wasn't sure exactly what would happen to the portal, but it would be nothing good; of that he was certain.

"We have to get in there," Incarnadine shouted, unsure of being heard. A six-legged, three-horned quasi-rhinoceros charged at him. He sprayed it with green fire; the thing fissioned into six smaller animals. He laid down a blanket of fire over these. Result: three dozen reduced-scale replicas, all maniacally bent on goring him in the ankles. They continued to replicate and reduce in size, Zeno's paradox coming into play. They would keep halving the distance to their target, but never reach it. Incarnadine stepped out of their path.

There was less and less to do. Another antique aircraft circled over-head, but was not quite so magically well constituted as its predeces-sors; its motor sputtered, then died, and the craft fell out of the night, crashing into the formal garden on the house's east side.

More monsters, these looking a bit threadbare: another reject from a Japanese sci fi flick; a dozen more hackneyed horrors from central casting; something that looked from the waist up like Lon Chaney's werewolf, but was web-toed and scaly in the other direction. It blew up very nicely. A second anomaly shambled toward them, looking for all the world like a gorilla wearing a vintage deep-sea diving helmet. Whatever movie it was from, it didn't get very far.

There came a lull in the action.

With a weary sigh, Trent sank to one knee. "Man, I'm bushed." He chuckled. "Getting old."

"I think we've just about broken their back."

Trent surveyed the field of battle, now empty. "No, they have some-thing left."

"I'd be willing to bet not. That last salvo had spell exhaustion writ-ten all over it."

"Maybe so. We'd best make a run for the house now before that vor-tex — " Trent reconsidered. "Hell, maybe we don't want to get to the house. I'm not sure I can deal with any continuum disturbances."

"I'm fairly sure I can," Incarnadine said. "Let's move."

Trent got up. "Whatever you say. You seem to be running the show now."

"I still need your help. Got your second wind?"

"I'm on my fifth, I think. I've lost count. You know, that inductance gimmick really — "

The earth began to shake, and thunder rolled across the meadow.

"Oh, hell," Trent said. "Here comes the finale."

The thunder reached a crescendo, then a brilliant flash lit up the countryside.

All Hell came at them. Incarnadine looked out across the meadow and saw the Hosts of Hell in full battle regalia, arrayed to meet the foe. There were fiends, demons, hobgoblins, imps, and incubi of every description. Some sat astride great horned beasts of battle, some rode fantastic metal engines. Most charged on foot, screaming bloody mayhem.

Incarnadine flamed the first wave. They went down easily enough, but there were simply too many of them. He prepared himself for death, reciting the first lines of the Prayer of Leave-taking.

He looked up and saw a burnished curving blade poised to strike. The scaled horror that wielded it regarded him with molten red eyes.

"Now you will die, Haplodite scum," the thing said to him.

"You send me to a better place, tiresome one," the King replied.

"You — you. . . .!" The thing was beside itself with rage. But it did not strike.

"What seems to be the matter, O Fearful One?"

"You . . . *shit!*"

Incarnadine laughed. He laid his palms on the thing's horny chest and pushed. There was almost nothing to push against. The matinee monster fell over like a papier-mâché dummy.

He materialized a sword and swung at another bugaboo. It split down the middle, revealing its chintzy hollowness.

"Spell exhaustion!" he heard Trent yell. "Inky! They've shot their wad! They're just buying time."

"The house is about to go!" he shouted back. "Let's get up there!"

It was easier said than done. They were flapped, batted, and swatted at by hosts of bogus fiends, all about as substantial as paper dolls,

and as dangerous. But there were thousands of them, and they succeeded in getting in the way.

Trent and Incarnadine hedge-hopped through the formal gardens, then encountered more ersatz boogeymen on the croquet court. They pushed, kicked, and bulled their way forward, finally reaching the outer perimeter of the auroralike phenomenon. Once inside it, the cheapjack monsters disappeared.

Invisible fists pummeled them, jostling them this way and that. Fierce gusts of wind arose and tore at them. Leaning into the wind, they staggered forward. After fighting their way across a brick patio, they reached the back door.

Incarnadine began waving his hands. Trent tried the handle. The door opened. Trent grinned at his brother.

"You probably still can't spell 'magician.'"

"I was always an overachiever."

At that moment, the bottom dropped out of everything.

House Over the Borderline

"Barnaby?"

"Huh?"

"Wake up."

"I'm up. Whaddya want?"

"What do I want? We were kissin', and then you go and fall asleep on me!"

"I didn't fall asleep."

"Yes, you did!"

"I'm sorry. I feel like I haven't slept in a thousand years."

"Yeah, me, too. But I was beginning to like what we were doin'. A whole lot."

"You mean this stuff?"

After they parted, she said, "Yeah, that stuff. And a couple of other things you were startin' to do."

A strange flickering light suddenly dawned through the window.

"Uh-oh," Deena said.

"That was quick. Sun just popped up, I guess."

"The sun don't pop up, never."

"Look out the window."

"You look out the window!"

"I'm tired, Deena honey."

"And I ain't? Oh, damn it, all right."

Deena got to her knees and leaned out over the nightstand and peeked out the window. Then she dove back into bed.

"What was out there?" he asked.

"Don't ask!" she said.

The bedroom door burst open and the demon they had encountered in the closet came scampering in. It went directly to the window and threw up the sash.

"Excuse me, folks, but it's time to bail out," the fiend said as it clambered up onto the sill. "So long!" It jumped off and was gone.

"Don't that beat everything," Deena said.

"You know, he wasn't such a bad sort, once you got to know him."

"Kiss me again, fool."

The demons were dead. Very dead. In fact, they stank badly enough to have succumbed days ago, and looked it as well.

"This one just crumpled up and died, all of a sudden like," Snowclaw said (in his own language, but everyone seemed to understand him).

"Mine, too," Gene said. "Jesus. There were only two of them."

"There may be others," Kwip said.

"Nope," Sheila said. "Those are the two who were causing all the trouble. The rest was magic."

"What in the world is going on outside?" Linda asked.

They all went to the window.

"Now this is extremely interesting," Gene said.

Outside, the sun was a golden arch across the sky, the moon a pale silver bow. The landscape was alive. Saplings grew into giant trees, died, decayed, and fell in a matter of seconds. The seasons went by, one after another, in a flickering blur.

"We're traveling through time," Gene decided. "I guess."

"That's absolutely correct," came a voice from the far end of the living room.

Gene and his companions turned to regard the two men who had entered the room.

"Hello again," said the tall, handsome man with the beard.

"Lord Incarnadine!" Linda said.

"Yes. You remembered. I believe we met only once."

"Certainly I remember . . . uh, Your Majesty." Linda did a quick curtsey.

"And I believe this is . . . Mr. Ferraro?"

"Yes, sir."

"And . . .?"

"Kwip of Dunwiddin, Your Majesty."

"No need to kneel. Arise, Kwip of Dunwiddin!"

"His Majesty is too kind."

"And, let me see . . ."

"They call me Snowclaw."

"Aptly yclept. Stout fellow. And this charming young lady?"

"Sheila Jankowski, sir."

"Ah, it was you. You were doing quite a good deal of spellcasting in here, weren't you?"

Sheila blushed. "Yes, sir."

"Excellent work! You saved the lives of your friends, and quite possibly mine and my brother's. I'm sorry — ladies and gentlemen, may I present His Royal Highness Trent, Prince of the House of Haplodie, Protector of Zilonesia, Vice-regent of Ulontha, Beloved of the Gods, Holy Warrior, Keeper of the Stone of Truth-telling . . . and so forth and so on."

Trent said, "Those honorifics and fifty cents will get me a cup of decaffeinated coffee. Howdy, folks."

Gene said, "Uh . . . sir? May I ask a question?"

"Sure," Incarnadine said.

"What the hell has been going on?"

Incarnadine laughed. "That's going to take some explaining."

Linda said, "I want to know where *those* things came from." She pointed to the cadavers.

"From a very mysterious aspect, the nature of which we might never fully understand."

"Are they *real* demons? I mean — well, it's kind of hard to ask the right questions."

"I know what you mean. Are they truly supernatural? I don't know. I suspect the physical laws that govern their universe are radically different from most. They do have physical bodies, however, so, as I see it, the question is moot. I'm sorry I don't have many of the right answers."

"That's okay."

Incarnadine went to the window. "Don't let all this nonsense out the window faze you. Too much magic in one place tends to be a little destabilizing. Not to worry. We thought the trajectory might turn out

to be hyperbolic, but it isn't. The effect will start to rebound momentarily. There we go."

As he spoke, the sun stopped in the sky over what looked like a Carboniferous swamp. Then it began to move backward. Night fell, giving way to dawn a few seconds later. The sun streaked back across the sky, accelerating at a rapid rate. Soon the golden arch re-established itself.

"I'm getting a Big Mac attack," Gene said.

"As I said," Incarnadine continued, "not to worry. The house should return to normal spacetime in short order. Any other questions?"

"This is Earth, isn't it?" Sheila asked. "I mean, when we get back to normal . . . whatever it was you said."

"Yes, this is Earth. Your home. And no doubt you want to stay."

"Yes! I mean . . ."

"There is some doubt?"

"Well, I'm going to miss the castle." Sheila slapped her forehead. "I don't believe I said that." Then she realized the gaffe. "I didn't mean — "

Incarnadine chuckled. "I know exactly what you mean. And I've been meaning to solve the one-way access problem for a long time. Please accept my apologies for any inconvenience the delay has caused you. Now that we have the Earth portal nailed down, I think we should establish a permanent access to the castle. This house would make an excellent way station."

"Where is this place?" Gene asked.

Trent said, "The closest town is Ligonier, Pennsylvania."

Gene jumped up and down. "That's a stone's throw from my hometown!"

"Mine, too!" Sheila said.

Gene stopped jumping. "How the hell am I going to explain where I've been? I've been away almost a year."

Incarnadine thought about it. "Well, this is a problem. There are some possible solutions, though. As you can see, we're traveling through time. It could be possible to stop the house just shortly after the time you entered the castle. We could cut it as close as you like. Or, as an alternative, it's actually theoretically possible to tune a portal to permit time travel. You have to be careful to avoid paradoxes, of course. Meeting yourself coming the other way, that sort of thing. But in principle, it shouldn't be a problem."

"I'll opt for the portal method," Gene said. "I'd like time to change into something less Gothic."

"No doubt."

"Sir, what about the situation back at the castle?"

"Well, as soon as we get things squared away here, I'm going to return to the castle to finish some important business."

"My liege!"

Carrying a large leather-bound book, his index finger wedged inside it, Osmirik ran into the room and knelt at his liege lord's feet.

"Arise, good and faithful servant. Whaddya got there?"

"The spell, Your Majesty! The containment spell for the Hosts of Hell! Your ancestor, Ervoldt, used this ancient Tryphosite spell for confining evil spirits. I've done a rough translation of some of the more obscure lines." He fumbled with a few sheets of paper.

Incarnadine scanned the book. "Tryphosite, eh? You don't say. Ervoldt was a wise old coot, wasn't he? Yes, yes, I see. This should work. Excellent job, Osmirik. I knew I could count on you."

"I am only too happy to be of service to His Serene and Transcendent Majesty."

"This looks like it has a decay time of a little over five thousand years. No wonder Ferne unraveled it so easily. It was just about due to go on the fritz, anyway. Do you suppose if we made some modifications we could increase the effective time — say, here . . . and here?"

Osmirik looked over the King's shoulder. "Oh, I should say so, Your Majesty."

Incarnadine read the section through again, nodding. "Yes, it should work." He closed the book and handed it back to the librarian. "Thank you, Osmirik. I am forever in your debt."

Astonished, Osmirik accepted the volume. "His Majesty does not need a working copy . . .?"

Incarnadine smiled. "You needn't bother. I'm a fast study."

Awed, Osmirik bowed and backed away.

Incarnadine looked out the window. "The house will probably oscillate a little before it settles down to the present. A half hour, I'd say. Did anyone check out the kitchen? There might be something to eat in there. Is anyone as famished as I am?"

The house bounced for two full hours between the future and the past until eventually zeroing in on its target, the fleeting instant of the present. In the meantime, they ate a meal of canned food made tolerable by an excellent Chablis that Gene found in the cellar, along with many other drinkable spirits. Barnaby and Deena came down in time for dessert: canned cherries jubilee with a superb Napoleon brandy.

"There was more demons upstairs," Deena told them. "We saw one of them!"

"An incubus," Incarnadine said. "A technician, probably. Blue-collar type, not one of the warrior demons of the sort you people battled. Relatively harmless."

"Do you think any of them are still here?" Barnaby wanted to know.

"No," Trent said. "If the warriors died of spell exhaustion, the underlings didn't have a chance."

Deena told of the one who had jumped out the window.

"One chance in a million of survival that way. Not that it's any great loss."

They all agreed not to lose any sleep over it.

"How did they manage to fool your sister?" Gene asked.

"Well, their disguises fooled you," Incarnadine said. "Didn't they? But you're right, my sister should have known better. I suspect she succumbed to their influence a long time ago."

"You mean, she was a puppet?"

"No. The Hosts are persuasive. I've told you how, as young people, we all had a brief flirtation with them. She was acting in their interests all along, and I don't think she realized it. Of course, this in no way exonerates her."

Sheila said, "When you go back to the castle, you don't expect to have any trouble?"

"None," Incarnadine said, finishing the last of his wine. "I can beat them, and they know it now. Their only chance was to kill me, or keep me out of the castle. They couldn't do the former and they can't do the latter."

"Couldn't they — ?" Sheila shook her head, puzzled.

"No, they're licked. Sure, they could battle me every inch of the way back to their portal. But they know they'd lose in the end. I suspect they've totally withdrawn from the castle."

Sheila frowned. "It's so hard to understand."

"Yes, almost impossible. I don't pretend to understand them, nor do I fully understand everything that's happened. But if Ferne's still alive, I'm hoping to get some answers." Incarnadine sat back. "When I've finished in the castle, I'll send back word here, so you can come on through, if you wish."

"I'm leaving from here," Sheila said. "I've only been gone a few days."

"Fine. I'm sure you'll find a car in the garage. You're welcome to use it."

"I still think I should do a time trip," Gene said. "And so should Linda. Our folks will think we've come back from the dead."

"Well, it will take some time to set up," Incarnadine said.

Trent said, "There's no need for that, if you want to take another tack."

"How so?" Incarnadine asked.

Trent spoke to Gene. "Write a letter to your folks and make up some good excuse for your absence. It's no problem for me to take that letter and back-time it a year or so."

Incarnadine was surprised. "You've been dabbling in time travel?"

"Sending people back is a little beyond my skill. But dropping a few letters into the postal stream of twelve months ago would be a breeze."

"Trent, I think you've become the family's best magician."

"Coming from you, that's quite a compliment."

"I like the idea," Gene said. "It means we could just pile into the car with Sheila and drive home now. Those stories are going to have to be pretty good, though. Now, let's see. What wild yarn could we come up with?"

"Could somebody lend me plane fare to California?" Linda asked.

"No problem," Trent said. "Put it on my MasterCard."

"Thanks. You're very kind."

"We princes are naturally charming."

"He's been using lines like that for three hundred years," Incarnadine warned.

"Go to hell, Inky."

Incarnadine rose from the table. "I think it's just about time."

Castle

The two brothers stepped through the veil their sister had erected to block the portal. Being of the House of Haplodie, they were immune; no spell could keep them out of the castle.

They found their sister Ferne slumped in a chair in the parlor, three empty sherry bottles at her feet. She was polishing off the remains of a fourth. Seeing Trent, dim recognition formed in her eyes.

"'Lo," was all she managed, along with a twisted smile.

"Stay with her," Incarnadine said.

"For as long as I can," Trent said.

"What do you mean?"

"I can't stay in the castle for any length of time. It's the spell Dad laid on me when we had our difference of opinion. He banished me, Inky. Never told anyone. I guess he felt a little guilty."

Nonplussed, Incarnadine said, "What sort of spell?"

"Nothing much. It's just that if I stay here longer than, say, ten minutes, I begin to get a case of the paranoid heebie-jeebies. I just go quietly nuts and get this overwhelming urge to run screaming from the place. Very effective."

"Gods. I'm sorry, Trent. I wish I had known."

"Yeah. Well, I didn't tell anyone, for the shame of it all. Silly, I guess. It's not my fault Dad had it in for me."

Incarnadine felt restrained from commenting. "Uh, well, if you have to go — listen. Thanks. I'll never forget it, Trent."

"Don't mention it. Look me up next time you're in New York."

"I will."

They looked at each other for a long moment.

"Farewell, brother."

"Farewell," Incarnadine said. He turned and left the parlor.

He found Deems in the outer halls, along with the bodies of thousands of his men. Many had died of wounds, but more had succumbed to spell exhaustion. Judging from the number of enemy dead, they had given a good account of themselves, defending a strange castle in a foreign land.

Incarnadine took his overcoat off and covered his brother's body with it, then recited a prayer for the departed.

He walked a good distance into the castle before encountering carcasses of the previous invaders. The place already stank to high heaven. It would be a monumental cleanup job.

A whispering silence held throughout the castle. Death skulked in the shadows, but would not show its face. Time hung like cobwebs in the corners.

Incarnadine walked with purposeful stride. As he did, he got the feeling that someone or something was ahead of him, keeping just out of sight. He didn't see anything.

He knew exactly where to go. It was a long trip, and a lonely one. The years echoed in the halls, reverberating off stone-vaulted ceilings.

In a dim crypt in the nethermost reaches of the castle, he found what he sought. A black oblong lay inscribed in gray shadows. He approached it.

He heard his name called, far off, faint.

"No," he said.

Dim shapes swam within the portal, and a cold wind blew out of it. There came to his ears a faint wailing and weeping.

He ignored it, raising his hands. He began the spellcasting, reciting each line of the incantation crisply and distinctly. As he continued, the wailing grew louder and louder.

The spell was short, succinct, and to the point. He finished it with a flourish of his hands, and the sounds emanating from the portal ceased. He stepped forward and peered into the darkness. What had been a gaping hole was now a blank stone wall. He reached out and touched it. The portal was gone.

On his way back, he undid the protective spells over a few of the aspects his Guardsmen had retreated into along with most of the castle's local citizenry, and many of its Guests.

Tyrene, the captain of the Guard, was standing watch inside one of them. When the portal opened, Tyrene regarded his liege lord with some disgruntlement. Obviously he did not care for hiding out while the castle was overrun by invaders. But he had had his orders. Incarnadine did his best to assuage him and salve his wounded pride. Then he bade him sound recall.

Whistling a tune he had heard during his stay on Earth, he trudged up to his study to begin the job of bringing the castle back to life.

Throne Room

His serene and Transcendental Majesty sat in state upon the Siege Perilous.

"Bring the prisoner," he ordered.

The prisoner was escorted through the huge room and brought to kneel at His Majesty's feet.

"Arise," he commanded. Then he said, "Do you have anything to say on your behalf before I pronounce judgment on you?"

Ferne shrugged. "Not really."

"Perhaps you can clarify a few issues."

"If I can, I would be most happy to."

"Why did you do it, Ferne?"

Her laughter was low and private, as if no one could possibly share or understand it.

He said, "You will not answer?"

"Oh, Inky, what a question. I could give a hundred reasons. A thousand. I wanted your position, your power, your magic. I deserved it. Even if I didn't deserve it, I wanted it. But all of that is rather academic now. Perhaps the real reason is that I was desperate for something to do."

His Majesty pondered her answer.

"Perhaps I know what you mean," he said.

Her look was haughty. "Don't be so damned understanding! You couldn't possibly know! You're the type who's perfectly happy raising children and keeping house and wallowing in the mundane things of half a thousand worlds. I'm not. I hunger, I thirst for things you've never dreamed of."

"Do you claim to know my dreams?" he answered. "Do you claim to know me at all?"

"I don't want to discuss it, if you don't mind."

He nodded slowly. "As you wish. Tell me one thing, though. I'm a little unclear as to the chronology of the plot you hatched. When did you begin to bargain with the Hosts?"

"Does it matter?"

"Yes."

"I talked with them off and on for years, trying to think of some way to use them to my advantage. After all, they are a powerful force, and would make excellent allies. But I couldn't find a way that did not involve inordinate risks."

"So you settled on a lesser ally?"

"The blue things? As I told you, I had no thought of allying myself with subhuman rubbish. It was then that Deems and I struck our bargain. We simply needed the castle to be invaded. I simply picked one of the holes Father had sealed up. I remember. I was with him when he did it. He'd conducted an expedition into the aspect and had found a nascently dangerous militaristic culture."

"So you undid Dad's containment spell. But nothing happened immediately," the King said.

"No. The blue ones took their good time about it, plodding, unimaginative military types that they are. But then I had a stroke of luck. You popped off to Earth in search of Trent, whom you suspected. And then the blue ones attacked! Marvelous timing, but quite fortuitous. But when you refused to cooperate, I had a real problem. I had overplayed my hand as far as the blue ones were concerned. They were too powerful for Deems and me alone. The only alternative was to employ an even more powerful force to rid the castle of them, reserving you as a trump card against these new invaders. I thought I could keep you out of the castle. You were in a world where your magic did not work. I was the superior magician in that world."

"Didn't you think Trent would help me?"

"Never. I'm astounded that he did. And truly astounded by his talents."

"As am I. Nevertheless, he did help me."

She nodded sadly. "I should have seen it. I should have made it my business to find out what Trent had been up to during his exile."

"You knew of Dad's banishing him?"

"Oh, yes. It was supposed to be a secret, but I caught wind of it." She chewed her lip, perplexed. "But even if I'd known of Trent's powers, I would never have imagined that his hatred of you would have ameliorated over the years. You two had such terrible *fights* when you were young."

"We did. Sibling rivalry can certainly last into adulthood, but given enough time — and we are all very old indeed at this point — it passes, like all things in all worlds. No one can nurse a grudge forever. Except perhaps you, dear sister."

"I bear no grudge. It was simply something to keep me occupied in my dotage."

He chuckled. "You don't look the part of the aging dowager princess."

"Please! Don't compliment me when you are about to sentence me to death!"

His smile faded. "You deserve to die. You killed Deems, your brother. You misled him, manipulated him. . . ." He was astonished at her pained expression. "You feel some remorse?"

"Yes! Of course."

"I wonder if it's real. No matter. One more question. How could you have let Host agents infiltrate your base on Earth? If they had succeeded in assassinating me, your cause would have been lost."

She looked away. "I don't know. The irrational in me had taken over by then, I suppose. I suppose I wanted nothing but death at that point. Not for you, but for me."

"The irrational came to dominate your thinking a long time ago. Even the *thought* of striking a bargain with the Hosts is itself an irrational act. To entertain any such notion is tantamount to contemplating suicide."

"I suppose you're right," she said, her voice small and colorless. "You always are." She seemed on the verge of tears. But she composed herself and said, "What does it matter now?"

"It will matter in your future life, sister."

Her eyes filled with wonder, hope, and disbelief. "You . . . you would let me live?"

"I will not condemn a relative to death, especially a pretender to the throne. It always looks bad, no matter how weak the claimant's case. It would reflect badly on my kingdom, and my reign."

She looked at him a long moment before saying, "I can't fathom what your motivations are, nor can I imagine who would gainsay your right to condemn me to death. In fact, I should think the common run of opinion is that if you don't, you're weak, or mad, or both."

"Let those who would judge me do so and be damned. I hereby pronounce judgment on you. You shall be taken to an unstable area of the castle and put through the first aspect that appears. The gateway will be guarded until it disappears. Should you somehow find your way back into the castle, you will be laid hands on and put out immediately, in the aforementioned manner. Do you understand the nature of your fate?"

Her voice barely audible, she said, "Yes."

"May the gods have mercy on you. Take her away."

The guards made motions to lay hands on her. She halted them with a curt, imperious gesture. She stepped forward, mounting the two steps to the throne.

The King rose. She embraced him, and covered his mouth with hers.

Their embrace lasted but a few seconds. He broke it, a look of astonishment on his reddened face. Her smile was mysterious, as always. Then she laughed.

"Take her away," he said. "And leave, all of you."

He sat in the empty throne room for a long time, his eyes far away, his thoughts troubled.

Finally he said, "To hell with it."

Then he yawned and got up. He doffed his robe and draped it on the throne. Taking off the crown, he hung it at a jaunty angle on the left upright of the ancient oaken chair. He left the chamber by a secret back door.

The spiral stairs led up into the family residence. He walked to an area of wall bordered by two pilasters. Raising his arms, he muttered a short incantation. A portal formed in the wall, and he stepped through.

His son and daughter ran to embrace him. Then Zafra took him into her arms. Holding her, he looked out over the beach and got a powerful urge to go sailing that day, no matter how tired he was.

Then he remembered something. He had contracted to write a novel for Spade Books, and the deadline was in six months. Six months! Why, he hadn't written a word in thirty years.

He had never heard of a novel-writing spell, but he was fairly sure he could come up with one, after a little brainstorming.

Biography

John DeChancie

John DeChancie is a popular author of numerous science fiction/fantasy novels including the hugely entertaining CASTLE series and STARRIGGER trilogy. He lives in Pittsburgh, Pennsylvania.

Printed in the United States
5690

magpies made their awful sound, the traffic hummed on the main road some quarter of a mile away, and beyond the road, a large goods train rumbled slowly, but steadily, along the railway track, the driver occasionally sounding the two-tone horn. The air, thought the man, had a clean, winter freshness about it, with a trace of mustiness rising from the ground and an all pervading smell of charred meat. To his right something rustled in the undergrowth, a squirrel he assumed, for such creatures had reached pest proportions of late. He had learned that from the television, for he spoke to few people and did not read the newspapers. The man turned from the body and began the slow walk back to the road and to the public phone box and to dial 999. He had only ever dialled 999 once before, after running near naked along the same path and in a panic after Tommy Davies had failed to surface.

He encountered a woman coming the other way before he reached the road. She was older than he, well dressed, her dog was a pedigree golden Labrador. She avoided eye contact as they closed with each other, looking past him, nervous of him or aloof, probably both, he couldn't tell, but he said, 'I wouldn't go down there, missus.' The woman walked on past him, ignoring him, until he added, 'There's a dead body,' at which she stopped in her tracks, as smartly as a serviceman coming to attention. She looked at him. 'By the logs,' he said. Then he asked, 'Do you have a mobile phone?'

George Hennessey looked down at the body, by then it, and the two logs, being enclosed in a large inflatable tent. He found himself mesmerized by the sight until the flash of SOCO's camera brought him back to the here and now, alerted him to the present.

'Male, female?' he asked.

'Police surgeon said, male, boss.' Yellich answered softly, in recognition of the reverence of the location. 'He

took one look at the body, and said male, and pronounced life extinct at . . .' Yellich consulted his notebook. '11.10 this forenoon.'

'I see. I hope . . . hope he was dead before he was set on fire . . . for his sake. It's one of the deaths I fear.'

'Sir?'

'Being burned alive. I am not frightened of death, Yellich. It holds no fear for me . . . not in itself. The when of it does and the how of it does and this is one how I would be very pleased to avoid. The other is falling from a great height while conscious . . . So, I hope, for his sake, he was not alive when this was done to him.'

'Yes, sir, not a pleasant way to go.'

'Strange, don't you think?'

'Sir?'

'Well ponder . . . ponder if you will. There is no scorching of the logs or the ground . . . He wasn't set on fire here.'

'He wasn't, was he, sir? I see what you mean . . . he was carried here . . . like that.'

'Yes . . . a corpse is not a pleasant thing to carry, well, I imagine not, but a charred corpse? I understand the flesh just comes off in your hand . . . like a well cooked joint, just falls apart . . . And it's been left where it was easily found . . . not concealed. Well, hardly concealed . . . hardly at all. Found by . . .?'

'A local man, sir. He was rambling, just to get out of the house for an hour or so.' Again Yellich consulted his notebook. 'Richard Boot by name. We have his address if you need to talk to him, but he didn't see anything. A lady walking her dog allowed him to use her mobile phone . . . and we are here.'

'And we are here.' Hennessey paused. 'You can even smell the burning . . . just . . . the odour is still detectable. He must have been dumped in the night. But why go to all that trouble? Why burn the man so completely . . . then carry him to where he will be easily found?' He glanced at Yellich.

'Beats me, sir. There's a river here. If they had put him in the river it would have been longer before he would be found, if ever, once the rats got their teeth into him . . . If they gnawed into the stomach, released the gasses, he'd sink, making a very tasty meal for fish, rodents and micro-organisms alike.'

'So they were not worried about him being found . . . just did not want him to be found in a location that would link him to the perpetrators.'

'Yes, sir.' Yellich smiled at Hennessey. 'That has to be the answer.'

'So, he won't be related to anyone who did this, nor a friend, nor a business partner . . . nor an enemy even.'

'Yes, sir, I see where you are going.'

'Into areas of great difficulty. This is possibly a gang-land killing that will never be wrapped up. We'll likely identify him . . . then it will be a wall of silence. Nothing in the immediate area?'

'Constables are doing a fingertip search.'

'Yes, I saw . . . but no tracks that you noticed?'

'No, sir . . . the only footprints seemed to be of the man . . . Richard Boot and the lady dog walker. There was a frost last night, the ground would have been rock hard.'

'And the path leads to a road where a motor vehicle would have been parked, again without leaving any tyre tracks . . . and no houses close enough to be said to over-look the road where the path joins it?'

'No, boss . . .'

'Coming up against brick walls every way we turn, but let us not rush things. Somebody wanted this man dead, he had significance for someone . . . he meant something to somebody and at least some attempt was made to conceal the body, a token attempt, but an attempt. Didn't leave him on the side of the road for example . . . so whoever did this, didn't want an early discovery.'

The SOCO's camera flashed again.

'No, sir.'

'CCTV?'

'Not on this stretch of road, sir.'

Hennessey inclined his head. 'That would be too much to hope for, but then it might tell us something . . . it might imply local knowledge . . . Things are beginning to fall into place, Yellich.'

The curtain of the tent opened, a young and pale looking constable glanced at the charred remains as if unable to prevent himself from doing so and then looked at Hennessey. 'Dr D'Acre, sir.' He then stood back, holding the curtain, allowing Dr D'Acre to enter.

Dr D'Acre glanced at Hennessey and then at Yellich. 'Gentlemen,' she said.

'Ma'am,' said Yellich. The SOCO remained reverentially silent.

'Doctor,' Hennessey murmured softly, 'one corpse of the male sex, pronounced life extinct by Dr Mann, the police surgeon, at 11.10 this day. Death appears suspicious.'

'I'll say!' Louise D'Acre looked at the corpse. 'He has assumed . . . his body has assumed the classic pugilistic pose of a person who when alive, or shortly after death, was burned. You see how the hands have risen up like a boxer defending himself?'

'Yes.' Hennessey spoke softly.

'Well, that wouldn't have happened to that degree if rigor had established itself. If rigor had established itself, the spine would have curved and contracted like a matchstick which is allowed to burn along its length, but the arms would have remained by his side. So if he wasn't burned to death, he was burned very shortly after he was life extinct . . . within twenty-four hours. I am not going to take a rectal temperature; the thermal confusion caused by the incineration would make the exercise quite pointless. If you have finished here with photographs etcetera,

6

you can have him transported to York District Hospital . . . I'll conduct the PM as soon as possible.'

'All finished?' Hennessey turned to the white overcoated Scenes of Crime Officer.

'All done, sir.' The man, portly and middle-aged, beamed as he recounted, 'Colour, black and white . . . all done.'

'Good.' Dr D'Acre allowed herself a brief smile, with lips coated with pale lipstick. 'Will you be observing for the police, Detective Chief Inspector?'

'Yes,' Hennessey said, nodding. 'Yes, I will.'

Again he saw the man. He glanced out of the window and took a moment's break and watched the man. He seemed to be elderly, but strode out like a youth, two fields distant, but the silver hair was clearly evident. He had noticed the man before, always at the same time, about eleven in the forenoon, walking the path through Denny Wood. He turned back to the room.

The charred corpse lay on the left of the stainless steel table as viewed from Hennessey's vantage point at the side of the pathology laboratory. Hennessey was dressed in disposable green coveralls, as were Dr D'Acre and Eric Filey, the pathology assistant. Hennessey had encountered Eric Filey on a number of occasions whilst observing post-mortems for the police and had always found the youthful, rotund individual to be a cheery and warm personality; in complete contrast to all other pathology assistants he had met. All others, he had found, seemed to have let their work affect them; dealing with death, mortality, the essential frailty of the human body made them sour, humourless, cynical. Occasionally it had made them very fearful as in the case of one man Hennessey had met just once but who he remembered vividly because of the man's fear. This man had been a lowly assistant in a pathology laboratory for very nearly all his working life and then,

in his sixties, knew that if there was anything even remotely suspicious about his death, then his corpse would be examined. He knew which laboratory in which hospital his body would be taken to, which table it would be lain on with a starched white towel covering his genitals, which of his colleagues would assist which pathologist, which tools would be used to dissect his body. When Hennessey met him, he was fearful of going out of doors, rarely ventured out at night and never alone, always being accompanied by his patient and very dutiful wife. But not so Eric Filey, late twenties, quiet unless spoken to, and then would reply with warmth. He was efficient too, good at his job, evinced by the respect he was always given by Dr D'Acre and other pathologists. At that moment he, like Hennessey, stood, knowing their place, waiting for comments or requests from Dr D'Acre.

Dr D'Acre stood beside the stainless steel table dressed, as Hennessey and Filey, in green disposable coveralls with a disposable hat and foot covers. She reached a slender arm upwards and adjusted an angle poise arm which was bolted to the ceiling, until the microphone on the lower end of the arm was just above her head and central to the table. The room was brilliantly illuminated by florescent bulbs that shimmered behind perspex sheets affixed to the ceiling.

'Unknown adult of the male sex.' Dr D'Acre spoke with received pronunciation in a clear voice, evidently for the benefit of the audio typist who would be handed the cassette tape at the conclusion of the post-mortem. 'Today's date, twelfth of December . . . and give it a case number please.' She pondered the body. 'The body is covered with third degree burns, the deeper tissue below the skin is destroyed, subcutaneous fat and muscle tissue has been lost or severely damaged . . . this can be seen at a glance. The hair is almost completely burned away but sufficient survives to indicate that he had scalp hair above his ears and round the

8

back of his head, but the scalp was probably bald . . . the skin is leathery to the touch.' Dr D'Acre took a scalpel and probed into the thigh. 'The soft tissue has been partially consumed by the fire . . . the bone itself is not blackened . . . the period of incineration was not very long and there may even have been an attempt to extinguish the flames. The burning is extensive to the point that all parts of the body are grossly affected. If this fire had been left to run its course, the body would eventually have cremated, leaving only bones and internal organs. This fire was either extinguished . . . or . . . it took place in an enclosed space and the flames consumed all the oxygen and the fire expired before cremation occurred. There are a number of splits to the skin which seem similar to knife wounds but are in fact consistent with burning . . . They are where we would expect to find such splitting, the elbows and knees and they show no bleeding . . . so safely fire damage. I can detect no sign of ante-mortem injury –' she glanced at Hennessey – 'but the day is young. I think we all want to know whether this gentleman was mercifully deceased before he was incinerated . . . so let's find out.'

Dr D'Acre took a scalpel from the tray and drove an incision into the larynx of the corpse and opened the incision. 'Well, what we are looking for is soot deposits below the vocal chords . . . soot can enter the mouth of a corpse but it cannot pass beyond the vocal chords unless the person is breathing and here . . . here, you will both be relieved to note that there is no soot in the lower respiratory tract, so fortunately for this man, he did not die as a result of the fire. He was deceased before he was set alight . . . Rather rules out my suggestion that someone tried to put out the fire and lends weight to the corpse being burned in an enclosed space which had a finite supply of oxygen. Foul play, rather than an accident . . . at least it points that way. So, if the fire didn't kill him, what did? Well, there is no sign of trauma over and above the fire-damaged

tissue so we have to dig deeper . . . So let us first look at his skull.'

Again Dr D'Acre took the scalpel and drove an incision round the head, just above the ears. She then laid the scalpel in the tray at the foot of the table and with slender, latex-encased hands and fingers, removed the skin from the top of the skull. 'Just out of the oven,' she remarked with, what Hennessey thought, to be uncharacteristically dark humour. 'This fire didn't take place a long time ago, but that observation has been made earlier. The ease with which the skin peels from the bone serves to confirm it.' She laid the fold of charred and brittle skin beside the skull. 'Ah . . . and here we have the cause of death . . . well, a probable cause of death . . . massive fracturing of the skull . . . radial fractures like spokes of a wheel radiating from a central point. A flat surface . . . falling head-first on to concrete would have caused injuries like this, in the case of an accident, or a spade in the case of intentional injury . . . something flat and hard . . . This injury would have killed him outright. A single, forceful blow to the top of his head . . . the . . . blood hasn't cavitated.'

'Cavitated?' Hennessey repeated.

'Yes, in cases of burning of human bodies . . . and animal . . . the blood boils and is forced by the heat into the cavity between the brain and the skull. It doesn't look like blood by then, more like thick green soup, but that hasn't happened and that further indicates that the fire, while consuming his body, didn't last long. It seems to me that the fire was an attempt to conceal his identity. They may have thought that they had succeeded and contented themselves with what they had achieved rather than wanting to reduce the body further . . . no clothing . . . no trace of fabric . . . no zip fasteners melted to the body, no trace of leather or rubber on the feet . . . no wristwatch . . . all removed. He wouldn't have done that by himself in the winter . . . no naturist here . . . His clothing was removed

10

and why? Well, that is your department, Detective Chief
Inspector. I do no not wish to intrude.'

'Oh, intrude all you like, ma'am.' Hennessey raised his
voice slightly to allow it to carry across the laboratory.
'All help gratefully received, but I take your point, identity concealment seems to be emerging as an issue in this
case.'

'Well . . . let's help you all we can. Mr Filey . . . if you
could help me?'

Hennessey watched as Eric Filey and Dr D'Acre, with
seeming ease, rolled the charred corpse on to its side. Dr
D'Acre then took a tape measure and laid it the length of
the spine. 'Two feet eight inches,' she said, 'or approximately eighty-one centimetres. That would make him about
five feet four inches tall, but the fire would have caused
some shrinking, probably by as much as two inches. So,
he would have been about five feet six inches in height
or one metre and sixty-seven centimetres in European
newspeak. I can get a better idea of his height once I
measure the femur and tibia and other long bones and
from them deduce the height of the gentleman, but five
foot six is a close approximation, the spine being half the
overall height of a normally proportioned person and this
gentleman appears normally proportioned. Fashion models
with endless legs tend to upset that theory but, lucky them,
they are not normally proportioned. So . . . if we can roll
him back, please, Mr Filey?'

Again Hennessey watched the skill and apparent ease with
which the corpse was turned gently over on to its posterior.

'We'll look at the mouth . . . a veritable gold mine of
information.' Dr D'Acre took a length of stainless steel
and forced it between the teeth and then prised the mouth
open, causing a distinct 'crack' to the head as the rigor
was broken. 'Well, he's Northern European . . . or
Caucasian . . . the teeth tell us that and he has had recent
dental work . . . and British dentistry . . . so his identity

will be easy to confirm once you have a name and someone to tell you who his dentist was. Dentists are obliged to keep their records for eleven years, but this dental work appears to be quite recent . . . within two or three years I'd say . . . the fillings are not decayed. I'll extract one of his teeth, send it to the forensic science laboratory at Wetherby, they'll cut it in cross section and that will give them his age to within twelve months. So let's see what he had for his last meal. Better take a deep breath, gentlemen . . .' Dr D'Acre once again took the scalpel and drove an incision across the stomach allowing intestinal gases to escape with a loud 'hiss'.

'Smelled worse,' she said, 'and the presence of gas is further indication that the fire was of brief duration. The gases not smelling as strongly as they otherwise might means that this gentleman is recently deceased. This is not the case of a two-, three-, four-day-old corpse being set alight and then dumped; this gentleman was set alight soon after losing his life . . . and within the last twenty-four hours. He also ate shortly before he died . . . a substantial meal . . . which is still discernible . . . chicken, I think . . . yes . . . and vegetables, rice . . . peas . . . mushrooms . . . chicken curry. This man did not know he was going to die, he enjoyed a chicken curry and then met his end.'

Dr D'Acre stepped sideways towards the head. 'The facial features are unrecognizable and seem to have suffered more damage than the rest of the corpse . . . It's as if the accelerant was poured over the face to attempt to disguise, or even destroy the features, and flames spread out from there. I wouldn't say that this was a random attack – as you have said, Mr Hennessey, attempted concealment of identity is an issue here – but this is not gangland, it's too messy, too careless in my experience, and I dare say in yours. There is panic here; there is an absence of knowledge of forensic procedures . . . facial reconstruction now takes a matter of seconds with digital

imaging. All the computer operator needs is an X-ray of the skull and an image can be conjured on the screen within seconds. Used to take weeks building the face up using plasticine on the actual skull, but the depth of tissue is in the computer program; all the operator needs is the sex, race and age.'

'All of which you have kindly provided.'

'Except the age; Wetherby will give you that once I give them a tooth. We'll X-ray the skull before I extract the tooth . . . send the X-ray to Wetherby along with the tooth. So, adult, West European male, well nourished, addressed dental hygiene, was killed by a massive blow to the skull which may or may not have been deliberate . . . but then there followed a clumsy and as I said, apparently panic-driven attempt to conceal the identity of the person in question, and by someone not of the criminal fraternity. A criminal would not panic and would know of forensic techniques. The body was probably burned inside an enclosed space that was not combustible – a metal container, for example. There is no sign of clothing on the body. The fire was of brief duration and had he been clothed, some remnants of fibre would be present. Similarly, there is no metal as from zip fasteners or a watch etcetera . . . similarly no footwear . . . Again points to an attempt to conceal his identity.' She paused. 'I'll trawl for poisons as a matter of course, but I feel in my waters it will be futile, the massive fracturing of the skull seems to be the cause of death, as if someone crept up behind him and whacked him over the head with a spade, then panicked. So, over to you, Mr Hennessey, my report will be with you tomorrow, but that is the nuts and bolts . . . over to you.'

'Over to me.' George Hennessey halted just inside the door of the hospital and braced himself to meet the blast of cold air that was the wind, a bitter north-easterly that drove

across the city of York and the surrounding area. He screwed his fedora down round his head, buttoned up his overcoat and turned up his collar. Then he stepped purposely out of the centrally-heated cocoon that was the hospital. He strode down Gilleygate and instead of joining the walls as was his usual custom, knowing like every York resident that by far the speediest way to cross the centre of the city is to walk the walls, he chose to walk up Micklegate, believing the walls would be too exposed. 'Over to me.' Dr D'Acre's words rang in his ears. He thought of the victim, a male who ate well, and who cared for his teeth . . . such a man would be integrated . . . such a man would be missed . . . soon someone will be weeping.

He entered the main entrance of Micklegate Bar police station, nodded in response to the duty constable's deferential greeting of 'Good afternoon, sir', and opened the 'Staff Only' door and closed it behind him. He signed as being 'in' and checked his pigeonhole. There was nothing of importance, he thought: the usual reminder about saving money by writing on both sides of a sheet of paper, and notification of a retirement party for an officer he only vaguely knew. Such notices of retirement parties once held little significance for him but now he was silver haired and with liver-spotted hands . . . soon . . . very soon, the staff in the division would be plunging their hands into their pigeonholes and extracting a notice of a retirement party for DCI George Hennessey of Micklegate Bar police station. But not, he thought, not for a few months yet, a good few months at that. Time enough, he thought, time enough to crack the case of the charred corpse and a few more cases after that.

He walked on to his office, noticing that Yellich was not at his desk as he passed his office. In his own office he peeled off his overcoat and hung it on the coat stand, putting his hat on the peg above his coat. He kept his jacket on, the police station not, he found, being as generously heated

as was York District Hospital. He then picked up the phone on his desk and made two internal phone calls, the first to the collator asking for any recent missing person reports involving adult Caucasian males of about five and a half feet or one metre sixty-seven centimetres in height; the second call was to the press officer, and between them they created, word by word, a press release. It was done, advised the press officer, in sufficient time to be included in the early evening news bulletins of the regional television networks, and for the final edition of the evening paper. The local radio stations would be carrying the story on their hourly news broadcasts. He thanked the press officer and replaced the handset of his phone gently as his eye was caught by a solitary figure walking the walls, hunched forwards, in a blue duffel coat. Hennessey watched the man until he was obscured from view by the confines of the small windows of Hennessey's office. He then turned his attention to the task in hand, phoned the collator again, asked for a crime number and was given 12/161. He noted the number on his notepad along with the date, and ruminated that already, by the twelfth of December, there had been 161 crimes reported in York Division alone. Most, he knew, would be petty and non-violent and 12/161 would be the first murder, perhaps even the first serious offence. York, after all, is a seat of learning, a seat of justice and a cathedral city; it attracts tourists but it does have a rough underside on Friday and Saturday nights when the agricultural labourers and the coal miners come in from small towns in the Vale wanting their beer, women and fights. Despite that, 12/161 would be the first murder.

Case number 12/161 would also be unlike most murders which are products of fights in pubs or domestic disputes, where the death of the victim was not necessarily intentional, where witnesses often abound, and where the identity of the victim is known from the outset. Here the victim's

15

death appeared intentional; here efforts to hide the victim's identity had been made, clumsily so, but made nonetheless. Further, this murder was, as Dr D'Acre pointed out, unlikely to be gangland; it was too messy. That, pondered Hennessey, would equally both help and hinder the police. Gangland would know how to cover their tracks, the perpetrators of this murder did not; that would prove to be useful, but gangland members are known to the police. It is a rite of passage that every gangland member must have done prison time, and prison time means a police record, it means fingerprints and possibly DNA on file; all good assistance to any police investigation. The perpetrators of this crime, however, might be Mr and Mrs Clean; no flies on them at all.

He sat back, causing his chair to creak. There was more than one perpetrator, if only because it would have taken more than one person to carry the corpse to where it was found. Two men minimum could have done it but he had a feeling that more than two were involved. Having seen the crime scene, having viewed the body wedged grotesquely between two tree trunks, he felt it likely to have been a job undertaken by three or four persons. A conspiracy; and that would also equally both help or hinder the police. If the conspirators held firm, maintained a wall of silence, then the police would have an uphill task, but should one of the conspirators lose their nerve, or be tempted to talk by inducement of the promise of lesser charges being levelled, then . . . then the conspiracy is doomed. We shall see, said Hennessey to himself, what we shall see.

There was a tap on the frame of his office doorway. DS Yellich stood there, wrapped in an overcoat. Hennessey smiled at him. 'Come in, Yellich.'

'Thanks, skipper.' Yellich walked into Hennessey's office and sat on a chair in front of Hennessey's desk. 'Not a great deal to report, I'm afraid.'

'Oh . . .? Tea?'

'Yes, please.' Yellich rubbed his hands. 'That wind is a biter . . . not so cold out of the wind but . . . what's that term? Chill factor? The chill factor is high . . . time to dig out the thermals, methinks.'

'Methinks too . . .' Hennessey stood and walked to the corner of his office where a kettle, milk, teabags and half a dozen mugs stood upon a small table. He checked that the kettle contained sufficient water and then switched it on. 'So, anything at all?' He poured milk into two mugs.

'No, sir . . . fingertip search of the area proved negative . . . nothing to show for a lot of constables with numb fingertips. The gentleman who found the body was eager to help but more out of a need for human company, poor soul. Lives alone, never worked in his life, not a single day's work since leaving school. Didn't seem to be the employment-avoiding type, just no luck, but he couldn't tell us anything.'

'Well, I've contacted the press officer and the collator. Dr D'Acre confirms that he was dead before being set on fire; death was caused by a massive blow to the head. You don't take sugar, do you?'

'No, thanks, skipper.'

Hennessey placed a teabag in two mugs and added boiling water. 'Wetherby will come back with an age tomorrow once they have extracted a tooth, and Dr D'Acre will supply an X-ray of the skull.'

'Facial reconstruction?'

'Yes. One tea.' Hennessey handed Yellich one of the mugs. The other he carried with him as he returned to his chair.

'Cheers.' Yellich grasped the mug of hot liquid with two hands. 'So, if the fire wasn't the cause of death, then someone wants to conceal the person's identity.'

'Yes . . . I was pondering the same just a moment ago. Dr D'Acre was able to find indications that the fire was starved of oxygen, as if the fire was contained within a

small space, like a metal container . . . something like that. And more than one perpetrator.'

'Yes . . . I thought two at least to be able to carry the corpse from the road to where—'

The phone on Hennessey's desk rang. He let it ring twice before picking it up. 'DCI Hennessey.'

Yellich watched as colour seemed to drain from Hennessey's face, and his jaw seemed to drop. Hennessey scribbled on his notepad.

'Thank you . . . got that.' Hennessey spoke softly. He replaced the handset gently on to the rest and glanced at Yellich. 'We've got another one . . . another charred corpse. Opposite side of the city, out by Heslington Common.'

Yellich gulped his tea. 'Other side of York, as you say, boss, but has to be linked.'

'Oh, yes.' Hennessey drank his tea in mouthfuls. 'Can't be a coincidence. Well . . . we're wanted . . . no rest for the wicked.'

Yellich drove. The distance from Micklegate Bar police station to Heslington Common was short, just a ten-minute drive. Following directions, they arrived efficiently at the scene, the blue flashing lights of the police cars against a drab background providing a clear homing beacon on the last stage of the journey. They left the car and walked together, with Yellich a half step behind Hennessey, to where a blue and white police tape, tied to trees, had cordoned off a small area of ground within a stand of small trees and shrubs. Four constables and a sergeant stood by the tape; a turban-wearing man knelt within the confines of the tape. The trees swayed. Hennessey held on to his fedora, Yellich's coat collar butted his jaw. The sky had turned overcast.

As Hennessey and Yellich approached, the turban-wearing man stood and then bowed under the tape and stood again. He nodded at Hennessey and Yellich. 'Good day,' he said reverently with a faultless English accent.

'Good day, Dr Mann,' Hennessey replied. He glanced beyond the tape where he could see blackened limbs rising from the tall grass. 'Another charred corpse, I understand.'

'Indeed yes, of the female sex on this occasion. I have just arrived, summoned by the constables, and will confirm life extinct at . . .' Dr Mann glanced at his watch. '4.47 p.m. . . . 16.47 hours this day.'

'16.47 agreed,' Hennessey replied. Out of the corner of his eye he saw Yellich retrieve his notebook from his pocket and begin to take notes.

'The body is that of an adult female . . . charred . . . incompletely burned . . . no destruction of the skeleton . . . again, as was the case this morning.'

'I see. Well, thank you, sir.' Hennessey again glanced towards the charred corpse.

'I will take my leave now. I will forward my report to you forthwith.'

'Thank you, sir.'

Dr Mann inclined his head and walked away towards his car, carrying his black bag with him.

'Found by?' Hennessey turned and addressed the uniformed sergeant.

'Children, sir.'

'Children! At this time?'

'Truants, sir. They were quite shaken. I think they'll be in school next week.' The sergeant forced a smile, not inappropriately, thought Hennessey. 'Seems they realized that they can either make the most of their educational opportunities or they can find dead bodies. The former seemed to be the more attractive to them now. They were quite young . . . twelve, thirteen, four of them. They were on their way home after spending the afternoon on the common . . . saw the body . . . ran the rest of the way. Saw a police vehicle parked by the roadside and reported it to the constable. The constable

investigated and called it in. Myself and the other constable were in the vicinity, we were diverted to assist. I called SOCO, the police surgeon and CID. Scenes of Crime Officers are yet to . . . ah . . .' The sergeant glanced beyond Hennessey. 'Just arriving now, sir.' Hennessey turned and saw a white van with SOCO in large black letters on the side, approach the parked police vehicles.

'Alright.' Hennessey stepped forward. 'Let's have a look before they get to work with their cameras.'

The sergeant lifted the blue and white tape to allow Hennessey and Yellich to ingress the cordoned off area. The two CID officers stopped short of the corpse at a point where they had a sufficiently full and clear view. It was as Dr Mann had described: a corpse, clearly female, lying face up with arms and legs raised in the pugilistic posture of a burned corpse. It was completely blackened, facial features were indistinguishable, the scalp hair had been destroyed and again, so far as Hennessey could tell, after learning from Dr D'Acre's observations of earlier that day, there appeared to be no clothing upon the corpse, no remnants of fabric, no metal, no trace of footwear.

'Damn strange,' Hennessey muttered.

'Sir?'

'Well, why leave them so far apart, yet so easily discoverable? This corpse is marginally more concealed than the male corpse but only marginally, it would have been found easily enough . . . if not today, then tomorrow; the common is very popular with dog walkers and folk just out for a walk to clear the tubes. So why not just leave the two bodies together somewhere?'

'Strange, as you say, sir.'

'"Fire burn and cauldron bubble. Fire burn and cauldron bubble",' Hennessey mumbled, almost to himself. 'Well,' he said, louder now, 'we'd better let the SOCO

crack on. Can you please contact Dr D'Acre . . . apologize, but ask her to attend.'

'Yes, of course.'

'Then return to the station and ask the press officer to modify the press release, not one, but two charred corpses. In the name of the Creator I hope there won't be any more . . . two is sufficient. I'll remain here.'

It was Friday, 17.53 hours.

Two

Saturday, December 13, 9.27 hours – 23.10 hours
in which a successful marriage is explored and both George Hennessey and Somerled Yellich are at home to the gracious reader.

Hennessey reclined in his chair and read the reports. Dr D'Acre's report on the male victim contained no new information; it was rather a confirmation of the findings of the post-mortem: death was caused by a massive blow to the skull; the fire damage was post-mortem; a trawl for poison as a matter of course had proved negative. Dr D'Acre had toiled into the previous mid-evening to complete the post-mortem on the female victim, with George Hennessey once again observing for the police, and he was more than impressed to have received her report by 09.15 on the Saturday. She must have dictated it to the secretary at 8.30 a.m. and had it sent to him by courier. Again, the report added nothing to the findings of the previous evening: the victim was female, Western European, also had had British dental treatment. Her larynx was crushed, minor bones in her neck had been broken; she had been strangled. Like the male victim, she too had also eaten a curry just before she had been murdered. Interestingly, her fingernails, which had survived the fire, showed no sign of damage which would normally have been expected; 'So-called defence injuries,' she reported, 'are not present which,' she concluded,

22

'means that sadly there is no trace of her attacker's blood beneath her fingernails and hence no DNA to be obtained.' Dr D'Acre concluded that the absence of defence injuries suggested the victim was restrained in some way, or was perhaps unconscious. The report from the forensic science laboratory at Wetherby stated that the tooth from the male victim indicated his age to be fifty-seven years, plus or minus twelve months. An X-ray of the male victim, the reported added, was being 'worked up' to provide a digital facial reconstruction.

Hennessey stood and took the reports to Yellich's office. 'Busy?'

'The hit-and-run, sir.' Yellich looked up from the report that he was writing.

'Oh, yes.'

'Seventeen years old . . . everything to live for, now she's going to spend the rest of her life in a wheelchair.'

'Knocked off her bike, wasn't she?'

'Yes, sir . . . last Wednesday. No witnesses but the vehicle will have been damaged. We're talking to all the local garages; somebody will have been approached with a repair job to the front near-side bumper. What have you there, more work for I?'

'Reports from Dr D'Acre and Wetherby.'

'Already?'

'Yes, efficient is not the word.' Hennessey handed the reports to him and sat in the chair in front of Yellich's desk while Yellich read them.

'Husband and wife, do you think?' Yellich put the reports down on his desk.

'Probably. We haven't heard from Wetherby yet about the age of the female victim, but that's what I was thinking . . . a husband and wife . . . out for a curry on Friday night, not expecting any bad news and a few hours later, they are no longer with us and their flesh is cooked.'

'No indication of clothing on the female victim?'

'None . . . but look at Dr D'Acre's report on the female victim . . . notice anything? I mean in comparison to the male?'

Yellich held up the two reports side by side and glanced at one, then the other. 'Good Lord!'

'Yes,' Hennessey said and smiled. 'She towered over him. He was five foot six or thereabouts and she, statuesque goddess, was over six feet tall. They would have made a striking couple.'

'I'll say. So is this for me, legwork for the Detective Sergeant? Visit all the Indian restaurants in York?'

Hennessey shrugged. 'You can do if you feel in need of the exercise but . . . you know Napoleon Bonaparte?'

'Heard of him. We did British history at school.'

'Well, he conquered half of Europe and you know the two qualities he looked for in his generals?'

'Tell me.'

'Intelligence and laziness.'

'Really?' Yellich smiled.

'Well, my collection of military history is not immodest, as you know, and I have read such. He had no time for intelligent and hardworking generals; he reasoned that if someone was hardworking and intelligent then he was stupid.'

'Cynical.'

'Probably . . . nay certainly . . . but, like I said, this fella very nearly achieved what the European Community is only now beginning to achieve. You see, he thought that if the hardworking general was ordered to take the army to the other side of the mountain he would take it over the top . . . up one side and down the other.'

'Fair enough.'

'But the lazy and intelligent general would do no such thing. Being intelligent, he would realize that he had to come up with the goods if he wished to keep his generalship, but being lazy he would find the easiest way to

achieve that end, and so he'd take his army round the side of the mountain. Get to the same place with much less effort and that is in the interest of the army as a whole. Laziness and intelligence; believe me, that is a devastating combination of traits in any man.'

'Ah, I see where you are going, skipper. I can tramp round the city or I can use the phone.' Yellich smiled.

'Exactly. I'd leave it for an hour or so; they won't be open for business until lunchtime, but the managers will be at their desks by about ten. If you get a result, I'll be in my office.'

'Yes, boss.' Yellich made a long arm for the Yellow Pages that lay at the far corner of his desk.

Hennessey returned to his office, and with some reluctance, but also knowing the importance of same, he began to address his paperwork. Monthly statistical returns for November had to be concluded by the end of the following week; overtime claims for junior officers had to be approved; a reference for an officer who wanted to transfer to another part of the UK for personal reasons – Stoke-on-Trent, a godforsaken, soulless, nothing of a place in Hennessey's view, but his fiancée wouldn't leave her home town, so the cheery constable had explained. Hennessey thought the young man deserved a good reference and Hennessey would find pleasure in writing it.

He had concluded the reference and put it in his out tray for onward conveyance to the typing pool where the secretaries, equipped with state-of-the-art word processors, worked and typed, but which was still called the typing pool, when Yellich tapped on the door frame of his office.

'Got a result,' he said with a smile.

The Last Viceroy restaurant stood in Gillygate between two terraced houses.

'Wouldn't want to live there,' Yellich observed as he and Hennessey walked to the door of the restaurant.

'Oh?'

'Too near an eatery. Had a friend once . . . when he was renting before he bought his first house, had a flat above a Chinese restaurant. He spent a fortune on food and ballooned, just never stopped eating – the continuous smell of food from the restaurant, you see, made him feel constantly hungry. Something me and Sara bore in mind when we were looking for a flat when we were first married.' He pressed the doorbell.

'It may be them.' The proprietor was Asian, in his early thirties, but spoke with a solid Yorkshire accent. Second, third, even fourth generation migrant, thought Hennessey. He seemed keen to help the police. 'It is the description . . . tall woman and short husband . . . it is sometimes seen, usually the other way round. My sister will only go out with men who are taller than her. So the description did ring a bell . . . if it's them.'

'They being?'

'Mr and Mrs Dent. They are regular customers. They don't come into York to eat but often eat at the end of their working day before going home. We have been open for three years and they have been regular customers from the day we opened. They are both accountants; they gave me some advice once which saved me a lot of money but I can't say I am their client. I did ask if they would take my account but they declined, most politely, but declined nonetheless. They didn't want to mix business with pleasure. So they explained.'

Hennessey glanced about him. The restaurant was decorated with embossed wallpaper in a rich scarlet colour, with prints of India, the Taj Mahal, the Gateway of India; a portrait of Earl Mountbatten, the Last Viceroy, hung by the door to the kitchen from which clattering sounds and the smell of Indian meals emanated. The table at which they sat had a starched white linen tablecloth and neatly folded paper napkins.

'How old are they?' asked Hennessey.

'Fifties, I'd say. As Mr Yellich asked, the age is correct.'

'Where do they live?'

'I'm afraid I don't know except that it is in the Vale, a car drive from the city.'

'Where are their business premises?'

'Precenters Court, by the Minster.'

'Yes, I know where it is. Posh address.'

'Doesn't get posher.' The man, Ali Kahn by name, smiled.

'And they ate here last night?'

'Thursday, boss,' Yellich corrected.

'Yes, sorry, last Thursday evening.'

'Yes . . . definitely . . . two nights ago. Chicken Korma . . . neither of them like hot curry.'

'When was that?'

'Early to mid evening . . . they probably arrived at 6.00 p.m., waited to be served . . . we knew that . . . happy to let the rush hour die down. So they ate from 7.00 p.m. until about 8.00 p.m. . . . didn't drink, a pitcher of chilled water between them . . . again, that was usual.'

'How did they seem?'

'Seem?'

'Their manner . . . attitude?'

'Oh . . . quite normal. They didn't look particularly happy as though they'd come into big money . . . nor did they look particularly upset . . . just a couple. They always looked very happy together . . . Very calm and content in each other's company . . . a settled marriage. I envy them. Why the police interest in them, may I ask? They are a very proper couple.'

'We . . . well . . .' Hennessey paused. 'Let's just say that we think they can help us with our inquiries and we are sure they are a very proper couple, as you say.'

'Well, the people you should talk to are their employees in Precenters Court. Can't miss their door, Dent and Dent, Chartered Accountants.'

It was just a five minute walk from The Last Viceroy on Gilleygate to Precenters Court, but the two streets were a world apart. Busy, bustling Gilleygate of small shops and houses and Precenters Court, a quiet cul-de-sac of Georgian terrace houses just on one side of the road, facing the high brick wall that was the boundary of the grounds of York Minster. Dent and Dent, Chartered Accountants was easily found. An imposing black gloss painted door which had to Hennessey a warm feeling, despite the colour being associated with mourning and tragedy. The office lights were on, a secretary could be seen tapping on to a keyboard of a word processor. Hennessey tried the door. It was locked. He pressed the buzzer attached to the 'squawk' box set in the wall.

'Hello?' The voice was soft, female, welcoming. 'Do you have an appointment?'

'We'd like to see Mr and Mrs Dent.'

'Well, I'm afraid you need an appointment.'

'It's the police.'

'Oh . . . please wait.'

Hennessey and Yellich waited. The door was opened within a few seconds by a middle-aged man in a woollen suit.

'Mr Dent?'

'No. You are the police?'

'Yes. Is Mr Dent in?'

'No, Mr and Mrs Dent don't work on Saturdays, neither do we normally but we have a backlog to clear.'

'I see. Where might we find Mr Dent . . . and Mrs Dent as well?'

'Why, is there some trouble?' The man was slightly built, well dressed, and seemed to both Hennessey and Yellich to be very serious minded.

'Yes, in a word,' Hennessey replied, craning his neck to look up at the man who stood on the elevated step of the doorway of the building. 'Might we come in?'

'Well . . . yes . . . yes.' The man stepped aside and allowed Hennessey and Yellich to enter.

'Very impressive.' Hennessey swept his hat off as he entered the hallway, high ceilings, complex plaster cornices, a large chandelier, deep pile carpets, polished hardwood furniture.

'Yes . . . it's a lovely old building, Regency or late third Georgian, I believe. Must have been a lovely family home but now these buildings are too large for single family occupancy. I mean, who could afford all the servants?' the man said with a humour which Hennessey didn't expect to see. 'Masson.'

'Sorry?'

'Masson. My name is Bernard Masson, chartered accountant, but employed, not a partner.'

'So I gathered,' Hennessey said, smiling, 'otherwise the brass plaque would be Dent, Dent and Masson, I assume.'

'Yes . . . a partnership would be pleasant, so would one's own practice, but employee status has its compensations . . . security and peace of mind. Anyway, shall we go to my office?' Masson shut the heavy front door behind him and walked past Hennessey and Yellich, leading them down the long corridor. 'Very York,' Masson said as he walked with a purposeful stride.

'Sorry?' Hennessey followed in Masson's wake.

'Very York . . . this building . . . old York at least, narrow frontage, but the building goes back a long way, very deep. Frontage of about twenty feet . . . but forty or fifty feet from front to back, very York.'

'As you say. Any cellars?'

'Oh, yes . . . extensive cellarage, of course, but we are prone to flooding.'

'I thought you might be.'

'So we can't use them. The Minster is just on the other side of the wall, as you know, and a few years ago the Bishop of York rowed a small boat up the aisle

of the Minster to the nave . . . famous photograph of that event.'

'I seem to recall seeing it.'

'Well, with that level of flooding occurring once every four or five years, we can't use the cellar, except perhaps for storage of non valuable, non perishable items but that's all . . . such a pity not to be able to utilize all that space.' He turned into a room. 'Please take a seat.' He indicated a row of armchairs in front of his desk. 'We do like to ensure client comfort as well as satisfaction,' he explained, as if seeing the expression of surprise on his visitors' faces.

'Dare say that keeps you in business.' Hennessey sank into one of the armchairs. Yellich followed suit.

'Well, that's the name of the game, as in all businesses; a satisfied customer will return with more work.' He sat behind his desk, leaning back in a hinged, high back, blue executive chair. The window behind him looked out on to a small garden with a high brick wall beyond which were seen the backs and roofs of the houses of High Petergate. 'How can I help you?'

'By describing Mr and Mrs Dent.'

'Describing them?'

'Yes.'

'Well . . . both C.A.s, built up this partnership over twenty-five years, live quietly . . . out by Malton way.'

'Their appearance?'

'Appearance? That is a strange question.'

'If you'd answer it.'

'Well, Mr Dent, Anthony, he is a man of modest size in terms of height . . . smaller . . . shorter than myself. I am five feet eight inches. I still think in Imperial measurement, so Tony would be about five six I should think. Muriel, that is Mrs Dent, is a statuesque six foot plus. I look up to her, down to him . . . literally. I mean, not in any other way; they both have my respect as individuals

and professionals in what can be a stressful occupation at times.'

'I know what you mean. Do you have their address?'

'West End House, Great Sheldwich . . . that's in the Vale of York, off the Malton Road, the A64.'

'Yes.'

'Well, follow the A64 as far as High Hutton, turn right, you'll come to Low Hutton, turn left there . . . well, you have to because the road doubles back to the A64, but Great Sheldwich is just after Low Hutton.'

'You've been there?'

'Does it show? Yes, the Dents are very hospitable, have an annual dinner party for the staff each summer . . . lay on taxis to take us back to our homes, even the junior secretaries are invited. It's one of the ways the Dents make their employees feel that they are part of the crew, one of the team. Good policy. Christmas bonus . . . generous leave. If you work for Dent and Dent, then Dent and Dent work for you . . . that is their policy.'

'I see. Any enemies?'

Masson's brow furrowed. He looked directly at Hennessey. 'Now I am worried. I have been employed by Dent and Dent for nearly twenty years and for the first time we have police officers calling on us, asking me to describe the Dents and wanting to know if they have enemies . . . what is happening?'

'If you'd just answer the question.'

'Oh no . . . oh no . . .' colour drained from Masson's face. 'You don't mean they are that couple . . .?'

'That couple?'

'The regional news, last night . . . the burned bodies . . . found at separate locations . . . small male, tall female . . .'

'We don't know yet,' Hennessey said.

'We'd appreciate it if you would keep this to yourself,' Yellich added. 'We don't want good information to be contaminated by rumour.'

'Of course . . . of course, I have learned to be discreet
. . . one has to if one is a C.A.'

'Good . . . so . . . enemies?'

'None that I know of, either personally or professionally.'

'What do you know of their personal circumstances?'

'Live quietly, as I said, two children . . . now grown,
boy and a girl.'

'I see . . . Do Mr and Mrs Dent have offices in this
building?'

'Yes, on the first floor, the most sought after floor.'
Masson smiled. 'Above ground but not exiled to the attic.
Do you want to see them?'

'In time. I think we ought to confirm that we are talking
about Mr and Mrs Dent. If you could ensure no one goes
in their rooms.'

'Of course. They are locked anyway.'

'Ah.' Hennessey stood. Yellich did likewise. 'So, West
End House, Great Sheldwich . . .'

'You can't miss it . . . ask if you don't see it, it's *the*
house of the village.'

West End House did indeed appear to both Hennessey
and Yellich to be *the* house in Great Sheldwich. It was,
they found, unmissable. It was not so much that it was a
striking, imposing, impressive building in its own right
that made it stand out, it was more its setting. Great
Sheldwich appeared to be more of a hamlet than a village,
with small, badly neglected cottages either side of the
narrow road, some with old, decaying motorcars in the
driveway. The village had but two shops, one of which
was boarded up. No one, not one person was to be seen,
not out of doors, not peering at the strangers from behind
twitching curtains. The wind and threat of rain added to
the sense of desolation.

Beyond the twin rows of small cottages stood a large
house, set back from the road but clearly visible, a pocket

of affluence in an area of rural poverty. Yellich drove slowly through Great Sheldwich and turned the car into the driveway of West End House. Hennessey pondered the house as they approached. Edwardian, he thought, a clear break from the cluttered roof lines so beloved of the Victorians, and a return to the graceful symmetry of the third Georgians, but not a complete return; a small window here and there and tall chimneys at either side of the building indicated its age.

Yellich halted the car beside the front door and Hennessey and he left the vehicle and walked up to the front door, which Hennessey found disappointingly small for a building the size of West End House. Hennessey pulled the bell pull and a jangling sound was heard from within the building. Hennessey and Yellich glanced at each other and then stood facing the door. It was opened, eventually, by a small, thinly built woman in a black dress. 'What?' She squinted at Yellich.

'Police,' said Hennessey, and the woman, rather than turning her head to face him, turned her body in a series of short, jerky movements. 'We'd like to speak to Mr and Mrs Dent.'

'Can't.' The woman spat the word and made to shut the door.

'Why not?' Hennessey held out his hand and prevented the door being closed.

'Not in.'

The door was then opened wider and a taller, generously proportioned woman stood in the doorway. 'Can I help, gentlemen?' Her voice was strong, confident, warm. She turned to the first woman and said, 'Thank you, Gabrielle, just carry on in the kitchen, please.'

Gabrielle scowled at Hennessey and then turned and scurried away with her arms bent at the elbow.

'Sorry,' the woman said as she smiled, 'but she comes from the village, you see.'

'Ah.' Hennessey returned the smile. 'I see.'

'And you are?'

'The police.' Hennessey showed the woman his ID. Yellich also offered his but the woman declined it with thanks saying, that if one is genuine, the other must be.

'Are Mr and Mrs Dent at home? Gabrielle said they were not at home. Is that the case?'

'Yes, it is. Would you care to come in out of the cold?' She stepped backwards and to one side, allowing Hennessey and Yellich to enter.

'Thank you.' Hennessey took his hat off as he stepped into the foyer. He found the house to be unpleasantly cold; he had expected it to be warmer.

'I am Mrs Forester. I am . . . well, like a butler, but we don't use the term. I manage the house for Mr and Mrs Dent.'

'I see. Really, we'd like to talk to them.'

'I'm afraid I don't know where they are. They didn't return home Thursday night, which is unusual, but nothing to panic about . . . but I was beginning to worry and to wonder what to do for the best. I am due home today too . . . I can delay my return.'

'To the village?'

'Heavens no!' Mrs Forester looked indignant at the suggestion. 'No, I live in Malton. I took this job when Mr Forester passed on. It's a live-in position but I get to return to my house each Saturday until Monday lunchtime. No, don't live in Great Sheldwich . . . the village is just one big family. They know who is the mother of each child that's born but the father's name on the birth certificate is a best guess. The men work on the land, the women stay at home. I never go to the village . . . turn right at the gate and it's a straight run to Malton. I have a car you see . . . I am allowed to keep it in the garage, but I wouldn't want to go into the village, it's full of Gabrielles.'

'Is there a Little Sheldwich?' Hennessey asked out of curiosity.

'There was, it was depopulated by the Black Death. A team of archaeologists from York University excavated the area, but there's nothing to see.'

'The village is that old?'

'Apparently . . . the present houses are mainly nineteenth century, but the site of the village is . . . well . . . ancient.'

'I see . . . that is interesting . . . just an interest of mine, you see.'

'Local history?'

'Well, yes, and other areas . . . but you were expecting Mr and Mrs Dent back Thursday evening?'

'Yes. They have stayed out overnight before though, but what is strange is that they always phone and let me or Mr Gregory know.'

'Mr Gregory?'

'Their son . . . he lives in a cottage on the estate.'

'The estate?'

'Yes, Mr and Mrs Dent own a lot of the farmland around here. They do not farm themselves, but rent the land to farmers.'

'I see . . . and Mr Gregory . . . is Gregory his Christian name?'

'Yes, Gregory Dent, but he is referred to as Mr Gregory. He might know where his parents are. I'm sure I don't . . . but then . . . oh . . . they couldn't have phoned Mr Gregory, he was out last night with his young lady. Oh my, and the police asking after them. Oh . . . I'm going to have a turn.' She put her hand up to her mouth.

'I'm sure it's nothing to worry about, Mrs Forester.' Hennessey spoke softly. Privately he was beginning to think that there might well be much to worry about but he did not feel equipped to cope with Mrs Forester having a 'turn'. 'Would it be possible to see their bedroom?'

'Their bedroom?'

'Yes . . . a strange request, but I assure you there is a purpose behind it.'

'Well, they are missing . . . I am sure they would have phoned . . . it is very strange.'

'So . . . may we?'

'Yes . . . yes . . .' Mrs Forester turned and began to ascend the wide staircase. Hennessey and Yellich followed.

The master bedroom, as Mrs Forester referred to it as being, was of what Hennessey thought to be generous proportions, with a king-size bed opposite the door, two large wardrobes, two chests of drawers and a bathroom en suite. A dressing table stood between the bed and the first chest of drawers. Hennessey walked to the dressing table and picked up a hairbrush. 'I'd like to borrow this,' he said. 'May I?'

'Suppose . . .' Mrs Forester suddenly seemed to sound very weary.

'It will help us.' Hennessey took a large self-sealing cellophane sachet from his pocket and dropped the hairbrush inside. 'Tell me, Mrs Forester, what are the Dents' washing practices.'

'Washing practices?'

'Bath or shower?'

'Mrs Dent prefers to bathe . . . Mr Dent showers.'

'Do you mind?' Hennessey indicated the en suite bathroom. Mrs Forester meekly shook her head. Hennessey walked into the bathroom and to the shower. He pulled back the shower curtain and examined the plughole of the shower well and smiled as he did so. Taking a ballpoint from his pocket he hooked it round a small mass of hair that was trapped in the plughole. Upon examination they seemed to be short and grey. He placed them in a smaller sachet. He then returned to the bedroom. 'Do you have a recent photograph of Mr and Mrs Dent?'

'I don't think we do . . . the Dents are very private

36

people. I mean, you don't move into a house in Great Sheldwich to socialize . . . Dare say there is a form of community spirit in this village but it's not the sort of community I would want to be part of . . . oh no, dear me no . . .'

'Holiday snaps? Anything? It really doesn't have to be recent . . . anything that shows their facial appearance. Recent would be better, but not really necessary.'

'Well . . . in the drawing room downstairs . . . perhaps . . . there are some photo albums.'

'Sounds ideal.'

The photograph albums, richly bound in leather, contained family snapshots showing a middle-aged couple, she significantly taller than he, occasional photographs showed a younger man and a woman with them.

'Their son and daughter,' explained Mrs Forester. 'Mr Gregory and Miss Juliette . . . except Miss Juliette is now Mrs Vicary.'

'They don't look like their parents.'

'They are adopted. Mr Gregory and Miss Juliette are natural brother and sister. They were adopted by the Dents when they were infants . . . the Dents are the only parents they have known.'

'I see . . . well, if I can take this photograph?' Hennessey eased a colour print from the mounting fixtures at each corner. 'It's all that we need.' He handed the photograph to Yellich who saw that it showed Mr and Mrs Dent standing together, smiling at the camera. It was a close-up photograph, showing their heads and shoulders only; a little unimaginative as a photograph but Yellich saw why Hennessey had chosen it. It would be very easy to super-impose the skull X-rays on to the faces in the photograph. They would match or they wouldn't.

'You say Mr and Mrs Dent were private people?' Hennessey addressed Mrs Forester.

'Yes, I would describe them as private . . . they keep

themselves to themselves. All they seem to want is each other . . . very touching in a way . . . married for all these years and still love each other.'

'Few friends, then?'

'But that doesn't mean that they are unpopular, it just means that they are . . . private . . . like I said . . . a private couple.'

'Yes . . . enemies?'

'Oh, none that I know of, and really, I am not that close. I know them well as any housekeeper would after five years' service but not closely . . . not closely enough to know their enemies . . . if they had any, but they didn't act like a couple with enemies . . . always relaxed . . . never agitated . . . seemed to leave the house each morning with a certain confidence . . . just wanted to get to work. They seemed to care a lot for their employees.'

'Yes, we heard about the annual dinner party.'

'Oh yes, and the Christmas bonus, and a gift for each employee. It's easy to give money as a Christmas bonus but each employee got a gift as well, made them feel special . . . but you still haven't told me what this is all about.'

'It may all be about nothing, Mrs Forester. We'll know when we get the hair samples back to our forensic science people at Wetherby.'

'The photograph too,' Yellich added.

'Then we may or may not return. Where does Miss Juliette live . . . or Mrs Vicary?'

'In York.'

'And Mr Gregory.'

'On the estate, as I said. He has a cottage about a mile from here.'

'Notice anything about West End House?' Hennessey asked as he and Yellich drove away in the gathering gloom.

'No, boss.' Yellich switched the headlights on.

'It's on the east end of the village.'

'Well, that's Great Sheldwich for you,' Yellich grinned.

'Not a place I'll be visiting in my free time.'
'Nor me.'
It was Saturday, 16.17 hours.

George Hennessey's car started sluggishly. It had not after all been used all day, he being content to let Yellich drive. He drove out of the car park of Micklegate Bar police station. The traffic was heavy; it was approaching Christmas, it was Saturday. He should not be surprised, he told himself, that the traffic was so heavy, all these folk going home with Christmas gifts in the boot of their cars . . . and not a few, no doubt, worrying about the size of their next credit card bill. He joined the traffic stream and inched his way through the ancient city until he could escape on the A19 Thirsk Road, which by then required headlights. He drove to Easingwold and, exploiting a gap in the traffic, turned into a solid-looking detached house. From within the house a dog barked at the sound of the tyres of Hennessey's car on the gravel. Hennessey left his car and entered the house by the front door to be greeted warmly and enthusiastically by a black mongrel which he patted in return. He made himself a pot of tea and then left the house by the rear door, continuing to wear his hat and coat against the wind and the threat of rain. Oscar ran out of the open door, though a dog flap was provided for his convenience, and criss-crossed the rear lawn whilst Hennessey stood sipping a mug of tea.

'Well, this a rum one, to use an expression that amused you when you were new here, rum and no mistake. Man and woman burned . . . well, their corpses were incinerated, and found separately, miles apart, but they can't fail to be linked, and they are going to prove to be one Mr and Mrs Dent. We obtained hair samples from their house, from her hairbrush and the shower plughole in his case. Yellich had them sent off to Wetherby by courier; we'll get a result any time after midday Monday. Sent a photo-

graph of the couple too, just to belt and bracer it. Somebody wanted them dead . . .' He sipped his tea. He loved tea when it was consumed out of doors; he found it fortifying, uplifting. 'And not just dead, but their bodies destroyed as if to prevent their being identified . . . so nobody was after their life insurance.' He laughed at his own joke but there was truth there. It meant that probably, just probably, immediate family could be ruled out as being not under suspicion.

But only probably.

He returned to the house and settled down in the drawing room, having shut the world out by drawing the heavy curtains, and read more of the account of the first battle of the Somme. The volume was a recent addition to his library of military history; it didn't tell him anything he didn't already know, but he did enjoy its style, a collection of written testaments from survivors, some very moving, some angry, some matter-of-fact, some with a strange, emotionless detachment about a battle which cost 60,000 British casualties in the first hour alone.

Later, he supped on a good, wholesome stew and then, having fed Oscar, he took him for their customary walk, half an hour out to an open field, fifteen minutes for Oscar to explore off the lead, and a gentle stroll back.

Still later he walked out again . . . alone . . . into Easingwold to the Dove Inn and a pint of mild and bitter, just one before last orders were called.

Somerled and Sara Yellich sat side by side on the settee in the living room of their home in Nether Poppleton.

'Hate the weekends,' Sara said as she squeezed her husband's hand. 'He's so demanding . . . excited about Christmas. I can understand that, but even so, I am tempted to give in and let him soak up television. I know that's the wrong thing to do but I was close to it today . . . resisted,

but I was close. I was so pleased when you came home. I needed that walk, that hour to myself . . . it freed my mind up.'

'Walking does that. I'll take him out tomorrow . . . I have the day off.'

'I thought you might be going in . . . that case . . .'

'We can't do much until the identity is confirmed. We can't expect a reply from Wetherby until midday Monday. Come on, let's go up.'

'They've found them,' said the man. 'We knew they'd do that.'

'Will they identify them?' the woman asked.

'Probably . . . the fire went out too quickly . . . we didn't get the pile of ash we wanted. Should have put them in the river; let the fishes do the job for us. Should have, should have, should have . . .'

'Going to be a lot of that in the next few days,' she said icily. 'Going to be a lot of that in the next many years if we don't keep our heads.'

'We'll keep them,' the man said confidently. 'Don't worry, we'll keep them.'

It was Saturday, 23.10 hours.

Three

Monday, December 15, 12.30 hours – 16.15 hours
in which the wealth of the deceased is revealed and their family is met.

Hennessey sat at his desk reading one report whilst Yellich sat in front of Hennessey's desk reading the other. The reports were then exchanged. Hennessey read the second report and looked up at Yellich. 'Well, that's it. As we suspected, Mr and Mrs Dent of Great Sheldwich are no longer with us.'

'Appears not. Very quick of Wetherby to come back so speedily.'

'Yes, I must write and thank them. Positive feedback, as I believe it's called, but whatever it is, it helps the world spin and we all need it. Worked under a woman once – she was a watch leader when I was in uniform – had the attitude that no comments are to be made if something goes well or someone did well but you heard about it if something went wrong; it meant all her team received nothing but adverse criticism.'

'Horrible.'

'It was. It was the most dispirited team I was in. I learned from it . . . learned to give positive feedback.'

'I'll remember that, boss.'

'Well . . . we have bad news to break. Could be interesting because, as they say, always look at the in-laws before you look at the out-laws.'

Yellich smiled. He had heard the joke before but he always appreciated the great truth it contained. 'I'll just go and grab my coat.'

Fifteen minutes later, with Yellich once again at the wheel, Hennessey and Yellich were driving along a straight but narrow road across the winter landscape of the Vale of York: blackened, freshly turned soil, denuded trees, a skein of geese under a low, grey sky. Yellich turned off the A19 and drove into Great Sheldwich. As before, not a living person was to be seen, although on that occasion – he thought probably because he was there observing – he did manage to see not one, but two net curtains twitch at their passing. Yellich drove into the driveway of West End House. The two officers left the car, walked up to the door and pulled the bell pull. The door was opened by Mrs Forester who smiled warmly at them.

'I saw you coming up the drive,' she said, 'and wanted to get to the door before Gabrielle. She means well, but social skills are not her strong point.' She then assumed a more serious looking countenance. 'I assume your return is because Mr and Mrs Dent . . . I mean the identification . . . is . . . What is that word? Conclusive . . . positive . . .?'

Hennessey inclined his head. 'Well . . . I am afraid you must continue to assume what you want to assume.'

'Oh . . . because I am not family?'

'Yes.'

'I see . . . well, that tells me everything I need to know. So you'll be looking for family?'

'Yes. You mentioned their children?'

'Mr Gregory and Miss Juliette . . . but they are adopted.'

'They are family in the eyes of the law. If they had been fostered they would not have been considered family,' Hennessey said, 'but having said that, are there any blood relatives?'

'Mr Dent has . . . or had . . . brothers and sisters, as did Mrs Dent.'

Hennessey and Yellich glanced at each other. Yellich said, 'They were adopted . . . As you say, boss, in the eyes of the law that makes them kin.'

'Yes . . . we could do with both.' Hennessey turned to Mrs Forester. 'Do you know where the nearest blood relatives to Mr and Mrs Dent live; nearest in terms of distance?'

'Yes, Mr Dent's brother keeps a shop in Malton High Street, a motorcycle retailer's called Dent Bikes; can't miss it. Mrs Dent has a sister in York . . . I have her address; I'll get it for you. Won't you please come in?' She stepped to one side and allowed Hennessey and Yellich to enter the building. It was still unpleasantly cold inside and Hennessey pondered the size of the heating bill for the house probably explained the chill. Moments later Mrs Forester returned holding a small piece of paper which she handed to Hennessey.

'Bishopthorpe.' Hennessey read the note. 'Quite a nice area, Mrs Forester. Don't know the street, Hollyhock Avenue. Do you, Yellich?'

'Hollyhock Avenue? No . . . rings no bells with me, sir.'

'Very well, we'd be obliged if you would not mention our visit to anybody . . . anybody associated with the house or the Dents, that is.'

'Of course, I am a woman of discretion,' she replied with a smile. 'You may trust me.'

'That is appreciated.' Hennessey returned the smile. 'Well, since we are here and since the law recognizes an adopted person as next of kin . . .'

'You'll need to tuck your trouser bottoms into your socks.'

'Sorry?'

'Anticipating you.' Mrs Forester smiled. 'You are about to ask directions to Mr Gregory's cottage.'

'Yes.'

'Well, the car drive takes ten minutes but the walk across

the field at the back of the house takes less than five. It's very muddy this time of year, though.'

'We'll drive,' Hennessey said.

'Very well . . . right out of the gate, first right and first right again.'

'It'll take us more than five minutes to clean our shoes,' Yellich explained. 'It makes sense to drive there.'

'Ah . . .' Mrs Forester inclined her head at the logic. 'The name of the cottage is Larch Tree Cottage, white door, but it's the only building there at the end of the track.'

Both Hennessey and Yellich thought the man overacted; it was too much of a display. They were seasoned officers; they both felt they knew an act when they saw one. They had followed Mrs Forester's directions, found Larch Tree Cottage with ease, and the light from within and the smoke rising from the chimney told them that the occupier was at home. They knocked on the door and introduced themselves to the young man who answered the door. He was well built. Hennessey thought that women would be attracted to him. He broke down and wept at the news of his adoptive parents' death. He wept too much and too easily for Hennessey and Yellich to believe he was sincere in his grief.

'I knew something was wrong when they still didn't come home on Friday night. What happened?'

'Well, we were wondering if you could help us there?'

'Me?' Gregory Dent shot an alarmed look at Hennessey.

'Yes, Mr Dent, you.'

Dent sank back into his chair and gazed into the log fire. 'I . . .' He shook his head. 'They were my parents . . . I loved them very much. Why should I want to harm them?'

'How do you know they were harmed? We said nothing about them being harmed. We told you they were deceased; we said nothing about them being harmed.'

'Well . . . police . . . it must mean crime.'

'Not necessarily,' Yellich said. 'We notify of accidental death; not a pleasant duty, but we do it.'

'But that's a uniformed officer, alone.Whereas two plain clothes detectives . . . and senior officers . . . What is your rank, sir? Detective Chief Inspector, did you say?'

'Yes.'

'And you are a detective sergeant?'

'Yes.'

'Well, I don't know much about police work but I know enough to know that you two gentlemen with your rank would not call unless my parents' death was suspicious.'

Hennessey said nothing but conceded to himself that Dent had made a fair point.

'Anyway –' Dent waved a hand at the room – 'won't you take a seat? You make me feel tired looking at you stood up.'

Mumbling their thanks, Hennessey and Yellich sat in the two vacant armchairs. 'So,' Hennessey asked, 'when did you last see your parents?'

'Last see them? Friday . . . Thursday . . . Wednesday. Wednesday evening, I called on them on Wednesday. We had a matter to discuss. I left about nine o'clock. So what happened to them?'

Hennessey told him.

'That news item . . .' Dent pointed to a small television set which stood on a shelf beside the stone fireplace. His face paled again. 'They were burned?'

'Yes.'

'But after death . . . it said . . . after death.'

'Yes . . . they were not burned alive, mercifully. So, do you live here alone?'

'Yes.'

'Who owns the cottage?'

'My father owns it, or at least he did.'

'And with your mother also deceased, who will inherit your father's estate?'

'Well, the will has to be read but . . .' Hennessey thought Dent looked smug. 'I dare say me and my sister will get the lion's share . . . dare say that's some compensation for losing your parents.'

'I understand that you and your sister were adopted?'

'Yes. We were old enough to understand right from the outset. My parents couldn't have children, so they adopted a pair. I was five, my sister seven when we came to live at West End House. Our real name is Locke . . . with an *e*. Our parents . . . our natural parents, were killed in a car crash. The story was that my father was a keen rugby player, had a game, got drunk after the game, phoned my mother up to collect him, she took a taxi there, poured him into the back seat with the help of his mates, then less than a mile later they were dead. Killed outright in a collision with a lorry driven by a Frenchman. It was on the wrong side of the road. The frog didn't turn up for the trial and all the judge could do was to issue a warrant for his arrest if he set foot in the UK again; the European arrest warrant didn't exist back then. So, we were shipped off to a children's home. That was alright . . . wasn't anything special. I have no complaints about it. Then we were put up for adoption, the Dents visited us . . . The children's home was in Hull, you see. They signed the papers and we became Gregory and Juliette Dent. We had more trouble adapting to life in West End House than life in the children's home. We were what you'd call working class . . . East Hull . . . know it?'

'Not really . . . been there a couple of times,' Hennessey said.

'Same,' Yellich added.

'Well, we took to the children's home because we spoke their language, in their accent, but the Dents were upper middle class . . . we had some adjusting to do, and then they packed us off to boarding school. Just minor public schools, mine was in Cumbria, near Carlisle. Juliette went

to one in Norfolk. Lucky her, quite near Norwich. Do you know Norwich?'

'Can't say I do.' Hennessey was content to let Dent talk. He noticed the apparent grief had rapidly evaporated.

'Me neither.'

'Lovely city.' Dent smiled as if recollecting a pleasant memory. 'But not Carlisle . . . drab place . . . the only good thing about Carlisle was the railway station, not because that's the way out, but because it's always busy. We used to be able to go out of school on Saturday afternoons and I would often go the railway station just to watch the trains. Such a busy station; trains coming and going all the time . . . from north and south . . . east and west . . . passenger as well as goods traffic. That was my escape from school, but Juliette did better. She made friends at school, unlike me, and had Norwich to visit on Saturdays and public holidays.'

'Are you employed, Mr Dent?'

'You mean, what am I doing sitting at home in the middle of the afternoon on a weekday?'

'No . . . no . . . I meant are you employed?' Hennessey spoke solemnly. 'Many shift workers sit at home on a weekday afternoon.'

'OK, point to you. Yes, I am employed. I manage the campsite.'

'Campsite? Tents?'

'No . . . I should call it the caravan site. We have a site of static caravans, fifty static caravans out by Filey. People from Leeds and Sheffield rent them for a fortnight at a time with their children. Confess I wouldn't keep a dog in one but they're happy enough. The work is seasonal, keeps me busy in summer, then the site is shut down, some routine maintenance to enable the vans to weather the winter. That wind off the North Sea, I swear you'd think the vans were being attacked with crowbars . . . One little crack and the wind gets in and

widens it, so we repaint the vans as soon as the season is over, put bitumen on the roofs, seal them for the winter. When that's done, there is nothing else to do until the spring when the vans are valeted before the season starts. They're fenced in . . . and we have an old man keeping his eye on them in case the vandals get in, but they never do. The locals know that there's nothing in the vans . . . and who's going to go on the cliff top on a wild night in February just to break a few windows for a laugh? So they're safe . . . like my friend's sheep.'

'Sheep?' Hennessey glanced at the fire as a log crackled.

'School friend . . . made a fortune in the City, just bought and sold at the right times, then went green and bought an island in the Orkneys with just one house on it . . . quite a large house . . . put some sheep on the island which was criss-crossed with drystone walls and gateways in the walls allowing the sheep to roam all over the island. In the winter he and his girlfriend head south to France, the Mediterranean coast of same . . . leaving the sheep to fend for themselves.'

'They can do that?'

'Apparently . . . you see, there's very little snow in the Orkneys because of the sea's influence, so the sheep can always reach the grass, keep themselves well fed. There are no predators on the island, and the criss-crossing nature of the walls means that the sheep can always find a lee of a wall to shelter behind, no matter which way the wind blows. Rupert, my friend, and his girlfriend return in the spring for lambing. They're very green wellie, wax jacket types when in the Orkneys. So my vans are like his sheep. In the winter they fend for themselves.'

'And you put your feet up in front of a log fire?'

'Hard life, isn't it?' Gregory Dent smiled a very self-satisfied smile, Hennessey thought, very self-satisfied, too self-satisfied. A 'cat that got the cream' sort of satisfaction, a 'can't-touch-me' expression. Hennessey had seen

that expression many times, and many times he had disabused the wearer of the idea.

'But I do have other responsibilities. I am supposed to be the family member in charge of the house,' he pointed to West End House. 'Both my parents working, you see . . . but Mrs Forester is so . . . efficient . . . she does my job for me.'

'So you sit at home?'

'Most days in the winter. In the summer I have to be at the van site . . . my own little box to live in and those people who knock on your door at all hours, speaking in dialect, complaining about this and that. I am twenty-seven years old, I have got better things to do with my summers than spend them in Filey and with no end in sight . . . and there's Rupert Fullerton with his island in the Orkneys bought and paid for and his house in the south of France, also bought and paid for . . . same age as me . . . set for life.' His chin set firm, 'the cat that got the cream' look evaporated and was replaced by an expression that said 'injustice' and 'gross unfairness'.

'Time to do something about it,' Hennessey suggested.

'Well, things are now quite different . . . overnight they are different. I am sorry for the parents, they pulled us out of that children's home . . . Sycamore Lodge it was called.'

'Sycamore Lodge,' Hennessey repeated.

'East Hull . . . forget the name of the road. We were there for nearly a year . . . Hughes Street Primary School.'

'Hughes Street?'

'Yes . . . I wasn't unhappy there, better than at Brookfield.'

'Brookfield?'

'My boarding school, up by Carlisle from where I used to catch the bus into Carlisle, get off by the citadel, buy a platform ticket and spend the afternoon on the platforms of the railway station . . . Trains from north and south and east and west, remember. Wasn't a trainspotter though.

Could never see the point in writing train numbers into a little book.'

'So . . . your father had a business interest outside the accountancy practice?'

'Yes . . . not just the van site. He owned a garage, a petrol filling station, not a repair garage. He doesn't . . . didn't know enough about cars to run a repair garage; and he has a car park; that is money for nothing; concrete a bit of land and charge people to park their cars on it. I mean, what could be an easier way of making money? He owns a few houses he rents to students . . . another money-spinner; students pay for the house, you own it. Then he has quite a portfolio of stocks and shares . . . So he's worth a little money.'

'Any enemies?'

'What businessman doesn't have enemies? Seems the more successful you are, the more enemies you make. Seems like that anyway.'

'Anyone in particular?'

'I wasn't close enough to the heart of things to know.'

'I see . . . but you'll benefit from his death?'

'Oh . . . I hope so . . .' Again he smiled. Hennessey saw that 'the cat that got the cream' look had reappeared. 'I do hope so.'

'So where were you on Thursday evening?'

'With my girlfriend.'

'Where were you?'

'At her house. Alone.'

'Just the two of you?'

'Just the two of us.'

'We'll have to confirm that with her. And we'll also have to speak with your sister. If you could give us their addresses?'

'Gladly.' Gregory Dent stood and once again revealed himself to be a lithe and a muscular young man.

*　　*　　*

'Gregory phoned. He said you'd call.' The woman seemed pale, drawn. Hennessey thought she was in shock. 'Mummy and Daddy . . . you'd better come in.'

Hennessey and Yellich stepped over the threshold into what seemed to Hennessey to be a modest family home. The woman invited them into the living room and began to pick up cushions and put them down again, run her fingers through her hair and turn away from the officers and turn towards them again.

'We could call later,' Hennessey offered.

'No . . . no, please . . . I want to know what happened . . . Mummy and Daddy . . . please take a seat.'

Hennessey and Yellich sat in an armchair each, the woman sat on the settee chewing her nails. She wore faded denim jeans, sports shoes, a man's rugby shirt patterned in brown and yellow horizontal stripes. Her hair was combed back and fashioned into a small ponytail. Hennessey read the room. It was a little untidy, more 'lived in' he thought than abandoned, it was clean, prints of the French Impressionists hung on the wall. The room smelled of air freshener and furniture polish, but faintly so.

'You are Mr and Mrs Dent's adopted daughter?'

'Yes, Mrs Vicary, Juliette Vicary. My husband teaches at Trinity College, not as grand as it sounds . . . it isn't Trinity College, Cambridge, nor even Trinity College, Dublin, but Trinity and St Joseph's College of Education. It produces primary school teachers. My husband teaches a course in history. As well as developmental psychology and such, the students have to major in one academic subject . . . my husband teaches those who choose history.'

'I see.'

'He's not at home . . . he'll be back at about five if you need to talk to him.'

'Not really,' Hennessey spoke softly. 'I don't think there's any need to speak to your husband at all. We really want to know more about Mr and Mrs Dent.'

'Yes . . . but who would want to harm them?'

'Is the question we would like answering too . . . who would? Do you know?'

Juliette Vicary shook her head. 'No . . . no . . . I know of no enemies of theirs but Daddy had a finger in a lot of pies. He was more than just an accountant . . . he was a businessman.'

'So we found out . . . quite an empire.'

'Oh . . . hardly anything.' She forced a smile. 'I mean in the great scheme of things, hardly a multinational corporation. He was a small fish, very local, no business interests outside York. I don't think he planned to . . . Mind, he was looking forward to his retirement, so his planning days were over.'

'What was he going to do with his business . . . his businesses?'

'I really don't know.'

'You and Gregory wouldn't take anything over?'

'Oh, no.' She smiled and then glanced out of the window. 'No, I am the wife of a history teacher and we both want to start a family. I have no time to run a business, I am just not that sort to be a businesswoman, swanning around in a Jaguar. I doubt my learned husband would approve anyway. He thinks that teaching is a noble profession; he likes working for a salary. He has often said he wouldn't work in the private sector, he wouldn't want to work for the profit motive.'

'I see.' Hennessey relaxed in the armchair. He was struck by how different Juliette Vicary seemed to be from her brother. He detected the family resemblance, both tall, he well built, she not big boned, but not finely made either, and there, he thought, the resemblance ended. His first impression of this woman was that she was warm and genuine, while the impression he had of her brother was that he was neither. 'And your brother, would he have become responsible for your father's local empire upon Mr Dent's retirement?'

Juliette Vicary's head sank forward. She looked uncomfortable. 'No . . . you may as well know that ours wasn't a particularly happy home. I seemed to get on alright with Mummy and Daddy . . . I did well at school . . . I didn't want to go to university, I worked on a kibbutz for a while to get some life experience . . . sort of find myself, met Leonard and my parents approved the match. It's been a good ten years for Leonard and me . . . Children are a bit delayed, we've been trying . . . there's still time . . . but Gregory and Daddy . . . I think he was a disappointment to them . . . not Daddy's fault, nor Mummy's. You adopt a child . . . you adopt someone else's creation . . . but Gregory is feckless. That's it, he's my brother – full brother – and he is feckless.'

'He manages a campsite of static caravans.'

'Does he?' Juliette Vicary raised her eyebrows. 'You know him.'

'We do?'

'Yes . . . well, the police at Filey do. He stole money from the safe in the manager's office . . . quite a lot of money . . . two thousand pounds.'

'And he's still allowed to keep his job?'

'He has to be given a job . . . a nominal job, so Daddy thinks. If he doesn't, he'll only get into more trouble with you gentlemen. It keeps him out of trouble. Letting him think he's got a job and giving him a salary and a place to live . . . rent free as well, he pays nothing for his cottage, he's kept. If it wasn't for a man at the site, a man called Mayhew, Clarence Mayhew, the caravan rental business would have gone under years ago. He is the under manager of the site but to all intents and purposes he is *the* manager. I'm sorry, I am in a bit of a state . . .'

'Yes, I can appreciate how difficult this is for you.'

'Well, answering the questions isn't difficult . . . absorbing what has happened is. It doesn't seem real . . . it's like a dream. I am sure you see this all the time.'

'A few times.' Hennessey smiled. 'Not all the time, thank goodness . . . that would be too much to cope with.'

'I can imagine . . . but you see life.'

'Yes.'

'That's what an Israeli soldier once said to me on the kibbutz . . . soldiers don't get paid much but we see life.'

'Dare say we can say the same. So who would know the extent of your father's business dealings?'

'Only Daddy. His papers will be in the premises of the accountancy firm, but you'll need to be a Philadelphia lawyer to get to grips with them.'

'Dare say we could cope. Do we have your permission to look at them?'

'Do you need my permission?' She held her palm against her chest.

'Yes . . . either yours or Gregory's.'

'You are the surviving heirs,' Yellich explained.

'Oh, I suppose I am . . . I haven't thought that far ahead.' She glanced at the window, distracted by the sound of a car drawing to a halt outside her house. 'It's my husband; I phoned him at work . . . I told him about Mummy and Daddy . . . I told him you would be calling . . . He's obviously been able to get away. Excuse me.' Juliette Vicary stood and walked hurriedly out of the door.

Hennessey and Yellich heard the front door open and Juliette Vicary say, 'Oh, Leonard, the police are here,' and a male voice then issued words of comfort. The door shut with a click and a man walked down the entrance hall and stood in the living room.

'Mr Vicary?' Hennessey stood. Yellich did likewise.

'Yes.' He extended his hand. 'Please be seated, gentlemen,' he said as he shook Hennessey's hand with a firm but not a crushing grip. He sat on the settee; Juliette sat beside him, nestling into him. 'This is a tragedy,' he said, 'a real tragedy.'

'Yes.' Hennessey nodded. 'Two lives. Any life taken

before its due time is a tragedy, even elderly people, and a married couple still with much to live for . . . yes, a tragedy.'

'Yes . . . what happened?'

'Well.' Hennessey sank back on to the settee, 'details, as they say, are sketchy. Both were killed before they were incinerated.'

'Thank goodness.' Leonard slid his hand into his wife's. 'Sorry, I didn't mean it to sound like that . . . I am just grateful that they were not burned alive; that would be too terrible to contemplate.'

'It's alright.' Hennessey held up his palm. 'I know what you meant. We had the same fear and the same sense of relief, but one, Mr Dent, appeared to have been killed by a massive blunt trauma to the head. Mrs Dent appeared to have been strangled.'

'Oh . . .' Juliette's hand went up to her mouth. 'Mummy.' Leonard Vicary slid his arm round her shoulders and pulled her closer to him.

'Little else is known, so we're at the stage of tracing their last movements and inquiring into any person who might have had a motive to harm them.'

'Harm! I think they did a bit more than harm.' Leonard Vicary seemed to Hennessey to cut a striking figure; he was a man who appeared to be in his late thirties, he had a full head of white hair which was swept back and balanced with a striking white beard and moustache, and between them sat a strongly pointed nose. He spoke with an accent foreign to Yorkshire. Midlands, thought Hennessey, north of London but south of Birmingham, that sort of area. 'But anything we can do to help,' Leonard continued.

'So, just to eliminate you, where were you last Thursday evening?'

'Home . . . here.' Leonard Vicary spoke with finality.

'Just the two of you?'

'Yes . . . it's a pattern that has established itself during term time, especially towards the end of term as now. It's the job . . . I love teaching but it takes from you. At the end of the week, all I want to do is collapse in front of the television. Just me and Juliette and a bottle of chilled Frascati, before and during a meal and then a very early night . . . I mean about nine p.m., probably nine thirty or ten . . . We also stay in on Fridays and Saturdays. The town is full of youth then but Sunday evenings, when said youth is paying for the previous evening, and the pubs are quiet, then we stroll out to the Lockkeepers' Arms . . . know it?'

'No.'

'Near here . . . real ale . . . no music . . . no smoking allowed anywhere. A real gem of a pub . . . but Thursday we were at home . . . home alone . . . just we two . . . just as wc like it.'

'Just soaking up television?'

'Well, soaking up the screen . . . Don't watch a lot of television . . . Video we rented from the video shop or a DVD from the DVD shop.'

'What did you watch?'

'*My Father's Den* . . . New Zealand film . . . quite good.'

'I'll keep an eye out for it. So . . . you knew little of Mr and Mrs Dent's business dealings?'

'Little, close to nothing,' Leonard Vicary answered, 'especially me, I had . . . still have, no interest in the Dent Corporation.'

'It's hardly a corporation,' Juliette Vicary said as she glanced at her husband. 'A few small businesses in and around York . . . and it's not fair . . . they're dead, murdered . . . it's not fair to dismiss them like that anymore.'

'Sorry, sorry . . .' He squeezed her shoulders gently. 'Sorry.'

'You didn't approve of your parents-in-law?'

'I liked them as a couple – provided me with a beautiful wife – but I am not interested in business. I am a man of

57

modest beginnings. I am proud of my degree, our little house, all bought and nearly paid for by education, education and education . . . That's my world . . . not the world of finance and property and profit . . . So I especially, and we as a couple, know nothing of Mr and Mrs Dent's business dealings.'

'And it's only Daddy.'

'Sorry?'

'Only Daddy,' Juliette Vicary explained. 'It was only Daddy who had business interests; Mummy was a partner in the accountancy practice but not in anything else.'

'Ah . . . I see . . . so the person to ask is at the practice . . . back on Precenters Court?'

'Yes.'

'So when did you last see your parents?'

The Vicarys glanced at each other. 'Last weekend,' Juliette answered. 'We drove out for Sunday lunch . . . that's also a pattern . . . not every Sunday.'

'About once a month,' Leonard Vicary explained. 'About . . . not a regular as clockwork thing.'

'Did you and Mr and Mrs Dent have a good relationship, as son-in-law and parents-in-law?'

Vicary glanced at his wife, who held eye contact with him. She nodded slightly. Vicary then turned to Hennessey and said, 'Yes . . . yes, I did. He is a wealthy man . . . Sorry, was a wealthy man, and like all wealthy men, he naturally suspected my motives when he was told Juliette and I had got engaged.'

'He was worried that you might be after his money?'

'Yes, that thought must have crossed his mind and he tested me . . . he provided a modest dowry for Juliette and then left a substantial sum of money in a trust fund to be shared equally by his grandchildren upon their reaching the age of twenty-seven.'

'Twenty-seven?'

'Too young and they'll squander it . . . that was his thinking. I think he was right. If I was given a million . . .'

'A million!'

'I said it was a substantial sum of money.' Vicary smiled. 'If we have four children, they'll inherit a million each . . . if we have three . . . or two . . . or one . . . any equal shares of four million pounds.'

'And if we don't have children, we'll adopt,' Juliette Vicary added helpfully. 'That's a bit of a family tradition.'

'I see.' Hennessey smiled. 'I see.'

'And when he also found out that I was interested only in pursuing a career in teaching and not wanting to edge my way into his business empire, then I met with his approval and married his beautiful daughter.' Leonard and Juliette Vicary beamed at each other. 'So our relationship was warm . . . we enjoyed Sunday lunch at West End House.'

'So you won't benefit from his death or that of Mrs Dent either?'

'That remains to be seen . . . he might have left us a few drops of drinking water, but we are advised the flood has gone to a trust fund to give to human beings who have yet to be born.'

'The accountancy practice has no selling value,' Juliette Vicary explained. 'It's like a law firm; the money comes in from clients, keeps the owners and employees in work, but upon the owner's death or retirement, the firm will be wound up, the employees will find other positions, the clients other accountants. Only the premises will have some value but the concept of the business . . . none at all.' She paused. 'Oh . . . this is really . . . all too much to take on board, I still can't believe it . . . This morning Mummy and Daddy were alive . . . so I thought . . . now I am . . . now they are deceased and those news reports about the man and woman being burned . . . well, their bodies were burnt. I never, never in my wildest dreams thought . . . life has got very real . . . it feels very solid, colours are louder. I looked at the front lawn before you gentlemen arrived

and I found beauty in a blade of grass. I read that once, that a dying man can find beauty in a blade of grass. Well, I can tell you that suddenly bereaved people can find the same beauty in the same place . . . and yet you know, there is a dream-like quality to it all. I really need to lie down . . . Would you mind?'

'No.' Hennessey stood, Yellich also. 'This has been very useful . . . it has helped us.'

'Helped?' Leonard Vicary also stood. 'I can't see what we have done to help.'

'Background information . . . helped us to get the measure of the Dent household out there at Great Sheldwich . . . all grist to the mill.'

'Well, you know where we are if you think we can help you further.'

'Indeed.'

'I'll see you out.'

Bernard Masson furrowed his brow. 'Do you have that authorization in writing?'

'No,' Hennessey replied. 'Sorry, no . . . it's verbal but given before my sergeant here.' He indicated to Yellich who sat beside him in front of Masson's desk.

'If you don't mind . . .' Masson reached forward and picked up the phone on his desk, 'I'll confirm it. Ah, Penny, can you please phone Mr and Mrs Dent's daughter . . . the number is in our directory under V. Yes, Vicary . . . thanks, I'll hold. Sorry, but I must be certain you have the permission.'

'Of course.' Hennessey nodded. 'I would do the same.'

'Good of you. Oh . . . Juliette, sorry to disturb you, it's Bernard. May I say how sorry I am . . . we all are really . . . well, the police are here . . .' Moments later he replaced the phone and said, 'Well, as you say, on the authorization of their daughter and eldest child, you may have full access to all the papers in respect of the late Anthony Dent's business dealings. The only spare accommodation

60

is Mr Dent's office . . . or Mrs Dent's . . . bit like stepping into dead men's shoes.'

'Are you familiar with Mr Dent's business dealings?'

'His little empire?' Masson pursed his lips. 'I think I am . . . unless anything major has been withheld from me . . . I think I am.'

'We'll look at the documents, of course, but could you give us some idea of what we will find?'

'Lots of small businesses with low overheads and little time needed to devote to the management of same. Anthony's time was consumed almost wholly by the practice.' Masson tapped his desktop. 'This was his passion. He built it from scratch. He was a recently qualified accountant and was working for Wheeler, Perkins and Walsh – they have premises in St Leonard's Place, big firm, good firm but got a bit sloppy with one of their clients, a landowner, a gentleman farmer in the old tradition. Anthony phoned this gentleman one day, one weekend from his home and asked, "How would you like to receive a quarter of a million pounds?" This was some thirty years ago remember, probably two or three million in today's terms. The client replied, "What do I have to do?" "Nothing," says Anthony, "just give me your account." Turns out that the gentleman had been paying far too much tax. Wheeler, Perkins and Walsh just were not doing their job . . . they'd put a sloppy junior in charge of the account and for years he'd been paying far too much to the Exchequer. So Anthony set up alone, the client moved his account to Dent and Dent. Muriel and he were not yet married, though they were an item, and Anthony came up with the goods and this gentleman received a massive rebate. Christmas came early for him that year. Word spread and Anthony won some very wealthy clients among the landowning set in West and North Yorkshire. The cloth-capped pigeon-fancier typical Yorkshireman who goes to bed sucking on a rod of mild steel, well, that belongs to

South Yorkshire . . . possibly Leeds and Bradford as well, but in the Vale and the Dales there is some very serious old money . . . And Dent and Dent is *the* accountants to have. We are proud of our reputation . . . Our clients stay with us.'

'So how much are . . . were the Dents worth?'

'Pencil figure?'

'Alright.'

'All in . . . probably about ten.'

'Ten?'

'Million.'

Hennessey gasped. 'I knew he was well off, but not that well off.'

'Well, it's what he's worth in terms of his property portfolio. There is West End House . . . and that is a lot of property. It's not just the house, you see, it's the farmland that surrounds the house, then there is the caravan site . . .'

'Gregory's little area of responsibility.'

'Yes. Anthony did not just own all the caravans on the site, he also owned the site itself; that's quite a few acres of cliff top. If planning permission could be obtained to build on that, a hotel perhaps, then it would be worth a great deal of money. Then there is this building –' Masson waved a hand with an upturned palm – 'excellent condition, Regency, smack in the centre of York overlooking the Minster grounds. Already you are into six figures. Then there are the car parks . . . small by comparison, but city centre sites, again with planning permission . . . who knows what they could be worth?' Masson paused. 'Then there's land . . .'

'More land?'

'Oh yes, it's all land. Low maintenance business; farms that are let to tenant farmers for a modest rent, but Anthony owned the land, acres of private woodland, stretches of river banks on which he sells annual angling permits to use. The car parks are private, not staffed, they have a

barrier across the entrance and each person that rents a space has a key. So no need to have somebody there collecting the parking fees. The land he owns doesn't generate a great deal of income, but it's the fact that he owns it that makes him wealthy.'

'I see . . . so who would benefit from his death?'

Masson opened his hands and shrugged. 'I suppose that depends on his will. If he didn't leave it all to a cat's home and made a logical will, then in the event of the common calamity I would assume that his adoptive son and daughter would become handsomely well off.'

'Very handsomely, I'd say,' commented Yellich.

'What do you know of his children?' asked Hennessey.

'Little. Met both but know little.'

'Did Mr Dent ever speak of his children?'

'Often, as any parent would . . . not worried about Juliette, she made a good marriage to a man who is not interested in the business, but Gregory . . . Anthony was worried about him . . . called him feckless. He really didn't see Gregory doing anything for the business. Come to think of it, ten might be an underestimate . . . might be nearer fifteen . . . possibly above fifteen. Well, I'll get the papers.' Masson stood. 'Tell you who to talk to . . .'

'Oh?'

'Anthony's brother . . . out in Malton, owns a motor-cycle retail outlet.'

'Yes, we have heard of him.'

'They were close . . . he and Anthony. If Anthony did say anything of relevance, it would have been to his brother.'

'Thursday night? Last week?' The woman extended a slender finger upwards and then to her right as if indicating 'last week' was outside her home, somewhere in the narrow street. She was slender, like her finger, a mop of black hair over a balanced face. She kept the

central heating turned up so that on a day like that day, she was comfortable in a red T-shirt and cut down jeans. One leg she folded underneath her as she sat, the other extended until her bare foot rested on the varnished floorboards. Her home was a modest terraced house within the walls of the city, where it is said that there is a church for every Sunday in the year and a pub for every other day.

Hennessey and Yellich sat side by side on the sofa, being the only other seating available in the cramped room.

'Yes. I presume Mr Dent phoned you to tell you we'd be calling?'

'He might have done but I have only just returned from work. So, Thursday last week?'

'Yes.'

'You know, I find it difficult to recall, it's the sign of a busy life . . . I am a legal secretary. Let's see, Monday today, yesterday was a lazy day. I don't work on a Sunday, not out of any religious conviction, I just don't lift a finger . . . not even any washing up. The washing up from yesterday's meals still waits for me in the kitchen, a great pile of it. Saturday . . . Saturday I shopped, began to eat away at my Christmas shopping list.' She glanced at her ceiling of mauve painted plaster. 'I dread my credit card bill; it's going to be a belt-tightening winter for this little spendthrift. I come from a large family with many relatives to buy for. So, that was Saturday . . . spent Saturday evening wrapping them up, then had an early night. Friday . . . at work all day . . . I work at Banks and Webb.'

'I don't know that firm.'

'They don't do criminal work, there's no money in it, so you probably wouldn't have heard of them. Just civil law work.'

'I see.'

'So Friday night I stayed in . . . Thursday . . . yes, Gregory was here, we both had a quiet night in. He stayed

the night and left when I went to work. He returned to
the mausoleum.'

'The mausoleum?'

'That's what Gregory calls West End House.'

'So . . . tell us, Miss Thurnham . . .'

'Mrs. Sorry, I am Mrs Thurnham. I am separated . . .
divorce pending. When I am divorced, I will return to my
maiden name of Moss. Susan Moss. Can't wait to return,
my maiden name makes me feel clean. My marriage was
short and unpleasant; the name of Thurnham makes me
feel contaminated.' She shrugged. 'Anyway, tell you
what?'

'Are you a long time associate of Mr Dent's?'

'We've known each other for about six months, known
each other in the biblical sense for about four . . . being
of course the last four.'

'I see.'

'I was reluctant to get involved with anyone so soon
after separating from Baron William the brute, of York,
but Gregory has a charm about him, and I have my needs.
I want many pleasant memories to comfort me when I am
in my rocking chair.'

'Aye,' Hennessey sighed, 'none of us get younger, except
Merlin the Magician, and growing old is no fun but it's
distinctly preferable than the alternative. So you haven't
seen Gregory Dent since the news of his parents' murder?'

'No . . . I didn't know whether to call or not. I am not
very skilled on such occasions . . . Sometimes . . . well, my
parents are very cautious people and they told me over
and over again: "if you don't know what to do, do nothing"
or as they said, "if in doubt do nowt". So I did nowt.
Gregory knows where I am if he needs me.'

'Alright . . . do you know much about his relationship
with his parents?'

Susan Thurnham shrugged. 'Not good . . . edgy . . . I
think there were arguments. Gregory complained that they

were holding him back. He wanted more of his father's business empire; he felt it was rightfully his.'

'He did?'

'Yes . . . all he got was a silly management position at the caravan site on the cliff top. He wanted more than that; he's very ambitious, impatient to get on, but his parents are . . . or were . . . blocking him, so he said.'

'Interesting.'

'What happens now, I don't know. It will be dependent upon what his parents left him in their will, I suppose.'

'Indeed. Mrs Thurnham, I have to tell you this, that anybody who provides a false alibi is liable to prosecution as an accessory.'

She raised her eyebrows and smiled. 'Is that a fact?'

'Yes.' Hennessey stood. Yellich did likewise. 'Yes, it's a fact.'

Four

Tuesday, December 16, 09.00 – 16.30 hours
in which the good Chief Inspector has old wounds unin-
tentionally opened and later meets a sputnik, and Yellich
views an illuminating photograph.

'Dad advised them against it.' Robin Dent sat at his
desk, reclining in his chair. Hennessey cast an eye
round the office. He saw it to be neat, efficient-looking,
a little characterless, he thought. Behind Dent was a
calendar of photographs of motorbikes. December's photograph was of a powerful looking yellow machine with a
leggy girl in a Father Christmas jacket and hat sitting
astride it.

Hennessey felt uncomfortable in the shop. Personal,
deeply felt and unpleasant memories resonated. 'Really?'

'Really.' Robin Dent was, Hennessey noted, like his
deceased brother, short in stature. 'Yes, really,' he smiled.
There was, thought Hennessey, a warmth about the man.
'Mind you, Dad advised me against buying my first bike
and look where it got me.' He looked around him. 'I haven't
got the money that Anthony had with his empire but I
have done well . . . pulled myself up. We are both of
humble origins; never had a lot when we were growing
up. It makes you lust for wealth, not easy money, but
money. There is moral money and immoral money. Dad
was a lay preacher, a Methodist, was always one for the
right and the wrong of it. Talked about giving and the

67

importance to give of yourself. I could quite understand it when he didn't want me to get a motorbike, few parents like their children having bikes but really they are as safe as their rider.'

And that, thought Hennessey with anger, is not true. It isn't true at all. He managed to remain silent. He breathed in through his nose and smelled a cocktail of air freshener and furniture polish with a whiff of new leather, new metal and new rubber.

'So . . .' Dent continued, 'it was something of a surprise when he advised Anthony and Muriel against adopting. He said, you just do not know what you are bringing into the family, you do not know what damaged goods you are taking on board. You can't make a silk purse out of a sow's ear, that was his most often used phrase, which we thought strange. He was all for giving of yourself, helping others. We thought adopting a couple of orphaned children would have a place within his philosophy but how wrong we were. His notion of giving did not extend to compromising his own. He had a shrewdness about him which we only found out when Anthony and Muriel announced their intention to adopt.'

'Interesting.'

'Yes . . . it was . . . you're twenty plus and you find out something about your parents for the first time . . . it's a revelation.'

'So there was not a great age gap between your brother and sister-in-law and their adoptive children?'

'No . . . the age gap was enough to be parent and child but it wasn't a massive gap . . . but enough.'

'They gave up easily, or was there a clear medical reason for not having children?'

'Gave up?'

'Trying for a family.'

'Ah . . . no . . . they tried . . . had tests and found out that Anthony was sterile, he'd never have children. That was

a massive blow to Muriel . . . worse than if she was unable to have children, so she said, because she was able to reproduce but would never have children on her own . . . but she loved Anthony. It was a sacrifice she was prepared to make. Good for her, I say.'

'Yes, a noble gesture.'

'Not like our parents . . . there was quite a gap between us and them, particularly Dad. He was an elderly father but a strong man, just went on and on. He was killed . . .'

'I'm sorry.'

'So were we . . . he was knocked down by a motorcyclist. Ironically the motorcyclist bought his machine from this outlet. I sold a young man a machine that he rode into my father . . . It has given me something to think about.'

'I'll say.'

'But most of the bikes you see round here are purchased from me and it probably was Dad's fault. He stepped into the path of the biker – there were witnesses – and the biker wasn't doing anything wrong. The police didn't prosecute him; says a lot.'

'Yes.'

'He was tipped to make the century eventually, get a telegram from Buckingham Palace . . . but he had had a long life and he had lived it well, so his funeral was still a celebration of a life. He was eighty-four, so he might have been short-changed a little . . . but only a little.'

'Yes.' Hennessey nodded. 'Short-changed but only a little.' Again, difficult memories echoed and chimed, again anger at the unfairness of it all gripped at his chest.

'Well, he was very upset when he heard about Gregory and Juliette having been found in a children's home in East Hull. He said the Americans have a saying, "You can take the kid out of the ghetto, but you can't take the ghetto out of the kid".'

'Yes, thank you . . . I was aware of that.'

'Well, he seemed to have been proved correct. Anthony once said that he wondered what sort of monster we had brought into this family.'

'Meaning?' Hennessey sat forward.

'Meaning Gregory. He and Muriel never seemed to be worried about Juliette . . . but Gregory was always very difficult. There was always something amoral about him. If he wasn't given anything he'd take it but he wouldn't see it as stealing . . . tried to find a rationalization. He just wouldn't see it as theft, or lack of responsibility, or whatever. He'd been given a job to do, and he wouldn't do it because nobody else had been given a similar job . . . this was when he was a boy. Juliette would be given a reward for something; he'd take the same thing as his reward . . . played according to his own rules, which he made up to suit himself as he went along.'

'I have met the type.'

'Yes . . . in your line of work I imagine you have. But Anthony was fearful. He once said he thought that Dad had been right, he said he feared great trouble from Gregory . . . That was when he was still quite young, and the problem with adopting is that you can't un-adopt easily . . . and you can't split up siblings. They couldn't keep Juliette and send Gregory back, so they kept him, sent him to a Roman Catholic boarding school in the hope that a good infusion of popery would instil some sense of right and wrong in him.'

'Do you know how he got on at school?'

Robin Dent shook his head. 'I don't . . . Anthony never spoke about it, but Gregory left as soon as he could with few, if any, qualifications . . . he never mentioned any school friends to me. Seemed to come home expecting Anthony and Muriel to provide for him. Never took a job . . . Technically – legally – they could have shown him the door on his sixteenth birthday but that was either not

70

in their nature . . . or . . . and I hesitate to say this . . . or they were by then already frightened of him.'

'Had they reason to fear him?'

'Well, nothing was said but I did suspect he had been violent, more likely towards Anthony, but probably Muriel as well, and Anthony told me of the cats that went missing, often coincidental with the sound of a shotgun being discharged.'

'They had a firearm?'

'A 410 . . . licensed . . . to keep the vermin down on the farm.'

'Alright.'

'But over a period of twelve months, the four cats they had disappeared. At the time each one disappeared, Gregory was seen with the 410 as if busying himself shooting rats . . . and rabbits . . . and magpies . . . maybe a fox; that was the sort of job Gregory would do . . . use the 410, but anything constructive, long term, anything requiring a level of responsibility, no way, not Gregory.'

'How did the animals in the house react to him?'

'They kept out of his way. The old Labrador they had growled at him the moment he entered the house, and the little boy that he was then, he smiled at the dog growling at him, a really sinister smile. The dog died soon afterwards.'

'Interesting.'

'Isn't it? I thought you people always visited in pairs?'

'Not always, only when visiting suspects.' Hennessey stood. 'And you are not a suspect . . . just a provider of background information.'

'That's a relief.' Robin Dent also stood and he and Hennessey shook hands. 'Can't interest you in a motorbike? You don't see yourself as a "grey biker"? I am selling a lot of machines to retired couples and single men.'

Hennessey withdrew his hand. 'Definitely not.'

Yellich also collected background information. Mabel Johnson sat pale and drawn looking in her neatly kept house in Fulford. 'There was just the two of us, Muriel and Mabel Cross, the cross sisters . . . used to be a joke, you know like the one "I sometimes wake up bad tempered but mostly I let him sleep". A bit like that. We were the "cross sisters".'

Yellich smiled.

'My Nigel was a good man but he never amounted to much in life. This was what he achieved, this little house, before it pleased the Lord to take him from me. We sort of stayed still in life. Muriel and I grew up in a house like this, modest you might say. Nigel too grew up like this, lived like this . . . and . . . well, it isn't my turn yet, so I still live like this but Muriel did very well in her marriage . . . on every level. She and Anthony loved each other, they really were inseparable and what Anthony achieved . . . and to die like that. The paper said they were dead before they were burnt, is that correct?'

'Yes.' Yellich glanced around him. The house he saw was neatly but very prosaically decorated. He thought that there was little evidence of much, if any, imagination in the lifestyle of Mrs Johnson and her late husband, Nigel.

'Yes, that was the case.'

'Can you tell that? How?' Mabel Johnson was a frail looking lady, who, Yellich thought, was dressed older than her years. It was, he thought, as if old age had some appeal for her, some attraction and, unusually, she was anxious to reach it. But that, he thought, was better than middle-aged women who wore the short skirts of a teenager.

'Yes . . . if there are soot deposits in the trachea . . .'

'Trachea?'

'The throat. If there are soot deposits there it means the person breathed in smoke, which means they were alive when engulfed in flames . . . No smoke in the

trachea means that the person was not breathing when they were . . .'

'Engulfed in flames.' Mabel Johnson finished the sentence for Yellich. 'I see . . . and my sister and her husband had no smoke in their . . . trachea?'

'None.'

'You are not just saying that to comfort me?'

'No . . .' Yellich smiled again as he sat in the old armchair opposite Mrs Johnson. 'There was no smoke in the trachea. I was not at the post-mortem but I read the report.'

Mrs Johnson nodded and bowed her head, as if in prayer.

Yellich allowed a few moments of silence to pass before he asked, 'Do you know of anyone who would want to harm Mrs Dent, your sister?'

'Harm Muriel?' Mrs Johnson seemed shocked. 'Heavens, no. Why would you think that?'

'We don't think it, it's a possibility that we have to explore. We believe that your sister and her husband were murdered.'

'Murdered . . .' Mrs Johnson sank backwards. 'That word . . . never in my born days did I think that this family would be visited by murder . . . It is . . . it is like a stain that can't be removed. My Nigel, Mr Johnson, he succumbed to natural causes, there is no shame in that, but to have one of yours murdered . . .'

'Well, there is not necessarily any shame in the other. It happens all the time . . . sadly.'

'But natural causes, that is God's will. Murder can be prevented . . .'

How? thought Yellich. Please, please, please tell us how and we'll all sleep safer. But he kept his own counsel. Then he asked again, 'Was anybody threatening Mrs Dent, that you know of?'

'Not that I know of . . . Mr Dent, Anthony, he was the businessman, he'd have enemies, you would have thought.'

'That is an obvious avenue and is being explored, but

it appears that Mr and Mrs Dent were murdered at the same time. There was an attempt to dispose of the bodies . . . there was a motivation to murder them. If Mr Dent wasn't the target, then perhaps Mrs Dent, for some reason as yet unknown, might have been.'

'I see . . . I see . . . I can understand that way of thinking but I can assure you, Mr . . .'

'Yellich.'

'Yellich . . . a strange name. Quite pleasant but strange.'

'East European, we think, possibly a corruption of another name, lost in the mists of time.'

'Ah . . . but no . . . I cannot see Muriel making an enemy either in her private life or her professional life. She and Anthony were private people, had few friends but they liked it that way. She just didn't socialise enough to make enemies and an accountant doesn't make enemies . . . If a client is overtaxed the money is refunded and the taxman, the Inland Revenue, likes accountants because they speak the same language, they play within the rules. The Revenue doesn't want to cheat the taxpayer; the accountant doesn't help the taxpayer cheat the Revenue. So I can't see an accountant making an enemy of anyone.'

'Fair point.' Yellich nodded.

'I'd look closer to home if I were you.'

'Meaning?'

'Their children . . . those two . . . particularly that Gregory.'

'*That* Gregory,' Yellich echoed the phrase. 'You don't sound as though you like him.'

'I don't. I never did and I never will. I have to say that our parents . . . that is, Muriel and my parents . . .'

'Yes?'

'Our parents were more supportive of the notion of adopting than we believe Anthony's parents were. I think they realized Muriel's need to be a mother, even an adoptive mother . . . but I don't like Gregory. His eyes . . . there

74

was a look in his eyes, as though he was laughing at the world around him . . . and that's when he was just seven. The look in his eyes was, and still is, one of evil. Juliette less so, though I did detect a vicious streak in her on occasions but Juliette's problem when she was growing up was that she was easily led by her brother. Now she's away from his influence and has a good marriage, well, things are better for her . . . but when she was a girl, if ever she misbehaved it was because Gregory would have put her up to it. One moment and I'll show you what I mean.' Mabel Johnson levered herself up from the armchair with some difficulty. 'Don't need one of those spring buttoned chairs yet,' she joked, 'not yet.' Once on her feet she walked out of the room and seemed to Yellich to be able to manage the stairs with ease and he heard her rummaging about the room directly above the room in which he sat.

He waited. Once again he glanced round the room. Neat, tidy and clean, little to soften the room, he thought, a television set in the corner on a polished table with a lower level on which lay the *Radio Times*. Other than that, he saw no sign of any recreation in the room; no magazines, no books . . . just the television. The room was clean, no dust that he could detect, the green three-piece suite seemed to clash with the blue of the carpet but one person's taste is not another's, and the mirror on the wall above the mantelpiece seemed to be from an earlier era, as did the wood-encased clock which stood directly beneath the mirror. Outside a milk float rattled and whined by.

Mrs Johnson descended the stairs and stood in the doorway of the room. 'Shall we sit in the kitchen?' She held a cardboard shoebox under her arm. 'It's easier to do this in the kitchen.'

The kitchen was long and thin with yellow coloured wall cupboards and work surfaces. Definitely of an earlier era, 1960s thought Yellich. Against one wall of the kitchen was a table with a matching yellow Formica surface with

a metal framed upright chair at either end. Mrs Johnson sat at the further end, by the back door of the house, Yellich sat in the second chair opposite the gas cooker. There was no fridge. Quite remarkable, he thought, to encounter a household in Britain in the early twenty-first century that does not appear to have a refrigerator. It was as if the entire house was in a time warp, as if the Johnsons had moved in when newly married, decorated it and had then been content to grow old. The bathroom, he felt, was sure to have porcelain ducks flying across the wall.

'It's in this lot.' Mrs Johnson pulled the top off the cardboard box and revealed the contents to be an assortment of photographic prints, mostly colour, but some in black and white.

'Really?' Yellich began to protest, knowing that police time is valuable time.

'No . . . I want you to see this.' Mrs Johnson's long, bony fingers began to claw through the photographs. 'One day I am going to write on the back of these . . . you know, what each one is, where it is, that sort of thing. I will do it . . . one day . . . but this won't take long because I know what the photograph looks like, it's larger and it's black and white. Black and white prints work better sometimes, Mr Johnson said, and he used to be a very keen photographer. Many of his photographs are upstairs in albums; these are just snaps I took with my little camera. Now . . . ah, here we are.' She handed Yellich a black and white photograph. 'We had a day trip to the coast. That's our family as it was shortly after Gregory and Juliette joined us. That's one . . . you'll recognize it, I'm sure.'

'North Bay promenade, Scarborough.'

'Yes, it's as easily recognized by people in the north east of England as Brighton Pavilion is by folk in the south. Don't like the south of England. I feel as though I am cheating when I am down there . . . life's too soft . . .

but yes, that's where it is. The Corner Café as it used to be to the left . . . I took this snap.'

Yellich looked at the photograph, two men and a woman grinned at the camera, between them were a small boy and a small girl and Yellich saw then what Mabel Johnson meant. The girl, the young Juliette, held a bucket and spade and smiled sheepishly at the camera. There was, thought Yellich, an appealing sincerity about her, but the boy's eyes . . . the look therein chilled him. 'This is young Gregory?'

'Yes . . . see what I mean? Those eyes . . .'

'Yes . . . yes, I do.' Yellich pondered the facial expression of young Gregory. He was smiling as clearly asked by the photographer, but the smile . . . his smile of all the five smiles was transparently insincere. His eyes had a gleam about them, like a predator sensing an easy kill, it was as though the photographer amused him, as though he was not smiling for the camera, but rather laughing at it, as though he was looking down with huge condescension at Mrs Johnson and her 'little camera' and that, at the age of seven years. 'Yes . . . I do, I really do see what you mean. Not healthy at all.'

'That is what they brought into our family. We were only ever aunt and uncle; we didn't want to get any closer. I didn't see my sister as much as I would have liked, especially during the holiday times. We did visit when they had packed him off to boarding school, but not as often as I would have liked. We felt frightened of him . . . myself and Mr Johnson . . . we both said as much . . . didn't want to let him get close enough to damage us. You'll have heard about the dog?'

'The dog?'

'The old Labrador that died shortly after Gregory and Juliette joined the family. He was an old dog but had some years yet. Big Tom took an instant dislike to Gregory and was found curled up one day in the small wood by the house. No damage . . . no injuries . . . just lying dead.

Could have been natural, of course. Juliette was upset by the old dog's death, but Gregory wasn't ... seemed quite pleased, so Muriel told me.'

'Well, my boss is chatting to Mr Dent's brother now.'

'The motorcyclist?'

'I believe so ... yes.'

'Well, he'll tell your boss the same story. Doubtless he'll tell him about the cats as well.'

'The cats?'

'They disappeared ... four of them over time ... but once Gregory had been given a shotgun to play with ...'

'A shotgun! To play with!'

'Well ... to play with is my expression. It was a small bore gun ... a 410 I think they are called.'

'Yes.'

'To keep vermin down, a job they thought he might enjoy, to control him, to bring him into the fold. He was a teenager by then ... mid to late teens ... and then the four cats disappeared over a period of as many months. I am sure Robin will have told your boss about that.'

'I am sure he will have done.' Yellich stood and handed the photograph back to Mrs Johnson. 'I am sure he will have done. Thank you, this has been illuminating.'

It was Tuesday, 10.30 a.m.

Hennessey handed Yellich the file. 'I've met the type before.'

Yellich read the file, then closed it and said, 'So have I. Not guilty despite overwhelming evidence. We meet them all the time. I can never fathom their minds. What do you think we should do? Pull him in for a quiz session?'

Hennessey drew breath between his teeth. 'Don't know ... don't know.' He glanced to his side, looked out of his office window at the stone battlements of the ancient city. He thought how cold they looked, sharply angular under a low, grey sky. Perhaps they looked that way, he further thought, because it was that time of the year, that run up

78

to Christmas deeply felt by him in Jennifer's absence. Still after all these years. Though he had people to buy for: a son, daughter-in-law, grandchildren . . . and one significant other. Soon it would be time to send Christmas cards, not too early so as to seem needy nor too late to give the impression that the card was an afterthought. He sent about forty, and received the same number – not bad; he was as integrated as he wanted to be. He hadn't the emotional energy to be universally popular and jealously guarded his free time and his solitude and loved the evening walk with Oscar as much as Oscar appeared to relish it. He turned again to face Yellich who sat patiently waiting for Hennessey's response. 'Don't know,' he said again. 'The boy is clever, I don't want to start him . . . don't want to give him any inkling that he is under suspicion until we have proof positive.'

'If we get it!' Yellich raised an eyebrow.

'Yes . . . yes, you're right . . . we won't get a confession.' He tapped the file. 'Not if this is anything to go by. His prints all over the safe, and the window where he broke into the office, the money, all of it, found in his van at the site and he pleads not guilty because it was his money to steal. Have you ever heard the like?'

'Yes . . .' Yellich laughed, 'as we have said many times, "Have we heard the like?"'

Hennessey grinned. 'Point to you.' He paused, glancing in the opposite direction at the police mutual calendar on the wall, the open door into the CID corridor. 'I think we need more on this fella.'

'More, sir?'

'More. I mean . . . I have told you what Robin Dent told me, and you have told me what Mabel Johnson told you. Pretty much the same message, pretty much the same sort of impression. I would like to see the photograph you describe, the dog that died, the cats that disappeared, stealing money, which through some twisted rationalization

he believed was his. Three thousand pounds in the safe but he only took two thousand because that was what he believed was owed to him when in fact he wasn't owed a penny. He was employed on a fixed salary and wasn't entitled to directors' fees like his adoptive father and mother, so he broke in and took them anyway but left one thousand to show how honest he is . . . or was. We'll have better luck nailing this Johnny the more we know about him.'

'What do you suggest, boss?'

'A trip to East Hull.' Hennessey glanced at his watch. 'Midday . . . take an hour to get there . . . So we'll eat like the weary foot soldiers we are, then drive out to the children's home he was in for a brief period. The staff will have changed by now but we might be able to pick a moved on or retired brain or two. What are you doing for lunch?'

'Canteen, skipper.'

'Ugh . . . don't know how you can stand that stodge.'

'It's cheap.' Yellich stood. 'My wallet likes it very well.'

'Alright, meet here in about an hour, then we'll drive to Hull. Not my favourite city . . .'

Hennessey cloaked himself against the north-east 'biter' in coat, hat and scarf, signed out and left Micklegate Bar police station and chose to walk down Micklegate itself, assuming that his usual route, upon the walls, would still be too exposed and Micklegate, he reasoned, was not an unattractive uphill and then downhill walk. The narrow street, within the walls, had buildings that interested him, such as the ancient terraced houses on Priory Street, with their narrow frontage and far reaching floor space, the ancient churches and graveyards and the pubs. So, so many pubs, that have given rise to the 'Micklegate challenge' or 'the walk'. One must start at Micklegate Bar, and stop at each pub and have one half pint of beer, then move on to the next pub for another half pint of beer. So far no one, not even the most hardened drinker has made it to Bridge Street at the further end of Micklegate.

But this is York, Hennessey mused; at least the old city, the city within the walls. Shops in Micklegate sang forth Christmas with lights and greetings, although it was not until Hennessey had crossed the Ouse that he met the full onslaught of the season, where lights were strung across the street, and attached to lamp posts, where the streets and the pedestrian precinct were thronged, even at midweek, with shoppers carrying bulging bags, not, he found, with a look of joy, but with a look of single-minded determination. His Christmas was going to be low-key, but at least it would be very inexpensive. The principal gift he would be buying for his household, for example, was a leg of lamb to be roasted for Oscar's Christmas dinner. He walked down Coney Street to St Leonard's Square where street musicians playing whistles (badly) competed with a Salvation Army band whose brass renderings of the old favourite carols Hennessey thought faultless. He was not trained in musical appreciation but he stood a while and listened to 'Hark, the Herald Angels Sing' and 'God Rest Ye Merry, Gentlemen'. Turning into the wind, he walked into Stonegate and then left into an alleyway at the end of which narrow covered passage was the entrance to Ye Olde Starre Inn, York's oldest pub. Being of festive mood, Hennessey ordered roast turkey, roast potatoes and stuffing which he relished whilst sitting in a quiet corner beneath a framed print of a map showing 'The West Ridinge of Yorkshyrre, the moft famous and faire Citie Yorke, defcribed – 1610'. Replenished, Hennessey retraced his steps to Micklegate Bar police station. He found Yellich sitting at his desk reading the *Yorkshire Post*. 'Ready?'

'As I'll ever be.' Yellich folded the paper and laid it on his desk. He reached for his coat and hat. 'Want me to drive, boss?'

'If you would.' Hennessey turned. 'If you would . . . you know I prefer not to.'

* * *

Hennessey always experienced the same sensations when visiting the city of Kingston upon Hull, on Humber's muddy northern bank, dissected by its own equally muddy river. He sensed that he was going down into something. It was all there: the folk were the same; the traffic drove on the same side of the road as in the rest of the kingdom; the large department stores had the same names as the chains in other towns and cities, yet . . . yet . . . he always felt that there was something missing in respect of the city.

The man was friendly, warm, affable. 'It was a children's home,' he said, smiling with large eyes, 'but that's old hat now . . . all is down to fostering children in the community. The move away from institutional care started a long time ago. We still have a few homes but not as many as before and Sycamore Lodge stopped being a children's home many years ago.'

Upon entering Hull down Anlaby Road, past the hospital, turning left at the railway station, Yellich had then forged his way east through the city and by enquiring at post offices and estate agents, managed to find Sycamore Lodge on Swallow Road. The building was clearly Victorian and, in Hennessey's eyes, was a monstrosity of complicated lines and turrets and dormer windows that interrupted the roof line. The building of red brick seemed to squat heavily on the ground it occupied. The door was opened by a pale skinned youth of about sixteen years who spoke in monosyllables but eventually directed Hennessey and Yellich to 'the chief's' office. The interior of the building Hennessey found to be as complex as the exterior as he and Yellich followed the youth's directions down twisting, undulating corridors until they came to a door with a sign reading 'The Chief' pinned with a single drawing pin. Hennessey tapped on the door and a jocular voice said, 'Come in.' 'The chief' revealed himself to be a man of middle years, Afro-Caribbean, and warmly told Hennessey that children's homes were 'old hat'.

'These youths are school leavers,' he explained. 'Unemployed. In some cases already unemployable. This is a drop-in centre. We teach what we can: social skills, interview skills, but when we shut up for the day, they go home. It's non residential. The youths are here because it's better for them to be here than wandering the streets. It's too easy to get heroin and crack in Hull. We do that as well, advise about drugs, the dangers therein. We get ex-addicts to talk to them about life in the gutter. So, how can I help you? Your warrant card said York. One of our lads or lassies got their prints in York?'

'Possibly . . . but we are here looking to pick brains.'

'Won't find many of those round here . . . staff or users,' the man said as he smiled. 'I'm Payper by the way.'

'Paper?'

'Sam Payper.' The chief smiled. 'Pronounced like news-paper but spelled with a *y*.'

'Ah . . . I see . . . well, we need to speak to someone who worked at Sycamore Lodge when it was an old hat children's home. This is our first port of call.'

'Oh . . . I see.'

'About twenty years ago, probably a little more.'

'Again, I see. I think the only way to do that is to pick up networks.' He turned and reached for the telephone. He picked it up and dialled a six-figure number from memory. 'The building is still owned and run by Social Services,' he said as he dialled. 'Hull is one of those depart-ments, unlike London boroughs, where people stay, move on within the department but stay. This fella will be the one to ask.' He waited. 'Not at his desk. Oh . . . Harold. Hello, Sam Payper. Listen, I have two gentlemen with me from the bold constabulary of York. Yes . . . indeed.' Sam Payper turned and winked at Hennessey. 'Yes, they are keen to pick brains.' Payper laughed. 'Yes, that's what I said too but they are keen to interview someone, anyone who worked at Sycamore Lodge when it was a children's

home, about twenty years ago.' Payper listened then turned to Hennessey and asked, 'What specifically is your inquiry about? It could help track down the right brains for you to pick. Are you trying to trace a member of staff . . . or one of the children?'

'We want to find someone who recalls two children by the name of Gregory and Juliette Locke.' Hennessey saw no reason not to inform the helpful Sam Payper of their purpose. 'Brother and sister . . . came into care as orphans following a road traffic accident in which their parents were killed.'

'I see.'

'Left care when they were adopted by Mr and Mrs Dent, of Great Sheldwich, Vale of York.'

'Right.' Sam Payper spoke into the phone, relaying the information Hennessey had provided. Then he turned to Hennessey and said, 'I can hear them asking for you. As I said, it's just one of those departments . . . you work your way into the bricks. Ah . . . you've got a result? Perhaps . . . yes . . . hello . . . right, got that.' He scribbled on a sheet of paper then said, 'Thanks,' and replaced the receiver. He turned to Hennessey. 'Got a paper and pen?' Yellich reached into his pocket and extracted his notebook and ballpoint.

'OK.' Sam Payper leaned forward. 'Ada Beadnall was the officer in charge of Sycamore Lodge when it was a children's home. She has retired to the coast. There's quite a lot of land between Hull and the east coast even though Hull is a seaport. She lives out by Withernsea. They are phoning her at home right now to see if they can let you have her address. She may in fact phone here. I am sure she will be very curious . . . that will make her eager to help. I know I would if I were retired. It's all behind you, then you have a part to play again. The other one is Alex Davies . . . I know him . . . he's a good bloke. He started out in social work as an unqualified member of staff straight from university working here, then did the training

course and is now a middle manager with the Fostering and Adoption section.' Sam Payper tapped the paper he held in his hand. 'You know, he could be useful, he could fast track access to the file on those two orphans, they'll still be in the archives.'

'That,' said Hennessey, 'that would be very useful, very useful indeed.'

The phone rang. Sam Payper smiled. 'This will be Ada Beadnall.' He looked at the phone. 'Do you not think the ring has an insistent quality?' He picked up the phone. 'Sycamore Lodge,' he said. 'Yes . . . just here.' He handed the phone to Hennessey. 'Miss Beadnall, for you.'

Hennessey took the phone and indicated to Yellich that he wanted to use the notepad and pen. Yellich handed them to him and watched as Hennessey held the phone to his ear with one hand and scribbled with the other. Eventually he thanked the caller very much and replaced the handset. 'You were right.' He smiled at Sam Payper. 'She is very eager to help. She is at home at the moment.' He glanced at his watch. 'We don't have the time to visit both by the two of us so . . .' He handed Yellich his notepad. 'That is Miss Beadnall's address. Can you drive out and visit her?'

'Yes, skipper.'

'See what she can tell you about Gregory and Juliette Locke, as they were.' Hennessey turned to Sam Payper. 'Who did you say the other chap was?'

'Alex . . . Alex Davies. He works in the centre of the city. I can run you there.'

'Could you?'

'Of course.' Sam Payper picked up the phone and dialled a number. When it was answered he asked for Alex Davies in Fostering and Adoption, then he handed the phone to Hennessey. 'Suggest you make a courtesy call,' he said. 'Let him know you're about to call on him and why.'

* * *

Having arranged to rendezvous with Hennessey at the cafe-
teria in the once grandly named Hull Paragon Railway
Station, and by then the more modestly named Hull Railway
Station, Yellich drove out to Withernsea. The wind drove
keenly off the North Sea and bit into Yellich's cheeks as
he got out of the car and walked up the steps of the house,
being the address Hennessey had scribbled on his notepad.
The house was an imposing four-storeyed terraced house
that faced the sea, which was then choppy and grey. He
rang the bell and waited. The door was opened with a
flourish by a small, finely boned lady who Yellich thought
was in her mid-sixties. She had short, grey hair and a ready
smile. She moved with confidence and seemed thus far to
have escaped any ravages of rheumatism or arthritis.
'Police?'

'Yes.' Yellich nodded gently and showed her his ID.

'Ah . . . please come in.' Ada Beadnall stepped to one
side and shut the door hurriedly behind him. 'Shut the
wind out,' she said. 'I love living at the coast but the east-
erlies in the winter . . . they've got teeth.'

'So I feel.' Yellich smiled. Towering over her, he felt
very protective towards Miss Beadnall.

'Please . . . shall we sit in here?' She led him to a living
room with high ceilings that looked out over the North
Sea. 'You'll have tea? Please . . . I get so few visitors.'

'Well, thank you, yes.'

'Please take a seat.'

Yellich did so. He found the room cluttered but in a
neat and managed manner, as if the room was controlled
by a woman who encouraged growth and fulfilment of
potential. When tea arrived it was in a generous white pot,
accompanied by a tray of toasted teacakes spread with
paté.

'My . . .' Yellich said. 'Really, this is too generous.'

'Keep the cold out. Food is the best central heating

system the body can have. Are you wearing your thermals, young man? Weather like this . . .'

'No. If I lived here then I would, but I live in York, it's a little more sheltered there. Still a bit windy but nothing compared to Withernsea.'

'Yes . . . it's lovely in the summer.' She poured the tea. 'A walk along the beach in the very early morning . . . but you pay for it in the winter.' She handed Yellich a cup of tea. 'Do help yourself to a teacake. So . . . on the phone you said it was about Gregory and Juliette Locke?'

'Well, that wasn't me, it was my boss, but yes . . . we are interested in anything you can tell us.'

'Why? Are they in trouble?'

'Possibly . . . I'd rather not say too much just yet.'

'Well . . .' Ada Beadnall poured herself a cup of tea and sat back in her chair. 'My sister was a teacher, she is retired now, and she says that looking back over the years she remembers the good ones and the bad ones . . . the others just . . . well, failed to impress upon her memory. In social work it's pretty much the same and I remember the Locke children very well.'

'Good or bad?'

'Bad, very bad, particularly Gregory. Those eyes . . . large brown . . . so menacing, wouldn't let you get past them . . . just couldn't see his soul. I remember once we took in an arsonist.'

'An arsonist?'

'Yes . . . a boy who was then older than Gregory. He had absconded from another local authority's care and had been picked up by the police. They brought him to us and we kept him for a few hours whilst his social worker made arrangements to come and pick him up. In the telephone conversation with her it was clear that she thought we were a secure unit.'

'Secure?'

'The children were kept locked up.'

87

Peter Turnbull

'Ah . . .'

'When she realized that we were non secure she gasped and told us to have him transferred to a secure unit without delay. He was fourteen and had multiple convictions for arson, but I remember him because his eyes were exactly like Gregory Locke's eyes and also . . . frightening . . . Gregory and that boy just gravitated to each other, even despite the age gap. They recognized each other as kindred spirits.'

'Chilling.'

'It was very, but Gregory never actually did anything wrong or criminal. He was only seven anyway, but he just seemed to slide through each day without any bad behaviour that would have enabled the staff to get hold of his personality. We just could not make an assessment of that boy. I remember him well . . . one of the bad ones who never misbehaved, yet when he was in there, other children misbehaved in a way that was very out of character. Then after they had found a home with that couple in York and were discharged from our care, things just settled down again . . . back to normal. Staff commented on it. How we seemed to have been visited by someone or something that created a lot of trouble but never could be blamed for anything, as if the other children were responding to his personality . . . or were receiving messages from him that the staff were unaware of.'

'Messages?'

'On a psychological level . . . as if without actually saying anything, he was manipulating them.'

'I see. What was his sister like?'

'Healthier. She misbehaved but I and the staff always had the impression she was very easily led by him.'

'Interesting.'

'Very . . . like I said, you only remember the good ones and the bad ones and I remember Gregory Locke. I'll tell

88

you something else as well . . . they were orphaned, recently orphaned, but you wouldn't have thought it. No emotion, no grief, no distress, not from him. She was a little more timid but he just stepped over the threshold and cast his eyes about the building as though he was assuming occupation and control . . . at seven years of age. Do have another teacake.'

Hennessey thought Alexander Davies to be a sorrowful looking man. He was, thought Hennessey, a man in his mid-forties. He seemed to have made a perfunctory attempt at being 'office smart' but the unironed blue shirt which ill matched the loud red tie told of a man whose mind was elsewhere. His office was untidy, though in Hennessey's experience that meant little. In his capacity as a police officer he had visited many Departments of Social Work and in the course of doing so had learned that a tidy desk therein was something of a rarity. Alex Davies cast a glance at a photograph of a woman with two adult children which stood on the windowsill of his office. 'The Locke children?'

'Yes.'

'I actually remember them being admitted, but I left Sycamore Lodge shortly afterwards, went to Sheffield University for professional training. Big mistake, should have gone to sea like my father on the trawlers, got my ticket. I would have been a skipper by now. The fishing can be dangerous, but it's not as soul sapping as this game.' He slapped his desk. 'Anyway, I have sent down to the archives for the file on the Locke children. It'll take some digging out but I phoned the request as soon as I received your call.' He glanced at his watch. 'Should be here by now. Sorry . . . sorry . . . I am not really myself; I have just lost my wife you see.'

'Oh . . . I am sorry.'

'Yes . . . she was only forty-two, breast cancer . . . she was so brave.'

Hennessey smiled. He allowed Davies to see his smile.

'You smile at my misfortune, Mr Hennessey?' Davies's voice had an angry edge.

'No . . . no . . . I wouldn't do that. No, I smile because I am a sputnik.'

'A sputnik? A satellite? What do you mean?'

'Sputnik is a Russian word, it means fellow traveller.'

'I didn't know that.'

'Take it from me . . . it's an inspired name for a satellite travelling with planet earth through space.'

'Isn't it just?'

'Well, I too am a widower . . . I know what you are feeling, but you had a good marriage, your wife saw your children grow.'

'Only twenty years . . . and she didn't see them complete university and settle down.'

'Well, we were married for barely two years,' Hennessey said, 'and Jennifer died when our son was just six months old.'

Alex Davies put his hand to his mouth. 'I am so sorry, I must sound so selfish.'

'Don't worry . . . she'll never die in a sense, if you keep your memory alive.'

'Oh, I will.' He glanced at the photograph. 'What happened to your wife, if I might ask?'

'Natural causes too . . . in her case it was Sudden Death Syndrome.'

'I have heard of that, strikes young, very healthy people, life just leaves them . . . no one knows the medical cause.'

'Yes, that's it . . . Jennifer was walking through Easingwold, where I still live in the same house, it was a hot day, folk thought she had fainted and called an ambulance, but she was dead on arrival . . . twenty-three years old.'

'Oh . . .'

'I scattered her ashes in the garden then spent the next

few years landscaping the garden to her design. One of the last things she did was to design the garden. It was as flat and as dull as a football pitch when we bought the house, now it has orchards and ponds with thriving pond life.'

'Sounds very nice.' Davies smiled gently.

'I will not move . . . I talk to her each day. I return home and tell her of my day. An observer would think I was talking to myself, but I sense her presence . . . I really do. I have a significant other in my life, a divorced lady, a recent development which delights me . . . told Jennifer of her and just know she approves.'

'That is the attitude. You've given me something there, Mr Hennessey, thank you. Chloe would want me to pick up and carry on . . . find someone else in time, but I will always treasure her memory.'

'I am sure you will.'

There was a tap on Alex Davies' office door. It was opened without further invitation and a nervous looking bespectacled girl in a yellow dress advanced on Davies' desk and handed him a manila file. 'I was asked to bring this to you, Mr Davies,' she stammered.

'Ah . . . thank you.' Davies smiled as he took hold of the file. 'I appreciate it.'

The young woman quickly withdrew, leaving Hennessey and Davies alone again.

'I might not be able to let you look at this, not without a warrant . . . they are strictly confidential, you see.'

'Then why bring it out of the archive? I am sure I'll be able to obtain a warrant but I could have saved a journey if I had known I would need one.'

'Well, it depends on what you want. I might be able to let you have some information but not all. Information about their adoptive parents, for example, that would need a warrant.'

'Ah . . . I am not interested in them. What can you tell me about the Locke children?'

'We'll see.' Davies opened the file. 'Parents Richard and Linda Locke, died in a car accident . . . known to you.'

'Really?'

'Yes, there's a pre-sentence report from the probation service here, receiving stolen goods. I can let you have a look at that.' Davies took the report from the file and handed it to Hennessey. 'A career criminal by the look of that track.'

'Seems so . . . receiving . . . receiving . . . fraud . . . embezzlement. He did a bit of time . . . he was inside when . . . yes, when both his children were born . . . nothing violent, though.' Hennessey scanned the report. 'I do believe that violence leads to more violence but nothing here to indicate that Gregory Locke's early life was violent.'

'It is Gregory whom the police are interested in?'

'Yes . . . can't tell you why, but yes. Not a good role model but Gregory's father doesn't come across as a violent person.'

'Well, you don't have to hit someone to be violent.' Davies leaned forward and folded his arms, resting them on his desk. 'You can be violent in your attitude, in your speech, and I still remain struck by how indifferent to his parents' death did young Gregory Locke seem. Very detached, emotionally speaking. Some damage was done to him, some considerable damage – which is to explain his attitude, not to excuse it.'

'Yes . . .' Hennessey growled, though he was surprised to find that Davies as a social worker was not what he privately referred to as an 'abuse excuse merchant'. 'His mother was no saint either . . . she had a few convictions. It's referred to here . . . a joint prosecution for fraud.'

'Crimes of a devious nature, unlike more honest crimes like assault, if you see what I mean? The crimes here seem to be entered into with the intention of not merely getting away with it, but of avoiding all suspicion in the first place. If he grew up in that devious sort of

household it would rub off on him, he would become a devious adult.'

'But not violent?'

'I would say not but then I am not a psychologist.'

'Near enough,' Hennessey smiled. 'But this has been interesting . . . if only in that it points to the possible elimination of our prime suspect. Possibly.'

It was Tuesday, 16.30 hours.

Five

Wednesday, December 17, 10.25 hours – 14.30 hours
in which the investigation becomes greatly confused.

T he red recording light glowed, the twin cassettes of
the tape recorder spun slowly.

'The time is 10.25 a.m., the date is the seventeenth of
December. The place is Interview Room Two, Micklegate
Bar Police Station, York. I am Detective Chief Inspector
Hennessey. I am now going to ask the other people in the
room to identify themselves.'

'Detective Sergeant Yellich.'

'Ambrose Peebles, of Ellis, Burden, Woodland and Lake,
solicitors, attending in accordance with the Police and
Criminal Evidence Act 1985.' Peebles spoke confidently,
softly, with, thought Hennessey, perfectly enunciated
received pronunciation.

'Gregory Dent.' Dent spoke curtly, he smiled slightly,
his eyes had that reported glassy look, Hennessey noted,
preventing anyone seeing into them, to assess his soul.

'Mr Dent,' Hennessey began, 'you have been brought
to the police station in connection with the murder of your
adoptive parents, Anthony and Muriel Dent.'

'I have?' Dent smirked.

'You have. You are under suspicion.'

'Of . . .?'

'Murder.'

'Really?' Dent sat forward, smiling confidently.

94

'You have the motivation. Has your parents' will been read?'

'Where there's a will, there's a way, is that what you are saying?'

'If you'd just answer the question.'

'Yes, it has. I am a rich man now. I intend to visit the Porsche dealership at my earliest convenience.'

'What have you inherited?'

'Quite a lot . . . enough to see me out without doing a stroke of work for the rest of my life, if I am shrewd in my investments.'

'What did the will say?'

'Well, my sister and I inherit pretty much everything: the house at Great Sheldwich, the farmland that adjoins it, the business premises at Precenters Court, the caravan site and all those caravans, the other plots of land here and there, the car parks on the prime building land. If we can get planning permission for a hotel on the caravan site . . . Juliette and I talked about it last night. Neither of us wants to carry on with any of the businesses, though we might keep a couple of the car parks as a safety net, one each, to let some income trickle in, but we are going to liquidize the rest. I'm going south; London's the place for a young man with my sort of money.'

'Young man with your sort of money? You could not wait until your parents died of natural causes by which time you'd be middle aged.'

'Mr Hennessey,' Ambrose Peebles growled. He was a well-set man, in his fifties, expensively dressed in silk shirt and quality three-piece suit. 'I must protest. Do you have any evidence with which you can support your suspicions?'

'No,' Dent replied, holding eye contact with Hennessey. 'No, he hasn't because there is none to be had. I have a cast-iron alibi for the night of the murders. My girlfriend told me you had visited her. She has confirmed my alibi

for you.' Dent paused. 'All the time you are wasting on me is the time you could be devoting to apprehending the actual culprit. They were my parents . . . I have clear recollections of my real parents, I was seven when they died, but the Dents brought me up, paid for my education, took me into the family business. I want their murderer caught and brought to justice.'

'They didn't take you as far into the business as you would have liked, did they? A management position at the caravan site was as far "in" as you were allowed, and from which you stole.'

Dent's face hardened. A look of anger flashed across his eyes.

'Yes, we know about that . . . we have done some checking.'

'Shows how honest I am,' Dent said shrugging. 'Technically a crime . . . but morally, not so. You see I should have got director's fees as well.'

'But you were not a director. You were employed.'

'I was a member of the family. My parents got directors' fees of £2,000 after a period of trading. I was their son; I should have got the same, so I took it. There was £3,000 in the safe but I only took the £2,000 owed to me. Honest man.'

'The police charged you, the magistrates convicted you; they clearly didn't see you as an honest man. They saw you as a thief.'

'They were wrong. I took what was mine. If I was a thief, I would have taken the whole 3K.'

'Your parents were in your way. You got rid of them.'

'Oh yes? How? I was with Susan . . .'

'Just the two of you?'

'Yes.'

'Any independent witnesses?'

'No, I was with her, she was with me . . . we spent the evening alone.'

'But no one can verify that?'

'No.'

Hennessey paused. Then he asked, 'So, what happened to the cats?'

'The cats?'

'The cats belonging to the Dents, they disappeared over a period of a few months, coincidental it seemed with your taking the 410 to shoot vermin. And the dog that died shortly after you arrived at West End House, the dog that took an instant dislike to you. What did you do to him, you, aged seven years?'

Ambrose Peebles glanced at Hennessey. 'Really, Inspector, you have no evidence at all. A dog that died over twenty years ago . . . I mean . . . really . . . you are not just clutching at straws, you are grasping at thin air. I am not impressed.'

'Do we need to talk to Mrs Thurnham?'

'Dare say you can if you like . . . doubt she can tell you anything.'

'You are providing false alibis for each other, you're both implicated in the murders of the Dents.'

Gregory Dent smirked. 'That is preposterous. Susan has no motivation in the murders.'

'She'd share in your money.'

'That wouldn't be at all guaranteed. Possibly, possibly, if we were married, and she could expect some share of the money or a claim on it if we divorced . . . then, yes . . . perhaps, perhaps then . . . but as a mere girlfriend, even a promise of a share of any inheritance would be meaningless . . . can't enforce that.'

'Inspector,' Ambrose Peebles spoke softly, 'this is going nowhere. I must ask you to either charge my client with some offence or other, or release him.'

'Very well.' Hennessey reached for the stop button. 'This interview is terminated at 11.15 hours.' He pressed the stop button. 'Sergeant, will you please escort these two gentlemen to the door?'

Ten minutes later, in Hennessey's office, Hennessey said, 'He is up to his neck in those murders, Yellich, I can feel it . . . I feel it in my waters.'

'Probably, sir, but his brief is right, you'll need more than your waters to be able to nail him, and maybe the real culprit is out there . . . maybe we are not just barking up the wrong tree, we are in the wrong part of the forest.'

'Oh, you're right, you're right . . . the culprit is out there. He left five minutes ago on his way to the Porsche dealership. How much do you think he is worth?'

Yellich shook his head. He glanced out of the window of Hennessey's office; rain was falling vertically from a low, grey sky, causing the ancient walls to shine. 'Well, he has to split it with his sister, but he could realize eight figures if he liquidated, I'd say.'

'I'd say so too.' Hennessey stared ahead with a look of grim determination. 'That's one million reasons to murder his parents.'

'Don't close your mind too early, boss.'

'I'm not. That man is evil . . . I will be proved right.'

The phone on his desk rang, he snatched it up and Yellich watched as the colour drained from Hennessey's face. Hennessey listened and then mumbled his thanks and replaced the handset. 'There's been another.'

'Another, skipper?'

'Body . . . burned . . . charred . . . found just now . . . our attendance is requested.'

'Good old dog walkers.' The uniformed sergeant talked with a resigned attitude, as though he had seen it many times before. He was an elderly sergeant, close to retirement, Hennessey judged. He had a life-hardened look across his eyes and Hennessey thought that it would take much to make him smile. 'They find most of them. I tell you, sir, if it wasn't for dog walkers, a lot of bodies would never be found. Dog walkers, hikers . . . hikers too, but mainly dog walkers.'

Hennessey looked at the corpse, a male he thought, but he found it difficult to tell. It was face down with the chest raised off the ground as the arms and legs had contracted as the body burned. There was little else he could do, but view the corpse, as if by doing so he triggered the investigation process in his mind; it made the crime 'real' for him. He nodded and stepped outside the inflatable tent that had been erected over the body. The dour, humourless sergeant followed him. There was no need for a police presence inside the tent. The two men walked from the tent and ducked beneath the blue and white police tape which had been strung around the crime scene. He approached Yellich. 'Want to see it?'

'Not particularly, boss. I assume it is just like the other two and there will be photographs for me to study.'

Hennessey turned his collar up against the wind which blew from the east finding its way easily between the swaying trees of the small wood in which the charred body was found. 'Aye,' he muttered. 'It is just like the others, burned and blackened, burned to a crisp, dumped too, just like the others. No sign of burning on the vegetation and it was dumped next to a gorse bush. Ever seen a gorse bush burn?'

'Confess I haven't.'

'Terrifying, you'd think the plant was made of petrol. Had he been burned here, that plant would definitely have gone up in flames . . . So, dumped . . . like the others.' He turned to the uniformed sergeant. 'Anything of note?'

'I think there is . . . yes, sir. I'll show you.'

'Stay here and wait for Dr D'Acre please, Yellich, she's on her way.'

'Yes, boss.' Yellich thrust his hands into his coat pockets and stamped his feet. 'Damn cold,' he said, more to himself than to Hennessey.

'Walk about.' Hennessey smiled. 'But so long as you

remain in the vicinity of the tent . . . the police have to welcome the forensic pathologist.'

'Understood, sir.'

'OK, sergeant, what have you got?'

The sergeant led Hennessey along a pathway to the edge of the wood beyond which was a road, a narrow badly surfaced road, and beyond the road were winter brown ploughed fields and hedgerows, and beyond them the low skyline of the city of York. Between the wood and the road was a shallow stream, really no more than a trickle of water. A constable stood by the stream. He stiffened as Hennessey and the sergeant approached.

'The water has kept the ground here a bit muddy.' The sergeant stopped a little short of the stream. 'There are tyre tracks.'

'So I see.' Hennessey looked at the ground. The tyre tracks were short; very little muddy ground was to be had between the stream and the point where the soil was frozen. 'Better get Scene of Crime to photograph them.'

'Already done so, sir,' the sergeant said dryly.

'Good man.'

'I asked them if they'd take plaster casts once you had seen them.'

'Again, thank you.' Hennessey looked at the tyre tracks. 'Nothing distinctive,' he muttered, 'not even enough to say they have anything to set them apart from any other tracks . . . no uneven wear for example, no damage, but we can identify the make, that's a start.'

'Better than nothing,' the sergeant growled.

'As you say.' He looked about him. 'So, the vehicle reversed off the lane, had to; the dirt from the wheels is on the road surface . . . see it turning away to the right?'

'That's the easiest way to York from here, sir.'

'I see. Where would a left turn take you?'

'A small village . . . Anslow . . . then eventually the A19 to Thirsk or back to York.'

'I see . . . Well, assuming that this vehicle did convey the corpse, we can identify the tyre make and possibly the make of vehicle. The tyre tread is narrow.'

'Yes, small vehicle alright, sir.'

'The dog walker who found the body?'

'At home, sir . . . in Anslow. I have her details in my notebook. I would have asked her to remain but she was very shaken.'

'I can imagine . . . I can well imagine. She didn't tell you anything?'

'Nothing, sir. Pointed to where we would find the body, then gave her name and address and said she was going home.'

'Alright.' He turned to the constable. 'Continue to wait here.'

'Yes, sir.'

'Once the SOCO have taken plaster casts, can you report to the sergeant? But until then remain here.'

'Yes, sir.' He was a young man, about nineteen, thought Hennessey. This was probably his first murder. Hennessey knew it wouldn't be his last.

Hennessey and the sergeant walked purposefully back over the hard ground to where the inflatable tent was erected. He saw Dr D'Acre arriving. She was tall, slender and with good muscle tone, leggy, short cropped hair, serious attitude . . . She walked equally purposefully towards the tent, carrying a black Gladstone bag in her right hand. She and Hennessey nodded to each other as they met.

'Another, I believe,' she said when she and Hennessey were close enough to talk without raising their voices.

'Yes.' Hennessey nodded solemnly. 'In the tent.'

'Well, I'll see what I will see. If it is like the other two there will be little I can do here.' She had, thought Hennessey, a smooth, balanced face, wore no make-up save for a trace of very pale lipstick. 'I'll be conducting

the PM this afternoon. Will you be attending for the police, Chief Inspector?'

'Probably . . . if not myself then Sergeant Yellich. I want to go and talk to the lady who found the corpse. I should be free to attend. Sergeant . . .?'

'Sir?'

'If you'd see the lady pathologist to the tent?'

'Yes, sir.'

'Knew what it was as soon as I saw it.'

Hennessey had strolled into the village of Anslow and found it to be a ribbon of houses either side of the narrow road and little else, a small shop, a pub called The Bird in the Hand and a repair garage. Anslow. He opened the front gate and walked down a gravel covered path and in doing so, was reminded of a gravel covered driveway of a house in a small village just to the north of York. His feet crunching the ground caused a dog to bark from within the house. Gravel covered driveways and paths, and a metal gate that squeaks for the want of oil were, he thought, the two best burglar deterrents, save for a dog. He walked up to the door of the house, white painted, and rapped the black metal knocker. The door was opened quickly by a woman who, Hennessey thought, was in her forties. She was dark haired with a pale complexion and seemed to be large boned. An alert and well-fed springer spaniel stood at her feet barking at Hennessey. The dog was well cared for; Hennessey saw that in an instant: glossy coat, excellent muscle tone, not an ounce over-weight. A lucky dog to be this woman's pet.

'You'll be the police.' The woman spoke slowly with a distinct Yorkshire accent. 'I was expecting you.'

'Yes.' Hennessey showed her his ID.

The woman nodded and stepped aside and said, 'Alright, Toby,' at which point the spaniel stopped barking and sniffed at Hennessey's legs as he entered the house. The

woman shut the door behind Hennessey, closing it with a solid thud. The house was clearly very well built, probably in the 1930s, he thought. The woman led him into a sitting room which looked out on to the back garden, long, narrow and well tended.

'Please, take a seat.'

Hennessey sat and extracted his notebook from his coat pocket. 'You're Miss Eyton? Miss Paula Eyton?'

'Yes, I phoned the police. I knew what it was as soon as I saw it.'

'It is obvious . . .'

'Well, some folk might have had to do a double take, wait for a few seconds before fully realizing what they were looking at. But I knew immediately what it was; a charred corpse.' She paused. 'I was a firefighter for a few years. If you put out enough fires, you'll eventually put one out that has claimed lives.'

'Yes.'

'So I've seen the like before.'

'I see.' Hennessey glanced round the room. It was neat, clean. There were photographs of the dog in plentiful array, but no photograph of any human being.

'Yes . . . it got to me . . . firefighting is a highly stressed job . . . and I looked at the senior fire officers on parade with their bloodshot eyes . . . They had locked themselves away with a bottle, and I don't mean beer, slept it off . . . turned in for duty well the worse for wear . . . but it's the way they handled stress. A lot of deaths from heart attacks in the fire service, early deaths, men who died before their time . . . the job does that to you.'

'So I have heard.'

'Well, I got out but I took a few sights with me in my mind's eye . . . and charred corpses are among them. So the instant I saw it, I knew what it was. Called three nines on my mobile, waited until the boys in blue arrived, then gave my name and address and we returned home.'

'We?'

'Toby and me.' She glanced warmly at her dog. 'You can keep people. A dog gives you all you need and won't betray your trust.'

'So you take that walk daily? You and Toby?'

'Sometimes twice daily, depending on my shifts. I am a nurse.'

Hennessey smiled. 'Good for you.'

'It has its stresses but not like the fire service.'

'So the corpse appeared overnight?'

'Appeared?' Paula Eyton smiled. 'You make it sound like an apparition or as if it was conjured from thin air ... but yes, it was placed where I found it some time between 4.00 p.m. yesterday and about 10.30 a.m. this forenoon.'

'Alright.' Hennessey scribbled on his pad. 'Did you see anything out of the ordinary yesterday afternoon?'

'No ... smelled the body being burned, though.'

'Sorry?' Hennessey's jaw dropped. 'You smelled it being burned?'

'Yes.' Paula Eyton remained expressionless. 'Didn't realize it at the time but I smelled a distinct and unusual burning smell last night at about ten p.m. I didn't realize that I was smelling the corpse being burned, but putting two and two together, it must have been that that I was smelling. This is the country, farmers often have fires, burn all sorts. Fires are good things if properly used and only if properly used.'

'Yes ... only if properly used,' Hennessey echoed. 'Could you tell from which direction the smell came and how far away?'

'From over there.' Paula Eyton pointed to her back garden. 'Beyond the garden there is a sort of –' she shrugged – 'I wouldn't know how to describe it. It's a hotchpotch of an area, abandoned cars, an unofficial rubbish tip, but some allotments as well. If it wasn't burned

104

there, I can't think where else it would have been burned. Strange thing to do, burn a body then move it. Why not leave it where it's been burned?'

'Puzzles us too.'

'Unpleasant job. It's that that got to me when I was in the fire service, getting up close and personal to a burned corpse . . . the smell . . . and to touch them . . . the flesh crumbles in your hand.'

'You had to touch them?'

'Oh . . . yes . . . the firefighters lift the corpses into the body bags and zip them up, not the ambulance crew or the mortuary van crews, but the poor old firefighters, and it really was that which reached me in the end . . . Been there, done that, got the T-shirt . . . there are other T-shirts to be had . . . and for doing equally useful jobs.'

'How do I find the place you speak of?'

'From here? With great difficulty. I'll show you.' She turned to Toby and said, 'Walk,' and the spaniel barked and turned in tight tail-wagging circles with excitement.

Having donned a duffle coat, woollen hat, scarf and gloves, Paula Eyton walked with Hennessey from her house back in the direction of the small wood in which the body was found, and then, after a hundred yards, she turned to her left down a narrow path between a house and garden on the left and a ploughed field on the right.

'I'd tuck your trousers into your socks if I were you . . . it can be muddy in parts here even when it's as cold as this.' She strode on, she safely in hiking boots, also recently donned.

Hennessey knelt and did as suggested and then followed her.

Paula Eyton turned on to a second path. 'This is why I couldn't direct you,' she said. 'Lots of paths hereabouts.'

Hennessey, having caught her up, grunted his appreciation, though he felt he could have easily followed her

directions. Left out of the house, left on the path just before the field, left on to a second path; it was all that was needed.

The path led to a field which was as Paula Eyton had described, a hotchpotch of various land uses: waste tips, car dumps, a few tired looking allotments; an eyesore would, thought Hennessey, be an alternative description. 'If you'd allow me to continue alone?'

'Alone?' Paula Eyton inclined her head to one side. 'But I would have thought two people and a dog . . .'

'Alone,' Hennessey repeated. 'If you are correct and this is where the body was burned, then this is now a crime scene.'

'Ah, well, in that case . . .' She tugged the spaniel's lead. 'Come on, Toby, time to go home.' She walked away and then turned. 'Oh, sir . . .'

'Yes?' Hennessey also turned.

'The access road to this site is over there.' She pointed to the far end of the area of land as a gust of wind tugged the hair that protruded from the sides of her hat. 'It's the only way a vehicle can reach or leave the site.'

'Thank you.'

'And you could try Gladys.'

'Gladys?'

'Silver haired lady lives in the cottage.'

'The cottage?'

'The cottage . . . it's the only building on the road that runs to and from the site. She don't miss much, don't old Gladys,' she added in an affected accent. 'Not old Gladys.' She turned away and with her dark clothing, merged easily into the winter landscape.

Hennessey felt oddly alone. There were houses close by, the police were at the scene of the crime where the body lay under an inflatable tent, a mere fifteen minutes' walk away, yet he felt quite alone. The area had, he felt, a very lonely feel about it, very forlorn. Perhaps it was

the abandoned cars, or the mounds of discarded refuse. Perhaps it was the solitary nature of the allotments which were scattered, rather than nestling cosily against each other, or it was the rooks and crows that fluttered and picked amongst the rubbish. Perhaps it may have been the denuded trees of the wood beyond the site, or the way the wind blew coldly and relentlessly from the east under a low, grey sky. Or perhaps it was because on this site a body had been burned. Whatever it was, Hennessey felt very alone in the world; he would be very pleased to quit this area.

He strolled over the ground, skirting round the abandoned cars and mounds of detritus, following rough paths that had been created over the passage of time and very soon found what he had been looking for. He found an area of flat concrete, about twenty feet by ten, the foundation for a building that had in the event not been constructed, like a pillbox for the Home Guard to use to defend Anslow against Hitler's tanks, or an air-raid shelter for the citizens of Anslow to use to shelter from Nazi bombs; it seemed to Hennessey to be of that vintage. It was still solid but had an aged and sun-bleached look. In the centre of the apron of concrete was a blackened area, oblong in shape, longer than it was wide but with an ill-defined edge, the sort of blackening he would have expected to be the result of a body being laid out and then set alight. He plunged his hand into his coat pocket and took out his mobile. He unfolded it and keyed in Yellich's number. He disliked mobile phones, or brain fryers as he referred to them, irritants in pubs and buses and destroyers of the romance of a train journey, but there was no denying their usefulness. 'Yellich?'

'Yes, boss?'

'I think I have found the place where the body was burned. Can you send SOCO here?'

'Yes, boss.'

'It's towards the village of Anslow. Just before they reach the village . . . well, at the beginning of the village really, there's a path going off to the right-hand side between a ploughed field and the side of someone's privet hedge, take a left on to another path and follow it to an area of desolation.'

'OK . . . right down a path at the entrance to the village, left on another path . . . an area of desolation?'

'That's it.'

'Sounds like an ideal place to burn a body, skipper . . . has a very solemn feel.'

'Solemn is the word. There's something here that makes me shiver and it's not the wind.' He snapped his mobile shut and continued to prowl the area, looking at the ground from left to right and being careful to disturb as little as he could. Fifteen minutes later he noticed two men in high visibility jackets approach the wasteland. He raised his arm and walked towards them. 'Found me,' he said with a smile.

'Excellent directions, sir,' the older and taller of the two men replied warmly.

'Well, over here . . .' Hennessey led the two men to the concrete apron. 'Looks like a fire has been had here recently.'

'Smells like it too.' The older SOCO looked at the ground. 'I can smell it . . . very faint, but it's there . . . roast beef.'

Hennessey sniffed. 'Yes, you're right . . . this is the place. You know what to do . . . Photographs and then scrapings from the burned area . . . there will be human fat among the carbon.'

'He was deceased, sir.'

'You think?'

'The burned area is localized . . . well, he certainly wasn't conscious, just as with the other two.'

'The other two?'

'Last Friday . . . I attended the other two burned corpses. I assume they are linked?'

'Just do your job,' Hennessey spoke calmly but with an air of authority, 'and I'll do mine.' He walked away and as he did so, he once again took out his mobile phone and phoned Yellich.

'What's happening, Yellich?'

'The body is being removed now . . . tent is being deflated.'

'Good . . . good . . . get the uniforms over here, this seems to be more of a crime scene than your location.'

'Yes, boss.'

'Do a fingertip search of this site. I am going to see Gladys.'

'Gladys?'

'So I believe is her name. She lives in the cottage, being the only building on the access road to this . . . this area of desolation.'

'The cottage . . . access road . . . got that boss . . . so long as we know where you are.'

The cottage was easily found. As described by Paula Eyton, it was the only building on the access road to the area of desolation and to add to the distinctiveness it was, Hennessey saw, called 'The Cottage'. He walked up the concrete path and knocked on the door. There were two windows on the anterior of the cottage, one at either side of the door. The curtain to the left of the door moved as if in response to his knock. He stood on the threshold, looking about him at the trees to one side of the cottage, the ploughed field beyond, trees opposite. The nearest other dwellings were the rooftops of the houses of Anslow. The door opened wide, Gladys revealed herself to be a frail looking woman with short cropped, grey hair. She had a steely look in her eyes and her jaw was set firm in what Hennessey thought could be best described as determined.

'You really should have asked who I was before opening the door like that, Mrs . . .?'

'Gladys.' Her voice was cold, hard, but her mind was clearly all there, still firing on all cylinders. 'Just Gladys . . . and you are the police.'

'Yes.' He showed his ID.

'I don't need to see that, it's stamped on your forehead. I saw you, was watching you with that woman from the village, her and her dog. I saw her lead you up to the allotments. She was happy with you behind her and then you stood next to her and said something and she went back towards the village, her and her dog, and you had a good poke about the allotments and then you talked into one of those things that people carry these days, then you came straight here and you were not bothered who saw you. You're a policeman alright. You better wipe your feet and come in.'

Hennessey scraped the mud from the soles of his shoes on a metal bar beside the door then, stooping, he entered the cottage. He found it cold inside, dark and cramped. He followed Gladys to a small parlour where two upright wooden chairs stood in front of an open fire grate. Combustibles and a lump of coal lay in the grate. Gladys sat in one of the chairs and pulled a red shawl round her shoulders. 'Better keep your coat on,' she said, pronouncing 'coat' as 'koy-it'. A Leeds accent, Hennessey thought. Definitely not York, not from Sheffield way either where coat is pronounced 'koo-at'. 'It's chilly.'

'You should light your fire, Gladys.'

'Not yet. Take a seat . . . you make me feel tired standing there.'

Hennessey sat down in the second upright chair. It creaked as he allowed his full weight to rest upon it.

'Not used to such weight, that old chair. Used to be my man's . . . it's nice to see a man sitting in it again. No, I keep a cold house, keeps me healthy. People got by without

central heating for centuries . . . folks are just a lot of jessies now . . . I wear clothing to keep warm . . . I'll light the fire this after . . . I shouldn't burn coal but no one bothers old Gladys.'

'Very well, so long as you have heat if you need it.'

'I have. So you'll be wanting to know about the fire in the allotments last night?'

'Yes, yes, I would.'

'Used to be all allotments, forty, fifty years ago . . . all well tended . . . my man had one. Never tasted vegetables like the vegetables you grow in an allotment. Then one by one they got given up; no one wanted to take them over. Then a bit of rubbish was dumped, then another load, then the first motor was abandoned. There used to be thirty allotments on the plot, now there's five, and my husband's old allotment is home to an old car . . . aye . . .'

'The fire?' Hennessey pressed.

'What was burned, I don't know. Smelled . . . smelled wrong . . . went up quickly, in a flash. They used petrol I should think. Whatever, it went up with a whoosh. They stepped back smartly.'

'They?'

'A man and a woman. Did they burn it on the concrete?'

'Yes.'

'That was laid some years ago, it was going to be a storeroom for the allotment tenants but they couldn't get planning permission.'

'Oh, was that it? I thought perhaps . . .'

'Laid the foundations and then thought they ought to get permission to build the thing.' Gladys's chest heaved as she laughed. 'Silly sausages. Anyway, the concrete stayed . . . it looked to be about where the fire was.'

'Yes, it was.'

'About the only place you could have a bonfire.' Which, thought Hennessey, is more accurate than you know, having

once read that 'bonfire' is a contraction of 'bone fire', being the final disposal of the remains of a felon who had been hung, drawn and quartered. A bonfire was exactly what this lady had witnessed.

'Saw it from the window upstairs . . . at the back.'

'What time was that?'

'About eleven p.m. Not after midnight, I go to my bed at midnight as the bells chime . . . and I don't get up until dawn, not for nobody. Just Gladys in her old cocoon, snug and warm. So it was before midnight but late . . . heard the van first.'

'The van?'

'Like a small car, but a van . . . I know the difference.'

'Yes.'

'I heard it turn into the lane. Never seen it before but the driver seemed to know where he was. I thought another car was being dumped . . . watched it go. White . . . it was white . . . no writing on the side . . . sure of that . . . so then I went upstairs and saw nothing, it was all hidden from view, then whoosh . . . a flash of flame and in the light of the flame I saw two figures. I thought . . . I thought male and female, then the flames died down after a few minutes, then it was like they were put out. The figures started to smother the flames . . . then it was dark . . . then, some time later, after the van drove back down the lane, didn't see it but heard it. Gladys was well abed by then.'

It was Wednesday, 13.20 hours.

George Hennessey walked across the car park of York District Hospital, digesting a hurried but satisfying lunch. He glanced to his right as he walked towards the slab-sided, medium rise building. His heart warmed as he saw it, that beautiful old lady, a red and white Riley RMA circa 1947, the only car of its type in the city, nay in the Vale of York. One lady owner, lovingly serviced by a garage whose proprietor had made the owner promise him

first refusal should she ever decide to sell the vehicle. It was an offer said lady owner was pleased to give, if only to ensure high quality maintenance, knowing that she would never sell the vehicle: it had belonged to her father and she, in the fullness of time, was going to bequeath it to her son. It was not, Hennessey pondered, as he turned once more towards the building, every heirloom that does 10,000 trouble-free miles from year end to year end, requiring little more than an annual service and a change of tyres.

He pushed open the door of the hospital building and was met by a blast of warm air which caused him to instantly remove his hat, scarf and gloves, and to fully open his coat front. He walked down the softly echoing corridor, undertaking a walk he had taken many times before but did so with a lightness of step despite the heavy task ahead. He walked to the Department of Pathology and after presenting at the reception desk, walked down a smaller corridor and tapped softly on a door.

'Come in.'

Hennessey entered the room. It was a small, cramped office.

'Knew it was you.' Dr D'Acre glanced up at him. 'It wasn't just that I was expecting you but more that I would know that knock anywhere. The classic copper's knock, tap, tap . . . tap. Do take a seat.'

Hennessey sat beside her desk, noting a photograph of three children and a second photograph showing a horse which, even to Hennessey's untrained eye, looked to be a magnificent animal. 'I must alter my style.' He lowered himself on to the chair, holding his hat, gloves and scarf on his lap.

'So . . .' Dr D'Acre leaned back avoiding eye contact with him. 'Number three?'

'Possibly . . . it is going to throw a spanner in the works if he or she . . .'

113

'He.'

'I see . . . well, if he is not connected in any way with Mr and Mrs Dent.'

'You're thinking a serial killer?'

'Yes. If he is not connected, then yes, I am afraid that's what we are looking at. Just when we had someone in the frame . . . at least getting into the frame . . . just needed a push.'

'Oh?'

'Yes . . . the first two victims were husband and wife.'

'I know.'

'Yes . . . sorry. They adopted two children . . . one, the boy, Gregory, is a chilling piece of work. Set to inherit millions upon his adoptive parents' death . . . amoral . . . His adoptive parents' cats disappeared, their dog died shortly after he arrived and shortly after it had growled at him.'

Dr D'Acre raised her eyebrows and allowed herself uncharacteristic eye contact with him. 'I wouldn't dismiss that. I mean an animal's reaction to someone.'

'Oh, I don't . . . we don't. Can't use it as evidence of course, but it points us in the right direction. People reporting paranormal experiences have done the same . . . but it was a very brittle alibi.'

'Oh?'

'Yes, his lady friend said she was with him.'

'I see.'

'But there was no other independent witness. She's as cold and hardhearted as he is and they are an item. She stands to gain much from his bereavement, even if he pays her for her alibi and then they go their own separate ways. That is a very brittle alibi.' He glanced around the cramped office, neatly kept desk, calendar on the wall. 'So that was the state of play until, as you suggest, number three turned up. It was going to be a question of putting pressure on the alibi, see if it would break.

We advised his lady friend, Susan Thurnham, the ice maiden, of the consequences of aiding and abetting, especially in a crime as serious as murder – double murder, in fact. She just smiled and said "Really?" or "Is that so?" or some such nonchalance. But now with number three on the slab . . . no wonder he is cocky and she self-assured. If there's no connection between the victims, we are looking at a serial killer.'

'Well, I wish you luck. I can tell you that the victim is a male, probably late middle age or even elderly, he was not burned where he was found . . .'

'Yes, we believe we have identified the location where the body was burned. It poses another mystery.'

'Oh?'

'Well . . . the location of the burning seems to have been an area once given over to thriving and productive allotments, now given over to the unlawful disposal of waste, old cars and other refuse . . . and which is reasonably well hidden from the road. And further, which is less than a quarter of a mile from where the body was found.'

'So, why move the body at all? Is that what you mean?'

'Yes. A curiosity more than a mystery, but it's intriguing.'

'Well, I would say there's either a good reason to move the body or no logical reason at all. It might be just a panic reaction kicking in. Dare say all will be revealed. Well, I took a rectal temperature, despite the evident thermal confusion, which indicated recent death, within hours of him being found, but I don't like to be drawn on the time of death as you know. So all I will say, is that it was within hours of the corpse being discovered, and anything else I can tell you will have to wait until after the post-mortem. Well, Mr Filey will have prepped the body by now. Shall we get changed? I'll see you in the theatre.'

'Good old dog walkers.' Hennessey stood.

'What?' Dr D'Acre shot a glance at him.

'Oh, nothing . . . nothing . . . just an old man mumbling to himself.'

'Not so old.' She allowed herself a rare smile. 'I'll see you in there.'

It was Wednesday, December 17, 14.30 hours.

Six

Wednesday, December 17, 23.10 hours
in which Somerled Yellich meets a mystic and the gracious
reader is privy to George Hennessey's ghosts.

Sometimes, Somerled Yellich had found, sometimes, you
just know who you are talking to. This, he felt, was
one such case.

'It's now twenty-four hours.' The woman was elderly,
tearful, agitated. 'I just know something bad has happened
to him.'

'When did you last see your husband, Mrs Harthill?'

'Yesterday morning. He went out . . . for his walk . . .
he's got high blood pressure and the doctors told him to
take exercise as a way of controlling it. Don't have to go
to a gym, he said. I mean, a gym at Arthur's age, but it's
not necessary he said, a good, brisk twenty-minute walk
each day, that ought to do the trick, and Arthur . . . he
always went the second mile, you know . . . so he went
out for a forty-minute walk each morning, only really bad
weather would keep him in.'

'Don't talk as though he is no longer with us.' Yellich
spoke in as reassuring a manner as he could muster, but
he had to concede that Mrs Harthill's concern was probably with some foundation and his 'inner voice' as he
often called it, or 'his waters', knew that Mr Arthur
Harthill was at that moment a charred corpse in the
pathology laboratory at York District Hospital, probably

117

then being or indeed having been, dissected to establish the cause of his death, if it was, by some means, not the fire.

'He walks out by the wood, you see . . .'

'The wood?'

'Penny Wood.'

'OK.'

'But he never returned. Always the same walk. He takes it when the weather's fine, so I know the route and I went looking for him, calling his name . . . Arthur . . . Arthur . . . I called . . . no reply, and the wood is clear this time of the year.'

'Clear?'

'No leaves.'

'Ah . . .'

'You can see all around you, but it's like the earth swallowed him up or he's been abducted by them aliens like you hear about on television. Vanished. We grew up together . . . same street . . . we used to play together when we were four or five years old, now we are both seventy. We've known each other for sixty-five years, married for fifty of them. We always said when the first one went, the other wouldn't be too far behind.'

'Mrs Harthill . . .'

'He's gone . . . I know he's gone.' She opened her handbag and took out a photograph and handed it to Yellich. 'It's the most recent.'

Yellich took the photograph and looked at it. He saw Mrs Harthill glance from side to side as if seizing the opportunity to look at the interview room, spartan and functional as it was: a desk, three upright chairs, hessian carpeting, two-tone orange walls, light above dark. The photograph showed a slender, cheery-looking man digging a garden.

'Side on,' Yellich commented.

'Yes . . . it's a game we play, taking photographs of each

when the other isn't looking; we've got some grand snaps like that over the years. Isn't it any use?'

'Oh . . . it's of use. May we keep it?'

'Yes, that's what I brought it for, for you to keep.'

'Thanks.' Yellich clipped the photograph to the file he had opened on Harthill, Arthur, missing person. 'Do you have a photograph of Mr Harthill showing his face?'

'Like a passport photograph?'

'Yes . . . but a bit larger.'

'Yes.' She nodded. She was a small, frail looking woman, finely made, with short, close cropped silver hair, but she seemed to Yellich to have a strong character, a woman, he thought, who could weather a severe storm and possibly she had indeed done so, but he also felt that she was quite correct when she said that she and her husband would die within a short space of time . . . in her seventies . . . together since childhood, one would pine without the other. 'Yes, I can let you have quite a lot like that, photography is our passion.'

'Just one good one will do.' Yellich paused and then asked, 'What did your husband do for a living?'

Mrs Harthill hesitated before answering and then said, 'So, he is dead? I am right; he's a corpse somewhere, isn't he?'

Yellich made to speak but remained silent.

'You wouldn't have asked that question if he was just a missing person . . . not at his age. You've got a body of a man that you can't . . . that you don't know who it is . . . his identity. That's the word, his identity . . . you don't know his identity.'

'Possibly.' Yellich looked at the surface of the table. 'We possibly have . . . a male was taken to the mortuary of the York District Hospital earlier today.'

'Oh . . . my. Well, he was a surface worker.'

'A surface worker?'

'At the colliery . . . Wistow Pit. He wouldn't ever go

119

into the cages and go underground but he worked on the surface. Less money but he wasn't bothered. He was safe on the surface. He always said that mining is a safe job, though you hear about accidents because often a large number of men are lost, but if you want a dangerous job, go and work on a farm, that's what Arthur would say. He said, on average, one person a week is killed on British farms . . . one agricultural worker. Fifty miners a year are not killed . . . and we got our monthly ton.'

'Monthly ton?'

'Each worker and retired worker at the pit gets a ton of coal a month, left in our driveway, and Arthur or me would put it in the coalhole, shovel it in, one shovel full at a time . . . was a half-day job. Really, we could have left it where it was because no one would steal it. Coal Board houses, you see. Everybody worked in the pit, every home had a ton of coal put in their drive each month, but we had to move it because it was an eyesore. It was a condition of receiving it . . . it had to be put in the coal-hole out of sight and the drive swept up. What happened?'

'To the man? I can't tell you. I won't tell you until . . . unless it is your husband, then I will, but we may be jumping the gun . . . but . . .'

'But.' She fixed him with a keen, piercing stare. 'But what?'

'Well, I would like to drive you home, see where you and Mr Harthill live.'

'Lived,' she said. 'We used to live there. I still do . . . but not for long, I think. Not for long.' She stood. 'I am feeling tired, anyway . . . won't complain when my time comes. Come on.'

Yellich had never been to the Throwley estate before. He found it a strange, but not uninteresting experience. The houses he saw were drab, uniformly so, grey with small and often unkempt gardens. What Yellich did find fascinating was the smell of burning coal which lingered

in the air of the estate, smelling it even before he halted his car. When he did halt the car outside Mrs Harthill's house and left the vehicle, walking with her up her drive to the rear of the house, he, for the first time in his life smelled air that was heavy with coal smoke. He understood how it could be harmful to health and clearly understood then the need for smokeless zones, but he had to concede that the smell had warmth about it. He thought the smell welcoming and homely. In the neighbouring drive was a pile of coal, just as Mrs Harthill had described.

'They're away,' Mrs Harthill explained, as if apologizing for her neighbours. 'They'll put it away when they get back. Their daughter lives in Cornwall, she's having her first baby, they're going down for the event. They went down as parents and hope to come back as grandparents.'

'Ah . . .'

'You have children?'

'One . . . a boy.'

'Plan any more?' She fished into her coat pocket and withdrew a large mortice key which she placed into the lock of the door.

'No,' Yellich replied softly, 'no. Myself and Mrs Yellich are content with the one.'

'He'll need a brother or a sister.' She pushed open the door, forcing it with her shoulder. 'Arthur was going to fix this door . . . it jams.'

'He's got special needs.' Yellich assisted her to open the door. 'So . . . one it is. We couldn't manage with two.'

'Special needs? You mean he's simple?'

'Well, that's not the term . . .'

'Sorry . . . there's a girl like that on the estate . . . she always seems such a happy soul . . . bless her.'

The house was neatly kept. Mrs Harthill had made up a fire before she left the house, safely behind a fireguard.

It had settled by the time she and Yellich returned, into a bed of hot coal and gave out what Yellich found to be a very solid form of heat. Mrs Harthill peeled off her coat. 'Can't beat a coal fire,' she said. 'My sister and her husband live in York on the Tang Hall estate . . . you'll know it.'

'Oh, yes.'

'Aye . . . they got a lot of bother on that estate.'

'Yes.'

'Her house has central heating and gas fires . . . it's not the same.'

'I can tell.'

'Not used to coal fires? You'll be too young to remember them.'

'Yes, we were like your sister, gas fires and central heating.'

'Well, give me coal . . . despite the mess you have to clear up each day. So, what can I do? What can I do to help you catch Arthur's killer?'

'Mrs Harthill, we still don't know it is your husband.'

'It's him.' She touched her chest, 'I know . . . in here I know. I told you, Arthur and I knew each other since we were pre-school age and yesterday, about midday, I felt a sensation . . . not a physical thing . . . up here.' She pointed to her head. 'Up here I felt . . . a feeling that I couldn't recognize . . . I have never felt it before in my life and so I didn't know what it was, but it's stayed, it hasn't gone away and this morning I knew what it was . . . it was loneliness. No wonder I didn't recognize it . . . loneliness. I've heard folk talk about it, I've read of things called lonely hearts' clubs, never knew what they were but now I do . . . it's Arthur. For the first time in fifty years I woke up alone, alone in my bed, alone in my house. He was killed about midday yesterday . . . in the middle of his walk. Not natural causes, either. I was alone very suddenly. I felt as if I had been robbed of something. I wouldn't have felt like that if

he had had a heart attack . . . that would have been sudden
. . . possibly . . . but this was sudden, sudden . . . just before
the midday news came on television. Sudden . . . but it was
not fair, like I had been robbed . . . like something had been
stolen from me. If Arthur had had a heart attack, I wouldn't
have felt that I had been robbed. I would still have missed
him but it would have been different.'

'I see.' Yellich held eye contact with Mrs Harthill, once
again being impressed by her strength of character and
sharp mind.

'We were spiritualists,' she explained. 'We were both
that way inclined for a long time. We just feel things that
other folk don't seem to feel. I just know that he was
killed at noon yesterday.' She paused. 'You know, I think
I could take you to the very place he was killed.'

'Oh . . .?'

'Yes. We used to walk at the same speed, we could
follow his route. He left here at 11.30 a.m. yesterday
morning, so we walk for half an hour, that's all we have
to do . . . and I know where that will take us. Half an hour's
walk from here will take us to the one place on his route
which can't be seen . . . what's that word?'

'Overlooked?'

'Yes . . . overlooked. It's not long, about twice the
distance from here to the bottom of the garden.' She pointed
to the window.

Yellich glanced out of the window at a flat expanse of
lawn which terminated at a wooden fence, beyond which
was the garden belonging to another house on the estate,
from the chimney of which smoke rose to be caught and
whisked away by the wind. About thirty feet, he thought,
that would be twice the length of Mrs Harthill's back
garden. More than enough space to murder someone, drag
their body deeper into the wood. 'Yes, alright, we'll do
that . . . but first . . .'

'A photograph . . . full face.'

'Yes, please, and, if you have one, a strand of his hair.'

'A strand of his hair?'

'Yes, if you could find one . . . perhaps from the bath plughole, or from his comb. We could confirm . . . I mean, if he is the gentleman that was admitted . . . whose corpse was brought to the hospital this morning.'

'You could tell if it's Arthur . . . just by a strand of hair?'

'Yes . . . well, we can't, our scientists can . . . out at Wetherby . . . that's where they are based, but yes, it will confirm identity, probably more than the photograph.'

'I'll get his comb.'

'Here,' Mrs Harthill stopped. 'Here . . . this is where Arthur would have been at midday yesterday. I can't say that I feel anything . . . but I never have been sensitive to location. Arthur was . . . you know we'd be walking and he'd stop and say something happened here . . . something violent . . . he'd be sensitive like that. I never was . . . but I see ghosts that other folk don't see . . . that is my curse.'

'Curse?'

'I thought it was a gift when I realized I was seeing ghosts, but it has become a curse . . . I feel no sense of presence here . . . though this is where Arthur would have been at about midday yesterday.'

Yellich glanced at the path ahead of him. It was indeed a perfect place for an ambush. The path was sunken and curved; it was not overlooked by any building nor any roadway or pavement. The wood was generously covered in shrubs, few, very few with leaves, but sufficient shrubbery to conceal a body from the view of any person walking the pathway if it was dragged far enough and then perhaps covered with something, a sheet of corrugated iron, an old carpet, left as if selfishly fly-tipped. The path emerged on to a road, Yellich could hear the cars. Overpower an elderly man, conceal his body, return at night, carry the body the

short distance to a waiting vehicle and drive it away to where it was burned. 'We'd better walk back the way we came.'

'Why? It's quicker to carry on, brings you back to the estate. Arthur was just ten minutes from home.'

'Yes.' Yellich turned to her. 'I can smell the coal fire smoke from here, but this is a crime scene. I'd rather not contaminate it any more than it has already been contaminated. So, if you don't mind . . .?'

A lone crow cawed.

Hennessey sat back in his chair, cradling the mug of tea, listening to what Somerled Yellich said.

'So,' he said as he glanced out of the window at the ribbon of street lamps on Micklegate and the last remnants of daylight in a dark sky, 'too late to do a fingertip search today, as you say . . . but tomorrow?'

'First thing, skipper. I don't think the crime scene will get contaminated overnight . . . no one will visit it. I mean, if the felon or felons dropped something incriminating and it hasn't been picked up yet, it will still be there in the morning.'

'Yes . . . well, can you get the comb off to Wetherby by courier? Dr D'Acre sent tissue samples to them with a case reference number. Ask them to match them to the DNA from the comb, if you would and if they can. Listening to what you have said, I tend to think they will, though that does rather throw a spanner into the works.'

'You think a serial killer, sir?'

'Yes.' Hennessey placed the mug on his desk. 'Yes, I am beginning to think that way. No link between Mr Harthill and the Dents?'

'None that we could find. Mrs Harthill doesn't know them and they are a different social class. The Dents were senior professionals living . . . well, you remember their

house . . . West End House in the east end of the village of Great Sheldwich.'

'Yes.'

'Well, the Harthill household was the opposite end of the social ladder . . . almost. A Coal Board owned house, when there was a Coal Board, owned by a mining company now. Still burning coal; never came across a lot of coal fires before, it was interesting – the smell in the street, the solid feeling of the warmth.'

'Yes, it would have taken me back to Greenwich, we burned coal in our fire . . . all Londoners did . . . terrible smogs though. When the smoke from the thousands of coal fires mingles with fog, whenever there was a fog, it was called a smog, cobbling together the words smoke and fog.'

'I see.'

'Caused many fatalities. People who had chest problems at the best of times succumbed, forced the passing of the Clean Air Acts and the introduction of smokeless fuel, but nothing beats coal for warmth, provided you can get rid of the smoke. I would like to have smelled coal fire smoke once more. Pockets of coal-burning houses still exist, Grassington for one, but I didn't know about the Throwley estate . . . out by Wistow, you say?'

'Yes, boss.'

'Might take a trip out there one day, a lesson in modern history for myself. Well, back to business, the post-mortem on the third victim . . . apparent third victim provided the same result as the PMs on Mr and Mrs Dent.'

'Dead before being burned?' Yellich drained his mug of tea and placed it on Hennessey's desk.

'Yes, fortunately for him, no soot in the trachea, death was caused by a massive blow to the head, he was struck from behind. The pathway seems a likely murder place you think?'

'Yes, it runs the risk of someone coming along unexpectedly but that section of the path cannot be overlooked,

it would be a good place to do it. Drag the body into the shrubs, out of sight from the path, return after dark to collect the corpse and remove it to where it was burned.'

'Local knowledge.'

'Sorry, boss?'

'Local knowledge . . . that wood.'

'Penny Wood.'

'Yes, the stretch of sunken pathway, the desolate allotment site, the move to the other wood where it was found, that all says local knowledge, as does the location where the Dents were found . . . by the river, I mean. No one . . . no one in their right mind would go near a river, or any stretch of water at night, it's far too dangerous unless they knew exactly where they were, unless they knew every square foot of ground and I can't see Gregory Dent having that level of knowledge – he's too much of a playboy type.'

'Seems so . . . seems we were barking up the wrong tree with respect of Mr Dent. Wrong part of the forest completely, as you said.'

'So what now, boss?'

'Well, if you'll organize the fingertip search tomorrow and have the comb sent to Wetherby, I'll go and see the Commander . . . We need an "ologist".'

Yellich smiled. 'Yes, boss.' He stood and left Hennessey's office.

Hennessey, somewhat wearily, walked to the office of Commander Sharkey. He tapped reverently on the door.

'Come.' The voice had an imperious tone and the answer came only after a noticeable pause.

Hennessey opened the door and approached Sharkey's desk. 'A word, please, sir.'

'Of course, George, take a pew.'

Hennessey sat in one of the chairs in front of Sharkey's desk. Once again the desktop was neat, not a thing out of place. Sharkey, younger than Hennessey, was as usual,

impeccably dressed; behind him were framed photographs, one of a younger Sharkey as a junior officer in the British Army and a second of Sharkey in the uniform of the Royal Hong Kong Police.

'So –' Sharkey sat back in his chair – 'what can I do for you, George?'

'Well, to cut to the chase, sir, I think we need help. As I said to Sergeant Yellich just now, we need an "ologist".'

'A psychologist?'

'I believe that is the . . . title, yes, sir.'

'A forensic psychologist?'

'Well, someone who can tell us how a criminal mind works . . . how a felon ticks.'

'A forensic psychologist.'

'You have to approve the funding, sir.'

'Yes . . . so why do we need the services of the "ologist"?'

Hennessey told him.

'I see.' Sharkey leaned forward when Hennessey had finished talking. 'So, three murders . . . all similar, no connection between the first two and the third, but the first two were husband and wife?'

'It seems to be the beginning of a pattern. I'd like to stop it before it gets worse.'

'Yes . . . yes, I can sympathize . . . and serial murderers have been known to target members of the same family. So yes, I'll set the wheels in motion. Do you have anyone in mind?'

'We've used Dr Joseph at the university before, sir. She was very helpful the last time.'

'Alright, leave that with me.' Sharkey wrote on his pad. 'What is her first name?'

'Kamy . . . short for Kamilla, spelled with a *k*.'

'Alright . . . now, George, since you are here, how are you finding things?'

128

'I am not ready to police a desk, sir. I am on top of things. You have told me about your maths teacher at your school, Johnny Hay.'

'Taighe.' Sharkey nodded. 'Taighe, Johnny Taighe. Yes, just when he should have been allowed to soft-pedal into his pension they piled on the pressure. Poor bloke deserved retirement . . . he'd earned it teaching practically all his working life but always lower school, then they make him teach senior school for national qualifications.'

'Couldn't handle it.'

'No . . . I think about him often as I get older. He made more of an impact, more of an impression than I thought at the time.'

'Yes, that happens.'

'Poor old boy . . . equipped to carry the sort of load you put on a milk float and they give him the sort of load you would put on the back of an articulatcd lorry.'

'Well, I am well up to the job still, sir. I hear my pension calling my name but I am not ready to go yet.'

'Good . . . well I won't let what happened to Johnny Taighe happen to any one of mine. So, if you feel that you are losing the edge, if it should come to feel too much, you know where I am; we'll work something out.'

'I appreciate it, sir, but I walked out of the Navy after National Service by walking off a destroyer in Portsmouth Harbour, not from behind a desk, and I'd like to walk into retirement from the coalface of police work. My career has always been one of criminal investigation . . . I'd like my last day in the job to be just that.'

'Very well.' Sharkey held up his hand. 'Just so long as you know that you can knock on my door. So what about the nick as a whole, anything I should worry about? I had my fill of corruption in there. He pointed to the photograph of himself when in the Royal Hong Kong Police. 'I wasn't in that organization very long, thank goodness,

but I was there and part of it. If you were in it, you were part of it.'

This time Hennessey held up his hand. 'Sir, with respect, I am certain there is no corruption here. I would have sensed it, I am sure. I really think that you can sleep at night on that score.'

'Well, thank you, George. I find that reassuring. So, I'll acquire funding for Dr Joseph's services, let you know when you can make contact with her.'

Hennessey stood. 'Thank you, sir.'

Hennessey returned to his office, collected his hat and coat and drove home to Easingwold. He disliked driving for one tragic and highly personal reason, and the slow, halting rush-hour drive on that dark evening he found less than pleasant, but his heart leapt as he approached his house because there, half on and half off the kerb stood a BMW in German racing silver. Whoever was awaiting him at home would more than compensate for the irritating drive.

Later, after handshakes and the How are you's, George and Charles Hennessey sat in the kitchen of George Hennessey's house, the same house in which Charles had grown up.

'Copycat?' Charles sipped his tea and reached for a toasted teacake.

'Probably . . . if it's not a serial killer, it has to be a copycat. I don't know which is worse. A serial killer won't stop until he is caught or he "matures", so I once read, but it means just one felon to catch. A copycat will probably stop at one but it means an entirely separate additional investigation. Ah well, keeps us busy.'

'No shortage of work for you to do,' Charles said with a smile. 'And keep us busy.'

'What are you doing at the moment? Still in Sheffield?'

'No . . . no . . . that trial finished. We won an acquittal.'

'Good for you.'

'Well . . . yes, chalk it up but it wasn't a pleasing case.

We knew he did it, but it was our job to make the Crown work to prove their case and we managed to do that. The jury must have agonized but in the end there just was insufficient evidence to make his prosecution safe. The Crown's case was like a colander . . . had too many holes. It was as though they had hoped for a lazy defence team because they knew he was guilty.'

'Instead they got you. You always were a fighter.'

'Well, me and my junior; he's going far at the bar, he's like a pit bull terrier. He cross-examined the police witness. He's still very junior but his technique is awesome, you could almost see the senior police officer backing up against his attack. You'd think he was a QC with decades of experience. I am learning from him, but I think he should develop a more sophisticated approach. I enjoy tripping witnesses up with a calm and deceptively gentle approach, it lowers their guard. My junior's approach ensures that their guard is always well up, but it's not often that a senior police officer looks cowed in the dock . . . Anyway, the felon walked. In Scotland it would have been a "not proven" verdict. Very useful third verdict they have up there, but here and in Wales it is only guilty or not guilty. Couldn't convict on the evidence presented . . . too fragile . . . so they had to acquit, but that didn't mean to say he was innocent and his sneer when the foreperson said "not guilty" said so.'

'It happens. He walks only to be nailed for something else at some future date.'

'Oh, indeed. No . . . this week I'm in Bradford and this time we are also going not guilty, but this time I really do believe our client to have been wrongly charged, so we are fighting for the right reason. We're giving it everything we've got. I would be very upset if this man is convicted.'

'The case against him must be strong.'

'It is . . . motive, witnesses . . . He has no alibi, he also has a previous criminal record for acts of violence, so he's no saint, but that doesn't mean he's guilty of this offence. Anyway, we'll do what we can and lodge an appeal if the jury find against him.'

'Anyway, how are the children?'

'Fine . . . thriving, barrelling through their milestones, wanting to see Grandad again.'

'And Grandad wants to see them again. Soon.'

'This weekend?' Charles Hennessey raised an eyebrow.

'Mmm . . . possibly.'

'Ah ha . . . your lady friend, whom we still haven't met.'

'Well, it is my weekend off, one weekend in five when I don't have to work Saturday or Sunday. We had planned something, but this case . . . burning elderly people . . . no leads . . . dead-end alleys every way we look.'

'Well, you should take time off, you deserve it. It's only now I have children that I realize how hard it was for you, bringing me up alone.'

'I had help.'

'Childminders . . . not the same as a partner. So you deserve a rest, enjoy your weekend.'

'I will, if I can, but my friend will understand. I confess my retirement looms not like an end but a beginning. I will have so much time to do all the things I want to do and a good pension to enable me to do them. I intend to start each morning with a warm bath; no more falling out of bed and pulling on my clothes as if on automatic pilot, and driving to work whilst still half asleep. Not a lot of driving either, that is going to be the best part. Everything I need is in walking distance. I'll take the bus and the train if I need to go anywhere.'

'Uncle Graham's death really did affect you, didn't it?'

'Yes . . . me and Graham . . .' George Hennessey bit

his lip. 'Yes . . . as you know, there were eight years between us, so we never had that sibling rivalry that occurs when children are born within a year or two of each other. Him and his beloved motorbike . . . used to help him clean it on Sunday mornings, then he'd take me up to town, see the sights: Trafalgar Square, the Palace, the Houses of Parliament, across Westminster Bridge and back to Greenwich. Then one day, when I was . . . well, a lad, he rode away one night and I never saw him again. Your grandparents identified the body but the last I saw was a coffin being lowered into the ground on a summer's day . . . Same as your mother's funeral, except of course she wasn't buried – she's out there in the garden so she could watch you growing up. But yes, there is a gap and yes . . . yes, it has left me with an abiding dislike of the internal combustion engine whether two wheels or four . . . whether two stroke or four . . . a life for a patch of oil.'

'We've never really spoken about it before. Is that what caused the accident?'

'So we were told, though accident investigation is much more sophisticated now, but at the time we were told he hit a patch of oil on the road, lost control . . . a few inches either way, he might have missed it. You'd have liked him, he had a very warm personality and was wasted in the bank . . . but he was getting out, much to the dismay of our parents who thought the bank was "safe", which it was. It wasn't Graham, he was too creative to be a banker. He had applied for art college, he wanted to be a photojournalist . . . he would have been good at that . . . he would have taken some impressive, heart-stopping photographs . . . but . . .'

'But . . .'

When Charles Hennessey had warmly taken his leave, George Hennessey settled down to his evening. After briefly telling Jennifer of his day, briefly because the east

wind was biting, he prepared a simple but wholesome meal and digested it whilst sitting in front of a fire of faggots he had collected and allowed to dry. He sat down to read a book that had been in his collection of military history for many years but which he had only by then found time to read. It was an intriguing account of the Gallipoli campaign of 1915 told from the Turkish perspective. It had been translated into English in 1935 and was, Hennessey thought, written with an economical and very readable style and lavishly illustrated with maps and ink drawings. He thought it a gem of a book and an utter steal for the few pence he'd paid for it from a stall in the open market in York one summer's day. He had squandered money on occasions but over the years he had found that squandering was compensated by bargains acquired and money well spent. That book was one such bargain, and an example of how great joy and satisfaction can be had in exchange for a modest outlay.

Later, his meal settled, and Oscar fed, they walked together, man and dog, half an hour out, fifteen minutes allowing the mongrel to explore a small copse and half an hour back. Later still, George Hennessey, collar upturned, scarf around his neck and hat screwed on tight, walked into Easingwold for a pint of brown and mild at the Dove Inn. Just one before last orders were called. On the return journey he remembered to check a report he had read that one of the seven stars of the Great Bear had begun to flicker as its first stage of dying. He saw that it was so, that the most famous of the constellations was soon, though probably not even in his grandchildrens' lifetime, going to be six stars.

'There has to be another one.'
   'Another!'
   'Yes . . . soon . . . tonight. The plan is working . . .

don't you see it's working. There is no other way.' The
man paused. The woman beside him smiled. 'Don't you
see, there is no other way ... we have to see this
through.'

The fourth person in the room put his hand to his head
and groaned.

'Doesn't matter how many you kill,' said the first man,
'you still only serve one life sentence ... and if we keep
our heads, if we stick to the plan, we won't serve any
sentence at all. Just one more, that will do it. Just one
more.'

Wilson Weston walked home along Bad Bargain Lane
towards Tang Hall. He thrust his hands deep in his
pockets, the wind tugged at his wispy, grey hair, and
sliced through his clothing and chilled his bald head. He
wished he had brought his cap. He walked on; he would
soon be home, very soon be home. He wasn't a young
man, if he was young he would have run, run to keep
warm, run to get out of the wind, but not anymore, those
days were gone ... but the lights of the Tang Hall estate
were ahead of him. The van drove past slowly and halted
a little way ahead. The man thought it suspicious. It was
a van, a two-seater; he might be being offered a lift by
a good soul were it not for the fact that as the van passed
he saw, very clearly, that the passenger seat was occupied. There was no other reason for any vehicle to stop
on Bad Bargain Lane, there were no buildings, just fields
at either side. Wilson Weston halted. He was suspicious.
The van had seemed to halt for some reason in relation
to him. There was nothing coincidental about the vehicle
stopping, no other foot passengers, or any other vehicles
on that dark, starlit night to make the van draw to a halt
just ahead of him. The van lay between Wilson Weston
and home, just sitting there, white exhaust fumes rising
briefly from the tail pipe before being snatched away by

the wind. He stood there. The van remained motionless. Then the white reversing lights came on, the van whined towards him in reverse gear and Wilson Weston intuitively knew that there was nothing to be gained by running.

Seven

Thursday, December 18, 10.15 hours – 22.47 hours
in which a breakthrough is made and the kind reader is privy to the joy in the life of Somerled Yellich and also the joy in the life of George Hennessey.

George Hennessey stepped out of the white inflatable tent and looked around him. Sergeant Yellich looked at him, waiting for a lead, a response, as did a number of constables and a sergeant, but all Hennesscy could do was absorb the scene – woodland – and note the weather: low, grey sky, cold easterly wind. He approached Yellich. 'Woodland again.'

'Yes, sir.'

'Four . . .'

'Yes, sir . . . in almost as many days.'

'And again it was a dog walker who found the body.'

'Yes, sir, understandable though . . . I mean, this time of year, mid-week, the only folk who go into woodland are dog walkers.'

'Dare say.' He turned and noticed a line of houses in the middle distance. 'Better do a house-to-house along that street, somebody might have seen something.'

'I'll get on it, boss.'

'Good. Who is this guy . . .?'

'Persons, sir.' Yellich smiled.

'Sorry?'

'Persons . . . we have already concluded that this is the work of at least two persons.'

137

'Yes . . . sorry . . . so, who are these people?'

Yellich shrugged. 'I'll organize a fingertip search of the area . . . then start the house-to-house. Dr D'Acre is expected.'

'Yes, thank you . . . thank you.' He replied in an absent-minded, detached attitude. Again he asked himself, Who are these people? Movement to his right caught his eye, he turned and saw the slender figure of Dr D'Acre, followed by a constable who carried her Gladstone bag. She was solemn-faced with what Hennessey saw to be a determined look about her. She allowed herself brief eye contact with Hennessey as she closed his personal space. 'Good morning, ma'am.' Hennessey touched the brim of his hat.

'Chief Inspector.' She wore short hair, no make-up and carried herself erect; there was not even the slightest leaning forwards or hunching of shoulders as, Hennessey had often noticed, with many tall women. She wore green coveralls, solid, sensible shoes, and a woollen hat. Unusual for her, noted Hennessey, rarely having seen her in a hat, but he could understand the need for it; the wind was a biter. She glanced at the tent. 'Another burned corpse, I understand?' She took her bag from the constable with a nod of thanks.

'Yes, Doctor.' Hennessey walked back to the inflatable tent and held the flap aside. Dr D'Acre stooped and entered the tent. Hennessey followed. The corpse was lying on its side and had, when contracting in the flames, adopted the classic pugilistic pose.

'Male.' Dr D'Acre knelt and placed her bag on the ground. 'Placed here but not burned here: the grass is not fire damaged and it's unusual for a burns victim to be on their side, though this is probably not a burns victim. If the pattern is establishing itself, this gentleman was deceased when he was set alight, so his body was burned after death, we hope. Again, the burning is not as exten-

sive as it might otherwise have been . . . again, there is a sense that the fire was not allowed to run its course. Either it was put out, or died out because of lack of oxygen.' She opened her bag and removed a rectal thermometer. 'This might give some indication of the time of death but . . . well . . . we have had this conversation before.'

'Yes, indeed.' Hennessey smiled. 'The cause, yes, but the when . . . no . . . just a very wide approximation.'

'Well, when he was last seen alive, and when his body was found, is as good an approximation as anything I can offer, as I have said many, many times before, but a rectal temperature and a ground temperature is part of the procedure . . . so . . .'

'Understood and appreciated.'

'I understand . . .' Dr D'Acre said as she inserted the thermometer into the rectum of the corpse, 'I understand that the third victim . . .'

'Mr Harthill?'

'Was that his name? Well, the third victim was burned out of doors.'

'Yes.'

'Well, he too was not burned as badly as otherwise might have been the case so, if he was burned outside, there was no shortage of oxygen.'

'No . . . no, there wouldn't be, would there?'

'Well, that means that the fire was extinguished, it didn't die from oxygen starvation.'

'So it was put out?'

'Yes . . . smothered by blankets or similar . . . or doused with water. For some reason, the fire was not allowed to run its course.'

'What possible reason?'

'Ah . . . that, Chief Inspector, is your territory.' She extracted the thermometer and took a note of the reading. 'This man is not long deceased, probably alive less than twenty-four hours ago. Well, I have done all I need to do

here. If you have taken all the photographs you want to take, we can have him removed to York District and I'll commence the post-mortem. Will you be observing for the police?'

'Yes, ma'am, Yellich's knocking on doors.'

'Any idea of his identity?' Dr D'Acre stood.

'Not yet, ma'am, but someone will report him missing. I am sure . . . Of that, I am very sure.'

Somerled Yellich 'got a result' at only the third door upon which he knocked. The house, like the other houses in the street, was a compact, semi-detached, owner-occupied house that he believed to have been built in the 1930s. In the main they were 'ribbon development' houses constructed along the arterial roads leading out of the towns and cities with occasional short offshoots, like branches from a tree. The houses of this type had small front gardens, a larger rear garden, and originally had a wooden garage for the family car at the top corner of the rear garden. These houses were held up by the modern historian as an illustration of the fact that the so-called 'hungry thirties' were only hungry in highly localized areas of heavy, traditional industry. Elsewhere in Britain, people enjoyed the prosperity of being able to afford to buy a house of the ilk that Yellich was calling on and were also able to afford a mass-produced car from Dagenham or Cowley to put in the garage. A few could even afford foreign holidays.

Yellich walked up to the yellow-painted front door of the house and rang the bell. He didn't hear it ring inside the building and so knocked on the door and caused a dog to bark. A few moments later a tall and very thinly built man opened the door. He seemed to Yellich to be in his late fifties. He looked quizzically at Yellich but didn't speak.

'Police.' Yellich held the pause before speaking. He showed his ID. Still the man didn't answer.

'Calling on houses to see if anyone saw anything. There was an incident in the woods last night.'

'An incident?' The man spoke with a strong, local accent but seemed to Yellich to be disinclined to give much of himself.

'A body was found. We suspect foul play.'

'Ah.' The man paused.

'Did you see anything, sir?'

'Aye . . .'

'You did?'

'Possibly.'

'What?'

'Motor car . . . white van.'

Yellich's heart missed a beat. 'Where? When?'

The man nodded. 'The other side of the wood. The wood has a couple of entrances for children to access it, and folk to walk their dogs. I don't like going into the woods by myself in case I am taken for something I'm not, but I like to get out of an evening . . . helps me sleep if I take a walk and there is pavement all round the wood. Only these houses overlook the wood, Greaves Wood, it's called, but turn left at my gate, brings you up to the main road. Walk along the main road and take the first left into Watch Lane, and Watch Lane curves round and joins this road. So I do that walk when I can, when the weather is dry. Takes me about an hour to get round . . . then I sleep well. The entrance to the wood, one of the entrances, is off Watch Lane.

'Was in two minds about doing it last night; it was dry but cold . . . but . . . I knew I'd sleep better if I did the walk, so put on my long johns and a pullover and my old duffel coat and went out . . . got quite warm after a while, so I walked down Watch Lane and saw a white van draw up outside the entrance to the wood, just a narrow path between houses, but it was dark, a few lights from the houses but not many street lamps and no street

lamps at all anywhere near the entrance to Greaves Wood. I stopped walking and nudged into some shrubs . . . vans . . . cars . . . vehicles . . . they don't park there, not at night. It just looked suspicious.'

'Yes.' Yellich nodded his head slowly. 'I know what you mean.'

'You would do . . . as a copper. Anyway, I watched, and these two figures got out of the van. They went round the back, opened the door and took out this large bundle.'

'Bundle?'

'Well, it was wrapped in a sheet . . . or a carpet . . . took two of them to shift it . . . carried it into the woods. I stayed there, snuggled into the shrubs. It was very odd by then but not so odd as to have to call the police because Greaves Wood is used for fly-tipping, folks dump their old mattresses and televisions and wait for someone else to clear it up. The council has a blitz every now and again, so I thought fly-tippers, not a 999 call, and I don't have one of those pocket phones that young people carry to use to ruin the evening in the pub for everybody else. It would have taken me half an hour to get back home . . . so I just watched.'

'Understandable.'

'Anyway, the two people came back and eventually they drove off. Didn't see me.'

'Eventually?'

'Aye . . . the man was upset . . . he looked weak at the knees, staggered across the road, didn't want to get in the van . . . took his gloves off and held on to the front gate of the house opposite the entrance to Greaves Wood.'

'Took his gloves off?'

'Yes . . . why? Were you thinking of fingerprints? I watch crime dramas on TV.'

'Yes, I am. What time was this?'

'About eleven thirty.'

142

'That's less than twelve hours . . . they could still be there. Can you show me which gate?'

'Aye. Are we walking?'

'No, I'll have a car collect us.' He took out his mobile phone. 'Two persons?' Yellich jabbed his phone. 'A man and . . . a woman? A boy?'

'A woman.'

'Age?'

'Well, adults . . . but younger rather than older.'

Yellich spoke when his call was answered and requested a car to pick him up. 'Did they speak?'

'Aye, the woman said, "Hurry up, you can be sick at home". That was when he was leaning on the gate looking like he was going to faint. She was in control alright . . . she drove the van.'

'You didn't hear a name, or anything?'

'No . . . posh, though.'

'Posh?'

'Aye . . . posh . . . no accent, talked like the newsreaders talk . . . English, but no accent other than an English accent. I'll get my coat.'

'Have you seen this?' Dr D'Acre handed Hennessey an early edition of the evening paper. 'I see you gave a press release.'

'We had to.' Hennessey leaned forward and took the newspaper from Dr D'Acre. 'Wow . . . talk about lurid headlines: "The Cremators' Fourth Victim"? That will push up sales.'

'I imagine it will.' Dr D'Acre stood. 'Doubtless even the international press will be contacting you soon. No story moves newsprint like a serial killer. Well, shall we get on?'

'Yes, indeed.' Hennessey laid the paper on Dr D'Acre's desk in her small, cramped office and stood. 'I'll see you in there.'

* * *

'Difficult.' The Scenes of Crime Officer dusted the wooden gate. 'Exposure to the atmosphere never helps. Car thieves leave the windows of the car open to destroy any latents they might have left behind; that's if they don't torch the thing . . . which is what they did to mine.'

'Really?'

'Yes, really, Sergeant Yellich. My old VW . . . just wannabe car thieves, learning the trade, no car thief worth his salt would steal an old, rusty VW, but these boys all have to learn an apprenticeship.' The SOCO stood back and picked up his camera with a flash attachment from behind his case and photographed the latents. 'Two hands,' he said. 'Palm prints on this side of the gate, fingerprints on the other. The man gripped the gate like this . . .' He made a motion of gripping the gate with both hands when standing with his back to the road. 'Gripped quite hard too.'

'That corresponds to what our witness said.'

'I'll ask the householders for their prints for the purposes of elimination, but who grips their own front gate like that? I mean, not many . . . not many in my book.'

'Nor in mine.' Yellich turned away from the gate. 'Nor in mine.'

'The deceased is an adult male,' Dr D'Acre spoke for the benefit of the microphone, 'extensively burned . . .'

It proceeded to be a very rapid post-mortem, for Dr Louise D'Acre said she knew what to look for. Having identified the deceased as being European in terms of ethnicity and being approximately five feet ten inches or one metre seventy-three centimetres tall, allowing for more shrinkage than usual, 'because fire tends to contract the human body', she then determined that because of the absence of carbon deposits in the trachea that the fire was post-mortem. She then peeled the skin from the skull, having made an incision around the circumference above

the ears. 'Yes, it's always easy if you know what to look for . . . massive force trauma to the rear of the skull . . . something linear . . . an iron bar . . . not a hammer, with a focussed point but, as I said, a long, thin instrument, but an instrument of strength. He has a thick skull; it would have taken some force to inflict this injury . . . quite some force. It is one of the thickest skulls I have seen.'

'Didn't know skulls varied in thickness.' Hennessey stood against the wall of the pathology laboratory dressed in the requisite green paper coveralls, head, body and feet.

'Oh, yes.' Dr D'Acre turned in his direction. 'Of varied thickness, quite varied. There is a condition known as "eggshell skull" of extreme thinness. Folk don't know they have such a condition until they bump their head and cause a fracture, which sometimes is fatal. Did a PM on a young boy once, one of the ones I remember. You were present, weren't you, Eric?'

'Yes.' Eric Filey, the portly and jovial mortuary attendant, who was similarly dressed to Hennessey, nodded grimly, as he held a thirty-five millimetre camera with a flash attachment. 'Yes, it was one of the ones you tend to remember.'

'Irate father smacked his son round the head . . . flat of his hand . . . all of us have been tempted to do it and many of us have done it . . . killed his son outright. Felt sorry for the father . . . he was distraught, loved his little boy . . . he was suicidal, but that boy had an eggshell skull. It was a skull of such thinness that any accident in the rough and tumble of childhood may have . . . nay, would likely have been fatal. I was able to say that to him . . . it helped him in his grief a little . . . well . . . that is a long-winded answer.' She paused and considered the corpse which lay face up on the stainless steel table, one of four in the room. 'That is my conclusion, Chief Inspector . . . death from a massive

blow to the skull . . . burning was post-mortem. I'll fax my report to you as soon as possible.'

'Appreciated.'

'Do we know who it is?'

'Wilson Weston, is his name.' The man was agitated. 'He's my father. He's not at home. There's nowhere else he can go . . . nowhere he has to go. He's not wandered in the head.'

The constable tapped his pen on the missing persons report pad. 'If you'd wait a moment please, sir. We don't take mis. per. reports in respect of adults unless they have been missing for twenty-four hours but, in this case I think our CID officers might want to speak to you.'

'Why . . .?' The man's face drained of colour.

'If you'd take a seat, please, sir?' The constable went to the office behind the enquiry desk and picked up the phone and dialled a four figure internal number. 'Front desk here, sir,' he said when his call was answered. 'PC Banks. There's a member of the public here, wanting to make a mis. per. report . . . Less than twenty-four hours yet . . . Yes, sir, and adult, but the reason I am alerting you is that the description given fits that of the Code Four One of this morning, thought you might want to interview him? Yes . . . yes . . . thank you, sir.' PC Banks replaced the handset and walked back to the enquiry desk. 'Detective Sergeant Yellich will be out to see you, sir.'

'Thanks.' The man, sitting on the bench wringing his hands, nodded.

Moments later Yellich stepped into the public area and briefly spoke to PC Banks who pointed to the man sitting on the bench. Yellich approached him. 'Mr Weston?'

'Yes.' The man stood.

'Shall we talk in here?' Yellich opened the door of an interview room and Weston stepped in and sat down. Yellich sat opposite him.

'It's my father,' the man said with agitation.

146

'Whoa . . .' Yellich held up his hand. 'Let's take things one step at a time.'

'Sorry.' The man was thick set, wore an army surplus woollen pullover and denims, feet encased in solid, sensible winter boots. He rested a folded windcheater on his lap. His hands were fleshy with short, stubby fingers which were heavily nicotine stained.

'So you are?'

'John Weston, fifty years of age . . . unemployed . . . living on Alain Street, Tang Hall, number 127.'

'I see.' Yellich wrote on his pad.

'And your father is missing?'

'Yes.'

'He is?'

'Wilson Weston . . . he's eighty . . .'

'Wilson?'

'Yes . . . it's a strange Christian name, it caused him problems all his life and he never forgave his parents for giving him that name, but there's always been a Wilson Weston as far back as we can trace and the curse fell on him . . . that's how he saw it anyway, as a curse.'

'I see.'

'That's why he called me John. I was the only boy of my generation so I escaped. Mind you, I wouldn't really have minded. John is such an ordinary name. I've often fancied a strange name . . . I might have amounted to something if I had had a strange name to grow into . . .'

Yellich smiled, 'Try Somerled.'

'Is that your name, sir?'

'Yes, spelled *s o m e r l e d*, pronounced "sorley" . . . It's Gaelic. Anyway, why do you believe your father is missing?'

'He's not at home. He lives alone . . . he's a widower . . . has a one-person flat on the Tang Hall estate as well, Allington Close, number 25. He is good for his age, he goes out for a walk each night. I don't mean evening . . . I mean

147

night . . . to the end of Bad Bargain Lane and back, about half a mile. Not the full length of the lane but to where it crosses over the motorway . . . turns round and comes back, no matter what the weather. Except snow . . . can't walk in snow. So if there's thick snow he stays in, but always complains he feels the lack of "fresh".'

'Fresh?'

'Air . . . he likes a good lung full of fresh air each day . . . or night in his case. He's not at home this morning. I called round . . . I have a key. He didn't answer the door so I let myself in. I call on him every day, just to check on the old fella. He wasn't home, bed not slept in, mail on the floor not picked up, remains of the meal he'd had for supper in the kitchen sink, no sign of breakfast. He washes up each morning, you see, sir, that's his habit, his routine. Lets the dishes pile up in the sink then washes them all each morning after breakfast. Waits in for me to call each morning, then goes to the social club for lunch – it's a council run thing, does lunch for pensioners, ensures the old lads and lasses get at least one good meal each day of the week. Not open weekends. But today's . . . what? Thursday, so he would have waited in for me. His mind is as sharp as a tack. So I walked along the lane . . . not there. Mind, if he had been lying there after a heart attack or a stroke, somebody would have found him by the time I got there, but I had to do it.'

'Yes.'

'No trace of him. Phoned the hospitals . . . no one admitted . . . but you are seeing me?'

'Yes . . . there's no easy way to say this, so I'll just say it . . . a gentleman was murdered in the night, his body was found this morning. My boss is at the post-mortem now.'

'Post-mortem?'

'Yes.'

'Well, is it my father? If I could see him . . . I could identify him.'

'Well, that won't be possible, the body was damaged.'

'Oh.' John Weston sat back in his chair. 'You're not telling me . . . these . . . Cremators? I read the paper . . . no . . . no, not my dad?'

'We haven't identified the body.'

'Oh . . . no . . . no . . . no!' Weston buried his head in his hands. When he had sufficiently recovered, Yellich asked him if he had anything that could provide a DNA profile of Wilson Weston.

'What sort of thing are you looking for?'

'A hair from his scalp . . . that would be ideal.'

'Where could . . .?'

'A comb, hairbrush . . . bed sheets.'

'I'll look.'

'No . . . could you take me to your father's home?'

'Yes.'

'Did your father have any enemies?'

'Who would want to murder him?'

'Yes.'

'No . . . in fact he was a very quietly living man since my mother died . . . that was fifteen years ago. Moved into Tang Hall then, took his single person's flat . . . seems to be on nodding terms with most folk but not close to anyone. He's not the sort of bloke to rub folk up the wrong way.'

'Alright.' Yellich stood. 'I'll bring my car round to the front of the building. If you'd wait in the reception area?'

'It's not funny, George.' Commander Sharkey dropped the newspaper on Hennessey's desk. 'In fact, it's damned unfunny.'

'Yes, sir.'

'The "Cremators" indeed.' Sharkey sat in the chair in front of Hennessey's desk. 'So what progress have we made?'

We . . . we . . . Hennessey thought, there was not a great

deal of 'we' in it that might include Commander Sharkey. 'Well, we have made some progress . . . and in fairness, sir, it is still early days.'

'Four victims is not early days, George, these are serial killers.'

'Yes, sir, but with respect, this investigation is still only six days old.'

'It is four victims old, George, that's how old it is. So, what progress?'

'We have descriptions of the perpetrators and their likely vehicle, which will have been dumped by now or resprayed.'

'Yes.'

'Well . . . that's about it, sir. We allowed ourselves to get sidetracked a bit with the first two murders, the husband and wife, which was a double murder, a single incident, so the four victims represent only three crimes . . . but in the case of the first two there did at least seem to be motivation and a likely suspect, although it now appears that we were wrong.'

'Wrong?' Sharkey sighed.

'There was still only one crime at that point!' Hennessey allowed an edge to creep into his voice. He often heard his pension calling his name but never more earnestly or loudly than when he was with the officious commander who, senior in rank, was ten or fifteen years his junior.

'Very well. What's your next move?'

'A consultation with Dr Joseph at the university since you have obtained approval for the funding.'

'When?'

Hennessey glanced at his watch. 'Well . . . I should be leaving now, sir, if I am to be courteous and arrive on time.'

'Very well.' Sharkey stood and allowed himself a glance out of the small window of Hennessey's office. 'Tourists, in this weather?'

Hennessey followed his gaze and saw a small group of

elderly people who wore brightly coloured clothing, much more brightly coloured than any Briton would wear walking the walls. Probably Americans, he thought. 'Well, don't need heat and sun to enjoy ancient buildings or ghost walks, sir, and it brings in the money from year end to year end . . . not just for a few months each summer.'

'Dare say. Well, we must be courteous and so I'll let you get on . . . but I want daily progress reports.'

'Yes, sir.'

Hennessey had in fact a full ninety minutes before the appointed time of his consultation with Dr Joseph but he had seized the opportunity to rid himself of Sharkey's company. He had intended to drive the short distance from Micklegate Bar to the university campus at Heslington but, having freed himself from the commander's clutches upon a subterfuge, he needed to then vacate the building and, disliking driving even short distances, for reasons of which the gracious reader is already acquainted, he resolved to walk. The walk would in fact be quite pleasant, he decided, wrapped up against the wind with hat and scarf and overcoat, woollen trousers and good, comfortable and above all, dry footwear; it would indeed be very pleasant. A walk is good for freeing up the mind. For George Hennessey there had been times in his career that breakthroughs had been made towards the end of a sixty-minute stroll. For him a sixty-minute stroll problem was the equivalent of Sherlock Holmes' 'two pipe problems'.

Having signed out, he left the red brick Victorian building at Micklegate Bar, followed the walls of the ancient city to Ballie Hill. Again he enjoyed that particular stretch of wall which was always relatively free of other foot passengers, and which offered a delightful prospect to the north of proud and neatly kept terraced houses 'within the walls', and to the south, of the rooftops of the city and ending with a few paces through a small

copse which he always found enchanting. He crossed the flat and deceptively peaceful looking Ouse at Skeldergate Bridge and with some difficulty avoiding traffic, crossed into Tower Street and entered Fishergate. From Fishergate he walked into Kent Street of smaller terraced houses, which being without the walls, lacked the prestige and the value of similar properties within the walls, and from there walked on to Heslington Lane, past The Retreat operated by the Quakers and then appropriately or inappropriately, he thought, depending on one's point of view, entered Thief Lane of pleasant suburban houses which offered a view of the university buildings across the fields to his right. He turned gratefully into University Road and escaped the wind which had been blowing keenly into his face since he left Fishergate, and entered the grounds of the campus.

He enjoyed the walk within the grounds of the university, its square, modern construction, its angular clock tower, the lake on which were wildfowl, and noted few persons about, the institution by then being 'down' for Christmas. He stepped out of the chill wind into the warmth of a low-rise, centrally heated building and climbed a set of stairs to the first floor. He walked along the corridor until he came to a polished pinewood door on which was the nameplate 'Kamilla Joseph PhD'. He took off his hat, unwound his scarf, unbuttoned his overcoat and tapped softly on the door but could not resist using the well-honed knock of the police officer, tap, tap . . . tap.

'Come in.' The reply was prompt and reverential and warm. No imperious 'Come' after an equally imperious wait. Here was humility and, thought Hennessey, all the more humble since the expertise of Dr Joseph was of worldwide renown within the field of forensic psychology.

Hennessey entered the office. Dr Joseph smiled warmly at him and stood and extended her hand. 'We meet again, Chief Inspector.'

'Indeed.' Hennessey shook her hand. He found her grip

to be strong, though not over strong, which pleased him. He so detested those who give a 'wet lettuce' handshake with no grip at all.

'Please.' She indicated the chair in front of her desk with a sweep of an open palm and she too sat.

Hennessey noticed a neatly kept office, plants of a low maintenance variety, money plants, spider plants and cacti on the windowsill and also on her desk. Behind her on the wall was pinned an airline poster advertising Dr Joseph's native Brunei.

'Well . . .' She opened the file. 'I've not had a proper chance to study your report.'

'Yes. Very short notice . . . sorry.'

'No matter, I did what I could. Well, the terms "organized" and "disorganized" killer are now old hat but they still offer a useful starting point. So, there are now four victims, I understand? There's just three in the file.'

'Yes, Doctor . . . the fourth victim seems to us to fit the pattern . . . elderly . . .'

'Yes.'

'No known enemies according to his son who was interviewed by DS Yellich earlier today.'

'Alright.'

'No one would appear to benefit from his death; he was not a wealthy man.'

'Alright.'

'The gentleman was clubbed over the head, then by some means taken to a place we have yet to find, where his body was burned . . . definitely deceased when he was set alight.'

'Thankfully.'

'Indeed.'

'Then dumped in woodland.'

'So . . . attempt to conceal the identity by burning the corpse and once burned, it's discarded in a not particularly remote place?'

'Yes, that appears to be the case.'

'Incinerated to hide identity . . . a bit fatuous.'

'Yes. It didn't take us long to establish identity in all four cases.'

'So the perpetrators know little of scientific developments?'

'It would seem so.'

'Unlearned, perhaps?' Kamy Joseph raised her eyebrow.

'Perhaps.'

'Well, you see the problem I have with this dossier is accepting that the victims fit a profile. They are middle aged/elderly white persons, but beyond that there is more dissimilarity between the first two victims, Mr and Mrs Dent, and the second two. The first two are significantly more youthful than the second two victims, the first two were related, husband and wife, the second two are unrelated.'

'Yes . . . we can find no contact between the third and fourth victim.'

'The first two were professionally employed, wealthy and would be difficult to approach as a stranger . . .'

'Yes.'

'The second two were not at all wealthy and would be easier to approach, possibly less wary of being mugged. Was the fourth victim also attacked whilst walking in a remote place . . . alone?'

'Yes, he was . . . late at night on Bad Bargain Lane, edge of the city, fields either side.'

'You see, that strengthens my argument; I do not see a clear victim profile.'

'Not two independent teams of killers acting contemporaneously with each other?' Hennessey's hand went to his forehead. 'That would be too much.'

'No,' Kamy Joseph said as she held up her hand, 'don't jump the gun, Chief Inspector, don't rush your fences . . . just bear with me.' She paused. 'There are aspects of the

case which also don't add up. The first two victims . . .
husband and wife, very difficult to attack two persons as
a stranger, so the first crime would seem to have some
forward thinking, some planning to it. The weapon was
absent at the scene and the victims' bodies were transported. Those are characteristics of an organized killer but
such killers do not know their victims. The first two victims,
Mr and Mrs Dent, could only have been approached by
someone whom they knew. Some previous knowledge of
the victim is a characteristic of a disorganized killer, as
was once the term, as is the fact that the crime scene was
random and careless, and the body in each case was left
in the open, partially hidden, but not buried or dismembered and scattered. Also, in the case of a disorganized
killer, we would expect the weapon to be at the scene or
carelessly discarded, which it wasn't. That is one of the
reasons why forensic psychology has moved on from clas-
sifying killers as organized and disorganized . . . it just isn't
that neat, just isn't so clear-cut, but here . . .'

She patted the file. 'Here something else is going on.
In all cases there is a primary crime scene, a secondary
crime scene and disposal site . . . a tertiary crime scene.
That is consistent. That is a clear indication that we are
looking for the same two killers in each case.'

'Thank goodness for that.'

'And the crimes occurred at night?'

'Yes.'

'More commonality . . .?'

'Again, yes.'

'As is the attempt to protect the identity of the killers,
and their successful escape.'

Hennessey sat forward.

'I can also tell you that the perpetrators of these crimes
are local. They live in York or near York. They are
marauders, striking out of a base and attacking locally
. . . so it would seem to me. I feel that because of the

very short time window from the first two to the fourth and thus far final victim. A commuter, one who travels from his home some distance away would not attack as frequently, and their victims would also be more spread out, geographically speaking. The commuter would leave victims along the A1 from London to Edinburgh, for example.'

'I see.'

'Someone is in a hurry here, and not in a hurry to kill as many elderly people as possible.' She sat back in her chair. 'Something else is happening here.'

'What do you suggest?'

'Well . . . someone is at pains to convince you as rapidly as they can that you do in fact have a serial killer on your hands . . . which in fact you do, but not the randomly targeting killer he or they want you to think.'

'Camouflage killing?'

'That would be my guess, reading this file. I have read of such, but never come across one.'

'It's a new one for me as well.' Hennessey ran his liver-spotted hand through his silver hair. 'We are talking about the same thing here? Wherein a series of murders occur . . . they seem random . . .'

'Yes.'

'But one of the murders . . . just one, has a personal motive?'

'Yes, that's what I am thinking.'

'The others are random . . . the police think serial killer?'

'That's it.'

'And so the one person who has the motive to kill one specific victim is not a suspect?'

'Yes, so who would want you to rapidly eliminate him or them from your list of suspects?'

'Fellow called Gregory Dent.' Hennessey clenched his fist and brought it down on the arm of the chair. 'Damn him. It's all so clear now.'

'Better bring him in before another elderly person meets his maker marginally earlier than he would otherwise do.'

Yellich drove home to Huntingdon and parked his car outside his modest new-build house on the estate. He walked up the drive as the door opened and Jeremy ran out of the house to greet his father. Yellich stopped and braced himself for the impact just as Jeremy crashed against him with an arm-enveloping, head-burying hug of warmth and affection. Together they walked into the house and into the kitchen where Sara was preparing the evening meal. Yellich embraced his wife, and after eliciting the intelligence that Jeremy had been 'very good' since he was returned from school, Yellich, in keeping with established practice, changed into more casual clothing and took Jeremy for a walk. They walked into the old village and then to the playing fields by the parish church and to the stream, identifying plants and birds as they saw them. It had been hard for Somerled and Sara Yellich when they were told that their son would never be 'normal' and the sense of disappointment was profound, but great joy had come unexpectedly. That sense of childish wonder never left their son, that warmth, that faith in his parents. They also met parents of other children with learning difficulties who offered mutual support and from which grew valued friendships. It was, they had found, like a previously hitherto unknown world opening up for them. With affection and stimulation Jeremy, they were advised, could develop a mental age of twelve by the time he was in his early twenties and be able to live a semi-independent life in a supervised hostel.

Later, with Jeremy upstairs and sleeping the sleep of the just, Sara and Somerled Yellich sat together on the settee relaxing with a glass of wine each.

'And to think,' she said, 'to think, I would have been

Head of English in a comprehensive school by now if you had not dragged me off to the institution called marriage, intelligent females for the disposal of.'

'Would you turn the clock back if you could?'

'Nope . . .' She nestled her head into his chest. 'Wouldn't turn it back at all . . . not for one second.'

In the large kitchen of a solid half-timbered house in Skelton a man and a woman sat in silence with an empty teapot sitting on the table, as teenage and pre-teenage feet ran backwards and forwards until silence once again descended on the home. They talked softly and when, after thirty minutes had elapsed and no further sound had come from upstairs, Louise D'Acre smiled and said, 'Well, they're settled. Shall we go up now?'

'Yes,' George Hennessey said as he returned the smile. 'Yes . . . let's go up.'

It was Thursday, 22.47 hours.

Eight

Friday, December 19, 9.35 hours –
in which a jury deliberates and a middle-aged couple enjoy a cliff top stroll.

The twin cassettes of the tape recorder spun slowly, the red recording light glowed softly.

'The time is 9.35 hours, on Friday the nineteenth of December; the place is Interview Room Two in Micklegate Bar Police Station, York. I am Detective Chief Inspector Hennessey. I am now going to ask the other persons present to identify themselves.'

'Detective Sergeant Yellich.'

'Ambrose Peebles. Ellis, Burden, Woodland and Lake, solicitors, representing Mr Dent under the terms of the Police and Criminal Evidence Act 1985.'

'Gregory Dent.' He smiled and, thought Hennessey, he looked very confident, too damned confident, once again that cat-got-the-cream sort of confidence, trick-up-his-sleeve sort of confidence.

'Mr Dent, you have been arrested in connection with the murder of your parents—'

'Adoptive parents,' Dent interrupted Hennessey, 'adoptive parents.'

'Alright . . . with the murder of your adoptive parents Anthony and Muriel Dent of West End House, Great Sheldwich, and you have been cautioned. Is that correct?'

'Yes.' Dent nodded. 'Though I prefer the old caution
. . . the new one just doesn't have the poetry, somehow.'

'Let's stay with the issue,' Hennessey growled.

'OK.' Dent smiled.

Ambrose Peebles, portly, expensive suit, bespectacled,
glanced at Dent with clear irritation.

'You murdered your parents for a motive as yet
unknown, but probably greed. They were very wealthy.'

'Yes . . . they were. And now I am also wealthy.' He
held eye contact with Hennessey. 'I inherited half their
estate, the other half went to my sister.'

'So you had motive?'

'Yes.'

'You agree?'

'Of course, twelve million motives, though I confess I
didn't know they were that wealthy.'

'Twelve million!'

'The estate, over all, has been valued at approximately
twenty-four million. They were in possession of a large tract
of prime building land, in the centre of the city, and had
acquired other similar plots in neighbouring towns. It has
to be liquidized yet . . . so I am jumping the gun when I say
that I am also wealthy . . . but a matter of weeks, really.'

'Killing for money is as old . . .' Hennessey faltered. 'It's
. . . well, it's old, we come across it time and time again,
but why the other two? What harm . . .?' Hennessey paused
as he felt his anger rising. 'You see, it fell apart . . . it just
didn't look like a serial killer, despite what the papers called
you.'

'"The Cremators"? Yes, I read that.'

'It fell apart very rapidly. You made a number of errors
. . . our forensic psychologist saw through them. You might
have fooled the press but you didn't fool a psychologist.'

'What errors?'

Hennessey eyed Dent keenly. 'Am I hearing a confession?'

'Nope.' Dent smiled. 'But I am curious about the errors.'

'Why?'

'General interest . . . I am quite close to this case . . . I lost my adoptive parents, I am accused of their murder, I have a right to be interested. You would be interested too, if you were sitting here.'

'Well, I am not sitting there. You tried to pass off all four murders as the work of a serial killer.'

'Killers.' Dent relaxed in the chair. 'The newspapers spoke of a couple. "A murderous duo" I think they said . . . lurid . . .'

'Yes . . . you and Miss Thurnham.'

'Mrs Thurnham . . . she is not yet divorced.'

'Mrs Thurnham, we'll be talking to her next.'

'OK.'

'One of you will crack.'

'We will?'

'One of you . . . we will find evidence to link you to one of the murders.'

'You will?'

'Please, Mr Hennessey.' Peebles glanced at Hennessey over the rim of his spectacles. 'Please ask questions. This is not the time or place for threats.'

Hennessey nodded. 'Very well, did you murder Mr and Mrs Dent and two other elderly persons, namely—'

'No . . . no . . . no . . . no . . . no . . . and . . . no.' Dent's voice was calm, steady, unfaltering. 'No . . . I did not murder anyone.'

'We have only to find the white van.'

'If it's white . . . if it were mine, I would have re-sprayed it or burned it out. I would have reported it stolen . . . and by burning it, I would remove any evidence.'

'You hope so.'

'Well, I am after all allegedly . . . I repeat, allegedly, a cremator . . . an arsonist . . . a fire raiser . . . a fire setter . . . so I reckon I would set the van alight and burn any evidence

that would link me to one of the murders . . . if I was the murderer . . . if I was one of them.'

Hennessey reached for the off switch. 'This interview is concluded at 9.47 hours.' He switched off the machine and the red light dimmed and then vanished.

'So I am free to go?'

'No, we have twelve hours from the moment of arrest to decide whether to charge you. Please stay here.' Hennessey turned to the solicitor. 'Will you be accompanying us, Mr Peebles, or do we need a separate solicitor for Mrs Thurnham?'

'I can observe under the terms of the Police and Criminal Evidence Act . . . but if charges are brought, each defendant will then need a separate solicitor.'

'Thank you.'

Susan Thurnham, smartly dressed, sat impassively as Hennessey switched on the recorder and then invited all present to identify themselves for the tape. He then said, 'You know why you have been arrested, Mrs Thurnham?'

'Please make it a question . . . a clear question,' Ambrose Peebles spoke softly. 'PACE rules require such. A tape recorder can't hear a question mark.'

'Very well. Do you know why you have been arrested, Mrs Thurnham?'

'Yes.' She clearly wasn't giving anything away.

'And you have been cautioned? Sorry . . . sorry,' Hennessey held up his hand before Ambrose Peebles could object, 'and is it true that you have been cautioned?'

'Yes.'

'What do you know of the murders of Mr and Mrs Anthony and Muriel Dent?'

'Oh . . . they were first killed, then set on fire after they were dead . . . at a place still unknown.' She brushed her hair back.

Hennessey had to concede that she did look quite

fetching in her working clothes: pinstriped jacket and skirt, dark nylons and black shoes.

She continued, 'Then their bodies were dumped beside the river where they were found . . . that was about a week ago, yes . . . a week today in fact.'

'All of which was reported in the press.'

'Yes . . . which is all that I know.'

Hennessey paused. 'We know that this was a clumsy attempt to make the murders look like the work of a serial killer. Mr and Mrs Dent were murdered for a motive, two other elderly persons were murdered at random. We know that a couple was involved, a man and a woman who spoke with received pronunciation.'

'Oh yes, that was reported . . . I forgot that.'

'And you and Mr Gregory Dent can only alibi each other.'

'Well, that is an alibi . . . why are you wasting your time? Why are you wasting my time?'

'Because I believe that you and Gregory Dent murdered all four persons for the purpose of inheriting the Dents' fortune.'

'Well, all you have to do is to prove it. But I can tell you that you will not do so.'

'We won't?'

'No . . . you won't. There is no evidence to link us to the murders because we did not commit them.'

There was a warmth in her eyes, Hennessey had seen the look before. 'You are going to tell us something?'

'Yes . . . well, probably, I don't know for certain. I don't want to do your job for you, but sitting here it did focus my mind . . . but it occurs to me that someone else benefits from the death of Mr and Mrs Dent.'

'Their adoptive daughter?' Hennessey's jaw sagged.

'Well . . . doesn't she? And she is in a relationship . . . her husband . . . both speak with received pronunciation, a few short northern vowels but nearer to RP than accented

English and he, well, I understand that he drives to and from his job at the training college in . . .'

'A white van?'

'Well . . . it was white when I last saw it.' She smiled. 'So gentle a couple . . . so warm . . . the last person or persons you would think of being capable of multiple murder . . . but then I dare say, so was Jack the Ripper. Talk to the Vicarys.'

In the event it was Leonard Vicary who broke first. He cracked very easily. Whereas Juliette Vicary, bereaved early in life, a period in a children's home, then adoptive care, she had something of the ghetto about her, so Hennessey thought, more like her brother. But Leonard, a mild-mannered college lecturer, had never been in trouble with the police before. All Hennessey had to do was to leave him in an interview room for an hour or two, and when he returned, after being unable to extract a confession from Juliette Vicary, it was to find the man trembling with emotion, desperately holding back tears.

'So whose idea was it?' he asked gently, the tape recorder being switched on, all present having identified themselves again, and the place and time having been established.

'Gregory's . . . who else?'

'So, what was the plan?'

'To make it look like a serial killer was on the loose. Gregory said that he and Susan . . .'

'She was part of this?'

'Oh yes . . . very enthusiastic. Gregory said that he would invite suspicion, that would mean we would not be suspected, and because Gregory and Susan hadn't done the crimes, nothing could be proved, the case would go cold.'

'It would take a very long time for four murders to go cold, Mr Vicary, a very long time.'

'It sounded so simple. They made it sound so simple.'

164

'And the motive . . . money?'

'Yes, you've seen our house. It might look comfortable but we are struggling . . . a junior lecturer's salary is . . . low . . . and the Dents live a long time, that family make very old bones. Anthony Dent's father might still be alive now if he hadn't stepped in front of a motorbike. We'd have reached retirement before we inherited anything, and as Gregory and Juliette said, they were not their parents, anyway.'

'And you went along with that? So much for their money being kept in a trust fund for children not yet born.'

'Yes.' He pressed his hands to his eyes. 'Yes, Gregory, he has this way of making people do things . . . and Juliette . . . she's very pushy. Once we had killed the Dents we had to go through with the rest of the plan, no going back.'

'Who killed the Dents?'

Leonard Vicary shrugged. 'I did . . . banged them on the head with a golf club.'

'Where?'

'In our living room. We pretended to bump into them when they had had their evening meal and we invited them back to our house. Made sure of them by putting their heads in plastic bags. Carried them out, put them in the van, took them out into the country . . . doused with petrol . . . put the flames out before they went out, then brought the bodies back into the city and left them where they'd be found.'

'Why burn the bodies?'

'Gregory's idea. He said all serial killers have hallmarks, so we burned all the bodies . . . not totally incinerated them, just wanted a hallmark and a fire attracts attention, didn't want to let them burn too long . . . I've ruined my life.'

'Yes.' Hennessey remained softly spoken. 'Yes, you have . . . but a full confession . . . a guilty plea . . . statements implicating Gregory Dent and Susan Thurnham . . . play

your cards right in prison, you might breath free air while
you are still young enough to appreciate it.'

'Yes . . . everything you want.' He sat back. 'I feel better
for telling you . . . I couldn't have lived with myself. So,
where did we go wrong? What was the slip up that led
you to us? I have to know . . .'

'You didn't slip up. You were not even under suspicion
at all until Susan Thurnham suggested we chat to you.'

Leonard Vicary's face paled, he grabbed the edge of the
table, his jaw set firm. 'She fed us to you . . . they fed us
to you . . . all along . . . all along . . . that was their plan.'

Hennessey too felt a certain impact in the pit of his
stomach. He knew Vicary was correct. He saw it . . . he
saw it all now. So calculating, so mercilessly evil . . . but
proving it . . . proving it . . . that was going to be the
obstacle.

Due to the defendants inviting considerable local hostility,
it was requested by the defence, and not opposed by the
Crown, that the trial be moved to another location where
an impartial jury could be empanelled. Consequently, six
months after their arrest, Regina versus Vicary, Vicary,
Dent and Thurnham took place, in the middle of a heat-
wave, at Newcastle Crown Court. Leonard and Juliette
Vicary pleaded guilty to four charges of murder and each
collected four life sentences, to be served concurrently,
the judge recommending parole be considered only after
each defendant had served a minimum of twenty years
imprisonment. Gregory Dent and Susan Thurnham pleaded
not guilty to conspiracy to murder.

The white-wigged, black-gowned lawyer for the Crown
invited the jury to consider the cold and calculated manner
'which defies belief' by which the accused persuaded the
Vicarys to commit not one, but four acts of murder, and
then informed on them, 'like feeding them to the lions',
so that Gregory Dent would acquire his sister's share of

their inheritance, the law not permitting anyone to profit from crime. In the event of Juliette Vicary's guilt being established, her inheritance would automatically pass to her brother, Gregory Dent, there being no codicil in the will to allow Mr Anthony Dent's brother or any other relative at all to inherit anything of the estate of Anthony and Muriel Dent. 'The law of inheritance being quite clear . . . it is like a cross, it goes up and down before it goes from side to side,' he explained. 'In the absence of a will, parents and children inherit before brothers or sisters.'

'Not so,' said the equally bewigged and be-gowned counsel for the defence. 'It is, as my learned friend for the prosecution has himself stated in his own words, it is quite beyond belief that a man should manipulate his own sister into committing these crimes so that she would be disinherited, thus allowing him to inherit her fortune. Quite beyond belief. What is happening here, ladies and gentlemen of the jury, is that this is nothing more than a malicious attempt by the Vicarys to implicate Gregory Dent and Susan Thurnham in their crime, so as to soften the blow by dragging my clients down with them. It is nothing more than that. Further, a conviction for an offence of this magnitude requires proof, if it is to be a safe conviction. Proceeding on the balance of probability is simply not allowed . . . there must be proof, and there is no proof. There is no independent witness to the conspiracy being planned. It is but the word of two convicted murderers against the word of two people of good character. For that reason and that reason alone, a conviction would be wholly unsafe and I urge you to acquit both defendants.'

The jury retired and after three days of deliberation returned a majority verdict of Not Guilty in respect of both Gregory Dent and Susan Thurnham.

*   *   *

The middle-aged man and the younger, but only slightly younger, woman, strolled arm in arm along the cliff path enjoying the warmth of the evening.

'Those are his caravans,' said the man, 'see in the distance, little white boxes in the field?'

'Oh, really . . .?'

'Or they were his . . . he's sold them . . . he's liquidizing it all, they're moving south with their millions.'

'So unfair . . . setting up his sister like that, and her husband . . . and getting away with it.'

'Yes.' It was all the man felt he could say. 'Well,' he said after a pause, 'back to the hotel, a meal and an early night . . . would you like that?'

'Yes.' Louise D'Acre turned and smiled at George Hennessey. 'Yes, I would like that very much . . . very much indeed.'